Law and Philosophy Library

Volume 147

The Law and Philosophy Library , which has been in existence since 1985, aims to publish cutting edge works in the philosophy of law, and has a special history of publishing books that focus on legal reasoning and argumentation, including those that may involve somewhat formal methodologies. The series has published numerous important books on law and logic, law and artificial intelligence, law and language, and law and rhetoric. While continuing to stress these areas, the series has more recently expanded to include books on the intersection between law and the Continental philosophical tradition, consistent with the traditional openness of the series to books in the Continental jurisprudential tradition. The series is proud of the geographic diversity of its authors, and many have come from Latin America, Spain, Italy, the Netherlands, Germany, and Eastern Europe, as well, more obviously for an English-language series, from the United Kingdom, the United States, Australia and Canada.

Thomas Bustamante • Saulo de Matos •
André L. S. Coelho
Editors

Law, Morality and Judicial Reasoning

Essays on W. J. Waluchow's Jurisprudence and Constitutional Theory

Springer

Editors
Thomas Bustamante
Federal University of Minas Gerais
Belo Horizonte, Brazil

Saulo de Matos
Federal University of Para
Belém, Brazil

André L. S. Coelho
Federal University of Rio de Janeiro
Rio de Janeiro, Brazil

ISSN 1572-4395 ISSN 2215-0315 (electronic)
Law and Philosophy Library
ISBN 978-3-031-61878-9 ISBN 978-3-031-61879-6 (eBook)
https://doi.org/10.1007/978-3-031-61879-6

This Springer imprint is published by the registered company Springer Nature Switzerland AG
The registered company address is: Gewerbestrasse 11, 6330 Cham, Switzerland

Contents

About the Editors

Thomas Bustamante is Professor of Legal Theory and Philosophy of Law at the Federal University of Minas Gerais, Brazil, and Senior Research Productivity Fellow of the National Council for Scientific and Technological Development (CNPq), Brazil. He was a Global Research Fellow with a Fulbright Visiting Research Grant at the New York University, from 2020 to 2022, and a Research Fellow at King's College London. He holds a PhD from the Pontifical Catholic University, Rio de Janeiro. Some of his works in English appear in the *Canadian Journal of Law and Jurisprudence*, *Modern Law Review*, *Jurisprudence*, *Australian Journal of Legal Philosophy, American Journal of Comparative Law,* and *German Law Journal.* He has edited the books *New Essays on the Fish-Dworkin Debate* (with Margaret Martin, 2023), *Philosophy of Law as an Integral Part of Philosophy: Essays in the Jurisprudence of Gerald J. Postema* (with Thiago L Decat, 2020), *Democratizing Constitutional Law: Perspectives on Legal Theory and the Legitimacy of Constitutionalism* (with Bernardo Fernandes, 2016), *Argument Types and Fallacies in Legal Argumentation* (with Christian Dahlman, 2015) and *On the Philosophy of Precedent* (with Carlos Bernal Pulido, 2012).

Saulo de Matos is Professor of Legal Theory and Philosophy of Law at the Federal University of Pará, Brazil, and Vice-director of the Master and PhD Program in Human Rights of the same University. He holds a PhD from the University of Gottingen, Germany, and a Master's degree from the University of Heidelberg, Germany. His doctoral dissertation on the legal and political idea of popular sovereignty in modernity ("*Zum normativen Begriff der Volkssouveränität*") was published in Germany by Nomos Verlag in 2015. He was visiting scholar at University of California in Los Angeles (2013) and University of Gottingen (2017).

André L. S. Coelho is Professor of Legal Theory and Philosophy of Law at the Law School of the Federal University of Rio de Janeiro, in Brazil. He holds an M.Phil. and a Ph.D. in Philosophy from the Federal University of Santa Catarina, Brazil, with a Research Visit at the Goethe Universität of Frankfurt, Germany. He has previously taught at CESUPA and The University of Amazon, both in Brazil.

Contributors

Brian H. Bix University of Minnesota, School of Law, Minneapolis, MN, USA

Thomas Bustamante Federal University of Minas Gerais, Faculdade de Direito, Belo Horizonte, MG, Brazil
National Council for Scientific and Technological Development (CNPq), Brasília, DF, Brazil

André L. S. Coelho Federal University of Rio de Janeiro, Faculdade Nacional de Direito, Rio de Janeiro, RJ, Brazil

Kenneth M. Ehrenberg University of Surrey, School of Law, Guildford, UK

Imer B. Flores National Autonomous University of Mexico (UNAM), Instituto de Investigaciones Jurídicas, Circuito Mario de La Cueva s/n, C.U., Coyoacán, Ciudad de México, CDMX, Mexico

Michael Giudice York University, Department of Philosophy, Faculty of Liberal Arts and Professional Studies, Toronto, ON, Canada

Ronaldo Porto Macedo Junior University of Sao Paulo Law School, Sao Paulo, Brazil

Francisco Tarcísio Rocha Gomes Júnior University Center Christus (Unichristus), Fortaleza, Brazil

Matthew H. Kramer University of Cambridge, Churchill College, Storey's Way, Cambridge, UK

Breno Baía Magalhães Federal University of Pará, Belém, Brazil

Saulo de Matos Federal University of Pará, Faculdade de Direito, Campus Universitário, Belém, PA, Brazil

João Vitor Penna University of São Paulo, São Paulo, SP, Brazil

Jorge Sanchez Perez University of Alberta, Edmonton, AB, Canada

Xavier Scott York University, Department of Philosophy, Faculty of Liberal Arts and Professional Studies, Toronto, ON, Canada

Fábio Perin Shecaira Federal University of Rio de Janeiro, Faculdade Nacional de Direito, Rio de Janeiro, Brazil

Katharina Stevens University of Lethbridge, Department of Philosophy, University Hall, Lethbridge, AB, Canada

Ricardo Dib Taxi Federal University of Pará, Faculdade de Direito, Campus Universitário, Belém, Brazil

Introduction

Thomas Bustamante, Saulo de Matos, and André L. S. Coelho

Wilfrid Joseph Waluchow (or W.J. Waluchow) is one of the most important legal philosophers of our time. His insightful and original scholarship, expressed especially in his books *Inclusive Legal Positivism* (1994) and *A Common Law Theory of Judicial Review: The Living Tree* (2007), developed a powerful approach to legal and constitutional practice, shedding light on the theoretical commitments of legal positivism and the tension between fundamental rights and democracy in contemporary societies. Under the influence of H.L.A. Hart's jurisprudence, Professor Waluchow understands philosophy of law as an inquiry on how to understand, based on conceptual analysis, the implicit commitments that we undertake as participants of legal practice in constitutional communities.

Professor Waluchow got his Undergraduate and Master's degrees from University of Western Ontario, and his PhD from Oxford University, where he was the last PhD student supervised by Hart. He taught at McMaster University in Canada until his retirement. Besides the works in legal philosophy and philosophy of constitutional law, he published books in the field of bioethics (*Well and Good,* 2014; *Readings in Health Care Ethics*, 2012), and metaethics (*The Dimensions of Ethics*, 2003). His book *Inclusive Legal Positivism* is one of the most influential books of the twentieth century in analytical jurisprudence, since it successfully developed a new

T. Bustamante (✉)
Federal University of Minas Gerais, School of Law, Belo Horizonte, MG, Brazil

National Council for Scientific and Technological Development (CNPq), Brasília, DF, Brazil
e-mail: tbustamante@ufmg.br

S. de Matos
Federal University of Pará, Faculdade de Direito, Campus Universitário, Belém, PA, Brazil
e-mail: saulodematos@ufpa.br

A. L. S. Coelho
Federal University of Rio de Janeiro, Faculdade Nacional de Direito, Rio de Janeiro, RJ, Brazil
e-mail: andrecoelho@direito.ufrj.br

T. Bustamante et al. (eds.), *Law, Morality and Judicial Reasoning*, Law and Philosophy Library 147, https://doi.org/10.1007/978-3-031-61879-6_1

model for identifying valid legal propositions, namely the inclusive legal positivistic approach to law. According to this model, although the content of the law is necessarily determined by descriptive social facts (as postulated by the *social source thesis*), there is nothing in the structure of these descriptive social facts that prevents a legal system from incorporating principles or values amongst its criteria for legal validity.

In the interview published at the end of this book, Professor Waluchow considers his book *A Common Law Theory of Judicial Review: The Living Tree* as his decisive contribution to philosophy of law and constitutional law. Professor Waluchow's *Living Tree* is a philosophical response to the tension between fundamental rights and democracy, based on Hart's conceptual methodology and an egalitarian approach to the role of fundamental rights in democratic societies. His conception of a community's constitutional morality, which provides the basis for constitutional adjudication, has made an important impact on the contemporary debates on fundamental rights around the world.

The idea of this *Festschrift* in honour of Professor Waluchow emerged in result of a conference on some of the main topics of his legal and political works, held in Belém (Brazil) in February 2019, at the Federal University of Pará. Professor Waluchow was present at the conference to respond to all papers delivered at that time, and the authors were honoured with his careful comments and replies. After this meeting, the editors of this volume selected some of the papers of the participants in the conference and invited other contributors who historically helped to interpret, apply, and criticize Professor Waluchow's works. The book unites scholars from multiple countries, stages of their careers, and research interests. It encompasses the different and central issues of Professor Waluchow's thoughts in legal and constitutional theories, divided in three parts: the first part, *Waluchow's Jurisprudence Restated*, comprises six essays on Professor Waluchow's inclusive legal positivism; the second part, *Constitutional Reasoning, Political Morality and Judicial Review*, is dedicated to Professor Waluchow's philosophy of constitutional law, namely the debate on his work *A Common Law Theory of Judicial Review: The Living Tree*; and, finally, the third part, *Constitutional Morality Applied*, discusses the application of his theory on concrete issues of political and constitutional morality.

The book begins with a chapter from Matthew Kramer, one of the most prominent scholars in contemporary jurisprudence, who alongside Professor Waluchow is a forerunner of inclusive legal positivism. The chapter considers a distinction between two versions of inclusive legal positivism or, as Kramer prefers to call it, incorporationism: a moderate and an extreme version of incorporationism. According to extreme incorporationism, it is conceptually possible that a legal system "in which the sole criterion for the status of any norm as a law is the correctness of that norm as a moral principle" exists. Nonetheless, Kramer thinks that although this thesis is logically true, it is "extremely misleading and gratuitously obfuscatory". Notwithstanding the fact that this thesis is conceptually possible, "it is unsustainable as a matter of credible possibility" and should not be the focus of an interesting version of inclusive legal positivism.

In the following chapter, Kenneth Ehrenberg offers a more critical stance on Professor Waluchow's view. He develops a metaphysical argument against inclusive legal positivism based on some conceptual features of legal norms. He claims that Professor Waluchow's assertion that legal systems can incorporate a robust moral norm among the set of criteria of legal validity should not be accepted because it is conceptually inconsistent with the social fact thesis and the institutional character of law.

In a similar direction, André Coelho presents a Razian response to Professor Waluchow's critics regarding the classical debate between exclusive and inclusive legal positivism. His main thesis is that Professor Waluchow's objections against Raz's conception of authority and its connections with exclusive legal positivism responds to Raz's statements as if they were intended to be factually true, and not conceptually true.

A different direction is taken in the chapter by João Vitor Penna, which considers the implications of Professor Waluchow's distinction between "institutional" and "moral" forces of law. Penna believes, in agreement with Professor Waluchow, that a successful positivistic legal theory needs to address the problem of the institutional force of law, but at the same time this concern should not be restricted to theories of adjudication. Professor Waluchow's insightful construction of the institutional force of law does not support, therefore, the conclusion that its determination is not a proper task of analytical jurisprudence.

Another interesting reconstruction of the debate between Professor Waluchow and his main critics is offered in the chapter by Ronaldo Porto Macedo Junior, where the author examines Dworkin's responses to the objections that Professor Waluchow presented in *Inclusive Legal Positivism.* According to Macedo Junior, the final version of Dworkin's philosophy of law can be in part understood as a reaction to Professor Waluchow's inclusive legal positivistic model.

Another prominent scholar in the tradition of legal positivism is Brian Bix, who offers in his chapter a very thoughtful and considerate analysis of Professor Waluchow's inclusive legal positivism. The chapter considers the question whether inclusive legal positivism succeeds in its attempt to offer a distinctive vision of the nature of law, given the habitual accusation that it is swallowed by other positions like Dworkin's non-positivism. By carefully considering Professor Waluchow's version of legal positivism, Bix highlights the distinctive elements of this position. The conclusion is that it offers a view of law, legal reasoning, and legal validity which has been meticulously argued and defended, leaving it, for many, as the most attractive analytical theory of law.

The second part of the book, dedicated to the debate on Professor Waluchow's philosophy of constitutional law, starts with a chapter by Thomas Bustamante, who argues that regardless of their methodological disagreements law as integrity and inclusive legal positivism are on the same camp, and that the former can also provide a sound theory of precedent and adjudication. The appendix of the text, written three years after the main text, is probably the most important part of the chapter, since it offers the author's own analysis of Professor Waluchow's contribution to constitutional reasoning. There, Bustamante comments on a response that Professor

Waluchow offered to him in person and offers a pragmatic-inferentialist interpretation of Professor Waluchow's account of a community's constitutional morality. He claims that this account is not only plausible but also fully compatible with Dworkin's theory of legal interpretation, and that it leads to the conclusion that there is no harm in dropping the distinction between first-order and second-order judgments about law because legal reasoning must be 'detached', in Walhuchow's sense of the term, regardless of who undertakes the challenge of interpreting the law or the community's constitutional morality.

The following chapter by Imer Flores, provides a comprehensive review of some of Professor Waluchow's outstanding contributions to the field of legal philosophy and theory, mainly his account not only of the nature of law and of judicial discretion, i.e. inclusive legal positivism, but also of the justification of charter review, i.e. living tree constitutionalism. It offers an intriguing analysis of how Professor Waluchow's legal theory and philosophy of law hang together and complement one-another.

The next chapter, in turn, written by Saulo de Matos and Ricardo Dib Taxi, provides an analysis of the capacity of Professor Waluchow's theory to resist the so-called Alice's Paradox, which is a difficulty that emerges once one rejects the claim that the law has a fixed and stable semantic content. The chapter focuses on some aspects of Professor Waluchow's account of legal interpretation in constitutional law. The text seeks to reconstruct the background of the debate between theories of fixed meaning and theories of non-fixed meaning, in order to identify the main problems that each of these theories needs to deal for building a reasonable theory of constitutional interpretation.

In the same direction of the debate on the indeterminacy of Professor Waluchow's theory of constitutional interpretation, Katharina Stevens's chapter claims that Professor Waluchow's suggestion that judges can use the community's constitutional morality as a tool for constructing constitutional interpretations is closely related to the role that idealized audiences play in rhetorical argumentation theory. She holds that Professor Waluchow's judges are not sufficiently concerned with democratic legitimacy when they merely strive for answers about constitutional problems in harmony with the citizenry's existing moral commitments. Rather, they should conceive of themselves as public servants, submitting arguments to an audience of sovereign citizens who are, at the same time, the measuring stick by which the validity of these arguments is determined.

The final chapter of the second part of book, by Fábio Shecaira, defends Professor Waluchow's position against to the so-called "objection from diversity". According to this objection, the community's constitutional morality does not offer much in the way of guidance for judges in industrialized and culturally complex societies like Canada, the US, Brazil, etc. The purpose of the chapter is to analyse Professor Waluchow's recent attempt to refute the objection from diversity in a recent paper titled "Normative Reasoning from a Point of View".

The third part of this book discusses the application of Professor Waluchow's theory on constitutional morality, and it comprises four chapters considering four different dimensions of the debate.

Michael Giudice and Xavier Scott's chapter, without dismissing the claim that Professor Waluchow's living tree constitutionalism may constitute a reasonable method of interpretation in certain contexts, presents an objection to the application of the method to the Canadian context of *reconciliation* with indigenous peoples. The metaphor of the living tree, they argue, commits to 'bind Canadian constitutional law to certain fixed structures and practices in particular, and a European and colonial past in general'. It may constitute, on their view, an obstacle to reconciliation.

The next chapter, by Jorge Sanchez Perez, adopts a more optimistic interpretation of the capabilities of the living tree method to interpret indigenous practices, arguing that Professor Waluchow's idea of a community's constitutional morality is able to promote a global political morality that includes indigenous knowledge as a social fact. In this sense, Sanchez Perez stresses how Professor Waluchow's work gives us an important method to promote and engage with forward-looking agendas that can make the discipline more inclusive and open for future generations of scholars.

The penultimate chapter, by Breno Baía Magalhães, argues that although Professor Waluchow's central thesis on the nature of charters rights is primarily moral, its effectiveness and explanatory power seem to depend on elements relating to the institutional design of a constitutional tradition. Given this dependence on an institutional framework, he claims that the common law methodology will not find fertile ground to grow in constitutional experiences whose precedents are regarded as immutable rules imposed from top to bottom and where most constitutional rights cases are settled by an abstract form of judicial review.

Finally, in the last chapter of the book, Francisco Tarcísio Rocha Gomes Júnior discusses the possibility of using Professor Waluchow's theory of legal adjudication to understand the Latin American constitutional experience. The text presents three main concerns regarding the extension of Professor Waluchow's theory to Latin America: (i) a reflection on social and multicultural rights in the context of controversies around the legitimacy of a constitutional court; (ii) the idea that social and multicultural rights are not opposed to individual rights ; and, (iii) an argument that the protection of authentic intentions is relevant when there is political will which aims to render the constitutional empty and disregard the social commitments it undertakes.

This book ends with a spontaneous and rich interview with Professor Waluchow, where he tells us about his academic life, his relationship with H. L. A. Hart and other important legal philosophers during his PhD study in Oxford, and he responds to some of the critics presented in the chapters of this book. We know that this book cannot do justice to the importance of Professor Waluchow's contribution to legal philosophy, but we hope that it can at least contribute to spread the already remarkable influence of Professor Waluchow's scholarship and keep its spirit alive.

Thomas Bustamante is Professor of Legal Theory and Philosophy of Law at the Federal University of Minas Gerais, Brazil, and Senior Research Productivity Fellow of the National Council for Scientific and Technological Development (CNPq), Brazil. He was a Global Research Fellow with a Fulbright Visiting Research Grant at the New York University, from 2020 to 2021, and a Research Fellow at King's College London, from 2022 to 2023, with a grant from CAPES Foundation. He holds a PhD from the Pontifical Catholic University, Rio de Janeiro. Some of his works in English appear in the *Canadian Journal of Law and Jurisprudence, Modern Law Review, Jurisprudence, Australian Journal of Legal Philosophy, American Journal of Compartive Law,* and *German Law Journal.* He has edited the books *New Essays on the Fish-Dworkin Debate* (with Margaret Martin, 2023), *Philosophy of Law as an Integral Part of Philosophy: Essays in the Jurisprudence of Gerald J Postema* (with Thiago L Decat, 2020), *Democratizing Constitutional Law: Perspectives on Legal Theory and the Legitimacy of Constitutionalism* (with Bernardo Fernandes, 2016), *Argument Types and Fallacies in Legal Argumentation* (with Christian Dahlman, 2015) and *On the Philosophy of Precedent* (with Carlos Bernal Pulido, 2012).

Saulo de Matos is Professor of Legal Theory and Philosophy of Law at the Federal University of Pará, Brazil, and Vice-director of the Master and PhD Program in Human Rights of the same University. He holds a PhD from University of Gottingen, Germany, and a Master's degree from the University of Heidelberg, Germany. His doctoral dissertation on the legal and political idea of popular sovereignty in modernity ("*Zum normativen Begriff der Volkssouveränität*") was published in Germany by Nomos Verlag in 2015. He was visiting scholar at University of California in Los Angeles (2013) and University of Gottingen (2017).

André L. S. Coelho is Professor of Legal Theory and Philosophy of Law at the Law School of the Federal University of Rio de Janeiro, in Brazil. He holds an M.Phil and a Ph.D in Philosophy from the Federal University of Santa Catarina, Brazil, with a Research Visit at the Goethe Universität of Frankfurt, Germany. He has previously taught at CESUPA and The University of Amazon, both in Brazil.

Part I
Waluchow's Jurisprudence Restated

Incorporationism, Inclusivism, and Indeterminacy

Matthew H. Kramer

Abstract For three decades, Wil Waluchow has been one of the world's premier legal philosophers and in particular has been one of the world's premier legal positivists. In this essay, I explore the complexities of hard cases—cases in which there is substantial disagreement among judges or other legal experts over the correct answers to any questions at issue—in order to reflect upon the implications of those complexities for the legal-positivist theses which Waluchow has defended. The upshot is a more nuanced presentation of those theses.

1 Introduction

I am delighted to participate in a festschrift for Wil Waluchow, who is one of the world's foremost legal philosophers and also a major moral philosopher. He has incisively covered a lot of territory in moral philosophy—ranging from business ethics to medical ethics to meta-ethics—but, remarkably, his contributions to the philosophy of law have been even more profound and influential. He has established himself as one of the leading constitutional theorists in the English-speaking world, and his achievements in the field of general jurisprudence are even more redoubtable. Having been the final doctoral supervisee of H.L.A. Hart, he has played a huge role in defending and extending the tradition of legal positivism which Hart did so much to rejuvenate in the mid-twentieth century. Above all else, Professor Waluchow's magisterial 1994 book *Inclusive Legal Positivism* is the provenance of an entire subfield in general jurisprudence. It is a classic text that has served as a landmark for everyone who has written subsequently on the issues which it addresses. When I was producing my own books *In Defense of Legal Positivism* and *Where Law and Morality Meet*, I regarded *Inclusive Legal Positivism* as the most captivating and perceptive and elegantly written contribution to positivist jurisprudence since Hart's *The Concept of Law*. It will undoubtedly continue to be regarded

M. H. Kramer (✉)
University of Cambridge, Churchill College, Storey's Way, Cambridge, UK
e-mail: mhk11@cam.ac.uk

T. Bustamante et al. (eds.), *Law, Morality and Judicial Reasoning*, Law and Philosophy Library 147, https://doi.org/10.1007/978-3-031-61879-6_2

with great admiration as a point of reference by generations of jurisprudential scholars.

Alongside the formidable achievements of Waluchow as a philosopher is his endearingness as a human being. I first met him in the late 1990s, and I have found him to be a model of warm geniality and joviality ever since then. He seldom becomes angry, and he never raises his voice. He unremittingly exhibits solicitude for his students, many of whom recently paid tribute to him with a conference in his honor where they extended gratitude to him for his supportiveness as a mentor and a friend. (Like the writing of this paper, the convening of that conference took place during the worldwide COVID-19 catastrophe. Hence, it had to be conducted electronically.) His prowess as a scholar has been matched by his adeptness as an organizer of intellectual events, as he has hosted an array of major conferences and lectures that have led to high-profile publications. He has made McMaster University a global center of excellence in legal and political philosophy—an especially impressive achievement, given that McMaster does not have a law school.

I was initially inclined to write my paper for this festschrift with a focus on some areas of practical ethics which Waluchow has addressed illuminatingly. However, I have subsequently decided to concentrate instead on the area of legal philosophy in which his finest accomplishments have occurred: namely, the area of general jurisprudence. Indeed, I will concentrate more specifically on Inclusive Legal Positivism and especially on Incorporationism. Ever since the publication of Waluchow's 1994 volume, the phrase "Inclusive Legal Positivism" has come to be the dominant designation for both of the two doctrines just mentioned. Nevertheless, I shall continue here my practice of referring to them with the separate designations which I have employed. This paper will mull over some issues that arise from my previous work on Inclusive Legal Positivism and Incorporationism, in order to amplify and refine and modify that earlier work by pondering some complexities that are not fully explored therein. Though a recent essay by Waluchow (2022) was not aimed at prompting my present meditations, that essay is in fact what has inspired them. I shall say a bit more about that inspiration at the end of this paper.

2 Inclusivism and Incorporationism

Let us begin with the chief tenets of Inclusive Legal Positivism and Incorporationism, in formulations that slightly amplify those which I have presented in my earlier work on these matters. The vast majority of Inclusivists subscribe to the following thesis:

> *Inclusive Legal Positivism.* It can be the case, though it need not be the case, that the consistency of a norm with some or all of the principles of morality is a precondition for the status of the norm as a law in this or that credibly possible jurisdiction.

As is indicated in this thesis, the actuality of the state of affairs envisaged in it as a possibility is a matter that varies across jurisdictions. Also variable across jurisdictions are some salient aspects of that state of affairs. For example, the range of any moral principles involved—the range of any moral principles with which a norm must be consistent if it is to possess the status of a law—is likewise a jurisdiction-specific matter. Similarly variable is whether all laws or only some laws (if any) in a jurisdiction are subject to such a requirement of consistency.

While that requirement for legal validity is not inherent in the concept of law, it can be imposed as a threshold test under the Rule of Recognition in any particular legal system. Such a test is one of the criteria which the officials there use for ascertaining the law. Insofar as a threshold criterion of that sort is operative in any particular legal system, then, some degree of moral worthiness is a necessary condition for the legally authoritative force of each norm that is validated as a law within the system. Inclusive Legal Positivism, which readily accepts the possibility of such a state of affairs, is inclusive because it allows that moral precepts can figure among the criteria that guide officials' ascertainment of the law. Inclusivist theorists reject the view that all the criteria for law-ascertainment in every credibly possible legal system are focused on empirical sources. At the same time, the Inclusivists are positivists because they also reject the view that every credibly possible legal system does operate with some moral tests among its law-ascertaining criteria. An Inclusive Legal Positivist insists that such tests are contingent features, rather than essential features, of the systems of law in which they are applied.

Incorporationism is about a certain sufficient condition, rather than a necessary condition, for the status of norms as laws in particular jurisdictions:

> *Incorporationism.* It can be the case, though it need not be the case, that the correctness of a norm as a moral principle is a sufficient condition for the status of that norm as a law in this or that credibly possible jurisdiction.

Albeit the role of moral correctness as a sufficient condition for legal validity is not inherent in the concept of law, it can obtain under the Rule of Recognition in any particular legal system. An Incorporationist theorist maintains that moral principles regularly regarded by officials as legally determinative are indeed legal norms, notwithstanding that they have perhaps never been laid down in any explicit sources such as legislative enactments or judicial rulings. When officials do regularly engage in a practice of treating the moral soundness of norms as a sufficient condition for the legal authoritativeness of those norms, they have thereby incorporated moral principles into the law of their system of governance—even before most of the applicable principles have received any explicit and discrete recognition. Incorporationists, who unhesitatingly accept the possibility of such a state of affairs, are nonetheless legal positivists because they insist that the incorporation of moral principles into a legal system's array of norms is contingent rather than inevitable. This doctrine of Incorporationism is of course fully consistent with Inclusive Legal Positivism, and indeed the two are almost always embraced together by any theorist who embraces either of them.

3 Moderate Incorporationism Versus Extreme Incorporationism

In my previous writings on these matters, I have commended a moderate version of Incorporationism in preference to an extreme version (Kramer 2004, chs 1–4). That distinction between the two versions has heretofore been connected to a more familiar dichotomy, between easy cases and hard cases. However, one of the chief concerns of this paper is to investigate the complexities of that familiar dichotomy. Before we probe those complexities, this section will delineate the contrast between the two varieties of Incorporationism.

An extreme version of Incorporationism highlights the possibility of a system of governance in which the sole criterion for the status of any norm as a law is the correctness of that norm as a moral principle. Though such a thesis is true, it is extremely misleading and gratuitously obfuscatory. It is true because the envisaged system of law is indeed a possibility even in a sizeable society over a substantial period of time. Such a system is a logical possibility; its realization would not involve any logical contradiction. Yet the principal tenet of Incorporationism, as I have presented it above, does not refer to bare logical possibilities. It refers to credible possibilities (realizable in the actual world or in nearby counterfactual worlds). Logically possible though the system of law envisaged by extreme Incorporationists is even in a sizeable society over an extended period of time, it is not a credible possibility in any such society over such a period of time. Any credibly possible system of governance in a society larger than a handful of families will include criteria for the status of norms as laws in addition to any criterion focused on the correctness of norms as moral principles. Were that latter criterion the sole criterion, the ostensible system of governance containing it would not be able to function as a system of governance. Over vast areas of human life, that ostensible system would not provide sufficiently uniform guidance to people on how they are legally required or permitted to conduct themselves. Nor would it provide sufficiently uniform guidance to people on how they are able to exercise legal powers and on what the effects of exercising those powers would be. Though the correct principles of morality do furnish determinate answers to a myriad of questions, the understandings of those principles among the members of a credibly possible large-scale society will be profusely heterogeneous. Moreover, on countless points of detail, the correct principles of morality do not in themselves yield determinate answers. Such points of detail have to be resolved by recourse to conventional standards that have been laid down as authoritative. Precisely for these reasons, an array of laws beyond the correct principles of morality will be needed in any functional system of governance that presides over a credibly possible society.

Hence, notwithstanding that the thesis propounded by extreme Incorporationists is true as a matter of logical possibilities, it is unsustainable as a matter of credible possibilities. Consequently, that thesis is grossly misleading and obfuscatory. It trains attention on a bare logical possibility, and it thus tends to obscure the import of Incorporationism as a doctrine of general jurisprudence. The opponents of

Incorporationism could concede the bare logical possibility while rightly thinking that they had not conceded anything that detracts perceptibly from their general opposition to the doctrine. Given that a system of law like that outlined by extreme Incorporationists never has arisen and never will arise, an acknowledgment of the logical possibility of such a system is wholly undamaging for anyone who rejects the tenet of *Incorporationism* which I have formulated in §2 above.

Anyone favorably disposed toward that tenet is well advised, then, to adopt a moderate version of Incorporationism—as I have done in my previous writings on this topic. Instead of being concerned with the outlandish system of law on which the extreme Incorporationists bestow their attention, a proponent of the moderate version of Incorporationism maintains that there can credibly be a legal system in which the correctness of norms as moral principles is sufficient for the status of those norms as laws in the system's handling of certain cases. Unlike the thesis propounded by the extreme Incorporationists, this thesis of the moderate Incorporationists is an elaboration of the *Incorporationism* tenet in §2. It adverts to something that is credibly possible rather than to something that is just logically possible.

However, a proponent of moderate Incorporationism obviously has to precisify the phrase "certain cases" that has been used just above. In what sorts of cases, in a moderate-Incorporationist legal system, would the correct principles of morality be operative as laws which supplement the system's laws that have emanated from empirically ascertainable sources? To address this question adequately, a proponent of moderate Incorporationism has to mull over the complexities of hard cases—a task to which we now turn.

4 Hard Cases

In contemporary legal philosophy, the prominence of the distinction between hard cases and easy cases has been due partly to Hart's division between the core and the penumbra in Chapter 7 of *The Concept of Law*, and partly to Ronald Dworkin's emphasis on the disagreements in hard cases in *Taking Rights Seriously* and *Law's Empire*. In the present essay, I construe the contrast between hard cases and easy cases quite straightforwardly as follows. A case is hard if there is intractable disagreement or very widespread uncertainty among judges or other legal experts over the chief point(s) at issue within it. A case is easy if there is no such intractable disagreement or widespread uncertainty. Now, in connection with this very simple way of explicating the hard/easy dichotomy, several observations are germane.

First, the properties of hardness and easiness are clearly scalar properties. Either of them can be realized to varying degrees in any given situations. The scalar character of each property extends across several dimensions: the range or proportion of the legal experts among whom there is intractable disagreement or widespread uncertainty; the number and importance of the points to which the disagreement or uncertainty pertains; the persistence of the disagreement or uncertainty, whether over months or years or decades or centuries. Useful though a blunt distinction between hard cases and easy cases often is, it tends to obscure the dimensions along which each side of that distinction is scalar.

Second, and even more important, the hard/easy division is not tantamount to a distinction between cases in which the questions at issue are not determinately answerable and cases in which the questions at issue are determinately answerable. A case is easy if (1) all or nearly all experts concur on the answer(s) to any question(s) at issue therein and (2) no significant uncertainty about the answer(s) is harbored by most of the experts. That state of affairs can obtain even if there is no determinately correct answer to any question at issue in the case, provided that a misapprehension about the determinate answerability of the question(s) is widely shared among the experts. Although the sharing of such a misapprehension is undoubtedly not very common, it is neither impossible nor risibly fanciful. Conversely, a case is hard if there is widespread disagreement or uncertainty among experts over the answer to any question at issue therein. There can be such disagreement or uncertainty even if the question is determinately answerable. Indeed, as I have argued elsewhere (2007, pp. 17–21; 2008, pp. 49–50; 2018, pp. 112–120, 128–130)—partly in agreement with Dworkin—situations in which legal experts disagree intractably over determinately answerable questions are not very rare. We can aptly recognize as much when we distinguish carefully between indeterminacy on the one hand and indemonstrability or uncertainty on the other hand, as I have done in the writings to which I have just cited. Indeterminacy obtains when there is no uniquely correct answer (or no confined set of determinately correct answers) to some question Q under consideration, whereas indemonstrability prevails when there is widespread and intractable disagreement among experts about the correct answer to Q. Uncertainty prevails when experts are widely unable to reach any confident conclusions about the answer to Q. Indeterminacy is often coupled with indemonstrability or with uncertainty, but they are far from indisseverable. In some of my previous work on this topic (2018, pp. 112–120, 128–130), I have reproached Hart for neglecting these distinctions.

Third, although some hard cases do not involve any genuine indeterminacy, quite a few do. Not only are there different types of indeterminacy, but there are also different levels at which it can arise. In particular, indeterminacy can arise at the level of the empirically ascertainable laws of a jurisdiction that are applicable to some point of contention *C* in a case, or it can arise at the level of any moral principles that would be applicable to that point of contention. If there is indeterminacy at the former level but not at the latter, and if the correct principles of morality have been incorporated into the law of the relevant jurisdiction to supplement the empirically ascertainable legal norms, then there is a determinately correct legal answer to *C* notwithstanding the indeterminacy that obtains at the level of the black-letter law. If the determinately correct answer is generally recognized among legal experts, then the case is easy. By contrast, if the determinately correct legal answer is something over which the experts persistently disagree or about which they widely feel uncertain, then the case is hard despite the availability of a determinately correct legal answer to the question on which it turns. Even so, given that the correct principles of morality have been incorporated into the law of the jurisdiction through past activities of law-ascertainment, a court will be acting appropriately if it has recourse to those principles and if it identifies the answer to *C* correctly. In so doing, it will have furnished the correct legal answer to the legal point in dispute—because the moral principle which yields that uniquely correct answer is endowed with the status of a law in the relevant jurisdiction, *ex hypothesi*.

Contrariwise, if there is no indeterminacy at the level of the empirically ascertainable laws, then the presence or absence of indeterminacy at the level of the correct principles of morality does not affect the availability of a uniquely correct legal answer to *C*. After all, a moderately Incorporationist system of governance absorbs those principles into its law not to supersede the empirically ascertainable legal norms but instead to supplement them. There is no occasion for the activation of that supplementary role if the black-letter laws themselves are sufficient to generate a determinately correct answer to *C*. Of course, the officials in that system of governance might fail to identify the uniquely correct answer to *C*. If they inaccurately believe that the black-letter laws do not supply any such answer, then they will presumably seek such an answer in the correct principles of morality. If they believe (whether accurately or not) that those principles likewise do not supply any determinately correct answer to *C*, then they will conclude that the case which hinges on *C* does not lend itself to being resolved by reference to the existing law. They incorrectly think that the case cannot be resolved by reference to the legal norms that emanate from empirically ascertainable sources, and they likewise think that it cannot be resolved by reference to any correct principles of morality that possess the status of legal norms in the jurisdiction. If the officials instead believe (whether accurately or not) that the correct principles of morality do furnish a determinately correct answer to *C*, then they will conclude that the case which hinges on *C* is resolvable by reference to the existing law. That conclusion as stated here is correct, even though it emerges in the context of a misapprehension about the black-letter law. Furthermore, the conclusion about the existence of a determinately correct answer is itself true even if the officials have not accurately identified that answer.

Complexities proliferate still further when we notice that the preceding paragraph has treated the judges and other legal-governmental officials in the relevant jurisdiction as if they are a monolith. Disagreements among the judges and other officials are clearly possible in a case that hinges on *C*, as in other cases. Perhaps some judges will recognize that the empirically ascertainable laws deliver a uniquely correct answer to *C*, while other judges reach an opposite conclusion. Among the latter judges, there might be further divergences over the question whether the correct principles of morality as supplementary legal norms deliver a uniquely correct answer to *C*.

5 Some Lessons to Be Drawn

When we take account of this blizzard of complications and the many cognate complications that have not been specifically broached here, we find that the distinction between hard cases and easy cases—understood in the quite straightforward manner in which it has been construed in this paper—is not really the germane distinction for a moderate version of Incorporationism. To be sure, it is to some extent a reasonable proxy for the germane distinction. That is, we can reasonably assume that intractable disagreement or widespread uncertainty is especially likely in circumstances where the black-letter law in application to some matter is indeterminate. Nevertheless, strictly speaking, the distinction between hard cases and easy cases is beside the point. That distinction is fundamentally epistemic, as it pertains to how judges or other officials perceive and handle various sets of circumstances that have to be gauged by them. If in relation to some set of circumstances the judges converge in their perceptions, a case involving those circumstances will be easy. Conversely, if the judges diverge significantly in their perceptions or if many of them harbor significant uncertainty concerning how the set of circumstances should be perceived, the case involving those circumstances will be hard. Hugely important though these epistemic factors are in the operations of legal systems, they are orthogonal to the factors that are decisive for moderate Incorporationism. (Let us also recall, in line with what has been said in the second paragraph of §4 above, that a blunt distinction between hard cases and easy cases simplistically glosses over the intricacies that arise from the scalar character of hardness and easiness.)

Instead of being focused on those epistemic concerns, a moderate Incorporationist element of a Rule of Recognition is focused on the presence or absence of indeterminacy in the black-letter law. As has already been emphasized, indeterminacy is not equivalent to—or coextensive with—indemonstrability or uncertainty. Indeterminacy in the law of a jurisdiction is an ontological phenomenon. It is a property of the contents and implications of the prevailing legal norms. If the contents of those norms are such that they do not supply any determinately correct answer to some legal question, then either every intelligible answer to the question is correct or else no answer thereto is correct. Such a state of affairs can obtain whether or not the legal experts in the jurisdiction are aware of its obtaining.

By contrast, indemonstrability and uncertainty—like the distinction between easy cases and hard cases—are epistemic phenomena. They are properties of the ways in which the contents and implications of the prevailing laws in a jurisdiction are construed by judges or other officials who give effect to those laws. When the judges or other officials construe the laws, they are arriving at higher-order interpretive beliefs about legal norms that are the products of their lower-order beliefs and attitudes and behavior. Because of the abiding potential for incongruities between the lower-order beliefs and the higher-order beliefs about those lower-order beliefs, and because the incongruities can differ significantly among judges, there is an abiding potential for the epistemic properties of indemonstrability and uncertainty to be out of line with the ontological property of indeterminacy.

How, then, does the presence or absence of indeterminacy matter in a moderately Incorporationist Rule of Recognition? The correct principles of morality, in the supplementary role envisaged for them by moderate Incorporationists, do not become activated in their status as legal norms unless there is indeterminacy within the black-letter law in application to some case that has come up for decision by adjudicators or administrators. If the empirically ascertainable laws fail to yield any determinately correct answer(s) to the question(s) at issue in such a case, there is an occasion for the active supplementation of those laws by the correct principles of morality. If the principles of morality also fail to yield any determinately correct answer(s) to the question(s) at issue, then obviously they cannot perform their supplementary role in the case at hand. Contrariwise, if those principles answer the question(s) determinately, the supplementary function of the principles in their status as legal norms can be performed—and it will be performed if a majority of the adjudicators or administrators identify the principles and their implications correctly. A case of this kind will probably be a hard case, but it might not be. In any event, its hardness or easiness is incidental to the pivotal combination of factors: namely, the presence of indeterminacy in the black-letter law and the presence of determinacy in the correct principles of morality with regard to any question(s) at issue in the case. Only through the combination of those two factors is the moderately Incorporationist standard in a Rule of Recognition properly invocable by the adjudicators or administrators whose system of law is underpinned by that Rule of Recognition. And only through the correct identification of each of those factors by the adjudicators or administrators will that moderately Incorporationist standard be given effect. (Obviously, the Rule of Recognition in any particular system of governance might not include a moderately Incorporationist standard. My remarks here are applicable only when the regnant Rule of Recognition in a jurisdiction does comprise such a standard.)

The reason why the indeterminacy/determinacy combination is the pivotal factor—and why the hard/easy distinction is beside the point—is that a moderately Incorporationist criterion in a Rule of Recognition addresses any cases in which there are no empirically ascertainable laws that can correctly be invoked as bases for decisions in those cases. A moderately Incorporationist standard in a Rule of Recognition provides that, in such cases, the legal-governmental officials in the jurisdiction are both authorized and obligated to have recourse to the correct principles of morality as bases for their decisions. Unless those principles are themselves indeterminate on the points of contention in the cases under consideration, they can fill the lacunae left by the indeterminacy in the black-letter law. Now, this lacuna-filling function of the correct principles of morality under a moderately Incorporationist Rule of Recognition is focused entirely on what the law is rather than on how the law is construed. Occasions for the fulfillment of that function arise when and only when the points of contention in legal disputes are not covered determinately by the black-letter law, irrespective of whether the indeterminacy is recognized by the adjudicators and administrators who have to rule on those disputes, and irrespective of whether the adjudicators and administrators agree with one another on how the disputes should be resolved. Thus, because the distinction between hard cases and easy cases is centered not on what the law is but instead on the presence or absence of disagreement (or uncertainty) among experts about what the law is, it has no bearing on the applicability of a moderately Incorporationist standard in a Rule of Recognition. Decisive instead is the presence or absence of indeterminacy in the black-letter law.

6 Some Further Lessons

In light of what has just been argued, we can discern that some of the pronouncements in my earlier work on Incorporationism have been misleading at best. For example, in the Introduction to my book *Where Law and Morality Meet*, I announce that I will endeavor to "highlight the credible possibility of legal systems in which the laws for dealing with hard cases are incorporated moral principles" (2004, p. 6). To be sure, I thereafter evince a firmer understanding of the proper focus for an exposition of moderate Incorporationism, as I advert to a moderate "Incorporationist Rule of Recognition which establishes that moral worthiness is a sufficient condition for the status of norms as legal norms in hard cases that cannot be resolved by reference to legal norms from other sources" (2004, p. 28). Even then, however, my inclusion of the adjective "hard" before "cases" is inapposite—notwithstanding that most cases which cannot be determinately resolved by reference to empirically ascertainable legal norms will indeed be hard cases. Moreover, I subsequently declare that "the lone plausibly stable [version of an Incorporationist Rule of Recognition] is that in which the Incorporationist criteria apply peculiarly to hard cases. If there are gaps in the source-based law that need to be filled, or if there are clashes or serious ambiguities in the source-based law that need to be resolved, then judges and other officials may well invoke moral principles in order to deal with such circumstances" (2004, p. 34). Although the second sentence in this quotation is fine, the first sentence therein is guilty of the chief misstep against which I have warned in this paper. As becomes apparent on the next page of *Where Law and Morality Meet*, my concern with fending off Dworkin's onslaughts against positivism is what led me into the aforementioned misstep (2004, p. 35):

> This [moderate version] of Incorporationism is particularly pertinent in the context of my overall discussion, where we are pondering ways of replying to Dworkin. As has been mentioned in the Introduction to this book, Dworkin focused entirely on hard cases in his early attacks on legal positivists for their alleged failure to acknowledge the salience of moral principles in the law. Even in his more recent work, where he expresses some doubts about the distinction between hard cases and easy cases, his whole dissection of positivism's ostensible shortcomings is informed crucially by his accounts of several difficult cases. Hence, a version of Incorporationism attuned to the occurrence of such cases is apt indeed for fending off Dworkin's challenges. After all, the paramount merit of those challenges is to highlight the knotty legal cruxes which judges handle by recourse to moral principles. If legal positivism is to be worthy of commendation as a jurisprudential theory, it must be able to supply an adequate account of the judges' reliance on outright moral principles for adjudicative purposes. Incorporationism in its moderate form is an endeavor to furnish just such an account.

This latest quotation leads into two further lessons to be drawn from this paper. First, my erstwhile invocations of the distinction between hard cases and easy cases have not been necessary for the pursuit of my main concern in my elaboration of moderate Incorporationism. When I have distanced myself from extreme Incorporationism, I have done so chiefly for the reasons indicated in §3 of this paper. That is, I have argued that any Rule of Recognition of the sort envisaged by the extreme

Incorporationists would fail to provide the degree of regularized guidance that is essential for the very existence and functionality of a legal system of governance. My general aim here has been sustainable without any conflation of the hard/easy distinction and the indeterminacy/determinacy distinction, for—as has been noted more than once already—there is a very considerable overlap between the former distinction and the latter. Most cases marked by indeterminacy in the black-letter law will be hard cases, and a substantial proportion of hard cases arise in circumstances where such indeterminacy obtains. Conversely, most cases marked by determinacy in the black-letter law will be easy cases, and most easy cases pertain to circumstances in which there is such determinacy. (Worth keeping in mind here is that the properties of hardness and easiness are scalar, as has been observed in §4 above.) Without making the mistake of treating the hard/easy distinction and the indeterminacy/determinacy distinction as if they were equivalent, we can aptly take account of the large area of extensional intersection between them. Because of the sizeableness of that extensional intersection, the basis for differentiating between the untenability of an extreme Incorporationist Rule of Recognition and the tenability of a moderate Incorporationist Rule of Recognition can be expounded perfectly well with reference to the indeterminacy/determinacy divide. Hence, the gravamen of my complaint against extreme Incorporationism is salvageable, and so is my championing of moderate Incorporationism as a superior alternative that defuses the problem which undermines the extreme position. Both my complaint about the extreme approach and my commendation of the moderate approach are severable from the misleading terms in which I have sometimes articulated them.

Second, among the many faults that can accurately be imputed to Dworkin in his capacity as a legal philosopher is that he greatly overemphasized the distinction between hard cases and easy cases in his critiques of legal positivism. Admittedly, in *Law's Empire* he remarked that "easy cases are. . .only special cases of hard ones" (1986, p. 266). Nonetheless, even in that text he set up his whole critique of Hart by railing against legal positivists for their putative inability to capture accurately the nature of the disagreements in hard cases. Furthermore, in *Taking Rights Seriously*, where his fourth chapter is entitled "Hard Cases," he equivocated on the nature of hard cases in somewhat the same manner in which I have occasionally equivocated in my *Where Law and Morality Meet.* On the opening page of that fourth chapter, Dworkin declared that a hard case arises "[w]hen a particular lawsuit cannot be brought under a clear rule of law, laid down by some institution in advance" (1978, p. 81). If we overlook the fact that clarity is an epistemic property rather than an ontological property, Dworkin's wording is largely focused on indeterminacy in the black-letter law rather than on disagreement. Had Dworkin persistently adopted that focus in his discussions of hard cases, he might have spared future jurisprudential theorists from conflating indeterminacy and indemonstrability. However, elsewhere in *Taking Rights Seriously* he adverted to intractable disagreement as the defining feature of hard cases, and he thus understood the hard/easy distinction in the same way in which I have understood it throughout this paper. In the Introduction to that book, for example, he informed his readers that "there are hard cases, both in politics and at law, in which reasonable lawyers will disagree about rights, and neither will have available any argument that must necessarily convince the other" (1978, p. xiv). He was here clearly concentrating on indemonstrability rather than on indeterminacy. Thus, in addition to inducing future jurisprudential theorists to overemphasize the import of the distinction between hard cases and easy cases, Dworkin paved the way for those theorists to conflate indemonstrability and indeterminacy in their ruminations on that distinction.

7 Back to the Beginning

Some readers may have noticed that I have made no mention of Waluchow since the opening paragraphs of this paper. However, as I have indicated at the end of those opening paragraphs, this whole paper is prompted by a recent essay of his. In a footnote in that essay, Waluchow recalls an early article in which he propounded a version of extreme Incorporationism. He writes: "Professor Kramer's arguments against extreme Incorporationism have led me to think that my conclusion. . .may have been too broad – and that perhaps I should have restricted its reach to hard cases in all but fanciful, imaginary societies where moral agreement is far more prevalent than we find in modern, pluralistic societies" (Waluchow 2022, p. 126 fn 6). I applaud this retreat from extreme Incorporationism, but during the retreat Professor Waluchow should not focus on hard cases as such. Instead, he should limit the reach of Incorporationism to cases in which the black-letter law is indeterminate. In so doing, of course, he will be limiting its reach to cases that are mostly hard.

References

Dworkin, Ronald. 1978. *Taking Rights Seriously*. Cambridge, MA: Harvard University Press.

———. 1986. *Law's Empire*. London: Fontana Press.

Kramer, Matthew. 2004. *Where Law and Morality Meet*. Oxford: Oxford University Press.

———. 2007. *Objectivity and the Rule of Law*. Cambridge: Cambridge University Press.

———. 2008. When is There Not One Right Answer? *American Journal of Jurisprudence* 53: 49–68.

———. 2018. *H.L.A. Hart: The Nature of Law*. Cambridge: Polity Press.

Waluchow, Wil. 2022. Matthew Kramer and Inclusive Legal Positivism: Dancing on the Head of a Pin. In *Without Trimmings: The Legal, Political, and Moral Philosophy of Matthew Kramer*, ed. Visa Kurki and Mark McBride, 125–148. Oxford: Oxford University Press.

Matthew H. Kramer is Professor of Legal & Political Philosophy at the University of Cambridge and a Fellow of Churchill College. He is the Director of the Cambridge Forum for Legal and Political Philosophy, and a Fellow of the British Academy. Professor Kramer holds a J.D. (with high honors) from Harvard University Law School and a Ph.D (in Legal Philosophy) from the University of Cambridge. His multiple books include *Freedom of Expression as Self-Restraint* (Oxford, 2021), *H.L.A. Hart: The Nature of Law* (Polity Press, 2018), *Liberalism with Excellence* (Oxford, 2017), *The Ethics of Capital Punishment* (Oxford, 2011), *Moral Realism as a Moral Doctrine* (Wiley-Blackwell, 2009), *Where Law and Morality Meet* (Oxford, 2004), and *In Defense of Legal Positivism* (Oxford, 1999).

Inclusive Legal Positivism and the Fallibility of Officials

Kenneth M. Ehrenberg

Abstract Wil Waluchow has advanced perhaps the most convincing argument in favour of what he eloquently termed 'inclusive legal positivism', the view that a given legal system could make legal validity depend on moral truths. This chapter refocuses the case for the opposing view of exclusive positivism on the metaphysical tension in seeing law as an institutional social fact and yet for its validity to depend on something that is not a social fact, developing an understanding of official mistake as a way of highlighting that tension. If legal validity itself is understood as a socially constructed status (something with which any legal positivist would agree), key officials (as a group) cannot be wrong about the criteria sufficient for institutional membership having been met. While the officials cannot be wrong about the sufficient conditions, they can be wrong about the necessary (gatekeeping) ones and the moral criteria that inclusive positivists say could be included among the criteria of validity are invariably understood to be necessary conditions. That might look like a point in favour of inclusive positivism, but it is only the sufficient conditions that are constitutive of legal validity. Two facets of legal decisions are then marshalled to buttress the case for exclusive positivism: that almost every legal decision is also a determination of validity, and that all such decisions are systemically treated as correct until reviewed by a court of superior jurisdiction (which is itself a sufficient condition for membership). The implication of this is that moral criteria, understood as gatekeepers for legal validity, cannot be constitutive of legal validity.

1 Introduction

My intuitions have consistently pushed me toward what Wil Waluchow elegantly termed 'exclusive legal positivism' ('ELP') and away from 'inclusive legal positivism' ('ILP'), championed by him, H L A Hart, and others. Had I learned the

K. M. Ehrenberg (✉)
University of Surrey, School of Law, Guildford, UK
e-mail: k.ehrenberg@surrey.ac.uk

T. Bustamante et al. (eds.), *Law, Morality and Judicial Reasoning*, Law and Philosophy Library 147, https://doi.org/10.1007/978-3-031-61879-6_3

subject from Wil originally, I might have found it more convincing, as I always found Wil's arguments in its favour to be the most challenging. Many believe that the debate between ILP and ELP has reached an impasse, with the current arguments for each side not being capable of convincing the other. I think that one way out of this situation is to avoid the practical and conceptual arguments that have been the main focus and return to the metaphysical claims at the root of legal positivism. In doing so, we will find a new reason for rejecting ILP that will be hard to resist without rejecting core commitments of legal positivism.

As those familiar with Waluchow's work will already know, ILP is the belief that it is possible (though not necessary) for a legal system to have a moral criterion among its criteria of legal validity, while ELP is the denial of this claim. That is, ILP says a legal system could make what counts as valid law within that system dependent upon morality in some way, such that a putative law that is unjust or immoral in some specified way will not be legally valid in that system. ELP says legal validity can never be made to depend upon morality.

The reason I always thought ILP the more difficult position to accept is that, according to legal positivism as I understand it, law is a social fact. Every proposition of law that describes the state of some legal system and has a truth value, gets that truth value from facts about events that took place (or didn't take place) in the society of which that system is a part. It might have been the fact that a legislature of that society voted in favour of a certain form of words, sometime after that legislature was itself constituted in accord with some other rules accepted socially (or at least by some key segment of society) as setting forth the terms of what is to be given the status of legality for that society. It might have been the pronouncement of a judge who followed similar rules in coming to occupy an office constituted by similar earlier rules. It might have been the absence of such a vote or pronouncement. But morality is not (merely) a social construct.[1] Assuming morality is something capable of truth, those truths do not depend solely on social events. Slavery is wrong, even for a society that practices it without opposition. And if morality is not something capable of truth, it is even more difficult to see how the truth values of propositions of law can depend upon it. But if law is a social fact and legality is a status that is given by social events (especially where those social events that are the truthmakers of legal propositions are generally understood to be conscious undertakings of people who make those legal truths[2]), it is hard to see how legal validity can depend upon moral truths.[3] While Waluchow and others who adhere to ILP might say that

[1] It is possible that some facets of what is understood to be morally good or bad are merely social constructs. But the way we deploy moral judgments and talk about moral goodness and evil assumes that what makes those judgments right or wrong is not always determined by social beliefs. Those ways of speaking could be mistaken, but in that case it is more likely that our moral judgments are not something capable of being correct or incorrect in the way we deploy them. This, of course, is the subject of a huge and ancient debate far beyond our focus here.

[2] I put aside the question of whether customary law can be understood in this way.

[3] I will assume morality is capable of truth in order to motivate the problem of whether officials can be wrong in situations where legal validity is supposed to depend on that truth.

since legal validity is what people make it, there is no reason they cannot make it depend on some kind of moral truth, I hope to show here that this is metaphysically incoherent.

In an earlier work, I detailed what I thought was Waluchow's strongest argument in favour of ILP at the time (Ehrenberg 2016a, pp. 94–96). It seemed that the debate between ILP and ELP is only really joined if we are talking about the inclusion of a robust moral norm among the criteria of validity, raising the possibility that officials tasked with validity determinations could get those determinations wrong. If instead the moral criterion is understood to be merely one of moral acceptability to officials or the wider community, then the system has simply made legal validity depend upon another empirical fact, which is in principle discoverable. If the moral criterion is understood to be simply the moral judgment of the official tasked with making the determination of validity, then the system has simply given more guided discretion to that official (Raz 1972, pp. 841, 846).[4] But if the moral criterion included among the criteria of legal validity is understood to be one of robust or critical—what Waluchow sometimes calls 'Platonic' (2008a, p. 66)—morality, then the system has apparently imposed a condition on legal validity that is beyond the power of officials to verify or to determine by fiat or personal judgment.[5] If possible, this opens space for all the officials of the system to be mistaken in at least some of their judgments of legal validity. This, in turn, means that legal validity in that system is no longer merely a matter of social fact, since truth values of propositions of legal validity can depend on moral truths, which are not merely social facts.

2 The Morality in Waluchow's ILP

Waluchow wants to split the difference. When the criteria of legal validity include what appears to be a moral criterion, it refers to the wider community's shared 'true moral commitments', where 'true' describes the commitment as deeply held and reflected upon, without implying anything metaethical (Waluchow 2008a, p. 72). This splits the difference in that such moral commitments are presumably not beyond epistemic access. They are elements of positive morality and hence empirically discoverable, but are also not merely moral opinions that have not undergone tests for consistency with other moral convictions and depth of belief. The need for

[4] Elsewhere Raz calls it a 'directed power' (Raz 1994, p. 242).

[5] See Waluchow (2008a), p. 75: 'Some kind of positive morality is the only source [for judicial decisions requiring moral judgment] consistent with democracy, the rule of law, our epistemic limitations, and so on.'

such tests Waluchow calls 'the requirement of reflective equilibrium' or 'RRE' (Waluchow 2008a, pp. 71–72).

Much is made of moral disagreement, which would be expected as it is in the places of disagreement over our values that we are likely to spend the most time and energy trying to convince others of the folly of their ways. Not as much attention is paid to the vast swaths of moral agreement among values that are most deeply held. There is a good chance that, if everyone were to apply the test of RRE in a perfectly rational way, most moral disagreements would be resolved as the inconsistencies of certain beliefs with more deeply held convictions are uncovered. Of course, most people are either failing to apply RRE to some or all of their (mere) moral opinions entirely, or are failing to apply it correctly, and it is this that leads to (likely most, but probably not all) moral disagreement.

Waluchow argues that where the criteria of legal validity include a moral test of some kind, it means for judges to use the community's 'true moral commitments' to make those decisions. This is because judges have no privileged epistemic access to any objective morality (if such exists), and it would be neither fair nor prudent to have them deciding controversies on the basis of their own mere moral opinions (Waluchow 2008a, p. 75; 2015, pp. 34–35). This claim splits the difference because it sees the moral requirement among the criteria of legal validity as referring to an element of positive morality, but casts that positive morality in a more objective light as 'what most of [the community] *would think* were they more fully to engage RRE and attempt to reconcile their current belief(s) with their (overlapping) true moral commitments' (Waluchow 2008a, p. 75). Since judges are tasked with applying the subset of the community's true moral commitments that are embodied in the community's most basic laws ('the community's constitutional morality' or 'CCM'), it makes even more sense to have experts on the law parse those commitments for maximal consistency and apply them to controversies as they arise (Waluchow 2008a, pp. 76–77, 80, 81; 2015; 2018, p. 121). The key about CCM is that, while it is still a part of positive morality, it survives a test for consistency with key and deeply held moral beliefs and so has some characteristics of critical morality: where the criteria of legal validity include a moral criterion, an authoritative decision-maker can reasonably say that legal norms that do not withstand the RRE are legally invalid *ab initio*.[6]

[6]It should be noted that even under ILP, whether legal norms that do not withstand RRE are void when the inconsistency is noticed or void *ab initio*, is itself a choice to be made within the legal system. Hence a jurisprudential theory that aims to capture law wherever it is found should not depend on one choice rather than the other. But a theory that denies certain mistakes render decisions based on those mistakes legally invalid without the intervention of a higher decision-maker will have to explain how systems that choose to treat mistakes as void *ab initio* can do so. We will see later that this can be accomplished by saying the choice is itself the application of legal status and that there are strong metaphysical reasons for saying that the choice to treat the mistake as invalid *ab initio* is a retroactive application of that status declaration.

3 ELP Lets Down Its Guard

Exclusive legal positivists such as Joseph Raz and Scott Shapiro, have said that an inclusive legal positivist understanding of what happens when a moral criterion is putatively included among the criteria of legal validity would undermine the law's ability to guide behaviour, one of its primary functions. It would undermine law's ability to be an authoritative guide by requiring subjects to check directives against their own moral compasses (Raz 1994, p. 210), or it would undermine law's ability to make a practical difference in what subjects should do since it will be limited to telling them to do what they already should be doing (Shapiro 2000, p. 129). Since this behaviour guidance function is conceptually central to law, a picture of law that would undermine its ability to perform this function in such a fundamental way must be mistaken.

Waluchow's reply to these arguments focuses on their move from the metaphysical problem of reconciling moral truths and social facts to the practical issue of guiding behaviour. Since the attacks on ILP are claims that, if ILP were true, law would not be capable of performing its behaviour guidance function, they are vulnerable to a claim that law's difficulty in performing that function arises out of the nature of rules and not because of the inclusion of a moral criterion among the criteria of legal validity. Rules need to be general in order to be rules and not mere directives. They must be capable of applying to a wider variety of people and/or situations than a simple order given to an individual on one occasion. But the more general they are, the more they must rely upon vague terminology to capture the relevant parties and situations, and hence the less they are able to be interpreted by individuals who are unsure whether their situation is covered by the vague terminology. This is precisely why we need officials to make authoritative applications of necessarily open-textured rules to situations where their application is in doubt. But once we countenance the need for official interpretation to settle the law in cases falling into the 'penumbra of uncertainty', we are already acknowledging a limit on the law's ability to perform its guidance function until that determination is made (Waluchow 2008b, pp. 92–93). Hence, the threat to individual behaviour guidance by the inclusion of a moral criterion among the criteria of legal validity is there whether we think of that as making the law depend upon critical morality, Waluchow's positive but tested 'community's constitutional morality', or if we are only imagining it to increase officials' discretion. What's more, it is there even in systems without the moral criterion, a necessary tension at the heart of law. Including that moral criterion is therefore just another choice in how to strike a balance between the demands of generality and authority.

We might imagine the exclusive positivists complaining that the problems they have with ILP don't arise from the inclusion of a requirement of moral *acceptability* among the criteria of legal validity (which as noted would be empirically discoverable in principle), but rather from the claim that a robust norm of critical morality could be included. But this response is open to the retort that they brought Waluchow's reply upon themselves by couching their attacks on ILP in practical terms, relying on the difficulties such an inclusion poses for the law's performance of its behaviour guidance function. Once we have left the realm of the purely metaphysical problem of how a social fact can be made to depend upon something not socially constructed (if we are talking about critical morality), or upon facts that are not entirely socially determined (as might be suggested by the requirement that CCM consists only in those principles that objectively pass RRE), and start complaining that the law can't do its job when we include a moral criterion among the criteria of legal validity, Waluchow's reply has sharp teeth: The practical problems are the same whether we imagine the moral criterion to be robust and critical, the community's constitutional morality, or merely to be adding a condition of moral acceptability (either of the official making the determination, or of the wider society).

Earlier, I thought that the ELP reply that the problem with ILP arises from the inclusion of a robust moral requirement (rather than one of moral acceptability) was still the most convincing; I didn't fully appreciate the extent to which couching the ELP attacks in law's functionality (and hence making it a practical problem) undermines the force of the metaphysical intuition that there is a tension between saying law is a social fact and yet that its validity can depend upon something not a social fact (or at least not empirically demonstrable). So, let's grant for the moment that Waluchow's argument against the practical versions of the ELP arguments is successful and return to that metaphysical tension.

4 Official Mistake and the Case for ILP

One way to capture the metaphysical tension is to talk about the possibility and legal status of mistakes on the part of officials. If we include a criterion among the criteria of validity that is beyond empirical verification, we are introducing the possibility that all legal officials of a given community could be wrong about the validity of a legal norm or the truth of a legal proposition. Whether we are talking about critical morality or a community's constitutional morality that has met the requirement of reflective equilibrium (a test that judges can fail to implement correctly, or the result of which they can fail to understand), judgments deploying that moral criterion can be wrong.

Now, one might suppose that this state of affairs is impossible if the criteria of validity are, following Hart, set by the practice of officials simply making their validity determinations (Hart 1994, pp. 110, 255). If the criteria of validity are simply reflections of what the officials are saying is valid, then there doesn't seem to be any way that all of the officials could be wrong, just as the declaration of an umpire or referee in many sports determines the validity of a given play. It would seem that their determinations are *constitutive* of legal validity. The criteria are distillations of those decisions, an articulation of the rules they seem to follow in making their decisions. A departure from the apparent rules made by an official in a linchpin role (such as a constitutional judge) would be, in the first instance, a reason to re-examine one's articulation of the rules, rather than grounds for criticism of the official.[7]

But this supposition would overlook a key fact about the way the practice of officials sets the validity criteria. If the officials themselves are using a standard to make their judgments, then it seems more faithful to say that the standard they are using is a part of the validity criteria, even if their judgments are determinate of validity within the system. That is, if a rational judge would admit to having made a mistake if shown that her judgment was inconsistent with the standard with which she was trying to accord (notwithstanding the fact that the system still treats her judgment as dispositive), then it would make more sense to include that standard among the criteria of validity. If we are trying to track her practice, and her practice is to attempt to adhere to a standard in making her determinations, then her practice is what allows us to include the standard among the criteria of validity. Hence, while the validity criteria are a reflection of what the officials are using to make their determinations, it still makes sense to say that an official can make a mistake where her decision is not in accord with the criteria she is attempting to apply. On the other hand, if we want to say that a given decision is setting the validity criteria in that others are bound to adjust their decision-making to that decision, even if the official herself would have thought it wrong, then it might not make as much sense to say that decision is capable of being mistaken. So the decision-maker's attempt to track and reflect an articulable standard is a reason in favour of including that standard among the criteria of validity, while the finality of the decision (even if inconsistent with that standard) is a reason against including it. Since the finality of the mistaken decision is something that could vary among legal systems as well as the level of the court, this appears to be a point in favour of ILP.

Under any positivist interpretation, legal validity is a kind of status that is socially constructed. In some legal systems, it is understood to attach to any product of legislation or official legal decision-making where specified officials (their offices another form of status) follow the correct procedures. In others, further requirements (perhaps with content restrictions) are added onto the merely procedural ones. In either kind of system, legal validity is understood as bona fide membership in the legal system and therefore to carry whatever normativity the system would give to its members.[8] As a result of this, it is certainly possible for legal officials to be ignorant of certain facts that would determine legal status, or for them otherwise to make

[7] Of course, if you are yourself occupying a similar linchpin role and had a longstanding articulation of the validity rules that you had been following, the departure by your colleague would likely still be grounds for criticism. But for those examining the situation from the outside or occupying non-linchpin roles from which the system requires deference to decisions by those in the linchpin roles, a departure would be a prima facie reason to question one's understanding of the rules.

[8] Raz differentiates between legal validity and membership since the law can reach outside of itself to apply non-legal norms (Raz 1975, pp. 152–154). But this conception of institutional membership is slightly broader than his such that the incorporation of a non-legal norm renders it a member of the system.

mistakes about the truth of propositions of law. Consider the following example.[9] In most countries, what gets the status of legal tender is fixed by law. Generally, currency notes must be made of specified materials and in a specific design. Additionally, they must be made in a specified place and by specified people (officeholders). Hence, if I were to make an exact molecular copy of a banknote, except also give it a unique serial number, it would be indistinguishable from a legally valid banknote but would still be counterfeit. Even the highest legal official can certainly be mistaken about the correct legal status of this banknote.[10]

We might, however, imagine another kind of mistake. This would not be a mistake about the application of legal status to a putative member made based on the membership condition rules that specify which features it must possess in order to be bona fide. Rather, imagine a mistake about the constitutive rules of legal status themselves. Notwithstanding Ronald Dworkin's argument that many legal disputes are disputes over what we are here calling the membership (or validity) conditions for law (an argument positivists reject) (Dworkin 1986, pp. 5–7, 42–43),[11] most legal positivists don't really make metaphysical room for any serious mistakes of this second kind among key officials. The question is whether an official's validity determination using an apparent moral requirement is more like the mistake about the molecular counterfeit or more like the mistake about the constitutive rules of legal validity themselves. If it is the latter, then we would have to see if it is conceptually possible for a legal positivist to accept this kind of mistake, and what that says about the truth of ILP.

The reason this second kind of mistake appears impossible has to do with the nature of institutions (of which municipal legal systems are a clear example[12]). Institutions are social arrangements for the creation and assignment of statuses to people, events, objects, or even ideas and other abstractions, where those statuses are understood to carry powers to alter people's reasons for action.[13] They are created self-consciously and so the acceptance of the conditions specified as sufficient for creation of the institution make it the case that those conditions are sufficient for its creation (Thomasson 2003, pp. 588–590; Ehrenberg 2016a, p. 172). Since the existence of the institution depends on the collective acceptance and recognition by a specific set of people, it is their belief that those conditions have obtained that

---

[9] Discussed at Ehrenberg (2016a, p. 36).

[10] This assumes that the law specifying the requirements for legal tender does not contain a clause stating that official determinations of the legal status of specimens trump the possession of specified characteristics. But since this clause clearly does not exist in all legal systems, the possibility of this kind of error would still appear to be a point in favour of ILP.

[11] See also Patterson (2018, pp. 267–268), noting the need for legal positivists to account for the relationship between the rule that specifies the legal validity criteria and the rule's role in adjudication.

[12] *Pace* Neil MacCormick (1974, p. 105).

[13] Ehrenberg (2016a, pp. 32–34), citing Thomasson (2003) and Searle (1995).

makes it the case that the institution exists. Hence, *as a group*, they cannot be wrong about whether conditions sufficient for the institution to exist have obtained.[14]

The criteria of legal validity are constitutive of a legal system's institutionality in that they specify what gets the status of 'legally valid' and to carry the normativity that the system attaches to its members. They are the institution's membership conditions. To meet them is sufficient for membership within the legal system. Saying that the key officials, as a group, cannot be mistaken about their identity might appear to be another major point in favour of inclusive legal positivism. After all, if the officials all believe that the criteria include a moral requirement, or that a putative member (legal norm or application of a legal rule) is rationally consistent with the community's deeply held moral commitments, it would seem that belief cannot be mistaken. We are seeing that the officials cannot be wrong about the constitutive rules, even if they can be wrong about the empirical question of whether the rules have been met. So we appear to have a huge disjunctive point in ILP's favour: if an official mistake in the application of a moral criterion is akin to a mistake about whether a given specimen of currency is bona fide, then ILP is correct in saying that the moral criterion is a part of the validity criteria for the system and that judges can get it wrong. If, instead, an official 'mistake' in the application of a moral criterion is more like a 'mistake' about what the validity criteria are, then officials' collective belief about the presence of that moral criterion makes it the case that the system has that moral criterion among its validity criteria. The fact that this mistake is impossible entails that ILP is correct, or so it would seem.

5 A Deeper Metaphysical Case for ELP

As tempting as this argument for ILP is, however, it runs the risk of treating a necessary condition as if it were a sufficient one. The criteria of validity include enabling conditions that are usually procedural (e.g., anything passing a majority vote in Parliament), and also may include criteria that perform gatekeeping functions (e.g., may not be inconsistent with the written Constitution). While some enabling conditions may function both as sufficient and necessary conditions, I will be focusing on their role as sufficient conditions and so will refer to them as such. The gatekeeping criteria, however, function only as necessary conditions.[15]

Remember that an understanding of institutions tells us that it is only conditions functioning as sufficient for membership in the institution about the satisfaction of

[14] '[I]nstitutional kinds do not exist independently of our knowing something about them. ... [I]n the case of institutional kinds those principles we accept regarding sufficient conditions for the existence of these entities must be true. We are guaranteed freedom from complete ignorance and are preserved from error in many of our beliefs regarding the nature of institutional entities precisely because the principles accepted play a stipulative role in constituting the nature of the kind' (Thomasson 2003, p. 590).

[15] I thank Simon Palmer for alerting me to the need for this clarification.

which the relevant officials cannot be mistaken in their beliefs as a group. To see why it is only the sufficient conditions about which the officials cannot be universally in error, consider a potential supposed necessary condition the satisfaction of which we can have no direct knowledge: God must approve of the law for it to be valid. If God does not exist, then of course none of the laws are approved by God and hence none would be valid by this condition. If God does exist, no one knows for sure which (if any) laws God approves of, and hence officials can be massively and universally in error in their beliefs about which are approved. In neither situation are we tempted to say that there is no legal system present because of this criterion or the failure to apply it correctly.[16] So either there is universal error about the presence of this condition among the criteria of validity, or there is universal error in its application; those errors are perfectly possible and do not threaten the existence of the legal system. Rather, it is reliance upon beliefs in the constitutiveness and satisfaction of the *sufficient* conditions for membership that give the legal system its institutional existence. Hence, it is only about those that there cannot be universal error among the officials (Thomasson 2003, p. 590).

Some might be tempted by their memories of learning the contrapositive in first order logic to reply that all necessary conditions are negations of sufficient conditions for the negation of the other condition. Hence a criterion performing a gatekeeper function understood here as a necessary condition can be expressed as a sufficient condition for exclusion. That is, saying the law must pass a given test of morality to be legally valid is logically equivalent to saying failure to pass the test is sufficient for legal *in*validity. But either way it is expressed, the moral test is still a criterion for exclusion, and it is the criteria for *inclusion* (which we might also think of as enabling conditions) that are doing the metaphysical heavy lifting (as specifying what is sufficient for membership) in the assigning of institutional status. Waluchow himself acknowledges that ILP holds only that moral criteria can function as necessary conditions for validity, never as sufficient.[17] But what we are

---

[16]Lest it be thought that the theological example is doing something suspicious, take a more mundane necessary condition: 'all laws must be signed by the Queen to be valid'. The officials can be wrong either about the presence of this condition among the criteria of validity (where she signs no laws and yet the officials believe and treat many enactments as valid law), or about its satisfaction (where she has neglected to sign a given enactment and it is still treated as valid law, though there we are more likely to say that such treatment is the mistake). But where it is understood to be a sufficient condition, we cannot be wrong in saying that it is *enough* for her to sign the bill (that has met all other jointly sufficient conditions) for it to be a valid member of the system. It might be thought that the theological example would create problems for sufficient conditions as well since if the criterion was 'anything God approves of is law', everyone could apparently be mistaken about that condition or what God approves of. The point, however, is that officials are protected from massive error in their beliefs about what the sufficient conditions apply to, since it is those very beliefs that result in the institutional status being assigned to its members. Hence whatever they believe God approves of is legally valid as a result of that belief. See Giudice (2015, pp. 118–120), arguing recognition of officials is constitutive of legal validity.

[17]'Since there are, as far as I am aware, no versions of ILP that allow moral principles to serve as sufficient conditions for validity, defenders of ILP needn't concern themselves with the abundant

seeing is that it is only the sufficient conditions for membership about which officials cannot be generally mistaken. Once something is treated as a sufficient condition, meeting any supposedly necessary conditions is neither here nor there since the supposedly necessary conditions aren't able to perform their gatekeeping functions when the sufficient condition is met.

Therefore, metaphysically speaking, there's nothing wrong with the ELP retort that all officials can be mistaken in their belief in a moral requirement among the criteria of legal validity, since that requirement would function as a supposedly necessary condition. Yes, it's a kind of error theory in that it says that all officials can be mistaken. However, it's a theory that not only explains the error and how it is possible, but even how it might be perfectly understandable in those systems that putatively adopt a moral criterion. Mistaken beliefs in the existence or application of necessary conditions are not necessarily misguided; there may be very good reason for the belief in, and (attempted) application of moral criteria as necessary for legal validity by officials in some systems.[18] But those supposedly necessary conditions are not *constitutive* of legal validity the way the sufficient conditions are.[19]

Let us take stock for a moment. ILP introduces the possibility of officials being wrong in their validity determinations in a way that appears to be more than just an empirical error. Whether this is in the application of 'Platonic' morality or in a decision that a given piece of legislation is inconsistent with a community's constitutional morality because it is not rationally possible to reconcile it with that CCM via reflective equilibration, these are not empirically verifiable mistakes. We have seen that there are notionally two kinds of mistakes that we might think officials can make with regard to validity determinations: They can be wrong in the application of their agreed-upon validity criteria to a given instance (exemplified by the molecular counterfeit); or they can be wrong in what the validity criteria are themselves. However, we have also seen that there are some conceptual problems with this second kind of error. In general, errors about the satisfaction of conditions sufficient for membership in the legal system (legal validity) cannot be endemic among key officials, although errors about the identity or satisfaction of necessary conditions are possible and possibly widespread.

In discussing this second kind of error that appears impossible, I have said what is precluded is massive or universal error among key officials about the sufficient constitutive rules for legal validity. But of course, what we are usually talking about in the application of these criteria is the decision of one official or a small number.

---

absurdities that follow if we try to imagine that moral principles could serve this role' (Waluchow 2000, 79).

[18] On this point see Alexander (1990, 10), cited by Waluchow (2000, 59).

[19] One might take the argument of this chapter to offer instead a way to obviate the entire debate between ILP and ELP. It appears to show a way that ELP can admit ILP's claim that moral criteria can be included among the criteria of validity, so long as they are correctly understood as necessary but not sufficient conditions. But as such an admission would be a pyrrhic victory for ILP in that it comes at the cost of denying any constitutive role to such moral criteria in setting legal validity, it seems more correct to understand this as a win for ELP.

Plus, even if we do say that the moral criterion among the criteria of legal validity is a necessary condition in that it is performing a gatekeeping function, we might again appear to be saying that ILP is correct in that it is possible for the official making the determination to make a mistake in its application. As the moral criteria appear to be necessary conditions and the error of one official is not endemic, these considerations do not at first appear to pose any difficulty for ILP.

To see how these considerations do pose a difficulty for ILP, we must drill down a bit further into the nature of these decisions and their place within the legal system. There are two characteristics of official legal decisions that are important to note here. The first is that just about every legal decision that is not merely a determination of what non-legal facts obtained is a decision about legal validity.[20] If we imagine an adversarial system, with each side presenting an opposing argument over the state or application of the law, the official's acceptance of one side is holding that side's legal argument to be valid and the opposing side's invalid. Even in a completely non-adversarial system, we can imagine that officials will have interpretive options before them, among which they must choose one to recognize as legally valid, while rejecting the others as legally invalid.[21] The other important characteristic to note is that the system will treat those decisions as legally binding (i.e., legally valid and carrying whatever normativity the legal system endows them with) unless and until a court of greater authority (if one exists) strikes them down.[22] Every official (including those on that higher court) will treat the decision as sufficient for the validity of its holding until higher officials consider and invalidate it in their official capacity when called upon to do so (not ignoring that this might be done *sua sponte*).[23] So even if her decision is mistaken on the criteria she is

[20]This is not meant to imply that they are all hard cases or that they require an exercise of discretion. But every legal holding is an official declaration that one of a list of competing applications of law is legally valid, while its competing options are not.

[21]While these descriptions are using adjudication as a model for legal decisions, the non-adversarial analysis can also be applied to legislative decisions where the legislator believes herself to be constrained by pre-existing legal decisions or standards. Where the legislator is unconstrained (as in absolute monarchies, dictatorships, and systems adopting a Diceyan conception of parliamentary sovereignty (see Dicey 1982, pp. 3–4)), the legislative decision itself is considered fully constitutive of legal validity and hence not capable of mistakes in its application.

[22]This point is easily confused for Shapiro's notion of a 'general presumption of validity' (Shapiro 2011, pp. 202–203) that is enjoyed by legal decisions. But it should be distinguished, as I believe my point here is more fundamental and can help explain (if not supplant) his. Shapiro's presumption refers only to courts of superior jurisdiction and is only focused on the enforcement of decisions of lower officials. Since Shapiro is using this idea to underpin his claim that 'the law is a self-certifying planning organization', he is only concerned with the practical implications of the lower court decisions on enforcement for the execution of legal plans. It is therefore sufficient for him to understand it as a mere presumption. But we will see that the institutional metaphysics of law provide strong reasons for saying that it applies to all official legal decisions, not just for purposes of enforcement (but more broadly to determine what carries legal normativity), and that it is not a mere presumption rebuttable by a higher court—but rather a constitutive declaration that is alterable by a higher court.

[23]Michael Giudice makes a similar point in Giudice (2008).

attempting to track and she would admit as much, the institutional fact is that the decision is legally valid until modified since the bulk of officials cannot be mistaken in the identity or application of the conditions sufficient for legal validity and they are all treating her official pronouncement as sufficient for its validity. Hence the nature of the institution is to give the decision the status that comes with full validity until it is overturned. So even in systems where the overturned decision is understood to be invalid *ab initio*, that must be a retroactive invalidation.[24] This fact is a metaphysical truth that follows from the nature of institutions since the official treatment of the decision as legally valid prior to its being overturned is constitutive of its legal validity.[25]

To put this point in more Hartian terms, since the rule of recognition is a practice theory rule and judges' validity decisions are constitutive of the rule of recognition (in that these decisions are themselves the practices that form the rule of recognition), they cannot be making empirical mistakes (like the counterfeit money example) when they make a validity determination. Those decisions are afforded the status of legally valid by the institutional rules themselves. Where these decisions depart from the practices of the majority of other key officials, we must wait for another declaration to alter the institutional status of legal validity. Since these statuses are entirely socially constructed, whether to adhere strictly to linear time in the nature and operation of these statuses is a decision to be made by the institutional actors and designers. Hence, it is possible for the system to treat departing decisions as void *ab initio*, just as it is also possible for the system to treat departing decisions as void only from the moment they are declared to be inconsistent with the prevailing validity practices. But metaphysically speaking, since the institution treats the official's decision as the final word until a court of

[24]In further support of this point see Giudice (2015, pp. 129–131), quoting Peter Hogg (1997, pp. 801, 922). Waluchow uses the Canadian Charter to argue against this claim, noting that the Canadian Constitution Act, 1982 stipulates at 52(1) that 'any law that is inconsistent with the provisions of the Constitution is, to the extent of the inconsistency, of no force or effect'. Waluchow points out that the Act does not say this nullification happens when the inconsistency is noticed or declared and that 'inconsistencies do not begin to exist only when judges declare that they exist' (1991, 203). But these claims do nothing to belie my argument that it still entails a retroactive application of status. If the inconsistent provision was believed to be legally valid at the time of its adoption by the relevant officials and met the sufficient conditions for validity at that time (note the requirement of consistency under the Constitution Act is a necessary/gatekeeping condition, not a sufficient one), then the independent fact of its inconsistency cannot render it invalid from a metaphysical perspective as it retains its institutional status until it is declared inconsistent. The fact that there may be very good reasons for a legal system to treat the invalidity as effective from the adoption of the inconsistent provision is neither here nor there (that a system follows those reasons is a fact contingent on the design of the legal system) and does not call into question the metaphysical claims outlined here.

[25]It is true that non-officials might ignore the decision if they expect that it will be overturned. But even the fact that some instances of ignoring the decision are designed as test-cases to give higher courts the opportunity to overturn it (where the procedural rules of their system do not allow the higher court to invalidate lower court decisions *sua sponte*) attests to the fact that the system treats the decision as valid until the higher court overturns it.

higher jurisdiction declares it to be a mistake, a legal positivist accepting the social fact thesis and that law is a kind of institution should say that legal validity is fixed by the declaration of officials and not by consistency with a perceived set of gatekeeping necessary conditions.

The fact that a decision by one official is treated by the rest as sufficient for membership in this way and that every decision about a legal argument or application is also a validity determination solves the apparent problems for ELP. While a single official might be using her understanding of a moral criterion as a necessary condition and hence one she could be wrong about in its presence or application, her office (understood as a status that carries authority within the system) is treated as a sufficient condition for her decision's membership in the legal system by the rest of the officials.[26] They can't be wrong about that since their treatment of her decision as a sufficient condition is constitutive of it being that. So, while her decision in application of a moral criterion can be mistaken by her own lights, and it is unproblematic for her (or everyone) to believe in a moral criterion functioning as a necessary condition among the criteria of validity, it is the sufficient conditions for legal validity that do all the work. Those are made true and constitutive of legal validity by general official consensus of belief and treatment.

One might think these considerations could be embraced by ILP as a feature and not a bug. The moral criteria are functioning as gatekeepers or necessary conditions and hence are criteria the application of which officials can get wrong. This seems to be consistent with the ILP belief that the criteria of validity can have elements that are beyond reliable epistemic access or require the application of consistency tests that the official can get wrong. We seem to have made space for official error in the application of the criteria of legal validity, which is what the introduction of moral criteria would have done. The problem is that by saying officials can be wrong in the application *or presence* of these gatekeeping conditions, we are saying that they are not really constitutive of legal validity anymore. Once the authority of a single official's office is recognized as sufficient for the legal validity of her determinations, a mistake in the application of a gatekeeping condition becomes functionally equivalent to a mistake in the very presence of that gatekeeping condition. We're saying that there's no real difference between her misapplying a moral requirement and her being wrong about there being a moral requirement—which is to say, it's irrelevant to legal validity beyond her choice about how to apply it. But that is what

[26]In some systems, some or all decisions may not be treated as valid until a higher court decides upon their validity. In such cases, the argument simply applies at the higher level. Even if the lower court in such situations is attempting to track a moral principle directly, the legal status that carries normativity doesn't attach until the higher court rules. So, it is the higher court's ruling that is a sufficient condition, while any moral principles they are attempting to track are again supposed necessary conditions about which they can be mistaken. The recognition that lower court decisions might not be treated as valid in some systems until a higher court decides is a strong point against the generality of Shapiro's 'presumption of validity' mentioned above, in n 22, while not posing any problem for the considerations here. On the difficulties this presents for Shapiro, see Ehrenberg (2016b, pp. 335–340).

ELP has been saying all along: supposed moral criteria among the criteria of legal validity function at best as a guide to legal decision-making (as a directed power), and at worst simply to enhance official discretion, but are not constitutive of legal validity in any way.

It might be pointed out that these considerations only apply to the second kind of mistake, over the criteria of validity themselves, which legal positivism already has trouble accommodating (for good reason if it wishes to embrace an institutional theory of law). There's still the first kind of mistake exemplified by the molecular counterfeit currency note. Furthermore, I have noted above that my claim that all official legal determinations are also determinations of legal validity only applies where the determination is not merely about non-legal facts. So, if the official making a mistake in applying the community's constitutional morality is making a mistake about merely non-legal facts, then it would be possible for there to be facts about legal validity under those non-legal facts that are subject to universal mistake, just as all officials could be mistaken about the legal validity of a given piece of currency.

There are two reasons this solution does not work to save ILP. First, it is difficult to understand a decision about whether a given legal norm is consistent with the community's constitutional morality (consisting in its deeply held moral commitments that have passed the test of the requirement of reflective equilibrium) as being akin to a determination about whether or not some non-legal fact obtains, which is understood to be a criterion for some application of law. It is manifestly a decision about whether the putative legal norm is legally valid and hence a direct application of the criteria of legal validity (among which Waluchow holds we find the requirement for consistency with the community's constitutional morality in those systems that have chosen to include such a requirement). Even if we are to say that the characteristic of the putative legal norm that determines whether or not it is consistent with the CCM is a non-legal fact, it is not a decision about whether some aspect of statutory law has been triggered by that non-legal fact (as in the case of the molecular counterfeit). Rather, it is a direct determination of legal validity for that norm, which will be treated as sufficient for legal validity by the community of legal officials unless and until overturned. Approaching this first point from the other direction, whether a given decision is consistent with the CCM in a system requiring that consistency for legal validity to attach is, *ex hypothesi*, a legal (rather than a non-legal) fact according to ILP. (Recall that this was part of Waluchow's justification for having these decisions made by judges.) Hence, adherents of ILP could not rely on the mistake being about a non-legal fact to avoid the problem.

Second, I may have been unnecessarily pulling my punches when I excluded determinations of merely non-legal facts from the analysis. After all, even those determinations of merely non-legal facts are determinations of what facts obtain for the purposes of attaching legal status. Once again, such decisions are treated as sufficient for legal validity until overturned by a superior official. Returning to the example of the molecular counterfeit, it makes perfect sense to say that the specimen is a counterfeit and that all treatment of it as bona fide is in error, since we are applying the apparently necessary conditions of valid currency to exclude the counterfeit specimen. But once we apply any sufficient conditions to say that it is valid (perhaps the Chief Central Banker officially stipulating that the specimen meets all non-legal requirements), the situation changes. The legally determined non-legal facts may be at odds with reality, but it is those legally determined facts that now carry the relevant legal status. We have a conflict between a sufficient condition that assigns it the status of legally valid, and a supposedly necessary condition that excludes it—in which case the sufficient condition always wins.

The options open to ILP as a result of these considerations appear to be slim: Adherents could deny that law is an institution, which would be a tall order since institutional theory captures what legal positivists want to say about the nature of law so well. Adherents could deny some of the particular understandings of institutions that I give here. But that would also be difficult, as it is clear that official acceptance and treatment of members as carrying the normative status imparted by the institutions is sufficient for membership and having that normative status. And it is this realization that lies at the heart of legal positivists' understanding of basic validity rules. The other option would be to say that official mistake can render decisions invalid without the intercession of any holdings to that effect. But that would appear to suggest that legal validity itself is no longer entirely a matter of social fact and opens the decidedly anti-positivist possibility that all the valid laws of a given legal system go unrecognized by any official, or that every law treated as valid by officials in the system is actually invalid.[27]

6 Conclusion

We have seen that ILP is inconsistent with the institutional nature of law, which seems to be a core commitment of legal positivism. As an institution, the official recognition of conditions sufficient for legal validity cannot be fundamentally mistaken as that recognition is constitutive of the institution's membership conditions (which serve as the criteria of legal validity). ILP's claim that a given legal system can include a moral criterion (whether positive, positive but meeting the RRE, or 'Platonic') among its criteria of legal validity is invariably including the moral criterion as a supposedly necessary condition performing a gatekeeping function. But any mistake about the presence or application of supposedly necessary (gatekeeping) conditions has no effect on legal validity where the sufficient (enabling) conditions are recognized as present. So, even if officials are sincerely attempting to apply a moral criterion that they agree is necessary for legal validity, their recognition of some social fact (such as a single authoritative pronouncement) as sufficient for validity will always trump that moral criterion. Even their belief in and application of that moral criterion as a necessary condition for validity does not render it a truly necessary condition, since it cannot be necessary where a conflicting

[27] A similar critique of ILP is levelled by Giudice (2015, p. 117).

sufficient condition of social fact has been met. Hence, from an external perspective examining the metaphysics of law, a moral criterion cannot serve as a necessary condition among the criteria of validity. Waluchow's understanding of ILP might be a more accurate reflection of the internal perspective of officials, what they believe to be the conditions required for legal validity in systems that appear to embrace a moral criterion. But this analysis has shown that internal perspective to be metaphysically inaccurate, while offering a glimpse of why the official picture does not match the deeper reality of law.

Acknowledgment Big thanks to Michael Giudice for comments on an earlier draft, and to Alex Sarch and Simon Palmer for helpful discussions.

References

Alexander, Larry. 1990. Law and Exclusionary Reasons. *Philosophical Topics* 18: 5–22.
Dicey, A.V. 1982. *Introduction to the Study of the Law of the Constitution (First Published 1885)*. Indianapolis: Liberty Fund.
Dworkin, Ronald. 1986. *Law's Empire*. Cambridge, Mass: Belknap Press.
Ehrenberg, Kenneth M. 2016a. *The Functions of Law*. Oxford: Oxford University Press.
———. 2016b. Law as Plan and Artefact. *Jurisprudence* 7: 325–340.
Giudice, Michael. 2008. The Regular Practice of Morality in Law. *Ratio Juris* 21: 94–106.
———. 2015. *Understanding the Nature of Law*. Cheltenham: Edward Elgar.
Hart, H. L. A. 1994. *The Concept of Law*, 2nd edn. (first published 1961). Oxford: Oxford University Press.
Hogg, Peter. 1997. *Constitutional Law of Canada*. 4th ed. Toronto: Carswell.
MacCormick, Neil. 1974. Law as Institutional Fact. *Law Quarterly Review* 90: 102–129.
Patterson, Dennis M. 2018. Theoretical Disagreement, Legal Positivism, and Interpretation. *Ratio Juris* 31: 260–275.
Raz, Joseph. 1972. Legal Principles and the Limits of Law. *Yale Law Journal* 81: 823–854.
———. 1975. *Practical Reason and Norms*. London: Hutchinson.
———. 1994. *Ethics in the Public Domain: Essays in the Morality of Law and Politics*. Oxford: Oxford University Press.
Searle, John R. 1995. *The Construction of Social Reality*. New York: Free Press.
Shapiro, Scott J. 2000. Law, Morality, and the Guidance of Conduct. *Legal Theory* 6: 127–170.
———. 2011. *Legality*. Cambridge, Mass: Harvard University Press.
Thomasson, Amie L. 2003. Realism and Human Kinds. *Philosophy and Phenomenological Research* 67: 580–609.
Waluchow, Wilfrid J. 1991. Charter Challenges: A Test Case for Theories of Law. *Osgoode Hall Law Journal* 29: 183–214.
———. 2000. Authority and the Practical Difference Thesis. *Legal Theory* 6: 45–81.
———. 2008a. Constitutional Morality and Bills of Rights. In *Expounding the Constitution: Essays in Constitutional Theory*, ed. Grant Huscroft, 65–92. Cambridge: Cambridge University Press.
———. 2008b. Legality, Morality, and the Guiding Function of Law. In *The Legacy of HLA Hart, Legal, Political, and Moral Philosophy*, ed. Claire Grant et al., 85–97. Oxford: Oxford University Press.
———. 2015. Constitutional Rights and the Possibility of Detached Constitutional Interpretation. *Problema* 9: 23–52.
———. 2018. Normative Reasoning from a Point of View. In *Unpacking Normativity*, ed. Kenneth Einar Himma, Miodrag Jovanovic, and Bojan Spaic, 119–133. Oxford: Hart Publishing.

Kenneth M. Ehrenberg is Professor of Jurisprudence and Philosophy at the University of Surrey, United Kingdom. Prior to that he held appointments in philosophy and law at the University of Alabama and at the State University of New York at Buffalo. In 2010, he was HLA Hart Visiting Fellow at the Oxford Centre for Ethics and Philosophy of Law. He writes about the relationship between law and morality, the social ontology of law, jurisprudential methodology, and legal normativity and is the author of *The Functions of Law* (Oxford, 2016).

Responses to Waluchow on Raz

André L. S. Coelho

Abstract Since its publication in 1994, Wilfrid J. Waluchow's first book, "Inclusive Legal Positivism" (ILP), has been regarded as the best defence of that jurisprudential account. This chapter engages with Waluchow's arguments against Joseph Raz, particularly the criticism of his conception of authority and its consequences for the debate between exclusive and inclusive legal positivism. The aim of the chapter is to present: (1) a short summary of Raz's view on authority and his defence of exclusive legal positivism; (2) a response to Waluchow's criticism of Raz's view of the necessarily peremptory nature of authority in general, pointing out that, despite Waluchow being right about that, it might be the case that the authority law claims is, in fact, of the peremptory type; (3) a response to Waluchow's criticism of Raz's view of the necessarily peremptory nature of law's authority in particular, where Waluchow appeals to the role exceptions play in the enforcement of legal norms; (4) a response to Waluchow's criticism to Raz's analogy between law and arbitration, where Waluchow reminds the role coordination and consensus play both in arbitration and in law; and, finally, (5) an explanation of the true nature of the disagreement between exclusive and inclusive legal positivists, that I view as residing in their conceptions of "description," and why such disagreement is unlikely to be overcome.

1 Introduction

Wilfrid J. Waluchow's seminal work, *Inclusive Legal Positivism*, published in 1994, has consistently stood the test of time as the foremost defense of this particular jurisprudential perspective. In a realm populated by notable scholars such as Jules Coleman, Matthew Kramer, and Kenneth E. Himma, *Inclusive Legal Positivism* nonetheless retains its unrivalled status even after twenty-seven years. It is, therefore, no exaggeration to assert that delving into the intricate arguments presented in this

A. L. S. Coelho (✉)
Federal University of Rio de Janeiro, Rio de Janeiro, RJ, Brazil
e-mail: andrecoelho@direito.ufrj.br

T. Bustamante et al. (eds.), *Law, Morality and Judicial Reasoning*, Law and Philosophy Library 147, https://doi.org/10.1007/978-3-031-61879-6_4

masterpiece is not only relevant but also an indispensable endeavor for anyone who earnestly seeks to grapple with the intricacies of legal theory.

Waluchow devotes a substantial portion of the book to the polemical defense of inclusive legal positivism against its most prominent critics. His intellectual battle is fought on two distinct fronts, as outlined in the insightful introduction: interpretivism and exclusive legal positivism, epitomised by the figures of Ronald Dworkin and Joseph Raz, respectively. It is important to note that the present chapter does not delve into a defense of Dworkin's views. Instead, its primary focus is engaging with Waluchow's comprehensive arguments aimed at refuting Raz's perspective, with particular emphasis on the critical examination of Raz's notion of authority and its far-reaching implications for the exclusive-versus-inclusive legal positivism debate. It is my hope, therefore, that the present chapter will serve as a resource for those seeking an in-depth understanding of these intricate jurisprudential discussions and the pivotal role that Waluchow's work plays in shaping them.

In what follows, I outline the core themes of my analysis, each of which illuminates key aspects of the complex debate surrounding Joseph Raz's jurisprudential views and Wilfrid J. Waluchow's critical engagement with them.

First, I provide a brief overview of Raz's perspective on authority and his staunch defense of exclusive legal positivism. This basic exposition sets the stage for the subsequent examination of Waluchow's critique.

Second, I address Waluchow's critique of Raz's claim that authority is inherently peremptory. While I agree with Waluchow's observation, I argue that it is plausible that the authority ascribed to law may indeed possess peremptory characteristics, despite Waluchow's reservations.

Third, I consider Waluchow's objection to Raz's view of the peremptory nature of legal authority, focusing on the role of exceptions in the enforcement of legal norms. In doing so, I emphasize Raz's distinction between the authority claimed by the law and the authority law possesses, arguing that the former does not accommodate exceptions while the latter does, thus clarifying the essence of their disagreement.

Fourth, I address Waluchow's challenge to Raz's analogy between law and arbitration, in which Waluchow stresses the role of coordination and consensus in both contexts. In contrast, I argue that a more accurate account of law is one that emphasizes conflict and disagreement and thus sheds light on the true nature of legal phenomena.

Finally, I offer an explanation of the fundamental divergence between exclusive and inclusive legal positivists, which I identify as rooted in their contrasting conceptions of "description." I also explore the challenges inherent in reconciling these opposing views and suggest that such reconciliation may be an elusive goal.

2 A Brief Summary of Raz's Ideas

At this point, Joseph Raz's conceptualization of the authority of law and his vigorous advocacy of exclusive legal positivism have attained such a preeminent status within jurisprudential discourse that they would seem to obviate the need for any further explication. Nevertheless, the nuances of Raz's arguments, which Wilfrid J. Waluchow examines and to which I offer responses, are closely intertwined with a precise understanding of Raz's foundational ideas. Consequently, it would be unwise to omit a brief recapitulation of Raz's views before embarking on a more comprehensive exploration of the intricacies and implications of these debates. Thus, in the following exposition, I will provide a brief overview of Raz's perspective on the nature of legal authority and his resolute stance in favor of exclusive legal positivism, in order to lay the necessary groundwork for a more rigorous and detailed analysis of the divergent views and critiques that have animated contemporary jurisprudential discourse.

Following the work of H.L.A. Hart (1961, p. 100–110), there is a widespread consensus among positivist scholars that each legal system has a rule of recognition that serves as a guiding source for identifying the conditions under which a legal norm is valid. These conditions are commonly referred to as the criteria of legal validity. The central dispute between adherents of exclusive and inclusive legal positivism hinges on the crucial question of whether the criteria of legal validity can include moral considerations. Exclusive legal positivism staunchly maintains that it is conceptually impossible for law to incorporate moral criteria into its rule of recognition, thereby decisively separating law from moral considerations. Inclusive legal positivism, on the other hand, holds that while the inclusion of moral criteria is not mandatory, it remains conceptually possible and, in certain legal systems, a factual reality.

Joseph Raz emerges as a prominent proponent of exclusive legal positivism, so it is imperative to examine the foundations of his perspective in order to understand why he is so adamant that the inclusion of moral criteria within the scope of the law's validity is an impossibility. Central to Raz's argument is his conception of the authority of law, which serves as the linchpin of his argument. Raz posits that the assertion of law's authority is not merely a contingent attribute, but a conceptually necessary feature (Raz 1979, p. 93–94). It is precisely this conceptual necessity of law's claim to authority, juxtaposed with the inherent incompatibility of moral criteria with such claims, that leads Raz to the inescapable conclusion that the integration of moral criteria into the legal domain is inherently a conceptual impossibility.

It would be no exaggeration to say that Raz actually has not one but several versions (at least three, according to the most reliable commentators on his work as a whole) of the main argument about how authority acts in terms of second-order reasons and why this nature of authority makes law incompatible with moral criteria. It is not the intention of this brief summary to decide which of these versions is ultimately more convincing, nor to commit to defending Raz's argument against

Waluchow's rejoinders in only one of these versions. I would therefore like the following explanation to be seen as a summary of a basic version that is more or less present in all of the fuller versions of the argument. This lowest common denominator of Raz's argument will suffice for our purposes in the later sections of the chapter.

Raz describes authority as having the capability to create exclusionary, second-order reasons, which negates the agent's first-order reasons for acting differently and which unilaterally decides what the agent must do. While first-order reasons are the pros and cons that the agent weighs and compares in their balance of reasons, authoritative directives (while functioning as second-order reasons) render first-order reasons and their balance irrelevant. Authoritative directives attain a preemption (replacement) of those reasons, becoming the sole determinant of the agent's action.

According to Raz, authority implies a preemption of reasons, a substitution of the subject's reasons for acting with those given by the authority's directives—in this case, the norms of law. This statement depends on Raz's theory of practical reasons, which divides them into first-order and second-order reasons. First-order reasons are reasons to do or not to do something, which can have more or less weight. When there is a conflict between reasons to do and not to do, it is decided by weighing the reasons, taking into account which sum of the reasons (the sum of all the pros or all the cons) has more weight. Second-order reasons, on the other hand, are not reasons for doing or not doing something, but reasons for considering or disregarding first-order reasons.

In the case of the second-order reasons that are of most interest to Raz—namely, exclusionary reasons—they cancel out or remove the balance of reasons, replacing the first-order reasons against their determination (but leaving intact the first-order reasons that weigh in favor of that same determination). Thus, an agent can have first-order reasons for and against robbing a bank. If no authoritative determination were made, the agent would decide whether or not to rob the bank based on the comparative balance of these first-order reasons. However, the legal rule that criminalizes this conduct by assigning a corresponding penalty acts as a second-order reason for the exclusionary type, cancelling out the first-order reasons for robbery but maintaining the preexisting contrary reasons. The agent then has first-order reasons against robbing the bank and a second-order exclusionary reason that, on the one hand, cancels out the reasons in favor of the robbery and, on the other, replaces them by adding a second-order reason for giving up the robbery.

If confronted with other exclusionary reasons, reasons of this type don't have weight, but rather a hierarchy, greater or lesser. For example, the authority of the law prevails over that of the individual over himself, or of a boss at work, or of a parent in the family. They don't alter or contribute to the balance of first-order reasons, but they do replace (preempt) the balance of reasons with what they determine. This is the thesis of preemption, which Raz formulates as follows: "The fact that an authority requires performance of an action is a reason for its performance which is not to be added to all other relevant reasons when assessing what to do, but should replace some of them." (Raz 1994, p. 214)

A short example will help to clarify this. If a lawyer working in a law firm is unsure whether to file a motion to subpoena a witness, she is unsure because there are compelling pros and cons. In order to reach a decision, the lawyer is likely to weigh and compare the pros and cons (her first-order reasons for acting) in a balance of reasons and conclude which side is weightier in terms of both strategic advantages and other moral, legal, or political considerations. Alternatively, if, getting closer to the fatal decision deadline, the lawyer's employer intervenes, puts an end to the impasse, and instructs her to file the complaint anyway, any pros and cons she had been considering so far become irrelevant and her reason for acting from that point on is based solely on the employer's instruction (her second-order reason for acting).

According to Rawls, the claim that the lawyer, by obeying the order of the employer as her boss (i.e. by obeying the order of an authority), has abandoned her first-order reasons in order to treat only the employer's order as a second-order reason for action—that is, she has engaged in preemption of reasons—is compatible with the claim that the lawyer is following the course of action that presumably still best satisfies the reasons that apply to her in the situation. This is because the order given by the authority is supposed to have taken into account the reasons for and against and to have reached a final decision that represents a superior judgement of knowledge. Therefore, the lawyer is not entitled to reexamine the reasons in order to reopen the decision. This is also why, by deciding to act as instructed, the lawyer is in a better position to take into account the reasons relevant to her than she would be if she tried to decide for herself which side of the balance of reasons had more weight:

> The normal and primary way to establish that a person should be acknowledged to have authority over another person involves showing that the alleged subject is likely better to comply with reasons which apply to him (other than the alleged authoritative directives) if he accepts the directives of the alleged authority as authoritatively binding, and tries to follow them, than if he tries to follow the reasons which apply to him directly. (Raz 1994, p. 214)

Such an example also helps to distinguish between persuasion (an attempt to influence the agent's balance of reasons) and command (an exercise of authority that overrides that balance of reasons and unilaterally determines what the agent is to do). If the boss had tried to persuade the lawyer to file the complaint, she would have insisted on the first-order reasons, the pros and cons, to show that one or the other was more compelling. But because the boss did not use persuasion but authority, she gave an order, took the decision out of the lawyer's hands, disregarded the result of her weighing of the reasons, and replaced her first-order reasons with the exclusionary second-order reason of doing what she was ordered to do.

Raz maintains that law always claims authority over its subjects in the sense that it always expects those subjects to treat legal norms as exclusionary, second-order reasons for action. Law never leaves it to the subjects to decide whether or not what the legal norm commands is the best course of action. In other words, it never presents itself as yet another first-order reason to be taken into account in the subjects' balance of reasons. The very existence of a valid law implies that whatever reasons the subjects previously had to act this way or that have become irrelevant in the eyes of the law, because the only relevant reason now is to obey the law's commands.

Two additional remarks are necessary at this point. One is to make clear that Raz is not saying that every valid legal norm should be obeyed no matter what, only that such treatment is what the law claims or expects of its subjects. The other is to emphasize that, according to Raz, such a claim to authority is conceptually necessary, in the sense that law would not be law if it did not claim authority. This is because, unlike morality, which is obligatory by means of persuasion, law is obligatory by means of preemption, and preemption cannot be achieved without authority.

Moral propositions and moral criteria, according to Raz, are never capable of doing this. Moral reasons are first-order reasons to be taken into account in the balance of reasons, or are the supposed result of the balance of reasons. But they are never second-order reasons that overturn such a balance. Moral reasons appeal to persuasion, not to authority. If true, they are certainly obligatory, but on the basis of reasons that the agent is supposed to understand and agree with, not on the basis of authority.

To take a single example that has become famous in the literature of ethics, neither Kant's statement that lying is always wrong nor Benjamin Constant's response that lying is sometimes acceptable can be declared true on the basis of authority. No one is a moral authority whose moral statements should be taken as moral truth regardless of the agent's considerations or disagreements. All they can do is provide the agent with a rational justification for their positions. Moral reasons never climb the vertical staircase of preemption; they only walk the horizontal path of persuasion.

It is only a product of logical inference to surmise that law can never incorporate moral criteria into its rule of recognition. As a matter of conceptual necessity, since law must always claim authority over its subjects, and morality can never be compatible with authority, it follows that law can never incorporate moral criteria. Hence, the conclusion is that exclusive legal positivism is the best jurisprudential account.

Take, for example, a constitutional rule that no law may be passed that imposes cruel or unusual punishment. Leaving aside the "unusual" part and focusing only on the "cruel," such a rule could be said to introduce a moral criterion into the rule of recognition of that legal system. After all, it clearly states that a law imposing cruel punishment is not to be considered valid, which means that "non-cruelty" (an apparently clear case of a moral criterion) has become a criterion of legal validity for laws. This is exactly the kind of example that inclusive legal positivists like to invoke.

According to Raz, because it's conceptually impossible for law to incorporate moral criteria, nothing like that happens. What is really going on is one of two things. Either the criterion in the case is not moral and persuasive, but legal and authoritative (not what moral reasoning would conclude is not cruel, but what the higher courts say it is: for example, the death penalty in the US); or the criterion is indeed moral, but it is invoked as something external to the law, without being "incorporated" into the law (in the same way that a French legal norm can be invoked by a US judgment without becoming part of US law). Either the morality of the criterion is apparent but not real, or its incorporation into law is what is apparent but not real.

This, in a nutshell, is the gist of Raz's ideas. Much was left unmentioned, such as the difference between de facto and legitimate authority, his service conception of authority, the separation between a (necessarily descriptive) theory of law and a (necessarily normative) theory of adjudication, and the difference between the legal point of view and judicial decision-making, among others—some of which were unnecessary for our purposes and some of which will be mentioned later in my critical examination.

3 Waluchow on Raz's Conception of Authority in General

A critical response to Joseph Raz's link between the authority of law and exclusive legal positivism is to challenge the notion that legal norms uniformly provide peremptory, exclusionary reasons for action. Wilfrid J. Waluchow develops this critique in two key steps. First, he posits that Raz's insistence on peremptory authority as the only reasonable account of practical authority is not a plausible position. Second, Waluchow argues that this all-or-nothing perspective does not align closely with the practical treatment of legal norms by officials and citizens, both of whom often pursue a more nuanced and flexible approach. If correct, this argument would challenge Raz's rigid characterization of practical authority and add depth to the discourse on the intersection of legal authority and inclusive and exclusive legal positivism.

The first argument resonates in everyday scenarios involving authority. In practical situations, when a supervisor instructs an employee to retrieve an item from the office, the employee is not expected to break down a locked door or enter the premises even in the face of a fire. This illustrates that the supervisor's instruction is not in itself an all-encompassing, exclusionary reason overriding all other considerations. It is crucial to recognize that the authority conferred by such directives—for there is nothing in the admission that these competing reasons also carry weight and must be taken into account that leads us to the conclusion that the supervisor therefore lacks any authority whatsoever—does not depend on the existence of peremptory, exclusionary, or preemptive reasons. This underlines the broader point that authority need not be absolute and based on such grounds alone. In fact, authority can manifest itself in different forms, and the absolutist paradigm represents only one possible conception among several conceivable types of authority.

In this context, I tend to agree with Waluchow. Joseph Raz presents his account as if it encompasses all forms of authority, when in fact it is primarily concerned with a single type: peremptory authority. To illustrate, both the authority of a supervisor over their employees and the authority of the law over its subjects are instances of authority. However, unlike the legal system, a responsible boss does not claim or expect, and reasonably so, that their employees should unconditionally obey their instructions, even when unforeseen, compelling circumstances dictate otherwise.

The above reasonable supervisor expects her command (in this case, to get something from the office) to override some reasons for disobedience, such as not wanting to or not agreeing that it is the best thing to do. But she is certainly not claiming or expecting that her command will override every possible reason for disobedience, including those she has not considered (the office was closed) or could never have considered (the building was on fire). This is not to say that her order lacks authority, only that it lacks authority of the peremptory type. This should be conceded without any reservations.

Joseph Raz's conception of authority might be less open to criticism in this regard if he explicitly admitted that the real scope of his theory concerns only peremptory authority. Such an approach would allow for the consideration of other, non-peremptory forms of authority in contrast to the peremptory model. These alternative forms could be explored on the basis of the nature of the first-order reasons they seek to negate or uphold—for example, whether they operate through preferential rather than exclusionary second-order reasons.

However, it should be remembered that while these critiques have successfully shown that many instances of the exercise of authority do not involve peremptory authority, they have not gone so far as to exclude peremptory authority as a possible type of authority that can be exercised in the real world. It is perhaps not the only model of authority, but it is still one model of authority. It is the form of authority that Raz particularly emphasizes and assigns to law as one of its essential claims.

4 Waluchow on Raz's Conception of Law's Authority in Particular

Waluchow's second claim similarly resonates with those familiar with the practical enforcement of law. The all-or-nothing characterization of peremptory authority departs from the usual treatment of legal norms within existing legal systems. It is not uncommon for legal norms to contain exceptions, whether explicitly stated in their language or arising from the interplay of other legal norms and judicial considerations. In cases where legal norms contain exceptions, certain first-order reasons for acting otherwise remain unaffected and continue to be relevant factors that may even outweigh the norms when applicable. This underscores the fact that such norms do not function as exclusionary, second-order reasons and highlights the nuanced and context-dependent nature of their authority in practice.

Waluchow explains that the presence of exceptions within legal norms does not negate their authoritative status, clarifying that legal norms retain their authority over both officials and citizens even when they allow for exceptions. This concept of being mandatory while allowing for exceptions applies to a substantial majority of legal norms, implying that a significant portion of the legal framework exercises authority without functioning as exclusionary reasons. As a result, the model of preferential rather than exclusionary authority that was previously proposed to explain the authority of a boss seems equally appropriate for characterizing the authority of legal norms.

At this point, it's important to note a shift in Waluchow's critique. His current critique departs from the notion that authority is not exclusively peremptory but is specifically concerned with the nature of the authority of legal norms. Consequently, the focus has shifted from a critique of Raz's conception of authority in the broad sense to a critique of Raz's conception of the authority exercised by legal norms.

Nevertheless, it is important to disentangle the critique at hand, which seems to conflate Joseph Raz's conception of the authority that law inherently claims as a matter of conceptual analysis with the authority that law actually exercises over officials and citizens in practice. Raz distinguishes between three distinct types of theories of law: those of validity, adjudication, and obedience, only the first of which is devoid of moral criteria. Crucially, Raz's concept of the authority of law is grounded in its conceptual nature as obligatory valid law, which seeks to describe what law in its essence requires or anticipates of those subject to it. This framework is not intended to describe the precise way in which law is enforced or obeyed in practice; rather, it elucidates what law *qua law* requires or expects of its subjects. Thus, to the extent that law requires or expects individuals to regard legal norms as second-order reasons that supersede and replace their first-order reasons, it posits authority of the peremptory variety, in line with Raz's conceptual framework.

This clarification places Waluchow's three examples of exceptions to legal norms in a different status. In the case of an exception contained in the legal norm itself, there is a second-order reason (the norm) for treating the first-order reason (the exception) as practically relevant. The same applies to an exception introduced by a second legal norm, since the norm–exception relationship results from the connection between two second-order reasons (the two legal norms forming a larger, more complete resulting norm).

The third type, however, wherein an exception is not prescribed by any legal norm, must be explained by a theory of either adjudication or obedience. According to Raz, because officials and citizens are responsible actors who use not only the legal point of view (which focuses solely on validity and authority), but also the wide range of their practical reason, they weigh legal directives against other considerations (undesirable consequences, unforeseen factors, etc.). Some of the non–legally prescribed exceptions are not what the law claims or expects, but are the effect of more compelling reasons that are taken into account despite what the law claims or expects.

It is therefore perfectly compatible for legal norms to claim peremptory authority over its subjects and to allow for exceptions. Either these exceptions result from the content of one or more legal norms of the system (being a product of the authority of the law, rather than an exception to it), or they result from compelling reasons other than the law, taken into account by officials and citizens as a matter of adjudication or obedience (and therefore outside the reign of legal theory and the legal point of view).

Furthermore, it is crucial to emphasize that the nature of the authority that law claims over its subjects cannot be accurately assessed by examining how these subjects interact with legal norms in practice. The way law is treated factually does not necessarily correspond to the conceptual claims it makes. Joseph Raz's argument underscores that the authority ascribed to law is the result of conceptual necessity rather than contingent factual circumstances. Thus, any assessment of the authority of law should be rooted in an understanding of its conceptual underpinnings, which may not always reflect its application in the real world.

5 Waluchow on Raz's Analogy Between Law and Arbitration

Joseph Raz presents an analogy between law and arbitration, drawing a parallel in which, in both scenarios, the parties involved acknowledge their inability to arrive at a solution independently. As a result, they abandon their original, first-order reasons for acting in various ways and instead commit themselves to abiding exclusively by the second-order reason represented by the arbitrator's decision, regardless of its specific content. This analogy serves as a conceptual framework to illuminate the distinctive nature of the authority vested in law and underscores the central role of second-order reasons in shaping the dynamics of compliance and decision-making within the legal and arbitral domains:

> Suppose that an arbitrator, asked to decide what is fair in a situation, has given a correct decision. That is, suppose there is only one fair outcome, and it was picked out by the arbitrator. Suppose that the parties to the dispute are told only that about his decision, i.e. that he gave the only correct decision. They will feel that they know little more of what the decision is than they did before. They were given a uniquely identifying description of the decision and yet it is an entirely unhelpful description. If they could agree on what was fair they would not have needed the arbitrator in the first place. A decision is serviceable only if it can be identified by means other than the considerations the weight and outcome of which it was meant to settle. (Raz 1994, p. 219)

Waluchow's critique of the analogy between law and arbitration introduces three distinct sub-arguments. First, he contends that arbitration is not only characterized by its peremptory resolution of disputes, but also encompasses a broader dimension focused on fostering respect, cooperation, and understanding. Arbitration can serve as a mechanism for building bridges and repairing relationships beyond the mere imposition of peremptory decisions. Second, Waluchow notes that in arbitration, it remains possible for an arbitrator to frame a dispute in terms of conflicting moral principles, leaving it to the parties to deliberate on the implications of the chosen principle. This flexibility differs from the all-encompassing peremptory nature suggested by the analogy. Third, Waluchow highlights a fundamental difference between arbitration and legal norms. Legal norms are often based on moral grounds that enjoy broad consensus, in contrast to arbitration, which may involve more contentious moral disagreements.

This is the point at which, in my view, Joseph Raz's analogy could potentially regain its potency, provided that two specific calibrations are made, both aimed at selecting appropriate examples to reach the desired conclusions. The first calibration concerns the choice of exemplary decisions.

It is true that arbitration can, and often does, incorporate elements of pedagogy, dialogue, and collegiality into its procedures. However, these instances do not necessarily embody the most robust or distinct type of authority that arbitration exercises—the very type that leads individuals to seek arbitrators in the first place. Similarly, while it is true that not all police arrests involve violence, the potential for such violence is integral to the definition of what constitutes a police arrest and the rationale for judicial authorities to order them. Just as peaceful arrests, regardless of their frequency, do not provide a particularly illustrative insight into the nature of police arrests, consensual arbitrations, regardless of their prevalence, may not serve as the most representative examples of the overarching nature of arbitration.

The second calibration concerns the choice of exemplary societies. The degree of moral consensus within a society directly influences the extent to which its legal norms are based on shared moral beliefs or dictate decisions individuals could make independently. Consequently, in societies characterized by a lack of moral consensus, the need for peremptory authority becomes more pronounced. It is conceivable that in a society in which moral consensus is extremely rare, a majority of its legal norms may settle disputes in ways that are beyond the capacity of individuals to resolve them independently. Such a society exemplifies the most extreme and distinctive form of authority that a legal norm can exercise. Therefore, it is in pluralistic and discordant societies that we witness the most exemplary cases of this authority.

In conclusion, then, by applying the double calibration that I have proposed, the type of authority that an arbitral tribunal exercises in its most exemplary decisions illustrates the type that law also exercises in the most exemplary societies—not those that are more frequent, but those that are most revealing of the type of authority involved in the decisions in question.

Of course, the double calibration argument depends on what exemplarity means in analytical investigations. What I am proposing here is perhaps analogous to (though completely independent of the plausibility of) Finnis's contrast between finding what happens in all possible cases and finding the central case whose features are more exemplary. With the important difference that I am defending what I consider to be the positivist version of Finnis's central case, which is the following: Law reveals its true nature not where social order and rational regulation are most successful, but where they are least successful. The true nature of law is to be sought in social contexts that have lost every other way for individuals to live together except through law.

In my view, this illustrates the rationale behind Max Weber's account of law as a purposive, rational institution. Weber's analysis begins with the recognition that modernity represents an ideal type characterized by the imminent erosion of shared trust and values within society. It also sheds light on why contemporary writers such as Jeremy Waldron and Scott Shapiro have given a central role to social disagreement within their positivist frameworks. It is worth noting, however, that they treat social disagreement as an empirical fact, whereas I see it as a heuristic device to enhance our exploration of the essence of law.

6 The Nature of Description and the Disagreement Between Positivists

In my interpretation of Joseph Raz's work, his particular brand of analytic philosophy encompasses two discernibly different intellectual endeavors, both of which are often referred to by the label "description." The first can be characterized as a conceptual or a priori description of law, while the second can be classified as a factual or a posteriori description of law.

The term "conceptual" or "a priori" description refers to a particular way of describing thing X that differs from the conventional approach of describing the characteristics that X typically possesses or that are attributed to X on the basis of widely held intuitions. Instead, it involves articulating features that are intrinsically bound to X by the compelling force of conceptual necessity. In other words, these properties are indispensable to the definition of X; without them, X would lose its essence and identity. To illustrate this, consider a cube: its fundamental definition requires the presence of six square sides, which inherently results in its having eight vertices. Describing a cube as having six square sides is an example of a conceptual description because it is undeniably true by virtue of the very definition of a cube. Conversely, to say that a cube has eight vertices is to extrapolate or extend the original definition in order to arrive at a conclusion that, although not stated in the definition, is implicit in it or can be derived from it by reasoned inference, and so is also an appropriate example of a conceptual description.

The other category includes the "factual" or "a posteriori" description of X, which ventures into the realm of synthetic propositions by drawing on one of three sources: common experience, historical evidence, or shared intuitions. Common experience is invoked when a sufficiently well-informed and experienced individual recognizes a proposition as true on the basis of life experience; for example, the widely accepted fact that law usually involves an element of coercion falls into this category. Historical evidence comes into play when a careful examination of our legal system in comparison with others from another time or place is sufficient to establish the generality or particularity of a certain feature. For example, the prohibition of murder as a general feature of all law, or the importance of judicial review as a particular feature of contemporary Western law, can be established by historical evidence.

Finally, a shared intuition arises when, even in the absence of extensive support from personal experience or historical evidence, a particular characteristic of X seems self-evident and resistant to counterargument. For example, the idea that the effectiveness of most laws depends on their association with sanctions seems intuitively compelling and difficult to dispute. These cases exemplify the realm of factual or a posteriori description, where empirical evidence and shared convictions illuminate the nature of X beyond the confines of mere conceptual necessity.

This distinction is of considerable value in exploring Joseph Raz's link between authority and exclusive positivism. It illuminates the difference between two kinds of statements: those affirming that law inherently claims an all-or-nothing form of authority, and those affirming that law lacks moral criteria for the validity of its norms. These statements do not constitute institutional descriptions (which would be empirical descriptions of institutions), but rather fall into the category of conceptual descriptions. They do not refer to the collective experience of dealing with the law, but revolve around inescapable assumptions about its nature, based on what is considered essential or definitional to its character as law. They are essentially a priori descriptions, immune to challenge by a posteriori observations or empirical evidence.

It is in the nature of a priori descriptions that, if they are true, they are also conceptually true, which means that no empirical fact can ever disprove them—for either that empirical fact illustrates the concept, carrying with it everything that is conceptually true about it, or it does not carry with it anything that is conceptually true about that concept, because it is not an illustration of it at all. You cannot disprove that a cube has six sides by showing a cube that has more or fewer sides, because either what you are showing is a cube and you are wrong about its number of sides, or what you are showing does have more or fewer than six sides, but you are wrong about it being a cube. Either way, you would be wrong, and you have failed to provide any disproof. Any alleged empirical disproof you provide will be reinterpreted in light of the a priori description, which is treated as conceptually true.

Now, here is how I see Raz's defense of the peremptory authority of law as a conceptual description of his claim. First, you start from a necessary feature of law. In this case, it is that law is obligatory, not optional or facultative.

Then you decide whether this obligation is peremptory or conditional. You can take the point of view of how the law is treated by officials and citizens, or the point of view of what the law claims just by being the law. The first is a posteriori and varies from one legal system to another. The second is a priori and unchanging. You therefore take the point of view of what the law claims and realise that every legal norm claims to be the sole and final reason for action unless it or another legal norm says otherwise.

Thus, the obligation that law asserts is peremptory, not conditional. This is not a feature of our legal system in particular, or of most legal systems known to have existed, but a necessary feature of law as law. To present itself as law is to claim peremptory authority.

Now, if one tries to dispute that by showing empirical evidence of how people usually deal with legal norms, I will state that this is about the authority that the law has, not about what the law claims. If shown some legal norms that explicitly admit they are not the only and final reason for action and should be followed only in the absence of some other, stronger reason, I would maintain that the fact that they explicitly admit this is further evidence that without this concession, their authority would be peremptory.

Although some may argue that this view of practical authority is too narrow and extreme, it is up to them to show not only that another conception of practical authority is possible, but that such an alternative conception is capable of being reconciled with the kind of obligation that law claims to have over our actions in the most exemplary cases. The battle must be fought on the conceptual, a priori level about law, and not on the factual, a posteriori level—or there won't be a battle at all.

This is also why I think that the exclusive/inclusive dispute is destined to spin around in repetitions and insistence: while one person might say, as a matter of factual description, that a legal norm prohibiting cruel punishment is a case of incorporation of moral criteria into the law, I would say, as a matter of conceptual description, that such incorporation is conceptually impossible and that, therefore, something else must be going on there (it is not a moral criterion except in its appearance at first glance; it operates in authoritative, not moral, logic; it makes use of moral content without incorporating it into the law, etc.). For some, incorporation is a fact that one first verifies and then use to change their conception of the law (like the weight or color of the cube); for me, incorporation is not a fact unless my conception of the law allows it to be true (it is like the number of vertices of the cube, which is not contained in the definition of the cube but can be obtained from it by inference or extrapolation).

In essence, I believe that Wilfrid J. Waluchow's critique of Joseph Raz's concept of authority and its association with exclusive legal positivism arises from an interpretation that treats Raz's claims as if they were intended to be empirically factual rather than conceptually true. It is important to note that Waluchow is certainly well versed in the a priori/a posteriori distinction and fully aware that Raz is presenting a conceptual argument about law. What may underlie this divergence, however, is a difference in preference as to which type of description of law is considered more relevant or valuable—with Waluchow placing greater emphasis on a factual description rather than a purely conceptual one. Or, better still, it may be that Waluchow's position is actually that conceptual description should be responsibly informed by factual description, striking a balance between the abstract conceptual framework and the empirical realities that inform our understanding of the law.

7 Conclusion

In this chapter, after summarizing Raz's arguments, I have conceded Waluchow's criticism that peremptory authority is not the only model of authority, while sustaining that it is one of the models that authority can take. I have shown that pointing out exceptions to the application of legal norms, whether by virtue of other legal norms or by the responsible practical reasoning of those who apply and obey the law, does not constitute an objection to the model of peremptory authority. I defended the analogy with arbitration, as long as we keep in mind the double calibration of focusing on exemplary decisions (those that arbitrate in cases of extreme disagreement) and exemplary societies (those that are traversed by extreme disagreement) to show the true nature of legal authority. Finally, I have explained how I believe that beneath the divergence between inclusive and exclusive positivism lies another, more complex divergence about the nature of the "description of law" that is relevant to legal theory. I hope that, in this way, the possible arguments that Raz, or a committed Razian, might use to defend his theory against Waluchow's objections will become clearer—notwithstanding the possibility that, after these clarifications, those who are in favor of the same emphases as Waluchow will be even more convinced of the correctness of their choice of side.

References

Hart, H.L.A. 1961. *The Concept of Law*. Oxford: Oxford University Press.
Raz, Joseph. 1979. *The Authority of Law: Essays on Law and Morality*. Oxford: Clarendon Press.
———. 1994. *Ethics in the Public Domain: Essays in the Morality of Law and Politics*. New York: Oxford University Press.
Waluchow, Wilfried J. 1994. *Inclusive Legal Positivism*. New York: Oxford University Press.

André L. S. Coelho is Professor of Legal Theory and Philosophy of Law at the Law School of the Federal University of Rio de Janeiro, in Brazil. He holds an M.Phil and a Ph.D in Philosophy from the Federal University of Santa Catarina, Brazil, with a Research Visit at the Goethe Universität of Frankfurt, Germany. He has previously taught at CESUPA and The University of Amazon, both in Brazil.

Waluchow on Institutional Forces of Law

João Vitor Penna

Abstract The chapter examines the idea of institutional forces of law, introduced by Wil Waluchow in *Inclusive Legal Positivism*. This concept is presented in Waluchow's theory to clarify Ronald Dworkin's suggestion that a theory of law must provide an account about the justification of state coercion. Waluchow argues that law has different kinds of institutional forces operating on judges and officials, which leads him to reject Dworkin's defense of a moral justification of coercion as a necessary part of a theory of the nature of law. Therefore, he concludes that it is one thing to say that a proposition is legally valid, and it is quite another to say that it is mandatory for judges. However, Waluchow gave no clear responses to two important questions related to that idea. First, given the various connections between institutional forces of law and the problem of the grounds of law, as a matter of a theory of law, it raises the question of whether these concepts are truly separate. Second, since the problem of the force of law is a matter of legal normativity, it leads us to inquire about Waluchow's explanation for the rise of legal obligations and the role of coercion in his concept of law. This paper concludes that any successful theory about the nature of law must also have an account of the institutional forces of law, at least at a minimum level that could describe how the law is obligatory for judges or citizens once we cannot conceive the law as merely a suggestion or advice.

1 Introduction

Over the past 50 years, the Hart–Dworkin debate has had a crucial impact on analytical legal theory, modifying our understanding of several themes and levels of discussion. Wil Waluchow's *Inclusive Legal Positivism*, published in 1994, is one of the most influential books that, engaging in the consequences of this debate, formulated a plausible, interesting, and fruitful theory of law.

J. V. Penna (✉)
University of São Paulo, Faculdade de Direito, São Paulo, SP, Brazil
e-mail: jvpenna@usp.br

T. Bustamante et al. (eds.), *Law, Morality and Judicial Reasoning*, Law and Philosophy Library 147, https://doi.org/10.1007/978-3-031-61879-6_5

After 25 years of publication of *Inclusive Legal Positivism*, we can clearly see its relevance to the theory of legal positivism in articulating one of its most coherent and powerful versions, which is a version of Hartian legal positivism that falls midway between Ronald Dworkin's and Joseph Raz's theories of law.

This theoretical project is based on a long discussion and critique of Waluchow's philosophical opponents. Waluchow faces Dworkin's well-known distinction between grounds and forces of law, introducing a thought-provoking concept: the idea of institutional forces of law. This concept plays an important role in Waluchow's legal theory as it aims to clarify Dworkin's intuition that the law must justify state coercion. Despite its attractiveness, however, Waluchow does not seem to have taken it far enough in his general theory of law, leaving his theory open to questions about how it deals with certain issues.

In this brief chapter, I will try to examine the notion of institutional forces of law and its role in a positivist concept of law within a Hartian tradition—to which Waluchow subscribes. I will begin, in Sect. 2, by briefly introducing Dworkin's concept of law and his distinction between grounds and forces of law. In Sect. 3, I will present Waluchow's critical remarks on the idea of "force of law," showing the distinction between law itself and its institutional forces and, thus, offering an overview of the claims he makes on the basis of this important notion. In Sect. 4, I will offer two comments on the institutional force of law that Waluchow would have to deal with in order to make his construction a more coherent and complete theory of law. Finally, in Sect. 5, I offer a conclusion that balances the implications these comments have for the theory.

Before starting, I would like to make a short remark. Waluchow's argument about institutional forces of law is associated with his criticism of Ronald Dworkin. Legal philosophers often examine this concept in the context of the controversy between these legal theorists, leading one to think that the main question in the notion of institutional forces of law lies in its methodological background. Given Dworkin and Waluchow's different views on the methodology of jurisprudence, some commentators believe that the debate between Waluchow and Dworkin on the forces of law is merely a product of their methodological differences (Perry 1996, pp. 369–374). Nevertheless, I believe there is more to the notion of institutional forces of law than a methodological disagreement between interpretivist and descriptive theories of law, inasmuch as the claim to distinguish between the "moral" and the "institutional" force of law is a substantive claim that can likely improve our understanding of important legal phenomena.

Thus, I propose a deeper analysis of the notion of institutional forces of law, taking a step away from Dworkin's specific concerns and evaluating the concept as a relevant feature of the broader notion of law. The idea that the power to change existing law can be distributed among judges is a very robust idea and entails several consequences for legal positivism. The aim of this chapter is to understand some of these consequences.

2 The Context of Waluchow's Argument About Institutional Forces of Law: Dworkin and the Justification of State Coercion

In *Law's Empire*, after criticizing what he describes as semantic theories of law and introducing his interpretive account of legality, Dworkin formulates his concept of law in order to provide a general and abstract claim that purports to be true for every conception of law. His concept is developed in these terms:

> The law of a community on this account is the scheme of rights and responsibilities that meet that complex standard: they license coercion because they flow from past decisions of the right sort. They are therefore "legal" rights and responsibilities. (Dworkin 1986, p. 93)

Therefore, Dworkin believes that any (interpretive) conception of law—like conventionalism, pragmatism, or law as integrity—must presuppose that, if there is law, there is also, on any level, a justification for the use of force.

Such a claim leads Dworkin to separate legal theory into two parts: 1) the *grounds of law*, which concerns those "circumstances in which particular propositions of law should be taken to be sound or true" (Dworkin 1986, p. 110); and 2) the *force of law*, which deals with "the relative power of any true proposition of law to justify coercion in different sorts of exceptional circumstance" (Dworkin 1986, p. 110).

Having introduced this difference, Dworkin claims that these two parts must support each other—that is, that every legal theory must give us an account of these parts. However, Dworkin points out that there is a general division of labor in the analytic tradition, in which political philosophers are usually concerned with problems about the force of law, while legal philosophers usually deal with questions about the foundations of law.

According to Dworkin, this division of labor is untenable because any legal theorist must presuppose, while formulating a theory about the grounds of law, a certain agreement about the force of law (Dworkin 1986, p. 111). At least in normal circumstances—when, for example, there is no controversy about justice—we can assume a rough agreement that we need to obey and apply the law. An interpretive conception of law only makes sense if we are operating under an assumption like this.

Therefore, Dworkin offers a distinction between the grounds and the forces of law, but he does not treat these notions as separable. They are only parts of a "full political theory of law" (Dworkin 1986, p. 110).

3 The Nature of Institutional Forces of Law

In *Inclusive Legal Positivism*, Waluchow argued that, despite being an important insight, the distinction between the force and the grounds of law faces some problems. Dworkin claims—according to Waluchow—that for legal positivism, it is one thing to say what the law is in a given case, and it is quite another thing to say that this law has some moral merit that can call upon our respect and our obedience (Waluchow 1994, p. 13). In this context, the central difference between Waluchow and Dworkin is that the latter believes that a successful legal theory must satisfy these two components, which is why he formulates the thesis that any conception of law needs to presuppose a justification for state coercion.

In Waluchow's view, Dworkin starts with a correct point in acknowledging that there is a difference between statements about what the law is and statements about which responsibilities citizens have in relation to that law. Waluchow thereby grants Dworkin's point and argues, in sequence, that we should accept a first important distinction: the difference between what the law is and the force of an existing law (Waluchow 1994, p. 33).

Nevertheless, turning his attention to the force of law, Waluchow introduces another distinction—that is, the difference between the "moral" and the "institutional" forces of law. According to Waluchow, institutional force is a characteristic of law that refers to the institutional powers and responsibilities judges have with respect to that law (Waluchow 1994, p. 33).

Waluchow intends to show the difference between law and its institutional force with an example (Waluchow 1994, pp. 34–35). He believes that it is not necessary to appeal to difficult or special cases to demonstrate the relevance or applicability of this concept, since we can simply observe and analyze the practice of precedents in common.

Waluchow invites us to imagine three judges with three different levels of hierarchy: a high-court judge, a middle-court judge, and a lower-court judge. We can see that the lower-court judge is obligated to follow the precedents defined by superior judges, but the high-court judge is not bound by the precedents of the intermediate court and can, if they think that it is legally required, overturn the previous ruling and create a new precedent for a case. Therefore, in a process in which a middle-court judge decides case C in manner X, lower-court judges will likely apply X regularly, and we can say that this precedent has institutional force over that court. Nevertheless, this same precedent does not have the same institutional force over a high-court judge, who might decide case C in a way that differs from X.

Thus, with this simple and ordinary example of legal practice, especially in the common law tradition, we can see that each of these hypothetical judges may have different powers and responsibilities in relation to the law, some of them being authorized to change it at various levels. This leads us to note that these multiple powers assigned to different judges illustrate a variety of institutional forces that operate differently on each one of these judges in similar legal cases. Therefore, Waluchow concludes that a sound legal theory needs to provide an account of the variety of institutional forces that operate over different judges at different hierarchical levels.

These judicial powers and responsibilities are essentially institutional and do not necessarily have a moral nature. In this sense, Waluchow distinguishes between the ideas of institutional force and moral force. It is perfectly plausible to say that a judge has no institutional power to change decision X—like the lower-court judge in his example—though the judge can have moral duty to do so. Thus, institutional force and moral force are different types of normative forces, in the sense of a system of powers and rights that are governed by norms of some kind.

Waluchow continues,

> Institutional force, as we have here defined it, is a function of the person's legal power (if any) to alter existing law so as to nullify its effect upon a decision. Moral force, as we have defined it, concerns the extent to which, if at all, there is a moral obligation to abide by the law's requirements. (Waluchow 1994, p. 39)

Therefore, we can conclude that the institutional force of law depends on the legal powers that are given to judges, which may vary according to this institutional hierarchy. The question now is how we determine the level of institutional force that operates over a judge. To answer this question, Waluchow introduces another distinction. He argues that we must distinguish between theories of law, theories of compliance, and theories of adjudication (Waluchow 1994, p. 40). In short, a theory of law is concerned with the nature of law and its relationship with morality, costumes, and use of force, among others; a theory of compliance is essentially normative and concerns the moral forces that law possesses over citizens and judges to guarantee its respect; and finally, a theory of adjudication is interested in explaining the variety of institutional forces that different sources of law possess over judges in certain contexts.

According to Waluchow, it is clear that we need a theory of adjudication to give us an account of the degree of institutional force that operates over different judges. It is this kind of theory that determines when judges have the legal power to overrule an existing law and create a new one. This is not the role of a theory of law, which is concerned with the background question of when a legal proposition is true.

These distinctions does not imply an absolute separation between the types of theories. Waluchow's claim is that they are "separate but connected" (Waluchow 1994, p. 64), in the sense that they are not identical theories and do not answer the same sets of questions. Therefore, Waluchow concludes that it is one thing to say that a proposition is legally valid and quite another to say that it is mandatory for judges. These are two questions that each need to be addressed by a separate theory, with its own methodology. Based on these distinctions, we can now understand the problems that Waluchow attributes to Dworkin's theory of law.

First, by referring only to the general notion of the "force of law," Dworkin cannot see that there are different kinds of normative forces related to law that operate over judges (Waluchow 1994, p. 38). The forces to which Dworkin refers are essentially moral forces. Waluchow does not deny the existence and operation of moral forces in legal decision-making, but these are not the only kind of forces that the law possesses. Judges are also influenced by forces that are essentially institutional—that is, internal to the law and founded on authoritative sources. This institutional force, according to Waluchow, is an important feature of law that we cannot ignore.

Secondly, by claiming that a legal theory must justify state coercion, Dworkin collapses a theory of adjudication within a theory of law, and this exposes him to three further problems: "(i) incoherence, (ii) an unnecessary proliferation of (indexed) legal rights, and (iii) an over-idealizing of law as whatever a mythical high-court judge would decide were the case before him" (Waluchow 1994, p. 58).

Therefore, Waluchow extracts from Dworkin an interesting account of the role of judges in adjudication and in identifying valid laws. However, he departs from Dworkin in assuming the existence of a variety of institutional forces in law (as distinct from moral forces) that are better understood if we separate theories of law from theories of adjudication.

4 The Role of Institutional Forces in a Theory of Law

Many philosophers examine Waluchow's theory and the idea of institutional forces of law in the context of his debate with Dworkin and Raz, as a useful argument for criticizing these theories. This approach takes the discussion of Waluchow's conception to its metatheoretical background, treating it as a mere methodological problem.[1] I wish, however, to bypass the methodological disagreements between Waluchow and Dworkin and consider the substantive debate between Waluchow and his adversaries.[2]

I hope that the significance of institutional forces of law is evident, as their existence substantially interferes with judges' work of applying law. This property and relevance justify my aim to examine the structure and implications of these forces. In fact, the importance of this concept cannot be underestimated for a coherent and comprehensive theory of law. Although this notion has been applied to criticize Dworkin, it also serves a valuable function in comprehending Waluchow's perspective on important themes, such as his account of judges' legal obligation to follow a currently valid law.

The core of what Waluchow claims about institutional forces is laid out in chapters two and three of *Inclusive Legal Positivism*, in which he tries to identify some problems with Dworkin's account by introducing the distinctions I presented above and by arguing that inclusive legal positivism can account for these

[1] Stephen Perry formulates a criticism of the idea of institutional forces of law, trying to prove that it is used against Dworkin as an argument that traduces a source-based view of Common Law, while against Raz it takes a moral-based view of this legal practice. Perry considers this a mistake, but he maintains that it has a methodological basis. See Perry (1996, pp. 376–378).

[2] In order to do this, I have to assume that Waluchow is right to treat those theories as doing the same methodological thing. At the end of chapter two of *Inclusive Legal Positivism*, he states, "In what follows we shall treat inclusive and exclusive positivism, together with natural-law theory and Dworkin's integrity theory as descriptive-explanatory theories of law, and assess them in these terms. Our principal aim is to show that inclusive positivism is a better descriptive-explanatory theory than its rivals so understood" (Waluchow 1994, p. 30).

distinctions in a more plausible and straightforward way. Nevertheless, I believe that the idea of the institutional force of law still requires some clarification. In this regard, I would like to address two points about this idea that, in my view, remain unclear.

The first is regarding the role of institutional forces in a theory of law. Waluchow argues that Dworkin perilously collapses three types of theories about law into one (theories of compliance and adjudication, for Dworkin, would be collapsed into a general theory of law). Waluchow, on the other hand, places the idea of institutional forces in the domain of a theory of adjudication, rather than in the domain of a theory of law (which is concerned with legal validity) or a theory of compliance (which is concerned with moral force). Nevertheless, it is likely that the concept of institutional force plays a more important role in a theory of law than Waluchow suggests.

Going back to the example of the judges, let us consider a valid legal proposition without any level of institutional force. In other words, imagine a singular law that fulfills all the requirements of a community's rule of recognition and that could be overruled in any case by any judge (i.e., from a high-court judge to a lower-court judge), because that judge would have no responsibilities with respect to that law. Could this singular law still be considered law? Probably not.

Such a hypothesis would be extremely implausible. It would be quite difficult to conceive that there could be a legal proposition a judge could absolutely ignore without being at least minimally responsible for applying it in certain cases. Every judge, when deciding that they should not apply a law, must at least treat that law as an institutionally important standard, which requires some institutional authorization to be overridden in a given case. Therefore, when we say that a higher-court judge, in the common-law practice of precedents, can overrule law L and establish a new one, this does not mean that there are no institutional forces related to L operating over that judge, but rather that L has less power over the higher-court judge than it has over the lower-court judge.

Waluchow agrees with that claim:

> There is, of course, reason to think that a legal system could not exist in which all judges were totally free at all times to change or depart from valid rules in any way they saw fit. But this is not my suggestion: the institutional forces of existing laws are often powerful and cannot be overcome. A system of absolute discretion in which no law had any institutional force at all could not be a system of law because there would be no general standards by which, on the whole, both private actions and judicial decisions could be guided. There would be no rule of law only, as Cardozo put it, "isolated dooms." (Waluchow 1994, p. 66)

These considerations might lead us to conclude that any law, to be law, must include at least a minimum degree of institutional force. Legal rules provide judges, at different levels and depending on the institutional arrangements, with some institutional powers and responsibilities related to these rules. The idea of institutional forces is, therefore, a conceptually necessary feature of law, making it a more central idea than acknowledged by Waluchow in *Inclusive Legal Positivism* and turning it into a matter for both a theory of law and a theory of adjudication.

As seen above, Waluchow might agree with this claim, but he would insist that it does not break the separation between the types of legal theory, as they might still answer different questions despite being connected in many ways. He argues that the three types of theories are not absolutely autonomous, as they are "separate but connected" (Waluchow 1994, p. 64). My argument, however, is that these connections are more important than he supposes, because they are concerned with central points of his theory of law.

A theory of law is a theory about what the law is in certain cases and what its relationship is with other realms, such as morality: the theory takes the law itself as its object of concern. In contrast, the idea of institutional forces of law represents a form of relationship that judges have with the law—that is, the powers and responsibilities judges have in their work of applying the law. In fact, it describes a relationship with law, not the law itself, that is governed by specific legal rules that are the rules of adjudication. This could lead us to think that institutional forces of law might be a topic for a theory of adjudication.

Even if law and its institutional forces are ontologically distinct, this does not necessarily imply that there is one type of theory that deals exclusively with each. A theory of law may have the law itself as its central object of concern and may also analyze other ideas that influence its object.

In order to argue that institutional forces of law are only a matter for a theory of adjudication, we would have to assume that the manner by which judges decide cases, which is influenced and governed by their relationship with the law (i.e., by the institutional forces of law), does not affect the law itself. We do not need to engage in a long methodological discussion of legal interpretation to see that this does not work well, as Waluchow's example of the practice of precedent in common law is sufficient for this task. At least in certain cases, some judges (like high-court judges) may have powers to create a new law, as they can overrule previous precedents and create a new one. If a judge can have the power to not treat a valid rule as legally mandatory, then the description of this power that judges invoke must be an important object of concern for a theory that purports to describe the valid law. Hence, identifying the existence and operation of the creative powers of judges, as well as those of legislators, is a task for a theory of law that is concerned with describing the conditions under which legal rules operate.

The scope of a theory of law cannot be strictly limited to the identification of the basic criteria for the validity of law (such as being limited to the criteria of a rule of recognition), but must also include arguments about what, based on these basic criteria, can modify existing law. Thus, the institutional forces of law must be the object of concern for a theory of law because, following Waluchow's definition, they constitute a central and necessary feature of law.

The second issue I want to address is about legal normativity, coercion, and institutional forces of law. The problem of normativity of law is a great debate in the history of legal theory that deals with what makes law mandatory, either for citizens or for judges. There is, I think, a close relationship between the problem of normativity and the institutional forces of law that Waluchow has not explored.

Dworkin distinguishes between grounds and forces of law in order to highlight two necessary and complementary parts of a "full political theory of law" (Dworkin 1986, p. 110). A theory of law must identify the conditions in which particular propositions of law should be taken as true (grounds of law) and the power that true legal propositions have to justify coercion (force of law). Legal theorists do not usually discuss the problem of the force of law because it is often the subject of a rough and implicit agreement in which, at least in normal circumstances, judges have the obligation to apply true legal propositions. However, there could be circumstances in which judges are morally obligated to do the opposite.

While explaining the Dworkinian distinction, Waluchow claims,

> The principles which provide the best "justification" of morally deficient settled law may yet be morally bankrupt. In such cases the answer to the hard question posed by a law's existence might be that a judge or citizen should act contrary to its requirements. The grounds of law do not, in such a hard case, impose justified requirements on the citizen, and most certainly do not license the use of force by the state or its agents. (Waluchow 1994, p. 12)

According to Dworkin, theories that focus only on the grounds of law, like traditional version of legal positivism, do not commit us to any claim about how citizens should behave or how judges should decide cases (Dworkin 1986, p. 112). This is, in these traditional views, is a matter for theories about the force of law. Therefore, if a single rule or the whole legal system has a low capacity to morally justify coercion, judges cannot be obligated to apply these legal rules. In other words, these legal rules cannot be legally mandatory for them. Hence, in Dworkin's concept of law, a claim about the forces of law provides an argument about the possibility of the state imposing obligations on citizens—that is, it is also an argument for the normativity of law.

Waluchow introduced the idea of institutional forces of law in order to replace the Dworkinian idea of forces of law as a morally engaged concept. The institutional forces of law have been defined as the various powers and responsibilities that judges have with respect to the law (Waluchow 1994, p. 33), which are essentially institutional rather than moral. It is a legal, not moral, force. Waluchow thus suggests that there is a way of justifying state coercion that appeals only to institutional demands, although he does not deny that moral forces could also exert an important force over judges.

The problem is that, by removing the moral-justificatory element from the idea of the forces of law and claiming that institutional demands are sufficient for law to function, Waluchow has left some elements out of his explanation of what a theory of law must incorporate. He provides no other element in the idea of institutional forces of law to explain the normativity of law and legal obligations. If institutional forces represent institutional powers and responsibilities judges have with respect to law, the argument makes no claim about what makes law mandatory and, especially, what role coercion plays in a general legal theory.

Dworkin claims that a theory of law must necessarily provide a moral and political justification for state coercion and that it is part of the job of this theory to provide and explanation and a justification of legal obligations. Waluchow, on the other hand, claims that forces of law could be sufficiently institutionally founded and that law therefore has the capacity to create legal obligations by itself. However, Waluchow's positivism has no explanation about how law can create these legal obligations for citizens or for judges without recourse to moral justification. This is an important point that needs clarification. In order to explain how citizens behave and judges apply rules, an argument about the institutional forces of law would have to be shaped as an argument about the normativity of law.

Waluchow also makes no claim about the role of coercion in his theory of law. The role of coercion in legal rules and in the formation of legal obligation is one of the most debated questions in analytical jurisprudence. However, this discussion lost much power in the Hartian tradition of positivism because his theory did not make it a necessary component of the concept of law, leaving this problem to the dominium of the minimum content of natural law.[3] Hart and Dworkin never engaged in a debate about the role of coercion, but Dworkin clearly believes that this concept is central, claiming that legal coercion must be justified in order to provide an argument for the normativity of law. Waluchow, on the other hand, has not provided us with an argument about the necessity or contingency of coercion in a theory of law or about the role of coercion in the formation of legal obligation.

One could consider the problem of normativity and the role of coercion to be questions of a theory of compliance, in Waluchow's sense; he would therefore have something to say about that. However, I do not believe he has sufficiently addressed this important point. A theory of compliance is described as a theory that deals with "(normal or exceptional) moral force of existing law, both for judges and for private citizens" (Waluchow 1994, p. 30). Thus, this theory is concerned with the moral justification of state coercion (to use Dworkinian vocabulary) and has less to say about the necessary features that law must have in order to be considered coercive. We must remember here the Austinian starting point followed by Hartian tradition: "where there is law, there human conduct is made in some sense non-optional or obligatory" (Hart 1994, p. 82). I cannot speak to this further in this extensive discussion about the problem of coercion and legal normativity, but this is clearly an important question for which Waluchow's theory has no clear answers.

5 Conclusion

Waluchow's observations on the existence and the function of institutional forces of law provide an interesting account of normativity in a theory of legal positivism and an important piece of the debate against Dworkin. However, it seems that Waluchow's idea remains underdeveloped in several crucial areas.

My aim in the last section was to highlight two points Waluchow would need to address in order to provide a complete account of this idea. While Waluchow claims

[3] About this, Hart claims, "'Sanctions' are therefore required not as the normal motive for obedience, but as a guarantee that those who would voluntarily obey shall not be sacrificed to those who would not. To obey, without this, would be to risk going to the wall. Given this standing danger, what reason demands is voluntary co-operation in a coercive system" (Hart 1994, p. 198).

that we must distinguish between theories of law, theories of compliance, and theories of adjudication, and that these theories are "separate but connected" (Waluchow 1994, p. 64), he does not provide a clear argument about how this connection is established and how elements of other theories ought to be considered in a theory of law, which is his object of inquiry. Waluchow also does not speak to how institutional forces of law explain the normativity of law or the role of coercion in a concept of law.

My point, then, is that if Waluchow is right about the existence of institutional forces of law, a successful (positivist) theory of law must address that, and we cannot leave this concern only to theories of adjudication. A theory of law (i.e., a theory that is essentially concerned with the problem of the grounds of law) also must also speak to this concept, and the importance of this idea cannot be underestimated.

This argument could lead us to endorse an account of legal theory that would again collapse grounds and forces of law into one theory, as Dworkin has posited. However, that is not the aim of this chapter. I have solely tried to highlight points in Waluchow's theory that would require clarification and complementation in order to support his critique of Dworkin. Hence, these observations are not fatal to Waluchow's theory, because it would be possible to reorganize and formulate an account of this concept that appeals to past positivist theories without undermining Waluchow's metatheoretical background of a descriptive-explanatory theory of law.

References

Dworkin, Ronald. 1986. *Law's Empire*. Cambridge, MA: Harvard University Press.

Hart, H.L.A. 1994. *The Concept of Law*. Oxford: Clarendon Press.

Perry, Stephen R. 1996. The Varieties of Legal Positivism: Critical Notice: *Inclusive legal positivism* by W.J. Waluchow. *Canadian Journal of Law & Jurisprudence* 9 (2): 361–381. https://doi.org/10.1017/S0841820900003490.

Waluchow, Wilfrid J. 1994. *Inclusive Legal Positivism*. Oxford: Clarendon Press.

João Vitor Penna is a Ph.D. student in Philosophy and Legal Theory at the University of São Paulo (Brazil). He gained his M.Phil in Law at Federal University of Pará (Brazil) developing research about Theories of Justice and Tort Law. He is also a Barrister at the Brazilian Bar and Professor of Private Law. He has research experience in Legal Theory, Philosophy of Law, and Private Law.

Some Issues Concerning Waluchow's Early Critique of Dworkin in *Inclusive Legal Positivism*

Ronaldo Porto Macedo Junior

Abstract Professor W.J. Waluchow's *Inclusive Legal Positivism* (1994) is still one of the most insightful and robust defenses of inclusive legal positivism ever written. It is a landmark in all theoretical debates concerning the matter. The book's central issues and arguments have stayed at the core of the dominant debate on legal theory over the last 20 years, at least in the Anglo-Saxon tradition. It represents one of the most thoughtful responses to Ronald Dworkin's legal theory and also to his challenge first presented in "The Model of Rules," that of reconciling the fact that moral standards heavily impact adjudication with the legal positivist premise that law is grounded exclusively in social practices (and not moral values). A related consequence of this challenge is a methodological dispute concerning the descriptive/normative nature of the theory of law that has drawn the attention of many philosophers in recent decades. Even if some of his criticisms do not fully resonate with every reader, they still represent a standard for the questions that serious legal scholars must face in order to position themselves in the contemporary debate.

1 The Importance of the Book

Professor W.J. Waluchow's *Inclusive Legal Positivism* (OUP), first published in 1994 and reprinted in 2003, remains one of the most insightful and robust defenses of inclusive legal positivism ever written. It is a landmark in all theoretical debates concerning the matter. The book's central issues and arguments remain at the core of the dominant debate on legal theory in the last 20 years, at least in the Anglo-Saxon tradition.

Wil Waluchow's critique of Ronald Dworkin's legal theory presents one of the most thoughtful challenges to his ideas. However, as Waluchow acknowledges, its

R. P. Macedo Junior (✉)
University of Sao Paulo Law School, Sao Paulo, Brazil
e-mail: rmacedo@usp.br

T. Bustamante et al. (eds.), *Law, Morality and Judicial Reasoning*, Law and Philosophy Library 147, https://doi.org/10.1007/978-3-031-61879-6_6

point of departure is one (or one set) of the Dworkinian challenges[1] brought to legal positivism: the challenge of reconciling that moral standards heavily impact adjudication with the legal positivist premise that law is praxis grounded exclusively in social practices (and not moral values).

To respond to this challenge, Waluchow tries to find a middle ground between his two most important interlocutors, Joseph Raz and Ronald Dworkin. His effort to find this place requires him to face many methodological dimensions of the current debate in legal theory. He primarily faces what is now considered the "classical debates" on legal theory's descriptive/normative dimension and the character of legal theory and interpretation. His rich and philosophically demanding book is an engaged introduction to the epistemological nature of contemporary jurisprudence.

Waluchow's effort is similar to Neil MacCormick's early defence (expressed in *Legal Reasoning and Legal Theory*)[2] of the Hartian general theory against the Dworkinian (and Finnisian) challenges (MacCormick 1994). Waluchow states his intentions in the introduction of the book:

> I shall assume that Hart's theory that a rule of recognition lies at the foundation of all legal systems is more or less correct, and that Dworkin's critique of the rule of recognition as a conventional, social rule, indeed his critique of Hart's entire theory of social rules, can be satisfactorily answered, as I think it can to defend a Hartian version of inclusive positivism against two of its principal opponents. Raz and Dworkin (Waluchow 1994, p. 4).

This quote shows that Dworkin could have replied convincingly to some of Waluchow's critiques made in his earlier work and how some replies were expanded in Dworkin's later books, which were unavailable when *Inclusive Legal Positivism* was published in 1994. *Justice in Robes* (Dworkin 2006a) and *Justice for Hedgehogs* (Dworkin 2011) are fundamental in this respect. Of course, one cannot criticize Waluchow for not addressing arguments not fully developed by Dworkin in 1994. However, it is illuminating to understand how his objections can (and could) be addressed and were already presented in Dworkin's earlier works (especially "The Model of Rules," originally published in 1967 and later reprinted in 1977 in *Taking Rights Seriously* as "The Model of Rules II"), although not so clearly conceptualized as in his later books.

---

[1] Ronald Dworkin has made many challenges to legal positivism. Most commentators have acknowledged this fact. See Shapiro (2007). This understanding is also shared by Gerald Postema: "Inclusivist doctrine was developed to explain Dworkin's observation of the apparent incorporation of moral principles into law. It does so by accepting the incorporation thesis as possibly true, as far as the concept of law is concerned" (2011, p. 465). This reveals an important feature of the dialectic of the recent incorporation debate. The inclusive positivist approach arose in direct response to Dworkin's challenge to Hart's revision of positivism. From the outset, inclusivism looked for ways that philosophers committed to positivism could keep their positivist faith while acknowledging the force of Dworkin's most persuasive arguments.

[2] Maccormick's ideas profoundly changed in his later books, published more than 20 years later, especially in MacCormick (2005, 2007).

2 Dworkin's Challenge

Dworkin presented his challenge to Hartian legal positivism in his seminal essay, "The Model of Rules" (or "The Model of Rules II") (Dworkin 1977a, pp. 46–80). Dworkin built on judicial arguments to express that adjudicative legal reasoning is unavoidably moral. He took the famous case *Riggs v. Palmer* (115 N.Y. 506 (1889)) to present the structure of his major points. Elmer Riggs killed his grandfather and later sued for his inheritance. The New York court denied his claim, invoking the principle that "no man may profit from his own wrong." According to Dworkin, judges often appeal to moral principles without pedigree in legislation (formal legal validity) and ground their authority on these principles' own merits (justice, fairness, equality, integrity, and others),[3] that can prevail over (or trump) enacted positive law. Besides, argumentative controversy in legal discourse usually involves conceptual disagreements that require decisions concerning reconstructive interpretation (or an interpretive approach).

This critique has generated competing explanations among legal positivists. The divide among legal positivists has contrasted "exclusive legal positivists" and "inclusive legal positivists."[4] The exclusive legal positivist reaction, led by Joseph Raz[5] and others,[6] insists that moral principles sometimes applied in adjudication are extra-legal principles. Exclusivists agree with the pedigree thesis stated by Dworkin. However, they have rejected Dworkin's criticism using two types of arguments.: On one hand, they point out that customary law has pedigree (legal validity). Thus, they

[3] Dworkin states, "This is so because the legality of principles depends, at least sometimes, simply on their content. The origin of [the *Henningsen* principles] as legal principles lies not in a particular decision of some legislature or court, but in a sense of appropriateness developed in the profession and the public over time. Their continued power depends upon this sense being sustained. If it no longer seemed unfair to allow people to profit by their wrongs, or fair to place special burdens upon oligopolies that manufacture potentially dangerous machines, these principles would no longer play much role in new cases, even if they had never been overruled or repealed" (Dworkin 1977a, p. 40).

[4] This debate is sometimes referred to as "incorporationists" or "soft positivists" in opposition to "non-incorporationists" or "hard positivists."

[5] Joseph Raz, exclusive legal positivism's leading advocate, refers to his view as the commitment to the source thesis. The source thesis was first set out in Raz (1979, pp. 40–55) and received its most vigorous defense in Raz (1985), reprinted in Raz (1994). Raz further develops his position in Raz (1980, pp. 211–212; 1994, pp. 195–209, 238–253, 326–340; 1998).

[6] See Marmor (2002), pp. 83–96. Some theorists like Brian Leiter (2009) have even criticized Dworkin's interpretation of this case and the historical accuracy of his approach. However, even putting aside this polemic, Dworkin's use of the case can be taken as, at least, a hypothetical case that serves this theoretical argument against legal positivism. Dworkin replied to his critics on this matter but also offered new examples—ones less controversial and vulnerable to this kind of criticism in *Law's Empire*, mainly introducing the *TVA* case (Dworkin 1986, pp. 20–23) and Mrs. Sorensen's hypothetical case (*Justice in Robes*—Hart's postscript and the point of political philosophy—Dworkin 2006a, pp. 143–145). Even positivist Scott Shapiro has acknowledged that Dworkin's new arguments and examples are not vulnerable to the old criticisms made soon after *Taking Rights Seriously* was published in 1977 (Shapiro 2007, pp. 35–43).

can be seen as having an adequate source of social pedigree.[7] A second argument concedes that judges are sometimes legally obligated to apply principles lacking institutional pedigree. However, this fact does not compromise the pedigree thesis, as these are extra-legal principles. In this view, supported by Joseph Raz (Raz 1994, chapter 9), Dworkin's mistake was to assume that a legal system should be complete. Judges are often required to apply foreign law and scientific standards that do not belong to a national legal system. Moral standards function in an analogous way.

Inclusive legal positivists have followed a different theoretical route. Waluchow's remark exemplifies this track: "The version of positivism developed and defended in this book will be called 'inclusive legal positivism.' A distinguishing feature of inclusive positivism is its claim that standards of political morality, that is, the morality we use to evaluate, justify, and criticize social institutions and their activities and products, e.g., laws, can and do in various ways figure in attempts to determine the existence, content, and meaning of valid laws" (Waluchow 1994, p. 10). In this theory, morality is included within the possible grounds for establishing the existence and content of valid, positive laws—that is, laws enacted or developed by human beings in legislatures and courts of law or customary practice (Waluchow 1994, p. 10).

This view was developed as a reaction to Dworkin's claim that the practice of adjudication showed the incorporation of moral principles into law. According to Waluchow and other advocates of inclusivism, legal positivism does not prohibit moral tests of legality once morality is incorporated into legal order. However, this is a contingent fact, not a conceptual truth (Soper 1977, p. 473; Lyons 1977, p. 415; Coleman 1988, p. 81; Waluchow 1994). For Waluchow, the only necessary legal grounds of law are the conventional practices rooted in the rule of recognition.[8]

3 Robust and Modest Inclusivism

Postema correctly calls our attention to the fact that inclusivism has taken different forms. For him, "the limiting case, *incorporation by enactment, holds that moral principles are incorporated into law when lawmakers or constitution-makers explicitly enact them*" (Postema 2011, p. 465). This is the kind of inclusive positivism adopted by Waluchow. His defense of inclusive legal positivism stresses that the moral argument appears once a constitution incorporates principles that are the basis for legal interpretation and deliberation (Waluchow 1994, chap. 4–7). However, his

[7] Shapiro correctly stressed, "The weakness of this response, however, is that judges often take themselves to be obligated to apply principles that seem entirely novel. As Dworkin pointed out, no court before *Henningsen* applied the principle that automobile manufacturers are subject to a greater standard of care. Yet that court nevertheless felt compelled to apply that norm" (Shapiro 2007, p. 32).

[8] A similar general conceptualization of inclusive legal positivism is presented by Kenneth Einar Himma in Himma (2004, pp. 97–98).

ideas can also be characterized as a "supple version of incorporation by enactment" (Postema 2011, p. 465 note 5), at least insofar as his argument focuses on the role of moral argument in constitutional interpretation and deliberation. Incorporation by enactment is also called "modest inclusivism."

If we accept this characterization, a Dworkinian argument against Waluchow would come up quite directly. The challenge is based on the fact that judges have used principles with no enactment pedigree. The *Riggs v. Palmer* case is but one example of that. For this reason, most positivists have been inclined to adopt a more robust version of inclusivism. The alternative to modest inclusivism claims that a legal system may include a minimal moral adequacy test among its conditions of validity. Thus, fundamental principles such as fairness, justice, or dignity could be part of the law when they function as filters for the rest of the substantive norms of law. They would be like "filters" incorporated into positive law (Postema 2011, p. 465).

Contrasting this idea, "robust inclusivism" accepts the further possibility that the moral merits of certain principles can be enough to make them valid legal norms. Consequently, morality can be a sufficient condition of validity, as there is a legal practice of relying on the substantive merits of principles (this position is adopted by Coleman—see Coleman 2001, p. 114).[9] Once the two main forms of inclusivism have been established, it is important to understand how Waluchow frames his own inclusive positivism as a response to Dworkinian interpretivism and Razian exclusive positivism. This is the task of the next topic.

4 Waluchow's Inclusivist Explanation

As mentioned, Waluchow is one of the foremost supporters of the inclusive legal positivist view. Moreover, this view differs from the exclusivist, Dworkinian, and classical common-law explanations of the concept of law. These differences are twofold. On the one hand, both the Dworkinian approach (interpretivism combined with law as integrity) and Waluchow's inclusivism acknowledge that moral correctness is not in itself sufficient to make a principle a legal one. However, inclusivism does not require the substantive integration of principles in the body of law. Its requirement is less comprehensive than interpretivism—it requires only a conventional practice of appealing to moral arguments when legal reasoning is at play. Thus, the moral constraint in the inclusive positivist approach is weaker than integration but stronger than that imposed on legal reasoning by the exclusivist doctrine. This fact explains why Waluchow claims that his legal perspective "is

[9] As Postema synthetically puts this point, "Robust inclusivism is the view that it is possible for there to a legal system to exist in which the conventional rule of recognition includes among its criteria of validity not just a test of minimal moral decency, but the moral correctness of principles themselves" (Postema 2011, p. 465).

designed to show that there is a positivistic theory to be found somewhere between Raz's exclusive positivism and Dworkin's (natural) law as integrity" (Waluchow 1994, p. 11).

On the other hand, the inclusivist explanation tries to show that the Dworkinian explanation is not necessary and is not even the best description of the real practice of law. In his book, however, Waluchow argues that inclusivism offers a *possible* explanation and possibly the most accurate descriptive account of legal practice (and especially legal reasoning) in Canada and the United States.[10] It shows advantages if compared with both Razian exclusivism and Dworkinian interpretivism. Waluchow provides a methodological critique of Dworkin's description of law, even while acknowledging that the interpretive approach correctly points out some central features of legal interpretation.

Nevertheless, Waluchow acknowledges that even an interpretivism approach like Dworkin's could be modified to comply with his criticisms. He mainly rejects "Dworkin's suggestion that law be identified as a scheme of institutional, moral rights to decisions before courts" (Waluchow 1994, pp. 73–74) as presented in his major works published until 1994. Waluchow's critique of Dworkin's ideas is directly connected with the concept of law and the central features of legal theory. For him, both issues are connected to a misconception of the very nature of legal theory found in Dworkin's ideas. Should we consider legal theory a normative or a mere descriptive endeavor? This question will be addressed at once.

5 Waluchow's Criticisms of Dworkin

5.1 Descriptive or Normative Theory?

One of the main strands of Waluchow's critique of Dworkin's ideas concerns the "confusion" in *Law's Empire* about the descriptive-normative distinction in legal theory. According to Waluchow, "much of the current confusion within general jurisprudence results from differences of opinion concerning (a) what it is exactly that one is supposed to be doing in offering a theory of law, and (b) what it is that

[10]Positivists are, of course, happy to acknowledge many contingent connections between law and morality. Numerous laws (for example, those proscribing assault and theft) are pretty clearly restatements of moral principles. Nevertheless, there are unfortunately too many examples of valid laws, such as those governing apartheid in South Africa, that are incapable of moral defense. Positivists are also happy to say that judges sometimes decide difficult cases by appealing to principles of morality when the law's guidance is insufficient to settle the question at hand: they will merely insist that these legally binding decisions are sometimes also morally indefensible. Judges are not infallible. In both instances, we see a connection between law and morals, but one that is merely contingent. Whether, in deciding a case on moral grounds, a judge necessarily steps beyond positive law is, as we shall see shortly, a question that divides legal positivists. However, all agree that such appeals are often made and that they serve to illustrate yet another close but contingent connection between law and morality (Waluchow 1994, p. 81).

one's opponents are doing in articulating their theories of law" (Waluchow 1994, p. 4).

Waluchow endorses a clear-cut distinction that many legal theorists make between descriptive and normative approaches and ambition to a legal theory, and he attributes a shared mistaken understanding among contemporary legal theorists to Ronald Dworkin's influence in the debate. This alleged "mistake" of fusing descriptive and normative views led to other theoretical deficiencies in Dworkin's approach. His characterization is the following: "Hart's perspective, then, is that of an external observer out to describe and analyze a particular kind of social system, and the concepts in terms of which we conceive of it, in a philosophically illuminating way. Dworkin's perspective, by contrast, is that of a judge out to justify what he does in holding people liable for violating legal rights and duties" (Waluchow 1994, p. 13).

Consequently, for Dworkin, jurisprudence is only "the general part of adjudication," and "no firm line divides it from adjudication or any other aspect of legal practice" (Dworkin 1986, p. 90) Thus, for Waluchow, *the Dworkinian conception of law is thoroughly normative* (Waluchow 1994, p. 15).

Nevertheless, Waluchow acknowledges a dimension in which Dworkin's conception is also descriptive, since, to offer its essentially normative theory, Dworkin has to admit that there is some correspondence (fit) between his theory and the practice.[11] However, he points to mere empirical correspondence as the criterion of descriptiveness. According to Waluchow, Dworkin's mistake is connected to a misconception that merges two distinct questions about law. One is clearly in the realm of legal theory (what the law is), while the other is usually addressed by political philosophy (the force of law, or people's reason to obey the law) and is related to the legitimacy of the forces and reasons to obey the law. "Merging the two different questions" (Waluchow 1994, p. 15) is misleading and brings confusion to an accurate understanding of legal practice because they are conceptually different and require different methods of approach. One is based on empirical and descriptive methods, while the other requires a controversial debate on morality and value objectivity.

Waluchow's critique must be revised, because it overlooks an essential philosophical assumption behind Dworkin's account. Dworkin is primarily interested in showing how law is *a special kind of practice* that, for most theoretical purposes, cannot be described from a mere descriptive point of view. He is rejecting the kind of descriptive approach advocated by Hart and endorsed by most legal positivists.

Dworkin's point was already clear when *Inclusive Legal Positivism* was first published in 1994. In "The Model of Rules II," he calls attention to the fact that there is an essential distinction between *asserting a social rule* and *asserting a normative*

---

[11] "There is a descriptive element in Dworkinian conceptions, if only because any justification of a social practice like law must in some way characterize, or at the very least presuppose a characterization of what the theorist seeks to justify. The 'object' to be interpreted must in some way be identified, and this requires an element of description. Dworkin expresses the descriptive component of interpretation by saying that any adequate interpretation of a social practice like law must, to some significant though indeterminate degree, 'fit' the practice as it exists" (Waluchow 1994, p. 15).

rule (Dworkin 1977a, p. 50). He gives one example: The sociologist, when describing a rule, usually asserts a social rule. A judge, on the contrary, usually asserts a normative rule. Hart himself was aware of this distinction. However, "he denies that these two sorts of assertions can be said to assert two different sorts of rules." Thus, "when the sociologist asserts the existence of a social rule, he merely asserts its existence" (Dworkin 1977a, p. 50). When a judge asserts its existence, "he also claims that these practice-conditions are met, but *in addition*, he displays his *acceptance* of the rule as a standard for guiding his own conduct and for judging the conduct of others" (Dworkin 1977a, pp. 50–51). For this reason, "The difference between a statement of a social rule and a statement of a normative rule, then, is not a difference in the type of rule each asserts, but rather a difference in the attitude each displays towards the social rule it does assert" (Dworkin 1977a, p. 51).[12] This

[12] The full text is revealing and clear in stating this point: "But Hart's theory, as so far presented, is open to an objection that might be put in the following way. When a sociologist says that a particular community 'has' or 'follows' a particular rule, like the no-hat-in-church rule, he means only to describe the behavior of that community in a certain respect. He means only to say that members of that community suppose that they have a particular duty and not that he agrees. But when a member of the community himself appeals to a rule, for the purpose of criticizing his own or someone else's behavior, then he means not simply to describe the behavior of other people but to evaluate it. He means not simply that others believe that they have a certain duty, but that they *do* have that duty. We must, therefore, recognize a distinction between two sorts of statements, each of which uses the concept of a rule. The sociologist, we might say, is asserting a *social* rule, but the churchgoer is asserting a *normative* rule. We might say that the sociologist's assertion of a social rule is true (or warranted) if a certain factual state of affairs occurs, that is, if the community behaves in the way Hart describes in his example. But we should want to say that the churchgoer's assertion of a nonnative rule is true (or warranted) only if a certain normative state of affairs exists, that is, only if individuals in fact do have the duty that they suppose they have in Hart's example. The judge trying a lawsuit is in the position of the churchgoer, not the sociologist. He does not mean to state, as a cold fact, simply that most judges believe that they have a duty to follow what the legislature has said; he means that they do in fact have such a duty and he cites that duty, not others' beliefs, as the justification for his own decision. If so, then the social rule cannot, without more, be the source of the duty he believes he has.

Hart anticipates this objection with an argument that forms the heart of his theory. He recognizes the distinction I have drawn between assertions of a 'social rule' and assertions of a 'normative rule,' though he does not use these terms. However, he denies, at least as to the cases he discusses, that these two sorts of assertions can be said to assert two different sorts of rules. Instead, he asks us to distinguish between the *existence* of a rule and its *acceptance* by individual members of the community in question. When the sociologist asserts the existence of a social rule, he merely asserts its existence: he says only that the practice conditions for that rule have been met. When the churchgoer asserts its existence, he also claims that these practice-conditions are met, but *in addition* he displays his *acceptance* of the rule as a standard for guiding his own conduct and for judging the conduct of others. He both identifies a social practice and indicates his disposition to conform his behavior to it. Nevertheless, insofar as each refers to a rule, it is the same rule, that is, the Rule that is constituted by the social practice in question.

The difference between a statement of a social rule and a statement of a normative rule, then, is not a difference in the type of rule each asserts, but rather a difference in the attitude each displays towards the social rule it does assert. When a judge appeals to the rule that whatever the legislature enacts is law, he is taking an internal point of view towards a social rule; what he says is true because a social practice to that effect exists, but he goes beyond simply saying that this is so. He difference depends on the context of the use of the language of rules. The sociological context of use differs from the judge's context of use of the language—they belong to two different language games.

Dworkin presents another example when he analyzes the many conceptions of "liberalism" that can be found in the historical, political, philosophical, and sociological debate about it (Dworkin 1974).[13] According to Dworkin, the historical meaning of the concept of liberalism is different from the normative, interpretive, and value-based concept of liberalism that he endorses in that text. This is not to say that a descriptive, sociological concept of liberalism is impossible or useless, but rather that it differs from the normative one.

Dworkin clarifies his ideas on the matter by introducing some essential conceptual distinctions in *Justice in Robes*, published in 2006.[14] There, Dworkin points to the semantic ambiguity that the concept of law involves, which expands its "confusion effect" to the theory of law itself: "Unfortunately the English word 'law' and parallel words in other languages are used in so many different ways, we have so many distinct concepts that we use those words to employ, and the interrelationships among these concepts are so problematic and controversial, that different theories about the connections between law and justice are often answers to very different kinds of questions" (Dworkin 2006a, p. 1). This confusion creates a new source of philosophical errors: "This semantic misfortune has caused a good deal of confusion in legal theory" (Dworkin 2006a, p. 1). I suspect that Waluchow is among those affected by this misfortune, especially for not acknowledging the different contexts for conceptions of law (and other normative concepts such as liberalism, freedom, and life).

For this reason, Dworkin (2006a, p. 2) specifies the meaning that he deems most important for discussing his *interpretive conception of law*—namely, the *doctrinal conception*. The law in the doctrinal sense refers to "the concept of 'the law' of some place or entity being to a particular effect: we use that doctrinal concept when we say, for example, that under Rhode Island law a contract signed by someone under the age of twelve is invalid or, more controversially, that American constitutional law permits the President to order foreigners suspected of terrorism to be tortured" (Dworkin 2006a, p. 2). Therefore, he refers to our use of the concept of law when we formulate legal propositions with truth values. These propositions are typical in the discourse of judges, prosecutors, and attorneys.

What Dworkin seeks to emphasize, therefore, is that the meaning of propositions of law (which, being propositions, have a truth value)[15] directly affects how the law

signals his disposition to regard the social practice as a justification for his conforming to it" (Dworkin 1977a, pp. 50–51).

[13] This review was revised and reprinted under the title "Liberty and Liberalism" in *Taking Rights Seriously* (Dworkin 1977a, pp. 259–265).

[14] The book *Do Xadrez à Cortesia*, or *From Chess to Courtesy* (Macedo Junior 2013), especially chapter six, develops these arguments more fully.

[15] Dworkin analyzes the bipolar nature of propositions from the logical point of view in Dworkin (1977b), republished as Dworkin (1978), and again in Dworkin (1985, pp. 119–145).

is understood. In Wittgensteinian terms, this means that the proper concept of law depends on the language game and the use of the concept that is in place in each practice. Thus, it is possible to use a purely descriptive concept of law. We often do this when we describe a sociological concept of law. This usage is not wrong per se. However, this is not the kind of concept we need (and use) when we are describing the argumentative practices that constitute the law we want to discuss, which include the practices and arguments that demonstrate the rules of Brazilian or English law.

Additionally, the truth value of the proposition we make inside the practice of law depends directly on the concept of law that one has and, in particular, on the type of concept it is.[16] This reasoning explains why, when we ask whether same-sex or same-gender couples have the right to marry according to Brazilian law, it is essential to acknowledge that we are not using purely descriptive sociological concepts of law and marriage. In such a context, Brazilian law is best understood as a doctrinal concept that simultaneously carries normative and descriptive meanings.

In short, a doctrinal concept of law relates to the linguistic context in which a truth value is required for propositions of law. When we try to describe what Brazilian or English law is in that proposition, made in the context of a court judgment, the doctrinal concept is the type of concept at stake. This conceptual distinction is important.

On the one hand, this is relevant from the practical point of view, given that it affects how a question will be decided, as stated in the analysis of the cases *Riggs v. Palmer*, *TVA* (437 U.S. 153 (1978)), and *Henningsen* (*Henningsen v. Bloomfield Motors*, Inc., 32 N.J. 358, 161 A.2d 69 (N.J. 1960)). In a case like *TVA*,[17] for example, Justice Burger and Justice Powell disagreed with the question "What is law?" Both agreed they have the legal duty to apply the law. However, they disagreed about what law is and what the grounds of law are. They had a theoretical disagreement, as they disagreed about precisely what kind of concept law is. On the other hand, the conceptual distinction is also important from the theoretical and descriptive point of view, given that the truth value of the legal proposition depends on our concept of law, which involves defining whether or not it includes moral evaluations and moral grounds. In Justice Powell's view, law includes moral

[16] He frames the question thusly: "It is important to decide whether moral criteria are ever, and if so when, among the truth conditions of propositions of law: the conditions that must hold to make such a proposition true. This is particularly important in political communities like our own in which important political decisions are made by judges who are thought to have a responsibility to decide only as required or licensed by true propositions of law. It matters particularly in such communities whether and when judges must look to morality to decide which propositions are true" (Dworkin 2006a, p. 2).

[17] After the discovery of the snail darter fish in the Little Tennessee River in August 1973, a lawsuit was filed alleging that the Tennessee Valley Authority (TVA) built a dam construction that violated the *Endangered Species Act*. The US Supreme Court ruled in favor of Hill. Justices Warren E. Burger and Lewis F. Powell, Jr., wrote two dissenting opinions, acknowledging different grounds of law that guided their decisions.

grounds, while in Justice Burger's approach, law is grounded exclusively on social grounds.

Dworkin also highlights the *sociological concept of law*. Here again, he returns to the example of the sociologist approach to law presented in 1972 (Dworkin 1977a, pp. 46–80). He refines and develops the argument, describing it as a kind of concept in his expanded "conceptography." We use the word "law" in this kind of concept to designate a particular type of social structure. The question is this: "We might ask, for instance, using that sociological concept, when law first appeared in primitive tribal societies or whether commerce is possible without law" (Dworkin 2006a, p. 3). In light of this, he states, "Different social theorists use somewhat different tests for identifying law in this sociological sense. Max Weber said that law does not exist where there are no specialized institutions of coercive enforcement, for example, and Lon Fuller said that there is no law unless certain minimal requirements of procedural justice are met" (Dworkin 2006a, p. 3).

It is crucial to notice that there is nothing wrong with the existence of this plurality of conceptions "in itself." What really matters is that we use the kind of concept required in the proper context of use. We can properly use a sociological concept of law (Hartian, for example) when we ask whether Common Law is more efficient than Civil Law. When trying to answer the question in this context, it might be helpful to use a conceptualization of law established exclusively by its social grounds. However, such a kind (sociological) concept of law would not be suitable for understanding the argumentative disagreement in the *TVA* case.

Dworkin explicitly acknowledges that in a great deal of sociological research, it may be helpful or even necessary to establish, *according to the purpose that one has in mind and the context of the use of language*, a stipulative definition (or a criterial concept) of the type of social structure that we must consider when we refer to a legal system. This use of the concept can be vital to organizing a research project, making historical claims, establishing correlations between social variables (such as economics and law, or religion and law, as Weber's works aptly demonstrate), or even showing the moral importance of certain practices. Nevertheless, Dworkin clearly warns that, despite the utility of this conceptual use in certain circumstances, we must be careful not to generalize its applicability to other contexts in which our analytic (and linguistic) purposes are different. In his words, "we must not make the mistake of thinking that there is some natural distinction of social kinds that marks off legal structures as having, just in themselves, some essential nature that these distinctions try to capture" (Dworkin 2006a, p. 3).

Indeed, this is the significance of the caveats in his polemic with Frederick Schauer over the role of institutions in the definition of law (Schauer 2009, pp. 35–44).[18] The Dworkinian interpretation is not exactly a rival view to classical sociological interpretation, as several critics (notably, Frederick Schauer)[19] seem to

[18] See Dworkin's answer to Schauer in Dworkin (2006b). See also Schauer (1996).

[19] See Dworkin's response to Schauer in Dworkin (2006b). The critical dialogue began with the publication of Schauer (2006), a review of Nicola Lacey's book *A Life of H. L. A. Hart: The*

suggest, but rather a philosophical approach to some reflective, normative, and evaluative interpretive practices, such as law. Classical sociological analyses can be highly relevant in determining the interpretive matters involved in legal practices. However, its approach must be completed and constitutes only part of (or a moment in) the interpretive activity necessary to describe what law is correctly. In this sense, contrary to Schauer's critique, Dworkin does not neglect the institutional dimension of law, but instead criticizes the limits of a conception of law exclusively grounded on this dimension when we try to describe the reflexive dimension of legal argumentation and, as a consequence, of an essential part of legal practice.

It is relevant to emphasize that the *sociological concept of law* is fine for Dworkin as long as it is used correctly and not as a substitute for the doctrinal concept. Another example of this kind of use is the following: Imagine a sociologist who wants to establish causal correlations between the *reduction* of social inequality and the *operation* of the Rule of Law. The sociological question might be as follows: Is there a positive causal correlation between the reduction of social inequality and respect for the Rule of Law? In order to answer this question, the sociologist might employ a stipulative concept of the Rule of Law, such as, "a political regime in which there is freedom of the press, separation of powers, an independent judiciary and the surrender of power through free and fair elections." This definition may be instrumental and practical for conducting research, and it poses no problems. Nevertheless, this concept would not be appropriate for determining the truth value of the proposition: "The investigatory powers of the Public Prosecutor do not violate the Rule of Law."

However, an additional point is that, depending on the kind of question that the sociologist of the law comes to formulate for their research, a criterial (or sociological) concept of law might be insufficient and inappropriate. By way of example, we might consider research on case law for which the understanding of the truth value of decisions might be a relevant element of the "sociological description."

Based on these distinctions, it is possible to identify some connections between these various conceptual uses, which, despite their proximity, are different. *They are grammatically distinct and not merely in their apparent or semantic meaning.* The grammar and the concepts' functions in different contexts of use (language games) confers them with either a mere descriptive sense or a descriptive-normative sense. In their proximity lies the root of the philosophical confusion that "stings" many of the users of such concepts. Philosophical error causes certain thoughts to fall victim to grammatical confusion related to different conceptual uses.

For Dworkin, there is an essential distinction between the doctrinal and sociological concepts of law. As mentioned above, "The doctrinal concept of law figures among the boundaries of the sociological concept in this way: nothing is a legal system in the sociological sense unless it makes sense to ask what rights and duties

Nightmare and the Noble Dream (2004). Neil MacCormick presents a less radical but similar objection in MacCormick (2007), pp. 296–297.

the system recognizes" (Dworkin 2006a, p. 4). This comment makes clear that Dworkin has in his mind a vital interconnection between the concepts, albeit not a reciprocal one. Therefore, "not every set of norms that deploys rights and duties is a case of law" (Dworkin 2006a, p. 4). The doctrinal concept is thus more restrictive than the sociological concept. According to the sociological concept, legal content is not necessarily legal from the doctrinal point of view. Dworkin argues that in the realm of a game such as chess (the example that he uses is the card game *Go Fish*), it makes sense to state that there are situations in which a player is obligated to move a piece or not; therefore, they might make a particular move because of the rule.

In the same way, in a sociological sense, it makes sense to state that there was Nazi law, even though, in many respects, "Nazi law" can be denied when we take a doctrinal concept as a reference point. For that reason, the two concepts each have a different philosophical status. Typically, the former is not a *contested concept*, and its truth conditions are more easily established by reference to reasonably precise sociological facts[20] or stipulative conventions regarding its meaning. That is not to say that there is no disagreement among sociologists of law based on divergent philosophical assumptions. It only means that conventional understandings have made its meaning more stable. An excellent example of a classic conventional meaning is the set of definitions found in chapter one of *Economy and Society*, in which Weber presents his "basic sociological terms" of comprehensive sociology (Weber 1978, pp. 3–24). The fact that these concepts of a criterial nature are commonly not contested does not mean that disagreements and controversies cannot exist. Disagreements can happen and do happen frequently. However, here, the nature of the controversy is different. In sociology, for example, there may be disputes regarding which concept best describes a social practice in all its complexity. However, there will rarely be an argument regarding which *conception* of a value among those used within a community best interprets the *concept* of that value (i.e., best identifies its evaluative "meaning or point" per se).[21] However, the same thing does not happen about the doctrinal concept since there can be disagreement regarding the truth conditions of a legal proposition that concerns precisely interpretive questions of this kind. Therefore, these have significant practical consequences.

It is also important not to understand that this distinction is not simply a novel way of presenting the distinction between theories of law and theories of adjudication accepted by Hart and Waluchow. Dworkin's point is that there can be useful descriptive theories of law, such as Weber's conception of law. However, only a particular descriptive-normative conception of law is able to give a fair and illuminating explanation of the concept of law used in its doctrinal context—one that takes

[20] See, for example, Cotterrell (1983).

[21] The argument here is based on a well-known distinction between concepts and conceptions, originally introduced by Gallie (1964, pp. 157–191) and further adopted by many philosophers, such as Rawls (1955), Hart in chapter one of *The Concept of Law* (1994), and Dworkin in chapter one of *Law's Empire* (1986).

into consideration the normative nature of que rule (the difference between a statement of a social rule and a statement of a normative rule, stated above) and the reflexive and interpretive feature of legal reasoning required to understand and apply them. Ultimately, offering an accurate conception of the doctrinal concept of law is legal theory's most important purpose and value (even though it is not its exclusive value).

For these same reasons, we can plausibly imagine a descriptive theory of adjudication. Usually, the sociology of legal interpretation offers this kind of approach. However, an accurate description of adjudication requires the acknowledgment of the normative nature of rules and the reflexive and interpretive method for the legal interpretation. In brief, doctrinal and sociological concepts do not merely reintroduce an old and well-known distinction between the theory of law and the theory of adjudication. The Dworkinian distinction shows that a fair, illuminating theory of law and a fair, illuminating theory of adjudication both require an understanding of the normative attitude adopted in the actions of the agents participating in legal practice. Waluchow's critique cannot cope with this distinction.

There is some family resemblance between a theory of law and a theory of adjudication, as both share the need for a normative rule understanding to offer a clear description of the practice of law. However, this does not mean that they are essentially the same. Furthermore, the normative rule attitude also requires that legal theory consider the intentionality (or point) behind the legal practice. The normative attitude includes the consideration of the force of law and its close connection with the requirement of legitimacy for accepting the authority of law. In other words, the authority of law is grounded on moral grounds, although not exclusively. Legal conventionalism and the service conception of authority cannot fully explain the normative roots of the guidance force of the normative rules in general, even if they can (in particular settings) explain why the law creates obligations.

In sum, Waluchow assigns Dworkin different functions to the concept of law related to different uses and kinds of concepts of law. This point of the critique connects to another: the distinction between grounds of law and force of law.

5.2 *Force, Grounds, and the Political Point of Law*

Waluchow credits Dworkin with being unaware of the distinction between the force of law and the grounds of law before criticizing his flawed idea that fuses the two different questions: "In explaining his claim that the grounds of law normally settle practical questions, Dworkin introduces us to a notion which plays a key part in his theory. He tells us the 'force' of law is 'the relative power of any true proposition of law to justify coercion in different sorts of exceptional circumstances'" (Dworkin 1986, p. 110). In hard cases wherein the grounds of law seem at odds with the requirements of moral principle, we must ask difficult questions concerning the law's power to justify coercion. Thus, "according to Dworkin, legal philosophers rightly concentrate on the grounds of law, while political philosophers are typically concerned with questions of its force. It is nevertheless Dworkin's view that a plausible legal theory regarding the grounds of law (a legal-grounds theory) will inevitably entail a fairly general answer to questions about what we might call the 'non-exceptional' or 'normal' force of law" (Waluchow 1994, p. 13).[22]

The problem with Waluchow's view is connected to his rejection of the accuracy of the kind of interpretative approach that law requires, since, for him, law can be interpreted as an external practice, much like a game of chess. It is crucial to note that even a chess game requires the acknowledgment of the Hartian *internal point of view*, which does not dismiss the "purely" descriptive nature of a chess theory. Waluchow is also well aware of this. However, according to Dworkin, the relevant point is that law is *not* like chess since it involves a self-reflective dimension in its practice. This self-reflective practice involves understanding, acknowledging, and attributing a political value in complying with the law. In other words, the value of law (its political point) is directly linked to the justification of the use of force. As argued elsewhere (Macedo Junior 2013, 2016), although chess is a social practice, it does not usually (at least not in its pivotal cases) involve disputes on the interpretive concepts. Quite the opposite: it is almost natural and intuitive to consider the game of chess based exclusively on its conventionally accepted rules or even rules set by an act of will from the agents.

Unlike other practices, such as law, chess does not involve an interpretive question associated with evaluative judgments (it is not understood from a conventional evaluative angle). For this reason, the argumentative and interpretive dimension of law is analogous to the social practice of courtesy (Dworkin 1986, pp. 46–49). The analogy with chess reveals a different logical grammar than the one used in the language game of courtesy. The trait that sets the social practice of courtesy apart from the social practice of chess is that the former includes an evaluative-reflective practice on a specific value on the part of the agents (that is, the *courtesy value)*, which is absent in the case of chess. In the case of chess, the conventional meanings of the rules are sufficient for the chess players to engage in the practice. In the case of the practice of courtesy, the interpretation of the meaning of the value of courtesy is required. It is not enough to refer the practice of courtesy to the conventional meaning of the courtesy value, as if we could check its proper meaning in a dictionary of courtesy etiquette. In arguing about the correct conceptualization of the concept of courtesy, we usually challenge its conventional meaning. In chess, the rules are made up of shared public standards, or "social rules," to use the terminology of H.L.A. Hart. In the case of courtesy, the shared behavioral standards are relevant, necessary conditions but are insufficient to correctly describe the activity's grammar. For the Hartian understanding of chess, it would be sufficient to record what the players understand about the rules they are subject to while playing. The chess example is perfectly appropriate to understand how a *criterial*

[22] A conception of law must explain the way that what it takes to be law provides a general justification for the exercise of coercive power by the state. This justification holds, except in special cases when competing arguments are exceptionally powerful (Dworkin 1986, p. 190).

concept works but is inappropriate to describe the functioning of an *interpretive concept* (Macedo Junior 2013, p. 298; Macedo Junior 2016, pp. 296–305).

An argumentative practice's distinctive trait is that it assumes the presence of arguments *about* the practices themselves. However, it is not simply the act of being courteous (for example, for a man to pay a young lady's bill or not) and the paradigmatic cases of courtesy—from whence come the rules that give the participants reasons to act—that must be considered in argumentative practice. Arguing, justifying, and challenging arguments about (and evaluations of) courtesy are part of the "courtesy game." An argumentative self-reflection exists here. The *argumentation practices* involved in the *practices of courtesy* only gain sense within the argumentative practices themselves, justifying and challenging the meaning and *conceptions* of the *concept* of courtesy. Finally, the arguments about courtesy are also parameters to determine the best conception of courtesy.

Therefore, for Dworkin, understanding an argumentative practice about an interpretive concept involves understanding the meaning that agents lend to the values and arguments involved in these practices, thus understanding the "internal" interpretation done by the agents. Waluchow misunderstands this recurrent *interpretive dimension* of the Dworkinian approach.

Waluchow, however, is not persuaded and insists:

> [F]or Dworkin, a legal theorist's job is not unlike that of a judge who sets out to interpret a statute or a line of precedents. Both must attempt to make their objects of study the best they can be to find in them as much moral value, i.e., moral justification, as they can. Both the judge and the legal theorist are trying to find something that licenses state coercion. The judge wants to know what justifies coercion in this particular case before him; the legal theorist wants to know what, in general, licenses coercion in all (or most) cases coming before the courts of a particular legal system or legal systems in general. So, according to Dworkin, legal theory is not essentially different from adjudication: it is just that the former is more general and encompasses more material than the latter. (Waluchow 1994, p. 32)

However, as previously demonstrated, this is not accurate—it is an overstatement. Even though Dworkin views jurisprudence as "the general part of adjudication, silent prologue to any decision at law" (Dworkin 1986, p. 90), there are different kinds of uses of the concepts of law and other evaluative concepts that can be described from a sociological or institutional point of view. Again, a sociological jurisprudence is possible and often helpful. There can be a descriptive legal theory, and its contributions can be illuminating. However, this kind of theory is not well-suited to a good description of the doctrinal sense of law.

This is not equivalent to saying that any kind of argument about values requires this type of interpretive approach, but instead that it is a central case (a pivotal case) for our understanding of legal arguments in the contemporary practice of law. Dworkin does not fuse the normative sense of the concept of law with its descriptive meaning, as stated by Waluchow. He simply points to the fact that the normative meaning is essential to a correct description of law in some significant (pivotal) contexts of the use of the concept of law. A sociological and mere descriptive conception of law could still be helpful in some contexts (for empirical investigations, for example). However, it is misleading and inadequate in other contexts of use (when they function as doctrinal concepts and a better, more complex doctrinal concept is needed).

5.3 Theory and Meta-Theory Engaged

Waluchow also accuses Dworkin of identifying the role of adjudication with the role of legal theory and, in so doing, confusing the very intellectual task of the legal theorist and the judge. He interprets Dworkin's account in this way:

> In his view, there just is no theoretically important difference between interpreting and engaging in a practice. Legal theory is not meta-theory, according to Dworkin. A legal theorist must, by the very logic of interpretation, "use the methods his subjects use in forming their own opinions about what [the practice] really requires. He must, that is, join the practice he proposes to understand; his conclusions are then not neutral reports about what [the participants] think but claims about [the practice] competitive with theirs." "[N]o firm line divides jurisprudence from adjudication or any other aspect of legal practice." (Waluchow 1994, pp. 23–24).[23]

Consequently, Dworkin is accused of merging the judge and the legal theorist approaches. Waluchow also stresses that,

> for Dworkin, a legal theorist's job is not unlike that of a judge who sets out to interpret a statute or a line of precedents. Both must attempt to make their objects of study the best they can be, to find in them as much moral value, i.e., moral justification, as they can. Both the judge and the legal theorist are trying to find something that licenses state coercion. The judge wants to know what justifies coercion in this particular case before him; the legal theorist wants to know what, in general, licenses coercion in all (or most) cases coming before the courts of a particular legal system or legal systems in general. *So, according to Dworkin, legal theory is not essentially different from adjudication: it is just that the former is more general and encompasses more material than the latter.* (Waluchow 1994, pp. 23–24, emphasis added)

Waluchow's claim is straightforward: Dworkin merges the task of the judge with the task of the legal theorist. Dworkin thinks that they only differ in the generality of their claims. However, his interpretation fails to account for the different uses of the concept of law that are at play in the descriptive and adjudicative contexts. As mentioned before, there can exist a purely descriptive theory of law as there can be a descriptive-normative theory of law. They can both function for descriptive purposes. However, when a judge bases their decisions on a merely descriptive concept of law (such as Kelsen or Hart's descriptive conceptions of law that Justice Burger might have invoked in the *TVA* case), the same concept functions as a doctrinal and normative concept. When this happens, due to the different contexts of use, it becomes normative, even though the legal theorists who conceptualized it intended

[23]The quotes inside this quote are from Dworkin (1986, pp. 25–26).

it to be merely descriptive. Using the concept in a different context transforms its type, changing its nature.[24]

Again, the new *conceptography* (the grammar of different kinds of uses and types of concepts) proposed by Dworkin in *Justice in Robes* and *Justice for Hedgehogs* (somehow partially anticipated in *Taking Rights Seriously*) helps explain the difficulties found in Waluchow's reading of Dworkin's *Law's Empire*. It is excessive to say that Dworkin *identifies* the judge's perspective with the legal theorist's approach. It is more accurate to say that judges use a doctrinal conception of law, which is deeply dependent on the theory of law assumed. This is a more appropriate way to understand Dworkin's famous motto: "Jurisprudence is the general part of adjudication, silent prologue to any decision at law" (Dworkin 1986, p. 90; Dworkin 1987, p. 14; Dworkin 2006a, pp. 36–48, 140–186; Dworkin 2011, p. 327). This interpretation reconciles the understanding of the different grammar and uses of the concept of law without accepting Waluchow's conclusion that, in Dworkin's view, there is pure confusion and plain identification of adjudication and legal theory. There is indeed no clear line separating them. However, this is far from admitting that the perspectives are identical, as Waluchow contends. It is vital to articulate that the insulation of different practices and beliefs is not absolute. The standards function as Wittgenstein's famous thread metaphor: a thread made of many different fibers, intertwined and setting patterns of family resemblances among them.[25] Dworkin offers a better account of the connection between the doctrinal and theoretical uses of the concept of law in his later works, only partially available to his critic in *Inclusive Legal Positivism.*

It might be helpful to remember that the usefulness of a more complex theory is not always evident in any context. Engineers today still apply Newtonian physics to

[24] Dworkin made a similar theoretical claim in "Is law like literature?" (reprinted as chapter six of *A Matter of Principle*, 1985). In this essay, he acknowledged that even a conventionalist conception of art (like "art is what the community of art experts believe art is") functions as a normative, interpretive pattern in the context of a dispute among art critics about the artistic value of a film like *Titanic* (Dworkin 1985, pp. 149–154). It could be a good or bad theory of art (or "aesthetic hypothesis," as Dworkin names it), but it is merely descriptive according to the creator's intentions. However, it still functions as an interpretive, normative conception of art in the context of the dispute.

[25] See Wittgenstein: "I can think of no better expression to characterize these similarities than 'family resemblances'; for the various resemblances between members of a family: build, features, the color of eyes, gait, temperament, etc., overlap and criss-cross in the same way.—And I shall say: 'games' form a family. And for instance, the kinds of number form a family in the same way. Why do we call something a 'number'? Well, perhaps because it has a—direct—relationship with several things that have hitherto been called number; and this can be said to give it an indirect relationship to other things we call the same name. And we extend our concept of number as in spinning a thread we twist fibre on fibre. And the strength of the thread does not reside in the fact that someone fibre runs through its whole length, but in the overlapping of many fibres. But if someone wished to say: 'There is something common to all these constructions—namely the disjunction of all their common properties'—I should reply: Now you are only playing with words. One might as well say: 'Something runs through the whole thread—namely the continuous overlapping of those fibers'" (2009, paragraph 67).

build bridges and cars—it would be a waste of time to use Einsteinian physics to make them. Newtonian models are simpler and sufficiently accurate for these purposes. However, the theory of relativity, which is much more complex, is required for making microchips, space stations, and astronomic observations. In our daily lives, we may not need a normative, interpretive (and self-reflexive) theory of rules to describe chess games or traffic laws. However, this is required (and makes a difference) in some pivotal hard cases (often in fundamental rights disputes in higher courts) that must be remembered by a better theory of law. Relativity physics also applies in the ordinary car-making process, but the theory of relativity does not show its descriptive advantages for the engineers who deal with it. Law as integrity and interpretation also does not show its clearest usefulness and highest accuracy in traffic law cases.

Furthermore, Dworkin also changed his understanding of the relationship between law and morals over time. In his later works, he rejected the idea that law and morals are two dominions with overlapping features and stated that law could be better described as a department of morals. In *Justice for Hedgehogs*, for example, Dworkin presents a more fully developed argument about the integration of the dominion of values (ethics, morality, and political morality) and claims that the reciprocal influence between them justifies labelling them departments of morals. Instead of different and independent dominions that sometimes overlap, we can understand them in a better way as departments that share "family resemblances," not separated by diverse essences that are distinguished by differences in scope, generality, and institutional dependence.[26] Dworkin rectified his ideas on this matter (the relationship between law and morals) and showed his way of understanding the relationship of different intertwined concepts more accurately and coherently. His new statement on this issue exemplifies how his conceptual critique became focused on the inadequacy of conceptualizing law and morals, and legal theory and adjudication as fully independent dominions.

This understanding should not be confused with a naïve identification of them but rather as suggesting that the lines separating the two practices (morals and law) inside two different concepts intermingle. Law is also a practice informed by its institutional dimension, which is insufficient to determine it (in an essentialist sense) completely. In other words, its institutional dimension is not a sufficient condition for the theoretical concept of law, even though it is a necessary one.

---

[26] He states, "There is a flaw in the two-systems picture. Once we take law and morality to compose separate systems of norms, there is no neutral standpoint from which the connections between these supposedly separate systems can be adjudicated. Where shall we turn for an answer to the question whether positivism or interpretivism is a more accurate or otherwise better account of how the two systems relate? Is this a moral question or a legal question? Either choice yields a circular argument with much too short a radius. . . . We have already noticed, in Chapter 8, the fallacy in these shared assumptions. We cannot solve the circularity problem of the two-systems picture through an analysis of the concept of law unless that concept can sensibly be treated as a criterial (or perhaps as a natural-kind) concept. But it cannot be" (Dworkin 2011, pp. 402–405).

This change in Dworkin's approach to the relationship between law and morals relationship the need to revise the accusation made by Waluchow that he merges political philosophy and legal theory, and the tasks of the judge and the legal theorist. The task of a judge before the law differs from that of the legal theorist. They differ in their commitment to dealing with concrete cases and generalizing about the law and legal reasoning. They also have distinct intellectual training and practical purposes. However, reasoning about concrete cases often requires interpretation, conceptual analysis, and philosophical sensibility, making judging and jurisprudential reasoning akin. The activity of the judge inevitably carries some philosophical questioning. In this sense, judges are not professional philosophers and cannot be. However, they have to philosophize, or at least responsibly assume their philosophical assumptions, in order to be good judges.[27] The outcomes of these philosophical efforts are particularly important when judges face hard cases rooted in theoretical disagreements. Nonetheless, a full development of this argument would require more than this brief comment.

Finally, introducing a more sophisticated conceptual apparatus in *Justice in Robes* advances Dworkin's strategy of preventing his ideas from falling victim to objections based on false problems. One of the most recurrent false problems concerns the debate about the existence of law in unjust regimes, frequently reintroduced into the debate through questions like the following: Did Nazi law exist or not? This question could be reformulated in a more classic formulation: "Is unjust law still law?"[28] From what has been seen up to this point, for Dworkin, this question cannot be answered if we do not specify beforehand which concept we are using to answer it; indeed, without such antecedent specification, raising the question may only generate confusion. For a traditional sociological conception of law (such as Max Weber's), a legal norm may be unjust and frequently is. According to the sociological concept, a discriminatory norm issued by the Nazi government is legal, despite being immoral and unjust. However, according to a doctrinal concept, the same norm would not be legal depending on the presupposed conception of law. Such is the case of a conception that interprets the principles of the political morality of a community as constitutive of the concept of law. Law as integrity is one possible description of the doctrinal conception of law that would allow challenging the legality of many rules posited by the "Nazi Regime."

[27] Dworkin fully develops this argument in "Must Our Judges Be Philosophers? Can They Be Philosophers?" (2001).

[28] The classical contemporary formulation of the question is done by Radbruch (2006b) and Radbruch (2006a). H.L.A. Hart directly addresses these issues and discusses Radbruch's idea, also called "Radbruch's Formula," in his well-known lecture "Positivism and the Separation of Law and Morals" (1958).

6 Conclusion

Waluchow's clear and profound critique of Dworkin's ideas has served a fundamental purpose of refining and deepening some of the most critical methodological features of the contemporary debate in legal theory. This chapter analyzed two basic claims about the descriptive nature of legal theory and the relationship between law and morals in the concept of law. Together with Jules Coleman's contribution (*The Practice of Principle*), Waluchow's book is one of the most potent defenses of inclusive legal positivism. Even if some of his criticisms are not fully convincing, they still represent the standard for the questions that legal scholars must face to position themselves in the contemporary debate. Furthermore, some Dworkinian responses and clarifications to many critiques made by Wil Waluchow appeared after the important book *Inclusive Legal Positivism* was published in 1994. They were, quite possibly, a reaction to it.

Acknowledgment Thanks to Yago Mina for revising a preliminary version of this text.

References

Coleman, Jules. 1988. *Markets, Morals and the Law*. Cambridge: Cambridge University Press.
———. 2001. *The Practice of Principle*. Oxford: Oxford University Press.
Cotterrell, Roger. 1983. The Sociological Concept of Law. *Journal of Law and Society* 10 (2): 241–255. https://doi.org/10.2307/1410234.
Dworkin, Ronald. 1967. The Model of Rules. *University of Chicago Law Review* 35: 14–46.
———. 1974. Did Mill Go Too Far? Review of *On Liberty and Liberalism: The Case of John Stuart Mill* by Gertrude Himmelfarb. *New York Review of Books*, 31 October 1974. http://www.nybooks.com/articles/archives/1974/oct/31/did-mill-go-too-far/.
———. 1977a. *Taking Rights Seriously*. Cambridge, MA: Harvard University Press.
———. 1977b. No Right Answer? In *Law, Morality, and Society: Essays in Honour of H.L.A. Hart*, ed. P.M.S. Hacker and Joseph Raz, 58–84. Oxford: Oxford University Press.
———. 1978. Is There Really No Right Answer in Hard Cases? *University of New York Law Review* 53: 1–32.
———. 1985. *A Matter of Principle*. Cambridge, MA: Harvard University Press.
———. 1986. *Law's Empire*. Cambridge, MA: Belknap Press.
———. 1987. Legal theory and the problem of sense. In *Issues in contemporary legal philosophy*, ed. Gavison, R. Oxford: Clarendon.
———. 2001. Must Our Judges Be Philosophers? Can They Be Philosophers? New York Council for the Humanities, 2000 Scholar of the Year Lecture, in Ronald Dworkin Papers (MS, 2071). Manuscripts and Archives, Yale University Library. https://archives.yale.edu/repositories/12/archival_objects/2979194. Accessed 19 September 2023.
———. 2006a. *Justice in Robes*. Cambridge, MA: Harvard University Press.
———. 2006b. Hart and the Concepts of Law. *Harvard Law Review* 119: 95–104.
———. 2011. *Justice for Hedgehogs*. Cambridge, MA: Harvard University Press.
Gallie, W.B. 1964. *Philosophy and the Historical Understanding*. London: Chatto & Windus.
Hart, H.L.A. 1958. Positivism and the Separation of Law and Morals. *Harvard Law Review* 71: 593–629. (Republished in Hart, H.L.A. 1983. *Essays in Jurisprudence and Philosophy*. Oxford: Oxford University Press).

———. 1994. *The Concept of Law*. 2nd ed. Oxford: Oxford University Press.
Himma, Kenneth E. 2004. Inclusive Legal Positivism. In *The Oxford Handbook of Jurisprudence and Philosophy of Law*, ed. Jules L. Coleman, Kenneth Einar Himma, and Scott J. Shapiro, 97–98. Oxford: Oxford University Press.
Lacey, Nicola. 2004. *A Life of H. L. A. Hart: The Nightmare and the Noble Dream*. Oxford: Oxford University Press.
Leiter, Brian. 2009. Explaining Theoretical Disagreement. *University of Chicago Law Review* 76 (3).: Article 5. https://chicagounbound.uchicago.edu/uclrev/vol76/iss3/5.
Lyons, David. 1977. Principles, Positivism, and Legal Theory. *Yale Law Journal* 87: 415–435.
MacCormick, Neil. 1994. *Legal Reasoning and Legal Theory*. 2nd ed. Oxford: Oxford University Press.
———. 2005. *Rhetoric and the Rule of Law: A Theory of Legal Reasoning*. Oxford: Oxford University Press.
———. 2007. *Institutions of Law: An Essay in Legal Theory*. Oxford: Oxford University Press.
Macedo Junior, Ronaldo Porto. 2013. *Do xadrez à cortesia: Dworkin e a teoria do direito contemporânea*. São Paulo: Saraiva.
———. 2016. On How Law Is Not Like Chess – Dworkin and the Theory of Conceptual Types. In *Democratizing Constitutional Law – Perspectives on Legal Theory and the Legitimacy of Constitutionalism*, ed. Thomas Bustamante and Bernardo Gonçalves Fernandes, 293–324. Dodrecht: Springer.
Marmor, Andrei. 2002. Exclusive Legal Positivism. In *The Oxford Handbook of Jurisprudence and Philosophy of Law*, ed. Jules L. Coleman and Scott Shapiro, 104–124. Oxford: Oxford University Press.
Postema, G. 2011. *A Treatise of Legal Philosophy and General Jurisprudence*. Vol. 11. Heidelberg: Springer.
Radbruch, Gustav. 2006a. Five Minutes of Legal Philosophy (1945). Trans. Bonnie Litschewski Paulson and Stanley L. Paulson. *Oxford Journal of Legal Studies* 26 (1): 13–15. https://doi.org/10.1093/ojls/gqi042.JSTOR3600539.
———. 2006b. Statutory Lawlessness and Supra-statutory Law (1946). Trans. Bonnie Litschewski Paulson and Stanley L. Paulson. *Oxford Journal of Legal Studies* 26 (1): 1–11. https://doi.org/10.1093/ojls/gqi041.
Rawls, John. 1955. Two Concepts of Rules. *The Philosophical Review* 64 (1): 3–32. https://doi.org/10.2307/2182230.
Raz, Joseph. 1979. *The Authority of Law*. Oxford: Clarendon Press.
———. 1980. *The Concept of a Legal System – An Introduction to the Theory of Legal System*. 2nd ed. Oxford: Clarendon Press.
———. 1985. Authority, Law and Morality. *The Monist* 68: 295–324.
———. 1994. *Ethics in the Public Domain*. Oxford: Clarendon Press.
———. 1998. Postema on Law's Autonomy and Public Practical Reasons: A Critical Comment. *Legal Theory* 4 (1): 1–20.
Schauer, F. 1996. Positivism as Pariah. In *The Autonomy of Law: Essays on Legal Positivism*, ed. R.P. George, 31–56. Oxford: Clarendon Press.
———. 2006. (Re)Taking Hart. *Harvard Law Review* 119: 852–883.
———. 2009. Institutions and the Concept of Law: A Reply to Ronald Dworkin (with Some Help from Neil MacCormick). In *Law as Institutional Normative Order: Essays in Honour of Sir Neil MacCormick*, ed. Zenon Bankowski and Maksymilian Del Mar, 35–44. Burlington: Ashgate.
Shapiro, S.J. 2007. The Hart Dworkin Debate: A Short Guide for the Perplexed. In *Ronald Dworkin: Contemporary Philosophy in Focus*, ed. A. Ripstein, 22–55. Cambridge: Cambridge University Press.

Soper, P. 1977. Legal Theory and the Obligation of Judge: The Hart/Dworkin Dispute. *Michigan Law Review* 75: 473–516.
Waluchow, W.J. 1994. *Inclusive Legal Positivism*. Oxford: Clarendon Press.
Weber, M. 1978. *Economy and Society*. Berkeley: University of California Press.
Wittgenstein, Ludwig. 2009. *Philosophical Investigations*. 4th ed. New York: Wiley-Blackwell.

Ronaldo Porto Macedo Junior is Professor of Jurisprudence at the University of São Paulo and a Professor of Law at Getúlio Vargas Foundation, both in Brazil. He has had his Habilitation (*Livre-Docência*) in Philosophy of Law at the University of São Paulo and holds a Ph.D in Law and an MPhil in Philosophy, both from the University of São Paulo. He has been Visiting Scholar at Harvard Law School and Visiting Researcher at Yale Law School. His books include *Do Xadrez à Cortesia* (Saraiva, 2013).

Competing Legal Positivisms, Methodology and Distinctive Visions of Law

Brian H. Bix

Abstract Wil Waluchow was (and is) one of the most significant figures in the "intramural" debate between inclusive and exclusive legal positivism, as well as a prominent figure in many other areas of legal and moral theory. This chapter will consider his contributions to the inclusive-exclusive debate, focusing primarily on one aspect of the debate: whether inclusive legal positivism succeeds in offering a distinctive vision of the nature of law. In the debate with exclusive legal positivism, inclusive legal positivism seems to have an advantage in the area of fit. For example, unlike exclusive legal positivism, inclusive legal positivism has no difficulty in accounting for constitutional judicial review or common law judicial legislation. However, the potential challenge to the inclusive approach is whether this greater fit with our legal practice (and the way we speak within and about our legal practice) is purchased at the cost of diminished significance. The concern is that inclusive legal positivism presents us with a theory of law which tells us very little about law. Throughout his writings, and particularly in his most recent works, Waluchow has responded to the charge of "no distinctive view of law." This chapter summarizes and evaluates this part of Waluchow's defense of inclusive legal positivism.

1 Preface

My first interaction with Wil Waluchow was over 25 years ago. I was only recently finished with graduate school, my doctoral thesis had the good fortune to be published (Bix 1993), but it had been largely, and perhaps appropriately, ignored. One of the few reviews I received was from this 'Wil Waluchow' (of whom I had not, at that time, been as familiar as I should have been), who wrote a 'Critical Notice' of the book in the *Canadian Journal of Law & Jurisprudence* (Waluchow 1996). The review began, 'It is not easy to summarize what this book is about' (Waluchow 1996, p. 397), and basically went downhill from there.

B. H. Bix (✉)
University of Minnesota, School of Law, Minneapolis, MN, USA
e-mail: bix@umn.edu

T. Bustamante et al. (eds.), *Law, Morality and Judicial Reasoning*, Law and Philosophy Library 147, https://doi.org/10.1007/978-3-031-61879-6_7

Despite—or, who knows, perhaps because of—this bracing introduction, I came to have the highest regard for Wil, as an incisive and reliable contributor to analytical legal theory, constitutional theory, and many other debates (as well as a deeply kind person, a great mentor to his numerous graduate students, an organizer of important conferences, and one could go on at some length!). It is a pleasure, and a great honor, to be able to participate in this *Festschrift*.

2 Introduction

Wil Waluchow is, without doubt, one of the most significant figures in the 'intra-mural' argument between inclusive and exclusive legal positivism,[1] as well as a prominent figure in many other areas of legal and moral theory. In this Chapter, I will consider his contributions to the inclusive-exclusive debate, focusing primarily on one aspect: whether inclusive legal positivism succeeds in offering a *distinctive* vision of the nature of law.

In what follows, Sect. 3 gives a brief introduction and overview to the inclusive-exclusive debate; Sect. 4 offers some general reflections on the construction of models and the evaluation of theories; Sect. 5 then focuses on Waluchow's views about inclusive legal positivism's view of law, before concluding.

3 The Inclusive Exclusive Debate: A Brief Overview

It is frequently stated that legal positivism is based on the separation of law and morality, or, put differently, that there are no necessary connections between law and morality. This is an imprecise way of presenting the point—for reasons that will be discussed at the end of this Section—but it will suffice as a rough starting point for explaining the difference between inclusive legal positivism and exclusive legal positivism.

If one wanted to negate a claim of necessary connection ('*necessarily* law has [or legal rules have] a certain moral content'), there would be two options. First, one could negate the *first* part of the asserted connection, by denying *the necessity* of the connection: one could claim that legal validity *might* depend on moral value, but that any such connection is *contingent, not necessary.*[2] Alternatively, one could negate

[1] Inclusive legal positivism (which is now the dominant label, in no small part due to Waluchow's book *Inclusive Legal Positivism* [Waluchow 1994]) is also sometimes called 'incorporationist' and 'soft' legal positivism; exclusive legal positivism is also sometimes known as 'hard' legal positivism. This Chapter will use the labels 'inclusive' and 'exclusive'.

[2] In this Chapter, the focus will be primarily on whether there are moral (or merits) tests for legal validity. John Gardner (2001) famously argued that the denial of such tests was the essential meaning of legal positivism. I think that this view unnecessarily discounts the theoretical

the *second* part of the asserted connection, by changing what is purported to be necessary to law: stating that it is *necessarily* the case that legal validity does not depend on moral content. The first position, that there *can* be moral tests for legal validity, but that any such tests are contingent, is 'inclusive legal positivism'. The second position, that it is necessarily the case that there are no moral tests of legal validity, is 'exclusive legal positivism'. It is generally agreed that the two versions of legal positivism arose as differing responses to Ronald Dworkin's attacks on H. L. A. Hart's version of legal positivism, in particular, Dworkin's argument that moral principles in fact play a role in determining legal validity (Dworkin 1977; Hart 2012).[3]

Waluchow summarizes the inclusive legal positivism position as follows: 'there is nothing in the very nature of law that rules out the conceptual possibility that a rule of recognition—whose existence and content are purely contingent matters of social fact—might, as a matter of further social fact, include conformity with one or more moral norms among its conditions for legal validity' (Waluchow 2009, p. 124). By way of contrast, Joseph Raz offers this summary of the exclusive legal positivist position: 'All law is source-based. ... A law is source-based if its existence and content can be identified by reference to social facts alone' (Raz 1994, pp. 194–195).

It is important to note that the debate between inclusive legal positivism and exclusive legal positivism is *not* a debate about what judges and other legal officials *should do*. Neither position entails a view (*eg*) that there should be more (or that there should be less) constitutional judicial review (based on moral standards), or that there should be more (or that there should be less) common law developments of the law through judicial legislation (based on moral standards). It is also *not* a debate about how judges should resolve disputes in a particular category of cases or generally about lawyers and judges should reason. The debate is at the descriptive and conceptual level, not the prescriptive level. To put the point differently, the debate is about *how to characterize* what judges are doing when they (*eg*) invalidate otherwise valid legislation, justifying that action based on moral language in a constitutional provision (Waluchow 2009, pp. 124–125).

The question in this debate between different forms of legal positivism turns on *how to understand* what is going on when a judge (*eg*) declares a statute to be void because it is inconsistent with a constitutional provision which contains a moral test

significance of possible overlaps of law and morality at two other levels: (1) whether a government *system*, if sufficiently unjust, loses its status as a *legal* system? (did the Nazis have law?, etc.), and (2) whether one must use moral evaluation in the construction of one's theory of law (can one's theory of law be 'morally neutral'?). The well-known debates between Hart and Joseph Raz on one side, and Lon Fuller, John Finnis, and Ronald Dworkin, on other side, display disagreements about all three levels (legal status of rule, legal status of system, construction of legal theory). *See, eg*, Hart (1958), Fuller (1958), Raz (2009), Dworkin (1977), Finnis (2011). However, more detailed discussion of three levels of connection or separation of law and morality must await another occasion.

[3]On the connection between Dworkin's critique of Hart and the inclusive-exclusive debate, *see, eg* Waluchow (2001), Waluchow (2020), Waluchow (2022, p. 127), Postema (2011, pp. 466–467).

(equality, due process of law, not-cruel punishment, or the like). An inclusive legal positivist would say that the judge has declared that the legislation is not valid law, *and never has been valid law*, because of its conflict with the constitutional guarantee. The exclusive legal positivist would say that the judge was authorized and directed to invalidate the law, but the law is not invalid until the judge acts. As will be discussed in greater length below, the characterization offered by the inclusive legal positivist more closely tracks the way most judges and lawyers speak about such cases, but the exclusive legal positivist's characterization can fit *what the courts do*, even if it diverges from *what the courts say (about what) they are doing*.

Just to follow up on the point left unfinished at the beginning of this Section, that it is inaccurate to equate legal positivism with the separation of law and morality: a few quick notes. There are a number of necessary connections between morality and law which legal positivists accept. For example, Joseph Raz lists among the 'necessary moral properties' of law: 'that rape cannot be committed by law', and that the formal (non-moral) properties of law (for example, rule of law properties, like those elaborated by Lon Fuller [1969, pp. 41–91]) may have moral *effects*, for example, making immoral state action less likely (Raz 2009, pp. 317–319).[4] Leslie Green adds other examples: 'Necessarily, law regulates objects of morality', '[n]ecessarily, law makes moral claims of its subjects', '[n]ecessarily, law is justice apt', and '[n]ecessarily, law is morally risky' (Green 2008, pp. 1047, 1048, 1050, 1052).[5] Necessary connections of this sort explain why many theorists now offer a definition of legal positivism that makes no reference to necessary or conceptual *separation*. For example, here is John Gardner's definition: 'In any legal system, whether a given norm is legally valid, and hence whether it forms part of the law of that system, depends on its sources, not its merits' (Gardner 2001, p. 201).

4 Models and Theories

By the nature of the project of theorizing, a theory offers a simplified picture of the object or practice it is a theory of. There is inevitably a trade-off, with the simplification offering a benefit as well as a cost; the hope is that the insight of the theoretical model will more than make up for the simplifying distortion. How much of a trade-off to make is not always easy to answer. Often, the philosophical debates regarding some topic or area of discourse will involve a choice between a theory or set of theories which seem better to fit the details of a practice, and a theory

[4]The emphasis on moral *effects* invokes the difference between 'identity questions' and 'implication questions', see Shapiro (2011, pp. 8–9). It is consistent with claiming that social sources alone *determine* the (content of) law that the law, so determined, might have (positive or negative) moral *consequences*.

[5]For further discussion of the 'myth' of 'no necessary connection', see Gardner (2001, pp. 222–225).

or set of theories which, while fitting the practice less well, seem to offer a clearer, more interesting, or more important claim about the practice.

Consider the two approaches (perhaps it is more precise to say 'sets of approaches') to rights, the interest (or 'benefit') theory and the will (or 'choice') theory (Kramer et al. 1998). Under the interest theory, one has a right when one is the beneficiary of another party's duty, or where there is a strong enough interest that is, or should be, protected (MacCormick 1977). Under the will theory, a right is present when one's range of action is protected by one's choice (whether to act or not, and whether to respond to violation or intrusion by bringing a court action) (Hart 1982). It is often pointed out in favor of interest theories against will theories that there are many things we are inclined to call rights that do not fit into a description emphasizing the agent's choice, as when we speak of the 'rights' of those legally incompetent to choose for themselves (*e.g.*, children) and 'rights' which are not subject to choice, because inalienable. The objection to interest theories, by contrast, is that they seem not to say anything very interesting about rights, the way will theories do. Will theories thus arguably make up for a certain lack of fit with the way we speak by having something more distinctive and interesting to say about the nature of rights.

Consider a second example, one closer to the debates within and about legal positivism. John Austin argued that law is the command of the sovereign (Austin 1995). This is, directly and indirectly, a very distinctive statement about the nature of law, but the theory is not currently widely accepted, primarily because of criticisms by H. L. A. Hart and others. Those criticisms focus on the many ways that the theory distorts the practice it purports to describe: that Austin's approach ignored the variety of laws (that laws can be both duty-imposing, power-conferring, and constitutive, and both primary and secondary); that it ignored the significance of the fact that many individuals accept the law, treating it as giving them reasons for action; etc (Hart 2012, pp. 18–25, 50–78). Because of criticisms like these, Austin's theory today has few advocates. The overall point, for our purposes, is however interesting or distinctive a theory's message, if it comes with too great a distortion of the underlying practice, it will be rejected.

Returning to the debate between inclusive legal positivism and exclusive legal positivism, one can see how the different approaches might be viewed under the above rubric. Exclusive legal positivism has a distinctive message about the nature of law, grounded on the relationship between practical reasoning, authority, and reasons for action. However, it appears to gain this distinctive message at the cost of a certain lack of fit with the practice, or at least with the way lawyers, judges, and citizens talk about and within the practice. This lack of fit is most salient in connection with many constitutional provisions—as their use in constitutional judicial review—and also, to some extent with common law reasoning; in those parts of modern legal practice in many countries, moral evaluation appears to be a necessary or sufficient conditions for rules to be legally valid or legally invalid. And legislation that conflicts with morally-laden constitutional tests is said to be 'void', not just 'subject to being invalidated' by a court.[6]

By contrast, as already mentioned, inclusive legal positivism seems to have an advantage in the area of fit, focusing on these sorts of cases. It has no difficulty in accounting for constitutional judicial review or common law judicial legislation (Waluchow 2009, pp. 124–125).[7] Waluchow, on a number of occasions, has emphasized 'the respects in which inclusive positivism seems to account better than Raz's exclusive version for certain salient features of legal practice' (Waluchow 1994, p. 6; 2022, p. 147).[8] Still, there have also been places where Waluchow has noted the aspects of legal practice where the inclusive approach may not fit as well as exclusive alternatives (Waluchow 2009, pp. 126–127, 133–134). One possible example where exclusive legal positivism arguably fits better ironically relates to the situation where exclusive legal positivism's fit is said to be worse: invalidation of statutes on constitutional grounds. While a court which holds a statute to be invalid because in violation of the constitution states that the statute was 'void ab initio', *prior* to the court's so holding, legal officials and citizens treat statutes that may appear to violate the constitution as still valid, *unless and until a court declares otherwise*. This practice in fact tracks the exclusive legal positivist's view of officials' having 'directed' or 'delegated' powers (Marmor 2001, pp. 64–65).

Returning to the initial point: even if it is granted that inclusive legal positivism generally fits our practices better than exclusive legal positivism, the potential challenge is whether this greater fit is purchased at the cost of diminished significance. The argument is that inclusive legal positivism presents us with a theory of law which tells us very little about law.[9] Inclusive legal positivism's residual message (when we allow that there *can* be a connection between moral merit and legal validity, as long as it is recognized that this connection is *contingent*, and

[6] At times, such language is found in the constitutional texts themselves. *See, eg, Canadian Charter of Rights and Freedoms* § 52(1): 'The Constitution of Canada is the supreme law of Canada, and any law that is inconsistent with the provisions of the Constitution is, to the extent of the inconsistency, of no force or effect'. And, of course, one can also find such language in court cases. *See, eg, Norton v. Shelby County*, 118 U.S. 425, 442 (1886) ('An unconstitutional act is not a law; . . . it is . . . as inoperative as though it had never been passed'.).

A related point regards actions done in violation of statutes later found to be unconstitutional. Waluchow cites the fact that convictions under such statutes are overturned, and that this is additional evidence for the better fit with our practices of inclusive legal positivism (Waluchow 2022, pp. 142–143). However, I think that the evidence here is less clear-cut, as courts (at least in the United States) will sometimes declare that certain constitutional decisions will have only *prospective effect* (thus, people earlier convicted under such statutes will *not* be released), and such conclusions have nothing to do with whether the judges in question favor inclusive legal positivism or exclusive legal positivism.

[7] See also Waluchow (1994, p. 6): 'Inclusive legal positivism offers a better account of the interpretation and application of constitutional documents like the *Canadian Charter of Rights and Freedoms* or the American *Bill of Rights*'.

[8] *Cf* Marmor (2001, pp. 64–65).

[9] A similar critique is offered in Postema (2011, p. 482).

grounded in the choices of legal officials) is that law's basic nature is conventional, that is, grounded primarily in social practices. The problem is that this is hardly a controversial view. As both inclusive legal positivist Matthew Kramer and natural law theorist John Finnis have pointed out, the conventional or social fact grounding of law is something that opponents of legal positivism have no problem endorsing (Kramer 2008, p. 249).[10] Does inclusive legal positivism have a view about law with which reasonable observers and theorists of other schools and approaches might disagree, or does it only offer views that are true in obvious or uncontroversial ways?

One way to see the challenge of distinctiveness is by noting that in some ways exclusive legal positivism simply makes *more claims* about the nature of law. As I wrote in an earlier piece:

> Advocates of exclusive legal positivism do not disagree with the . . . tenets of inclusive legal positivism just outlined. Advocates of exclusive legal positivism simply argue that more can be said about the nature of law, that there is more that all legal systems share, and must share, given the nature of law (Bix 1999, p. 27).

Ronald Dworkin, in a review of a book by Jules Coleman, in which Coleman defends a version of inclusive legal positivism, declares: 'Inclusive positivism . . . is not positivism at all, but only an attempt to keep the name "positivism" for a conception of law and legal practice that is entirely alien to positivism' (Dworkin 2002, p. 1656).[11] In the same review, Dworkin offers an objection similar to what we are considering in the present work: 'positivism rescued in this way can no longer claim to show what is distinctive about law and legal reasoning, because once we accept the strategy, we can easily regard any community's moral practices as resting on convention in the same way' (Dworkin 2002, p. 1660). While this Chapter does not inquire whether inclusive legal positivism is 'really positivism' (though it generally assumes a positive answer to that question), Dworkin's second line of objection does track the concerns of the present discussion. Does inclusive legal positivism offer a view about what is 'distinctive about law and legal reasoning'?

Consider, also, John Finnis's dismissal of all legal positivism (both inclusive and exclusive): 'Positivism does no more than repeat (1) what any competent lawyer . . . would say are (or are not) intra-systemically valid laws, imposing "legal requirements," and (2) what any street-wise observer would warn are the likely consequences of noncompliance' (Finnis 2000, p. 1611). Gerald Postema's judgment is comparable:

> [Inclusive legal positivism] has been defined exclusively by its opposition to positions on its two theoretical flanks [exclusive legal positivism and Ronald Dworkin's theory]. It offered little by way of a positive case for positivism as a theory of the nature of law, but rather

---

[10] *Cf* Kramer (2008, p. 249): 'Although legal positivists do insist on the conventionality of law, so does every minimally credible natural-law theory.'; Finnis (1996, pp. 203–204) (showing how traditional natural law theory affirmed the legal positivist 'dogmas' that there is no necessary connection between law and morality, and that the identification of the content and validity of law does not require resort to moral argument).

[11] Waluchow reviewed the same Coleman work. See Waluchow (2002).

assumes a plateau of commitment to positivism, relying largely on Hart's defense of a much more robust positivism. And it offered no positive case for its own endorsement of the truth of the incorporation thesis as an interpretation of the practice in familiar legal systems, relying largely on the persuasive power of Dworkin's original arguments (Postema 2011, pp. 466–467).

The charge, thus, is that inclusive legal positivism says only what is trivial and commonplace. While the general point of theorists is to persuade, if their theories persuade by only stating what is uncontested, then they have offered no substantial service. So we return to the question of whether inclusive legal positivism, at least in Waluchow's understanding of that approach, has anything substantial and distinctive to tell us about the nature of law.

5 Waluchow's Answer

In a recent work, Waluchow responded to a line of criticism similar to the one outlined in this Chapter. He offered the following defense of inclusive legal positivism ('ILP', with exclusive legal positivism abbreviated 'ELP'):

> (1) ILP better accounts for the conventional nature of law; (2) ILP offers a conceptual map of legal practice that is more consonant than ELP with the self-understanding expressed in the norms and practices of many legal systems; and (3) ILP better accounts for the variety of ways in which law is capable of structuring our practical reasoning and, as a result, serving our moral interests (Waluchow 2022, p. 130).[12]

The following discussion will focus primarily on the first point, with the other points treated more briefly.

Waluchow's argument about the conventional nature of law is that inclusive legal positivism is superior to exclusive legal positivism because it is more faithful to the conventional foundations of law (a core view of legal positivism). It is more faithful, the argument goes, in that inclusive legal positivism *does not put any constraints* on the content of the foundational conventions of the legal system; in particular, it leaves it open whether the rules of legal validity contain moral criteria or do not (Waluchow 2022, pp. 139–141).[13] This is meant to be a contrast with exclusive legal positivism, which *does* place constraints on the allowable conventions of legal systems: that these conventions cannot include moral criteria (or other 'merits' criteria) for the validity of legal rules.

One matter to note is that though legal positivist theories may focus on the social-fact or conventional foundations of law *more than* do other approaches to the nature of law, as discussed earlier, the conventional or social-fact grounding of law is a claim that many critics of legal positivism can and do affirm (Finnis 2000). At one

[12] In a footnote, Waluchow describes the first two arguments as already present in the literature, while he believed the third claim to be novel (Waluchow 2022, p. 130, fn 13).

[13] See also Waluchow 2022, p. 146.

point in a recent article, Waluchow endorses the following characterization of legal positivism by Kenneth Einar Himma: 'It "is the emphasis on law's conventionality that distinguishes positivism from other conceptual theories of law"' (Waluchow 2022, p. 139, quoting Himma 2001, p. 286). However, one might observe that this puts a lot of weight on the word, 'emphasis'. Is the claim, then, that though both legal positivism and its competitors accept the conventional nature of law, legal positivism is distinct because *it talks about it more*?[14] This does not seem persuasive.

Returning to Waluchow's argument about inclusive legal positivism and its (in Waluchow's view) appropriate openness regarding the content of conventions, he offers the following argument:

> [I]f, as positivism maintains, (1) the key to understanding law is its conventional nature. And if, as positivism further maintains, (2) the conventional nature of law rests ultimately on a social practice of recognition according to agreed criteria of validity; and (3) the concepts of convention and agreed criteria of validity in and of themselves neither entail nor require any substantive constraints on the nature of the criteria of legal validity upon which officials might agree; then (4) any theory, such as ELP, that dictates further, substantive constraints – beyond agreement and shared practice – on eligible criteria of validity, obscures the fundamental conventional nature of law (Waluchow 2022, p. 140).[15]

This is a nuanced argument, which must be approached carefully. It might be persuasive, for those who believe that any reduction of focus on conventionality undermines the power of the legal positivist position. Others might be less persuaded, observing that it merely points out that if (exclusive) legal positivism asserts more than one criterion for (the nature of) law, each criterion inevitably constrains or reduces the salience of the other criteria.

Waluchow, at one point, makes the parenthetical comment that to the extent that his argument about law's conventional nature shows inclusive legal positivism to be superior to exclusive legal positivism, by extension it also shows inclusive legal positivism to be superior to natural law theory and Dworkin's interpretive approach (Waluchow 2022, p. 141). However, for the reasons already outlined, this is not necessarily the case. If, for example, Finnis's natural law theory approach allows for a central place for conventions in the nature and content of law, while arguing that other elements (*e.g.*, moral evaluation) also have an important role, then it is far from

---

[14] I do not mean to be entirely dismissive of the possibility. One could think, in a quite different context, of two different political parties (not that far removed from (earlier versions of) the two main political parties in the United States), where both parties value liberty and equality, but one places greater emphasis on liberty and the other places greater emphasis on equality. The different in emphasis is important and is sufficient to distinguish the two parties' approaches. However, the political party example differs from the legal theory example in that the political parties' views are primarily *prescriptive*—where a difference in emphasis means a difference in policy prescriptions—while the implications or consequences of differences in the legal theories is less clear (given the point made earlier in the Chapter, that inclusive legal positivism and exclusive legal positivism offer different *characterizations* of the same actions, rather than different *prescriptions* for action).

[15] Waluchow then adds: 'At the very least, ... such a theory shoulders the burden of showing precisely why we must restrict criteria of validity to the type it specifies' (Waluchow 2022, p. 140).

clear that Waluchow's argument, that theories should not constrain the nature of the conventions at the heart of legal validity, in fact does offer any reason to prefer inclusive legal positivism to at least some forms of natural law theory.[16]

Waluchow's basic argument is thus that inclusive legal positivism is truer to legal positivism's emphasis on law's conventional grounding; it is, as it were, a 'purer' or 'more consistent' form of a conventional theory. Exclusive legal positivists would have responses: that there are reasons for restricting the criteria for validity, reasons based on the connections between law and authority or on the view that law must make a 'practical difference' in citizens' practical reasoning (Raz 1994, pp. 199–204; Shapiro 2000). Waluchow (and others) have argued at length against those lines of argument (Waluchow 1994, pp. 98–141; 1998; 2000; 2020; 2022, pp. 132–133; Coleman 1998, 2001; Kramer 2004), and this is not the occasion to repeat the exchanges.

A different sort of response comes from Andrei Marmor: that allowing moral criteria makes a rule of recognition *something other than a convention*. Conventions are, by their nature, specific and practical. Thus, there are conventional rules regarding what to bring to a dinner party (conventions which likely differ from one community to another), and conventional rules about which piece of silverware to use for the salad. 'But it would be very odd to suggest that there is a convention that you have to behave well, morally speaking, during the dinner party' (Marmor 2011, p. 95; 2001, pp. 51–54). Marmor adds:

> Reasons to behave morally well are there independently of any conventions. Conventions are norms that evolve to resolve cases in which the relevant social norms are underdetermined by reasons. If reasons completely determine the content of their corresponding norms, the norm is not a convention. And the same idea applies to the rule of recognition (Marmor 2011, p. 95).

Marmor notes that this argument is not (and is not meant to be) conclusive against inclusive legal positivism, only against its prescribed form of the rule of recognition as *conventional* (Marmor 2011, pp. 95–96). But it does raise problems for Waluchow if his argument (for the superiority of inclusive legal positivism and its distinctive view of law) is grounded on the purity or consistency of its message of conventionality.

The second theme of distinctiveness regards 'descriptive adequacy' (Waluchow 2022, p. 141): the greater consistency of inclusive legal positivism (relative to exclusive legal positivism), in connection to the way participants in the legal system speak about legal practices. The idea that inclusive legal positivism better fits our practices has already been discussed at some length in this Chapter, along with the observation that there may also be a few areas where inclusive legal positivism fits our practices *less well* than exclusive legal positivism.

---

[16] Dworkin's interpretive approach, and also Mark Greenberg's 'moral impact theory' (*eg*, Greenberg 2014), arguably offer more complex views about the connection between law and conventions. So the connection between those theories and Waluchow's arguments is, in turn, more complex.

Waluchow's third argument for inclusive legal positivism parallels his first. As the first argument was to the effect that if legal positivism emphasizes the way conventions are at the essence of law, why should we constrain what sort of conventions a legal system can have? Similarly, Waluchow argues that if law's function is (as Raz and others claim) about intervening in our practical reasoning, why should we not accept (as law) a system which 'recognizes certain, specific moral limits on its right to meddle in our practical reasoning'? (Waluchow 2022, p. 145). Though how much 'meddling' in our practical reasoning is the right amount, given the nature of law, again seems to go back to which theory best fits our practices (including the way we talk within law and our linguistic intuitions about which social systems deserve the label 'legal').

Waluchow summarizes his conclusion regarding inclusive legal positivism's distinctive view of law:

> ILP highlights a number of key features of law: (a) that law has the inherent capacity to facilitate our practical reasoning; (b) that there are a multitude of different ways in which it can do so; (c) that some of these find room for moral validity to play a role in establishing legal validity; and (d) that some of these latter options do so without excluding moral reasons entirely or (e) without fully collapsing legal validity into moral validity and robbing law entirely of its capacity to facilitate conformity with right reason (Waluchow 2022, p. 147).

In a sense, then, the argument comes down to '(a)' above: an (institutional practice) that 'facilitate[s] our practical reasoning'—with all the additional criteria simply noting the refusal to add further constraints.

6 Conclusion

Wil Waluchow has left a significant mark on constitutional law and theories about the nature of law. As to the latter, he is without a doubt one of the most important elaborators and defenders of inclusive legal positivism. This Chapter has explored an integral part of that defense, though one often overlooked. Instead of focusing on the detailed back-and-forth, point-by-point debate with exclusive legal positivism (analyzing the extent to which Waluchow and others have sufficiently answered the arguments raised by Raz, Marmor, and other advocates of the exclusive position), the present work looks at a different, but equally important part of the debate: the extent to which inclusive legal positivism provides a positive and distinctive view of law.

Waluchow has devoted more attention to this part of the debate than has any other defender of inclusive legal positivism, and his suggestions in the area are innovative and instructive. His primary affirmative point relates to law's conventional nature—undoubtedly a key aspect of the legal positivist picture. Critics might still question whether the proffered argument about conventions (like the argument about the role of law in practical reasoning) is more about rejecting the further constraints demanded by exclusive legal positivism than it is offering an affirmative view, but here, again, we are perhaps just showing different characterizations of the same matter—a theme, it seems, of the debate between inclusive legal positivism and exclusive legal positivism. In any event, the bottom line remains as it has been for some time: Waluchow's inclusive vision of law presents a view of law, legal reasoning, and legal validity which has been meticulously argued and defended, leaving it, for many, as the approach most attractive and persuasive among the analytical theories of law.

References

Austin, John. 1995. In *The Province of Jurisprudence Determined (first published 1832)*, ed. W.E. Rumble. Cambridge: Cambridge University Press.

Bix, Brian H. 1993. *Law, Language, and Legal Determinacy*. Oxford: Oxford University Press.

———. 1999. Patrolling the Boundaries: Inclusive Legal Positivism and the Nature of Jurisprudential Debate. *Canadian Journal of Law and Jurisprudence* 12: 17–33.

Coleman, Jules L. 1998. Incorporationism, Conventionality, and the Practical Difference Thesis. *Legal Theory* 4: 381–425.

———. 2001. *The Practice of Principle*. Oxford: Oxford University Press.

Dworkin, Ronald. 1977. *Taking Rights Seriously*. Cambridge, Mass: Harvard University Press.

———. 2002. Thirty Years On. *Harvard Law Review*: 1655–1687.

Finnis, John. 1996. The Truth in Legal Positivism. In *The Autonomy of Law*, ed. R. George, 195–214. Oxford: Oxford University Press.

———. 2000. On the Incoherence of Legal Positivism. *Notre Dame Law Review* 75: 1597–1612.

———. 2011. *Natural Law and Natural Rights*. 2nd ed. Oxford: Oxford University Press.

Fuller, Lon L. 1958. Positivism and Fidelity to Law - A Reply to Professor Hart. *Harvard Law Review* 71: 630–672.

———. 1969. *The Morality of Law*. New Haven: Yale University Press.

Gardner, John. 2001. Legal Positivism: 5½ Myths. *American Journal of Jurisprudence* 46: 199–227.

Green, Leslie. 2008. Positivism and the Inseparability of Law and Morals. *New York University Law Review* 83: 1035–1058.

Greenberg, Mark. 2014. The Moral Impact Theory of Law. *Yale Law Journal* 123: 1288.-1342.

Hart, H.L.A. 1958. Positivism and the Separation of Law and Morals. *Harvard Law Review* 71: 593–629.

———. 1982. Legal Rights. In *Essays on Bentham*, 162–193. Oxford: Oxford University Press.

———. 2012. *The Concept of Law*. Oxford: Oxford University Press.

Himma, Kenneth E. 2001. Law's Claim of Legitimate Authority. In *Hart's Postscript*, ed. J. Coleman, 286–309. Oxford: Oxford University Press.

Kramer, Matthew H. 2004. *Where Law and Morality Meet*. Oxford: Oxford University Press.

———. 2008. Is Law's Conventionality Consistent with Law's Objectivity? *Res Publica* 14: 241–252.

Kramer, Matthew H., Nigel E. Simmonds, and H. Steiner. 1998. *A Debate Over Rights: Philosophical Enquiries*. Oxford: Oxford University Press.

MacCormick, Neil. 1977. Rights in Legislation. In *Law, Morality and Society*, ed. P.M.S. Hacker and J. Raz, 189–209. Oxford: Oxford University Press.

Marmor, Andrei. 2001. *Positive Law and Objective Values*. Oxford: Oxford University Press.

———. 2011. *Philosophy of Law*. Princeton: Princeton University Press.

Postema, Gerald J. 2011. *Legal Philosophy in the Twentieth Century: The Common Law World*. Dordrecht: Springer.

Raz, Joseph. 1994. *Ethics in the Public Domain*. Oxford: Oxford University Press.

———. 2009. *The Authority of Law*. 2nd ed. Oxford: Oxford University Press.
Shapiro, Scott. 2000. Law, Morality, and the Guidance of Conduct. *Legal Theory* 6: 127–170.
———. 2011. *Legality*. Cambridge, Mass: Harvard University Press.
Waluchow, W.J. 1994. *Inclusive Legal Positivism*. Oxford: Oxford University Press.
———. 1996. Indeterminacy. *Canadian Journal of Law and Jurisprudence* 9: 397–409.
———. 1998. The Many Faces of Legal Positivism. *University of Toronto Law Journal* 48: 387–449.
———. 2000. Authority and the Practical Difference Thesis: A Defense of Inclusive Legal Positivism. *Legal Theory* 6: 45–81.
———. 2001. Legal Positivism, Inclusive Versus Exclusive. In *Routledge Encyclopedia of Philosophy*. Taylor and Francis. https://doi.org/10.4324/9780415249126-T064-1.
———. 2002. In Pursuit of Pragmatic Legal Theory. *Canadian Journal of Law and Jurisprudence* 15: 125–152.
———. 2009. Four Concepts of Validity: Reflections on Inclusive and Exclusive Positivism. In *The Rule of Recognition and the U.S. Constitution*, ed. M. Adler and K.E. Himma, 123–144. Oxford: Oxford University Press.
———. 2020. The Origins of Inclusive Legal Positivism. In *The Cambridge Companion to Legal Positivism*, ed. T. Spaak and P. Mindus, 491–500. Cambridge: Cambridge University Press.
———. 2022. Matthew Kramer and Inclusive Legal Positivism: Dancing on the Head of a Pin. In *Without Trimmings*, ed. M. McBride and V.A.J. Kurki, 125–148. Oxford: Oxford University Press.

Brian H. Bix is the Frederick W. Thomas Professor of Law and Philosophy at the University of Minnesota. He holds a D. Phil. (doctorate) from Oxford University, and a J.D. from Harvard University. He has published over 150 works, primarily in the areas of Jurisprudence, Family Law, and Contract Law, and his works been translated into eight languages. His books include *Jurisprudence: Theory and Context* (9th ed., Sweet & Maxwell, 2023); *A Dictionary of Legal Theory* (Oxford, 2004); and *Law, Language and Legal Determinacy* (Oxford, 1993).

Part II
Constitutional Reasoning, Political Morality and Judicial Review

Waluchow and Dworkin's Disagreement on Legal Theory, Precedent and Adjudication: A Family Affair

Thomas Bustamante

Abstract In this chapter, I address some of the criticisms of Dworkin that Waluchow raised in his book *Inclusive Legal Positivism*—in particular, (i) the response to Dworkin's methodological contention that jurisprudence should be regarded as a first-order interpretation of the law and (ii) the contention that Dworkin's "law as integrity" provides a deficient description of the practice of precedent, inasmuch as it does not distinguish between theories of law and theories of adjudication and creates a set of puzzles that cannot be resolved with Dworkin's interpretive account of the legal practice. In response to Waluchow, I argue that, regardless of their methodological disagreements, law as integrity and inclusive legal positivism are similar descriptions of the social practice of law, and that the former can also provide a sound theory of precedent and adjudication. The chapter is followed by an Appendix in which I consider Waluchow's more recent accounts of constitutional interpretation and political morality. In the Appendix, I offer a pragmatic-inferentialist interpretation of Waluchow's common law constitutionalism and argue that Waluchow may have reasons for dropping the distinction between first-order and second-order judgments about moral norms.

1 Introduction

Professor Wil Waluchow's contribution to legal philosophy scholarship has multiple fronts and cannot be analyzed in a single chapter. He provided one of the most forceful defenses of the position known as "inclusive legal positivism," which has become the dominant interpretation of H.L.A. Hart's opus magnum. Furthermore, his contribution to constitutional law and interpretation provides solid arguments for the legitimacy of judicial review and one of the most sophisticated models for

T. Bustamante (✉)
Federal University of Minas Gerais, School of Law, Belo Horizonte, MG, Brazil

National Council for Scientific and Technological Development (CNPq), Brasília, DF, Brazil
e-mail: tbustamante@ufmg.br

T. Bustamante et al. (eds.), *Law, Morality and Judicial Reasoning*, Law and Philosophy Library 147, https://doi.org/10.1007/978-3-031-61879-6_8

constitutional reasoning, based on a constructivist reinterpretation of common law reasoning. In this chapter, I focus on Waluchow's discussion of Ronald Dworkin's jurisprudence, in order to claim that there are more affinities between these influential jurisprudences than is usually acknowledged.

In *Inclusive Legal Positivism*, Waluchow offers a systematic defense of H.L.A. Hart's conception of law. One of the tasks of his book is responding to Dworkin's challenge to legal positivism without falling back into the strict conventionalist reading of the rule of recognition. This chapter addresses some of the criticisms against Dworkin that appear in the first two chapters of Waluchow's book—in particular, (i) the response to Dworkin's methodological contention that jurisprudence should be regarded as a first-order interpretation of the law (which differs from ordinary practical statements about the law only because its propositions are more general, not because it stands at a different level of analysis) and (ii) the claim that Dworkin's "law as integrity" provides a deficient description of the practice of precedent, inasmuch as its reluctance to distinguish between theories of law and theories of adjudication creates some unnecessary puzzles.

In response to Waluchow, I argue that, regardless of their methodological disagreements, law as integrity and inclusive legal positivism are in the same camp, and that the former can also provide a sound theory of precedent and adjudication. My argument proceeds as follows: in the second section, I present Waluchow's defense of analytical jurisprudence and the related critique of Dworkin's methodological views. In the third section, I discuss the distinction between moral and institutional forces of law, which Waluchow employs in response to Dworkin's objections against legal positivism. The fourth section presents a Dworkinian counterargument, and the fifth section demonstrates that both theories share similar commitments about the relationship between morality and law.

The chapter is followed by an Appendix, written three years after the main text, in which I comment on a response that Waluchow offered to me in person. In addition to responding to Waluchow's comment, I argue in the Appendix that his account of a community's constitutional morality (CCM) can be understood according to an inferentialist theory of meaning that justifies particular interpretations based on a holistic assessment of the relations between the commitments undertaken tacitly or explicitly by the participants in a rational normative practice. I subscribe to Waluchow's theory of constitutional interpretation, on the proviso it is interpreted in this way. I submit, finally, that my inferentialist interpretation of Waluchow's work is compatible with Dworkin's account of legal interpretation and that there is no harm in abandoning the view that there is a qualitative distinction between first-order and second-order judgments about law and political morality.

2 Waluchow's Defense of Analytical Jurisprudence

Let us begin with Waluchow's methodological point. Alongside Hart, Waluchow is convinced that jurisprudence should be analytical and descriptive and that the proper role of a legal theorist is to offer a neutral and uncommitted account of the grounds of law, with no specific concern for the moral force of valid legal statements and the normative reasons that one may or not have for complying with legal requirements. The point is not that the law's normative force is unimportant, but that our assertions about such force have to be distinguished from our propositions about the existence of legal norms. While questions of validity should be answered by a (descriptive) theory of law, controversies about the moral force of a (valid) legal rule belong to a (separate) theory of adjudication.

Waluchow's defense of Hartian legal positivism contrasts with Dworkin's basic meta-theoretical assumption in *Law's Empire*, which characterizes jurisprudence as an "interpretive" inquiry that assumes that part of the task of jurisprudence is to provide a moral justification for its ability to coerce.

Waluchow acknowledges that it is not the case that Dworkin's "law as integrity" simply lacks a descriptive account of legal materials. On the contrary, what separates Dworkin's methodology from Hartian jurisprudence is that the former assumes that pure description is *not enough*, in the sense that nothing can be correctly classified as law without the actual capacity to justify coercion by a judicial authority. The requirement of "fit" demands that the interpreter provides a descriptive account of the practice, although "the process of description is fundamentally governed ... by the goal of justification" (Waluchow 1994, pp. 15–16).

Therefore, according to Dworkin, legal theorists have a distinctive responsibility: they cannot provide an adequate description of the law without making a moral evaluation of its merits and undertaking a genuine effort to read the law in its best light. While arguing for theoretical propositions to describe the law, we should "deliberately permit our moral values and beliefs about the justification of state coercion to shape how we understand [the] social practice [of] law" (Waluchow 1994, p. 17). The point, once again, is not only that we should evaluate a theory according to epistemic values like simplicity, comprehensiveness, coherence, and so on, for it is difficult to think of an external and descriptive theory that would dispense with these values; it is, instead, the more radical contention that such a theory is fully committed—that is, it provides an argument from the same point of view as the *participant* of a legal practice. "In Dworkin's view," Waluchow argues, "it is just not possible to understand a social practice like law without engaging in it directly," for legal theory should not be regarded as a "meta-theory" (Waluchow 1994, pp. 23–24).

As Arthur Ripstein put it more recently, the core of Dworkin's conceptions of law, morality, and politics is his "resolute rejection of Archimedeanism" in any of these conceptions—that is, his reluctance to conceive the possibility of a second-order perspective to analyze the content of the practices he describes (Ripstein 2007, p. 7). A relevant disagreement between Dworkin and his positivist interlocutors has to do with the *status* of the arguments encountered in a theoretical account of a social practice like law (Ripstein 2007, p. 13). Hartian legal positivism claims that jurisprudence is "general" (in the sense that "it is not tied to any particular legal system or legal culture, but seeks to give an explanatory and clarifying account of law as a complex social and political institution with a rule-governed – and in that sense 'normative' – aspect") and "descriptive" (in the sense that "it is morally neutral and has no justificatory aims") (Hart 1994, pp. 239–240). In contrast, Dworkin maintains that a theory of an interpretive practice "is not essentially different from adjudication," although it can be "more general" and encompass "more material" than the latter (Waluchow 1994, p. 24).

Another controversial Dworkinian assumption is the view that legal theory is "not essentially different from interpretive theories in arts, or even from theories in the hard sciences like physics and chemistry" (Waluchow 1994, p. 25). According to Waluchow, "Dworkin provocatively suggests that all interpretive theories attempt to impose purpose and value on their objects" and that "interpretation takes different forms in law, literature, and science only because each of these enterprises has its own unique standards of value" (Waluchow 1994, pp. 24–25).

The difficulty in this comparison between science and law is neither that scientists are guided by evaluative judgments, nor that they sometimes attempt to make their interpretations the best they can be. It lies, instead, in the attempt to present the *data* (rather than the theory) in the manner that Dworkin suggests with his interpretive approach (Waluchow 1994, p. 25). Dworkin would be wrong to confuse the epistemic values we pursue in our theory with the properties of the objects that we purport to describe.

Waluchow seems to have a point here. Any approximation of legal and artistic interpretation to scientific interpretation cannot ignore the differences between these domains, as Dworkin would come to realize in more recent writings.[1] Perhaps Dworkin's flirtation with the idea of "scientific interpretation" stems from an incautious approximation to Hans-Georg Gadamer, who appears in a series of quotes in chapter 2 of *Law's Empire*. Although Dworkin does not share Gadamer's view that all knowledge is interpretive (Gadamer 2004, p. xxvii), the former might have been led by the latter to overstate the similarities between scientific reasoning on the one hand and the interpretation of arts and law on the other hand. Nevertheless, Dworkin clearly believes that the inner structure of scientific reasoning is not purposive, so "scientific interpretation" (as Dworkin called it in *Law's Empire*) is not "constructive," in the specific sense that Dworkin uses the term, and legal theorists should not use it as a model for their interpretive endeavors (Dworkin 1986, pp. 50–51).[2]

[1] See, for example, Dworkin (2011, p. 152), in which Dworkin is quite explicit in distinguishing interpretation from science, because while the former is "purposive, not just in the vocabulary of its claims but in the standards of its success," the latter is responsive to evidence, but not to the justifying goals of the interpretive inquiry.

[2] As Dworkin expresses textually in *Law's Empire*, the description of "artistic" and "conversational" interpretation "does not seem, at first blush, to fit scientific interpretation, and we might feel compelled, if we are attracted to the idea that all genuine interpretation is purposive, to say that scientific interpretation is not really interpretation at all" (Dworkin 1986, pp. 50–51). I think this specification is at odds with Gadamer's "universal" hermeneutics. Dworkin should have been more careful to specify which parts of Gadamer's hermeneutics he endorses and which parts he does not. There is at least one point of Gadamer's theory which is crucial to make sense of Dworkin's interpretive project, which is the thought that there is no sharp distinction between interpretation and application of interpretive concepts (Dworkin 1986, pp. 55).

Waluchow has a different stance: instead of arguing that legal interpretation is like artistic or literary interpretation, he advocates that jurisprudence should aspire to methodological neutrality, which is characteristic of scientific reasoning. If the point of jurisprudence is to provide a philosophically appealing understanding of the practice of law, it should not imitate the evaluative and relatively undisciplined methods of art critics and literature reviewers. Rather, jurisprudence would do best with the Archimedean standpoint that is typical of natural sciences. Waluchow finds it more attractive to distinguish between "trying to make the object of interpretation – i.e. the data – the best it can be, and attempting to make a theory about that object the best it can be" (Waluchow 1994, p. 26). Based on this distinction, he argues that, even though we might seek value for our interpretation (i.e., we might strive to make our interpretation a good one), it is awkward to suggest that in a philosophical inquiry about the nature of law we should do the same with the data we are required to analyze. In light of the possibility to choose between an "external" or "internal" view of jurisprudence, Waluchow believes that there is nothing in the object of our theory that should convince us to choose the latter and that we should not conflate our conceptual descriptions of valid law with our moral evaluation of its merits (Waluchow 1994, pp. 26–27).

3 On the Content and Force of Law

One of Waluchow's basic intuitions on this debate is that the question "What is the law on this matter?" is conceptually distinct from the question "What should citizens and judges do on this matter?" Even though sometimes we must settle the question of the content of law before making a moral judgment about what we ought to do in a certain case, each of these questions should be formulated separately. If we conflate the questions, unnecessary puzzles arise.

According to Waluchow, Dworkin did us a service when he distinguished the "grounds of law" (the truth-making conditions of a valid legal proposition) from the "force of law" (the law's capacity to create obligations and its power "to justify coercion" when it becomes necessary to uphold a norm) (Dworkin 1986, p. 110). A legal theory constructed from the participant's point of view fails to acknowledge important cases in which the law simply lacks a moral force, and some officials do not have a duty to follow a law (or might even, sometimes, have a legal duty not to comply with the law in its current precedent).

The practice of precedent illustrates this type of case in an intriguing way. To demonstrate this point, Waluchow introduces a distinction between two different forces a valid legal proposition can possess. One should distinguish the *moral force* of a legal proposition (described by Dworkin as simply the "force of law") from its *institutional force*. While moral force concerns "the extent to which, if at all, there is a moral obligation to abide by the law's requirements," institutional force "is a function of the person's legal power (if any) to alter existing law so as to nullify its effect upon a decision" (Waluchow 1994, p. 39). The easiest way to understand the institutional force of law is to analyze the effects of a precedent from a middle court. Consider the case of a legal system in which every judge can judicially review legislation and in which lower-court judges are strictly bound by the precedents of the higher courts, whereas higher courts can overrule lower-instance precedents on the ground that they are based on a mistake. Per Waluchow's positivism, it may well be the case that John (a first-instance judge) is bound by the precedent of an appeal court, while Mary (a Supreme Court justice) is permitted by the same doctrine to overrule such a precedent and settle a new law. To further specify this point, let us consider a precedent about the ambiguity of a concept that usually appears in the controversies of legal theorists: the concept of "vehicles." The Brazilian Constitution has a clear-cut provision authorizing member states to levy taxes on "self-propelled vehicles."[3] Suppose the Brazilian state of Pará decides to levy a tax on boats and private airplanes, in addition to the existing tax on "terrestrial" vehicles like cars, buses, motorcycles, and trucks. Suppose, further, that there is a middle-court precedent ruling that the constitutional provision authorizes the state to levy taxes only on owners of "terrestrial" vehicles and that the state lacks a Hohfieldian power to levy taxes on Janet's private jet.[4] What should Judge John and Justice Mary do in such a case? By Waluchow's account, the middle-court precedent has institutional force over Judge John but not over Justice Mary. While the former is strictly bound by the doctrine of binding precedents and therefore has no alternative but to follow the precedent, the latter has the legal power to overrule the precedent and might even be required by the law to replace such a precedent with a better rule. If the best constitutional interpretation requires that "terrestrial," "fluvial," and "aerial" vehicles be treated equally for fiscal purposes and that taxpayers contribute to the community according to their ability to pay (instead of the type of vehicles they drive), then Justice Mary—unlike Judge John—will be obligated to overrule the precedent and change the law. If the state Legislative Assembly enacts a statute to levy a tax on Janet's private jet, Judge John might be legally bound by the middle court's conclusion that such a statute is unconstitutional, while Justice Mary would likely issue an alternative directive.

According to Waluchow, cases like this demonstrate that a positivistic approach has an obvious advantage over a Dworkinian construction about the determination of the content of law. While a positivist explanation would identify the middle-court precedent as a valid law with different institutional forces over Judge John and Justice Mary, a Dworkinian reconstruction would be forced to admit that the precedent is law for Judge John but not for Justice Mary, as Dworkin eventually recognized when he claimed that "in some circumstances any accurate judgment about what the law is must in some way be indexed to refer to the level of the court in

[3] For more details, see the Constituição da República Federativa do Brasil, art. 155, III.

[4] This example is inspired by a real case decided by the Brazilian Federal Supreme Court, although the real case got its precedent from the highest court in the judicial hierarchy, rather than from a middle court. Brazil. STF, RE 134509/AM, Rel. Min. Marco Aurélio, j 29.05.2002, Pleno, DJ 13.09.2002, p. 64.

which the issue is assumed to arise" (Dworkin 1986, pp. 452–453). In a case in which a higher court has a "duty to overrule a precedent" but a lower court, under a strict rule of *stare decisis*, has no option but to follow the precedent, Dworkin believes that there are two ways a lawyer can describe the case:

> He might say (this is one way to put the point) that the law for the higher court is different from the law for the lower. Or he might say (this is another) that since the highest court has the last word, the law is "really" for the plaintiff, though she must appeal to have that law recognized and enforced. (Dworkin 1986, p. 453)

Given this statement about the pragmatic implications of the practice of precedent, there are two ways to deal with the apparent ambiguity of the concept of law, and Waluchow is satisfied with neither of them.

The first solution is the "indexing option": since Dworkin believes that law is always something judges can enforce, different judicial authorities would be in institutional positions that require them to operate with different notions of law. This implies that "the law for each is different from the law for the other" in the sense that "there is nothing which we can identify at any given time as the law bearing on Natham's case: there is rather lower-court law, middle-court law, and higher-court law" (Waluchow 1994, p. 52). Waluchow argues, therefore, that the indexing option leads to incoherence in Dworkin's jurisprudence. It appears to be at odds with the value of integrity, which is central to his own conception of law. How can there be a law conceived of as a "unified scheme of rights (and responsibilities)"—that is, as a "scheme which is to be applied consistently and equally" (Waluchow 1994, p. 53)—if the very concept of law has to be indexed to courts? In Waluchow's view, this question places Dworkin's "law as integrity" in an embarrassing position, for the very idea of a "community personified," which is elegantly presented in *Law's Empire* as a normative model, begins to fade: "The unity and integrity of law comes perilously close to vanishing on this account of legal rights" (Waluchow 1994, p. 54).

Would Dworkin's theory have a better fate under the second option? Under this option, the problem is not that different courts find different laws when a lower court is bound by a precedent while the upper court is empowered to overrule it. Rather, it is that the law is not constituted by the right to win under the lower court, but only at the highest possible court in a certain jurisdiction. To argue that someone has a right is to say that she has "right to win in the highest court," inasmuch as "rights are held against judges who preside over the highest court in the judicial hierarchy" (Waluchow 1994, p. 54). Waluchow's argument against Dworkin, here, is that most of the time citizens, officials and legal scholars would be working with an unsettled and idealized notion of law. Given the obvious fact that flesh-and-blood judges are not Hercules, and that the majority of legal controversies will never reach the Highest Chamber of the Supreme Court—in fact, most of them would not even reach a courtroom—the law which is valid here and now remains largely unknown (Waluchow 1994, p. 56).

Waluchow thinks that we need, therefore, to look for a single concept of law, one that is capable of settling on a clear and identifiable criterion of legal validity. Instead of looking for a theory of law that collapses into a theory of adjudication, failing to distinguish between the "institutional" and the "moral" forces of law, Waluchow believes it is more reasonable to offer a more modest jurisprudence, which is concerned only with the determination of the grounds of law. When we evaluate legal theories on their simplicity and explanatory capacity, Waluchow believes the best choice would be for a conceptual legal theory that postpones for a theory of adjudication any assessment of the merits of law.

4 A Dworkinian Reply

Let us turn now to Dworkin's response to Waluchow's criticisms. My point in the remaining sections of this paper is to argue for two controversial theses: *first*, Dworkin's most damaging objection to a positivist test for identifying the law works only against exclusive legal positivism, leaving the core assertions of inclusive legal positivism untouched; *second*, the survival of inclusive legal positivism does not entitle it to claim victory over Dworkin's "law as integrity," given that the most central claims of these two theories are almost identical.

To understand the first point, let us consider an argument that Dworkin raised against Hart before the publication of *Law's Empire*. In response to the Hartian claim that legal theory must be made from the external point of view (or, more precisely, from the "engaged external point of view"[5]), Dworkin sustained that that the concept of law "as it functions in our legal culture" is a "contested concept," and this circumstance alone makes it hopeless to develop a theory which is "'true' analytically just in virtue of the meaning of the word 'law'" (Dworkin 1984, p. 255). Because Hartians claimed otherwise, Dworkin thinks that they commit the fallacy of "essentialism" (Dworkin 1984, p. 259). According to Dworkin, law is not only a "contested" concept in the way linguistic philosophers use it, but also a "political" concept: "Law is a political concept not just because it is contested but because of the

[5]In *The Concept of Law*, Hart distinguishes between two senses of the "external point of view." According to the first, which Stephen Perry has called the "engaged external point of view," the observer looks at the practice with a hermeneutic eye. Although he wants to describe a practice from the outside, the observer, "without accepting the rules himself, asserts that the group accepts the rules, and thus may from the outside refer to the way in which *they* are concerned with them from the internal point of view" (Hart 1994, pp. 86–87). According to the second, which can be called an "extreme" external point of view, the observer simply describes the "regularities of physical behaviour," without regard to the acceptance of norms or the internal attitudes of the participants of the relevant social practice (Hart 1994, p. 90). According to Perry, Hart's view is that legal theorists must look at law from the "engaged external" point of view: "although Hart is not explicit about this, it is clearly just this kind of statement that jurisprudence requires in order accurately to describe normative practices and, in particular, law. This type of statement takes account of the internal point of view, but it is not made *from* that point of view; since the internal point of view is only referred to, not utilized, such external statements (and the theories of which they are a part) can be characterized as descriptive rather than normative in character" (Perry 1995, p. 103).

way it is contested. It takes its sense from its use: from the contexts of debates about what the law is, and from what turns on which view is accepted" (Dworkin 1984, p. 256, emphasis added). Hart will be wrong, therefore, if he is expecting legal theorists to reveal some sort of hidden essence of the law or purporting to describe the facts that make something a legal proposition in the way that we describe the laws of physics or natural sciences.

Is this charge of essentialism fair? It matters not, for my argument, to determine whether this is a sound criticism of Hart's theory before the publication of the *Postscript* to the second edition of *The Concept of Law*, since we need only to establish that it is a fair criticism of the way *exclusive legal positivism* describes the concept of law. While inclusive legal positivism admits that there are cases (perhaps the majority of cases) where "the identification of a rule as valid within a legal system, as well as the discernment of the rule's content and how it bears on a legal case, can depend on moral factors" (Waluchow 1994, p. 82), exclusive legal positivism is ontologically committed to the view that "all law is source-based," in the sense that a law's "existence and content can be identified by reference to social facts alone, without resort to any evaluative argument" (Raz 1994, pp. 210–211).

If exclusive legal positivism is right, "a jurisprudential theory is acceptable only if its tests for identifying the content of the law and determining its existence depend exclusively on facts of human behavior capable of being described in value-neutral terms and applied without resort to moral argument" (Raz 2009a, pp. 39–40). Although the social-sources thesis, in its strong version supported by exclusive legal positivism, is a thesis about the nature of law, it has an important methodological implication for the nature of legal theory. If exclusive legal positivism is true, the proper way to describe the law is by means of an external or "detached" normative statement. A statement is "detached," in the relevant sense, if it is made from a point of view that is distinct from the point of view of the participants of legal practice. One makes a detached statement of the law if one "uses normative language when describing the law and makes legal statements without thereby endorsing the law's moral authority" (Raz 2009a, p. 156). In order to explain this notion, Raz uses an interesting example of an expert in religious laws that does not share the religion she is trying to interpret. When an "orthodox but relatively ill-informed Jew" ask for the advice of her non-religious friend who is an expert in Rabbinical law, the question "What should I do?" clearly means what she should do according to the one who believes it, rather than the analyst. By presenting an answer, the expert is "simply stating how things are from the Jewish Orthodox point of view" (Raz 2009a, p. 156).

Exclusive legal positivism is committed to a detached methodology to identify the law because it implies that any other methodology would fail in what exclusive legal positivism considers the most important task of jurisprudence, which is to provide an amoral test for describing the law. This methodology is, on the exclusive positivist story, more than a methodological caprice; it is a constraint imposed upon the theory by the data such theory is set to explain. It is only *because* law is essentially a social fact (and essentially *only* a social fact) that an evaluative methodology will always fail in its description of the content of the law. By implication of its immutable essence, the law must be identified by a test that relies on a content-independent verification process (i.e., on a test that never appeals to the merits of a normative proposition). If the law generates preemptive reasons for action, then it must be the case that the identification of these reasons preempts any kind of evaluative or moral judgment.

As Dworkin plausibly argues, Raz's claim is presented as a *conceptual* claim, rather than as a normative argument (Dworkin 2006, pp. 198–210). Would an inclusive legal positivist necessarily be committed to such descriptive methodology? Although Waluchow (2018) more recently argued for a positive answer and explicitly defended that interpretive legal statements should be detached legal statements, I believe that there are at least some cases in which the answer is "no."[6] According to inclusive legal positivism, it is perfectly possible (perhaps it is even typical) that the rule of recognition incorporates moral considerations in its test to identify the validity of a legal provision: "moral values and principles count among the possible grounds that a legal system might accept for determining the existence and the content of valid laws" (Waluchow 1994, p. 82).

What happens when a legal system's rule of recognition incorporates moral facts in its test of legal validity? When this is the case, the answer to legal questions will inevitably depend on a moral judgment of the interpreter of law. For inclusive legal positivists, the law lacks a fixed essence in the way that Dworkin believes is unattractive. It is a contingent matter whether a legal system's rule of recognition incorporates such test, and whenever it incorporates there will be little difference between the process a Dworkinian adopts to find out the law and the process adopted by an inclusive legal positivist. If the law incorporates moral principles in the validity conditions of particular legal propositions, then something important happens no matter whether you are a Dworkinian or an inclusive legal positivist: one cannot understand the law only by making a detached statement in the way Raz suggested in his theory of law (i.e., a validity assessment that does not resort to any moral consideration). In legal systems which employ moral criteria of validity for its laws, even if you purport to describe the law from an Archimedean point of view—to explain, for instance, what the law means when it rules that something be done by a parent "in the best interest of his child"—your description will be defective if it fails to take up the moral responsibility of judging what these moral principles entail.

For inclusive legal positivists, it must be the case that the "framework" provided by the rule of recognition is created by a conventional practice of the participants. Nevertheless, as Jules Coleman expresses, it remains possible that there are disagreements about the content of this rule, including a disagreement that "might well be settled by an appeal to substantive moral argument about how one ought to

[6]I will leave my arguments in defense of this contention to this chapter's Appendix, wherein I propose to interpret Waluchow's concept of "community constitutional morality" according to Robert Brandom's inferentialism. For the moment, however, I will disregard Waluchow's recent endorsement of Raz's "detached legal statements" because I believe that it is an inconsistent element in his jurisprudence (which could be easily dismissed) and that it is not, for Waluchow's inclusive legal positivism, a conceptual necessity.

proceed and that may invite discussion about the point of the practice" (Coleman 2001, p. 99).

One should not be surprised by the fact that Dworkin quotes precisely this excerpt to make the most incisive criticism he has ever made on inclusive legal positivism. For Dworkin, Coleman's description "does not sound like positivism; it sounds like Hercules and his colleagues at work" (Dworkin 2006, p. 189). Although Coleman claims that (1) at the foundations of law lies a convention which specifies what are the grounds of a legal proposition, and that (2) the practice of law is a form of "shared cooperative activity" (in the sense of Michael Bratman)[7] that constitutes a "conventional social practice" in spite of the possibility of widespread disagreement about the "content of the criteria of legality" and their moral merit (Coleman 2001, p. 96; Dworkin 2006, pp. 188–198), his explanation would "eviscerate the idea of convention itself," inasmuch as "a convention exists only when each person acts in a certain way because others are acting in that way as well" (Dworkin 2006, p. 193). To summarize Dworkin's counter-argument:

> Coleman's version of legal positivism is best described as anti-positivism. He has wholly decamped from the philosophical heritage he undertakes to defend. He covers his retreat by claiming to remain true to the cardinal tenet of positivism, which is that law is always a matter of convention. But his use of convention pursues victory through surrender. His first strategy trivializes the idea of a convention and make it practically and theoretically useless. His second strategy, which hopes to convert cooperation into convention, fails because cooperation need not depend on convention, and because a legal system need not, as a matter of conceptual necessity, depend on full cooperation. We have made no progress in understanding the persistence of positivism's acolytes – in understanding why Coleman, for example, is so anxious to fly the flag of positivism that he is willing to abandon every article of its faith to do so. (Dworkin 2006, p. 198)

In spite of the fighting words between Coleman and Dworkin (neither of them is half as elegant as Waluchow, for instance), I think that Dworkin's response to Coleman shows a great deal of agreement between law as integrity and inclusive legal positivism. There seems to be two reasons to argue for this.

On the one hand (and perhaps more importantly), both under law as integrity and under inclusive legal positivism legal practice can be infused with moral disagreement about the content of the law, and there is no way to overcome this disagreement unless participants in legal disputes undertake a morally responsible judgment about the requirements of the relevant legal provision. If, for instance, a legal system incorporates a principle according to which administrative action has to be undertaken according to "public morality," like the Brazilian constitution does in article 37, then an important moral controversy becomes a part of legal practice, and the moral responsibility of any lawyer (no matter whether he is a practitioner, a citizen, a

[7] According to Kenneth Einar Himma, who first applied Bratman's ideas to the law, there are three characteristic features of a shared cooperative activity (SCA): "(1) each participant in an SCA attempts to conform her behaviour to the behaviour of the other participants; (2) each participant is committed to the joint activity; and (3) each participant is committed to supporting the efforts of the other participants to play their appropriate roles within the joint activity" (Himma 2002, p. 132).

judge or a legal theorist) will be to figure out what this moral principle requires in the case at hand.

On the other hand, neither Waluchow nor Dworkin puts forward an ontological and essentialist claim about the nature of the relation between law and morality. As I anticipated above, the claim at the heart of inclusive legal positivism is that there are *contingent* relations between law and morality. Even though these relations appear to be typical, there is nothing in the nature of law that rules out the possibility of a legal system that incorporates no principle of political morality in its criteria of legal validity. By the same token, law as integrity has never purported to be a theory of the ontology of law (on the contrary, it explicitly claims that there is *no fixed ontology* in law).[8] To be sure, law as integrity claims to be relevant only when we consider the "doctrinal" concept of law. A doctrinal concept of law, for Dworkin, explores "the concept of 'the law' of some place or entity being to a particular effect" (Dworkin 2006, p. 2). We use that concept not when we seek for a purely theoretical understanding of a controversial notion; rather, law as integrity's concern is a practical concern, since it is not presented as a general theory of the nature of law (in effect, it is a theory according to which law lacks a fixed nature and is an "argumentative" social practice) (Dworkin 1986, p. 13). A doctrinal concept, for Dworkin, is one that we use when we put forward political claims about the rights and duties we have towards one another, rights and duties that we tacitly assume are enforceable or at least worthy of judicial enforcement. A doctrinal concept, therefore, must be an "interpretive" concept, in the sense that our understanding of this concept depends on our ability to grasp the point or purpose of this concept (or the practice it describes) and read it in light of such purpose, to make it the best instance of the genre to which belongs.

But this does not mean, however, that there is a sound interpretive concept available for every situation in which we use the concept of law, or that there will never be a context where a non-interpretive concept (for instance, a criterial or conventional concept) might be preferable. If we want a historical or a sociological description of the law of ancient Rome, for instance, we would probably be better off with a criterial description of the conditions of validity accepted by Roman lawyers than with a struggle to adjust Roman law to its moral justification. Furthermore, if we look to extremely unjust legal systems such as, for instance, German Nazi law, then we would not be able to read it interpretively, given that under no conditions such law can be able to justify imposing an obligation on a given subject. As Waluchow explains, Dworkin seems to be using two different concepts when it comes to the explanation of wicked law:

> According to Dworkin, we have two senses of "law" within our language, and therefore more than one way to put the points we wish to make when talking about immoral regimes. One of these ways is captured by the positivists, the other by natural lawyers like Aquinas and Augustine. If by "law" we mean the elements of institutional history which serve as the

[8] Dworkin's claim, at least since his early response to Raz in "The Model of Rules II," is that the law lacks any "fixed set of standards of any sort" (Dworkin 1978, p. 76).

> "pre-interpretive" data of constructive interpretation of legal practice, then wicked law is indeed law (...)
>
> If, on the other hand, one means by the word "law" that which a non-sceptical, constructive interpretation of institutional history identifies as morally licensing coercive force, then wicked "law" does not quality for that honorific title. (Waluchow 1994, pp. 62–63)

Although Waluchow is unhappy with this "flexible" approach, which should be replaced by a positivist theory that is capable to provide a "univocal understanding of law" (Waluchow 1994, p. 64), he seems to be in agreement with Dworkin that moral justifiability is not an "ontological" or "essential" property of law; it is, rather, dependent upon the legitimacy of social practices and political institutions. The difference between Waluchow and Dworkin, therefore, is neither how they ordinarily see the law in a legal system that works reasonably well (for both will read such system in light of the moral principles which justify it), nor that one of them thinks that moral worth is a metaphysical or essential property of law.

There are more similarities than differences between Waluchow and Dworkin. When we dig deep into their theories, both regard the law from different points of view (Waluchow from an external, second-order, theoretical point of view and Dworkin from an internal, first-order, participative point of view), but in the end of the day they see the same object. This explains the fact that despite the puzzles of each of these theories, both retain a similar impression of plausibility, and both entail similar attitudes towards the practice of law. Even if Dworkin's objections to exclusive legal positivism are sound, inclusive positivism is unharmed by Dworkin's criticisms. The choice between Dworkin and Waluchow is based on a methodological preference. Let us discuss these methodologies in the next section, where I provide a Dworkinian explanation of the doctrine of binding precedents.

5 Explaining Precedent with Dworkin's Methodology

I return to the problem addressed at the beginning of this chapter. Suppose I am correct that inclusive legal positivism and law as integrity are seeing similar legal systems, although they look at it from different angles. If this is the case, none of these descriptions produces a knockdown argument against the other. Both produce a reliable picture of the legal system, but there is a price in each of these explanations of the character of law. At Sects. 2 and 3, I examined Waluchow's argument that Dworkin's explanation fails because it leads to a methodology that confuses a theory of law with a theory of adjudication, and to a poor description of what happens when a valid precedent binds a lower judge while is not authoritative upon a higher court. I believe, however, that this is also not a knockdown argument, and that Dworkin may have an interesting response. But before moving on to Dworkin's account of binding precedents, we must face another question. What is the problem that Dworkin sees in Archimedean theories such as Hart's or Waluchow's? Here's a statement of Dworkin's preference for an internalist conception of political concepts:

> The Archimedean story ignores the way in which political concepts actually function in political argument. They serve as abstract plateaus of agreement. Almost everyone agrees that the values in question are of at least some importance, and perhaps very great importance, but that agreement leaves open crucial substantive issues about what more precisely these values are or mean. (Dworkin 2006, pp. 148–149).

Dworkin's core methodological point is that when political concepts make a difference, they are used in an argumentative way. To put it in Wittgensteinean terms, this is a pragmatic concern about the grammar of the language game in which they figure when they appear in social practices and in political argument.[9] If I make an argument about what liberty is, my theory must be normative (on Dworkin's view) because I am not looking for a "theoretical as opposed to practical" understanding of the criteria some people might use to describe what liberty is. Rather, my claim is also a practical claim about what liberty entails or requires. Philosophers cannot claim neutrality in their explanations of interpretive concepts because their assertions fold back into the practice. And in ordinary political argument, the idea that I may somehow sacrifice my liberty never crosses my mind. The core of the matter is simply what liberty is or what it requires in the case at hand. It is because of the justificatory and practical role that political concepts play in our social practices that, for Dworkin, "philosophical analysis of political concepts cannot be shown to be descriptive in the model of scientific investigation into natural kinds" (Dworkin 2006, p. 153).

There seems to be an important reason, therefore, for Dworkin's methodological attitude. His basic assumption is that in legal argumentation questions of fidelity to law do not arise: we all assume that we are legally bound, that the law is capable of generating moral obligations, and that *legality* is a value. If we fail to acknowledge this point, we fail to understand how the concept of law really works in our political argument. Dworkin's methodological standpoint, therefore, is based on a pragmatic claim of fit between theory and practice. It is based on the claim that law is a political concept in the same way as justice, democracy, or liberty. This is why no Archimedean theory can explain it well:

> We can rescue the important questions of legal philosophy from Archimedean legal obscurantism by attacking them in this different way. We understand legal practice better, and make more intelligible sense of propositions of law, by pursuing an explicitly normative and political enterprise: refining and defending conceptions of legality and drawing tests for concrete claims of law from favored conceptions. There is no question of taking theories of law constructed in this way to be merely "descriptive." They are conceptual, but only in the normative, interpretive sense in which theories of justice, as well as theories of democracy, liberty, and equality, are conceptual. (Dworkin 2006, p. 170)

[9] I follow Ronaldo Macedo Junior in this interpretation of Dworkin. See Macedo Junior (2016). For a contrasting interpretation, which claims that Dworkin's view is inconsistent with Wittgenstein, see Patterson (1996, pp. 71–98). I have attempted to rebut Patterson's argument in a long footnote, in which I claim that it relies on an implausible regularist interpretation of Wittgenstein's solution to the so-called regress argument. See Bustamante (2021, pp. 12–14, note 48).

Given that the "doctrinal" sense of law (the only sense with which, for him, jurisprudence should be occupied) is assimilated to political concepts in general, Dworkin believes that this concept must be interpretive in the sense that it is descriptive *while* normative, in a way that is not possible to discriminate between these two features. When we disagree about this concept, our disagreement is both a theoretical and a practical disagreement, and the only way to resolve it is through a partly normative argument. This explains Dworkin's apparently shocking conclusion that "the cutting edge of a jurisprudential argument is its moral edge" (Dworkin 2006, p. 178).

What do we gain if we purchase Dworkin's theoretical package? We know that inclusive legal positivism, of the sort Waluchow defends, purports to gain conceptual clarity and philosophical accuracy. But what is Dworkin's advantage? I argue that we gain a theory more interesting from the practical point of view and more coherent with the way judges and participants understand the nature of legal argument (i.e., more in line with the claims they make and implicit assumptions to which are they committed). Nevertheless, this claim to a better fit between theory and practice cannot be vindicated unless one can show that Dworkin's theory of law is at least as capable as Waluchow's inclusive legal positivism of explaining what happens in the practice of precedent.

To come back to the example I used in Sect. 3, if Judge John and Justice Mary are both unsatisfied with a middle-court precedent that understands the concept of "vehicle" in a restrictive way (comprising vehicles with wheels such as cars, buses and motorcycles but not flying or floating vehicles like airplanes, helicopters and boats), how should they argue in support of their favored interpretation of the law? How should they explain their propositions about what the law requires in the current case? (To recap, our debate was whether these vehicles qualify as "self-propelled vehicles" for tax purposes.) As we recall, Waluchow will say that both Judge John and Justice Mary agree that the law, as it stands, is against the state's claim to tax Janet's private jet on the basis of the constitutional rule allowing it to tax vehicles in general. The difference is that Judge John is bound by the law while Justice Mary is not. Judge John might believe that the precedent that binds him is unconstitutional and may even write a detailed opinion showing to the higher courts his reasons to overrule it. But he still must argue that the wrong precedent is valid law, regardless of its unconstitutionality for its violation to the principles of equality and of taxation according to people's ability to pay. As Mark Greenberg puts it, inclusive legal positivism entails a sort of "atomism" in the determination of the content of the law, inasmuch as it takes for granted that "individual legal norms are explanatory prior to the content of the law as a whole" (Greenberg 2011a, p. 50). Could Judge John have argued in a different way?

Suppose Judge John becomes a Dworkinian. Suppose, further, that he is bound by the adjudicative rule that prevents him from changing the middle-court precedent he believes is wrong. How should he proceed if he is trying to convince Justice Mary to decide as he thinks is best? The best Dworkinian answer is that he must produce an argument about what the law is. Neither he nor Justice Mary will be persuaded by an argument according to which courts are allowed to change the law if they find it unattractive for political reasons. Given that questions of fidelity do not arise in legal argument, both will be assuming that one of the litigants has a *right to win the case*: not only a moral right, but a proper legal right to a final decision in her favor. If Judge John is to convince Justice Mary to adjudicate in favor of the state's government (and against Janet's attempt to get rid of ownership taxation on her airplane), he must struggle to claim that it is the law (rather than an independent morality) that establishes this right.

Will Judge John have to ignore Waluchow's contention that precedents may have different institutional forces? I do not think so. He could accept Waluchow's notion of institutional force and argue that although the law's institutional force is different from the force of purely substantive reasons, it is still a form of moral force. Judge John's duty to follow a precedent stems from a procedural rule that is based on a morally significant principle which establishes judicial hierarchy. If there is something in the legal system that prevents him from protecting someone's right in this case, it is just a *jurisdictional* rule that applies to the case at hand. In the current case, Judge John is bound by the precedent. He lacks jurisdiction to enforce the law. But he is still entitled to make a claim about what the law protects in the current case. For Judge John to convince Justice Mary, or the parties, or the audience of legal scholars, or the legislature, or the citizens in general, he must raise a claim about what the law (all things considered) requires in the current case. He must argue that the middle court has made a *legal* mistake. If he believes the law gives the state a power to tax Janet (provided that it does not violate principles of taxation such as strict legality, generality, non-retroactivity, and so on), he must argue for this interpretation and say that this is what the law really is, for otherwise he will not be able to persuade Justice Mary of his interpretation of the law. If Justice Mary is persuaded by his argument, on the other hand, she will not be entitled to claim for herself the power to change the law. If she sees herself as authorized to change the precedent, it is only because the precedent is illegal despite its unsuccessful claim to settle the law in a certain way. We cannot say that the precedent is law in an atomistic way, by looking only at an individual provision. Rather, the proper way to claim that something is legally obligatory requires a holistic assessment of the legal system. When regarded from the broad picture, the precedent was never part of the law. It might have been an institutional pronouncement that purported to be law, but it was not law in the proper sense because the law, after all, is a political concept like justice, or liberty, or democracy. The law is something whose sense derives in an important part from a system-oriented argument, not only from choice.

As we can see, Dworkin's conclusion that the middle-court precedent is not "law" once it is properly interpreted is consistent with the jurisdictional rule that prevents Judge John from changing the precedent in the current case. It is just as plausible as Waluchow's contention that the precedent has been law all along despite Justice Mary's legal obligation to overrule it. Although both propositions seem awkward on their face, they both make sense when further detail is provided. Neither Dworkin's thought that Judge John and Justice Mary are bound to make different statements of what the law commands they to do, nor Waluchow's thought that a precedent is "the law" despite its unconstitutionality has a better claim. They both seem strange at face value. But when we carefully reflect upon these theories, we see that there is a plausible explanation for these statements. If we attempt a charitable interpretation, both theories can survive.

Dworkin and Waluchow seem to have, therefore, a family dispute about how to characterize the law. They look at legal practice from different angles and yet see similar things. Furthermore, they seem to argue for liberal theories of interpretation and political morality that share a great deal of assumptions about judicial duty and adjudicative responsibilities. They are both in the same camp; they are part of the same family of theories and their most interesting disagreements are with the exclusive legal positivists that allow only institutional considerations in the determination of the content of the law (and with even more reason with those exclusive legal positivists who claim, like Scott Shapiro,[10] that legal reasoning must be "amoral" or hold, like Jeremy Waldron, that there are normative reasons for judicial textualism) (Waldron 1999, p. 145) or yet with the self-proclaimed "pragmatists" that allow, like Richard Posner, policy considerations in the construction of legal decisions (Posner 2003, p. 57).

6 Conclusion

As a conclusion, we can say that inclusive legal positivism and law as integrity share important assumptions. Neither of these theories is based on the essentialist assertion that law is made of social facts alone, and both allow for the empirical possibility of there being extremely unjust legal systems which may not deserve our allegiance and fail in their claim to generate moral obligations. Moreover, both would regard legal reasoning in a similar way, given that they agree that when law incorporates moral principles (which is what happens most of the times, and what happens in all the times Dworkin's theory can help us), we cannot determine the content of legal provisions without making a responsible moral judgment. When judged from their practical consequences, law as integrity and inclusive legal positivism do not differ much and lead to similar (liberal) theories of interpretation. Although it is true that they employ different methodologies to determine what the law is, when they look at most of our legal systems they end up seeing the same thing from different angles. Finally, Waluchow is wrong to suggest that Dworkin's theory is unacceptable because its account of legal precedent leads to irresolvable dilemmas. At first glance, Dworkin's implied assumption that there might be cases where lower judges lack jurisdiction to impose the law is just as worrying as Waluchow's assumption that sometimes these judges may have a legal obligation to disregard the law. But when

[10] According to Shapiro, the law's moral aim is to settle controversies that cannot be adequately resolved by morality. Hence, "the interpretation of any member of a system of plans [or laws] cannot be determined by facts whose existence a member of that system aims to settle" (Shapiro 2011, p. 311).

we look closer, both law as integrity and inclusive legal positivism have decent accounts for strictly binding precedents. These theories' responses to *stare decisis* and explanations of binding precedents are probably not decisive grounds for preferring either of them.

Acknowledgment I am happy to acknowledge the funding I received for the research that led to the publication of this chapter from the National Council for Scientific Development, CNPq, Brazil, Grants #423696/2018-1 and #306284/2020-0 and from FAPEMIG (a research supporting foundation of Minas Gerais state, Grant # APQ-02138-22.

Appendix: Waluchow and Dworkin on Interpretation of Political Morality

The conclusion of my chapter in this book was that Waluchow and Dworkin share some commitments that lead to similar accounts of the role of moral reasons in the practice of adjudication. They employ different methodologies to look at the same data but come to similar views. The force of moral reasons in adjudication is analogous and both theories can offer plausible explanations of the nature of law. It makes little practical difference which account one prefers, and no knock-down argument can be presented for either view.

In a conference in Brazil, Waluchow presented an interesting hypothesis in reaction to my argument. He suggested that there is a sense in which his account of constitutional reasoning and political morality is different from Dworkin's interpretivism. Waluchow's common law constitutionalism does not entitle judges to make first-order judgments of political morality. Their judgments are "detached" in the sense of Joseph Raz—that is, judgments undertaken from the "point of view" of a political morality that is endorsed by the community, rather than judgments that they themselves endorse when they purport to retrieve the truth about moral facts (Waluchow 2018, p. 124).

This is an intriguing response, which might either undermine my original claim or at least represent a change in Waluchow's views about morality and interpretation. But I believe that on closer inspection Waluchow's original views cohere with his later work, and that both remain proximate to Dworkin's philosophy of law. In Waluchow's earlier work he treated his debate with Dworkin as a *conceptual* debate about the nature of law. It was important for him to stress that "there is no logical connection between legal positivism and any particular theory of ethics" (Waluchow 1985, p. 205). He believed that if you grant Dworkin's theory of adjudication, nothing prevents you from accepting a positivist theory of law. Even if you commit to Dworkin's views that (i) judges should take into consideration moral principles when they adjudicate legal cases; (ii) there is no room for "strong discretion" in adjudication, given that judges are bound to employ these moral considerations; and (iii) judges must "develop and employ a 'theory' which best explains and justifies morally the settled decisions, rules and practices of their legal system," positivism will remain consistent with your interpretive approach (Waluchow 1985, p. 188).

Perhaps it can be argued that after *A Common Law Theory of Judicial Review* Waluchow draws a sharper line between his philosophy and Dworkin's theory of interpretation, since the former rejects the following three assumptions:

1) there must be a "truth of the matter" about moral facts for there to be objective judgments about morality;[11]
2) a judge's value judgments must coincide with her views and beliefs about the matters at stake (Waluchow 2007, p. 223); and
3) judges have a responsibility to make first-order moral judgments about these truths.[12]

Instead of these controversial assumptions, Waluchow puts forward six claims, which appear in his response to Jeremy Waldron and the "popular complaint" that judicial review "allows judges to impose their own subjective moral views":

4) "the rights to which a Charter refers are best viewed as rights of political morality established within what we'll call the 'community's constitutional morality'";
5) "the community can be wrong about what its own constitutional morality requires";
6) "a judge's views about what the morality requires in a particular case might, on the one hand, be correct, or at least better";
7) "when this is so, judges can be required by the Charter – the law – to enforce their own views of the community's constitutional morality against the erroneous beliefs of the community and its legislative representatives";
8) "when judges fulfil this duty, it is almost always misleading to view them as imposing *their own* subjective moral views";
9) "in enforcing their views about the rights of their community's constitutional morality recognized in a Charter, judges are in fact respecting, not violating, democratic principles" (Waluchow 2007, pp. 219–220).

[11] Waluchow's account of political morality and constitutional reasoning requires the existence of "true moral commitments" of a community's constitutional morality. Nonetheless, this "does not mean to suggest that they are 'correct' propositions or beliefs, only that they are ones to which we are truly committed" (Waluchow 2007, p. 224). In other words, as Waluchow expressed to me in private communication, it is possible to "identify X as a true commitment of the community without thereby suggesting or implying that X is true – indeed without implying that there is some truth of the matter with respect to X."

[12] In other words, Waluchow "does *not* believe that an interpretation of a body of law must, as Dworkin claims, be a moral theory of that object to which the theorist personally subscribes" (Waluchow 2007, p. 227, italics added).

I believe that Waluchow is right about these assumptions (although there is a sense in which assumption 3 can be plausibly defended). Nevertheless, Dworkin never held the assumptions 1 to 2, in the sense that Waluchow understands them, and can also be read as endorsing assumptions 4 to 9. The remaining disagreement concerns assumption 3, which matters little once one adopts either Dworkin's or Waluchow's account of interpretation.

It might be tempting to think that I am wrong if we take Dworkin's general statements about truth at their face value. Consider Dworkin's following statement: "that there are truths about values is an obvious, inescapable fact" (Dworkin 2011, p. 24). This appears to contradict Waluchow's attempt to remain agnostic on whether there is a truth of the matter about moral facts. Nonetheless, Dworkin's assertion loses much of its force when he adds that "there is only one way we can 'earn' the right to think that some judgment is true, and this has nothing to do with physics or metaphysics" (Dworkin 2011, p. 26). The proper way to argue for a moral truth is with further moral propositions, which should be interpreted not according to the vocabulary of metaethics, science or professional philosophy, but according to a more pragmatic attitude. When philosophers argue about moral facts, they usually have in mind a metaphysical concept of objectivity which commits the inquirer to a correspondence theory of truth. But Dworkin is careful enough to reject this view. Dworkin answers "What do moral facts consist in?" with what he calls the "ordinary view," which "insists that moral judgments are not made true by historical events or people's opinions or emotions or anything else in the physical or mental world" (Dworkin 2011, p. 29). Dworkin's theory of truth is a pragmatic theory which holds that "we can seek truth about morality only by pursuing coherence endorsed by conviction" (Dworkin 2011, p. 120). He adopts an interpretive or "ordinary" account of moral truth not because he believes there are moral facts "out there," but because of a practical necessity that derives from our responsibility to make judgments in the first place: "We cannot defend a theory of justice without also defending, as part of the same enterprise, a theory of moral objectivity. It is irresponsible to do without such a theory" (Dworkin 2011, p. 8). So when Dworkin argues for moral truths he is using a pragmatic concept that means "to describe method, not metaphysics" (Dworkin 2011, p. 121). His point is to show "how you must proceed if truth [in morality] is your agenda" (Dworkin 2011, p. 121).

This is a deflationary theory of truth, although perhaps Dworkin would be unhappy to describe it in that way. The only way to "rescue philosophical arguments about the nature of truth," he argues, is to "understand truth as an interpretive concept"—that is, to treat different theories of truth as interpretive claims: "The value of truth is interwoven in these [social] practices" (Dworkin 2011, p. 173). Therefore, if a correspondence theory of truth does not work for the practice of moral argumentation or value inquiry, then we should leave behind this "supremely abstract theory of truth" and characterize truth as "the intrinsic goal of inquiry" (Dworkin 2011, p. 177). Our abstract characterization of truth begins with a Peircean assumption, that "truth is what counts as the uniquely successful solution to a challenge of inquiry" (Dworkin 2011, p. 177). But this assumption should be adjusted to specific domains through "more concrete specifications tailored to each domain" (Dworkin 2011, p. 177). Although a common structure is presupposed, each domain contains its different standards of objectivity, which allow for appropriate judgments and validity conditions for one's claims (Raz 1999, pp. 118–160). In the domain of morality, Dworkin defines truth in the following sense:

> The truth of any true moral judgments consists in the truth of an indefinite number of other moral judgments. And its truth provides part of what constitutes the truth of any of those others. There is no hierarchy of moral principles built on axiomatic foundations. (Dworkin 2011, p. 117)

Dworkin regards morality, like law, as a practice in which the meaning of any particular proposition is *constructed* by its participants. When we argue in the context of an interpretive practice, we need not appeal to basic or ultimate moral facts. Our statements about morality are "statements within rather than about the enterprise of morality" (Dworkin 1986, p. 82). When I deploy an argument for a moral proposition (say, that slavery is wrong) I need not to show that some "atmospheric moral quaverings confirm my opinion, for example, or that it matches a noumenal metaphysical fact" (Dworkin 1986, pp. 80–81). Rather, "the practices of interpretation and morality give these claims all the meaning they need or could have" (Dworkin 1986, p. 83). As some interpreters have realized, this sounds like a pragmatic (yet not instrumentalist) conception of truth (Nye 2016; Decat 2015; Bustamante 2023), one that Waluchow may have good reasons to endorse. Waluchow's account of a community's constitutional morality is looking after precisely this type of methodological account of moral objectivity. His conception of a community's "true moral commitments" does *not* purport to be a correct *representation* of facts in the world, but rather a rational network of *commitments* that emerge as a form of social fact or pragmatic truth.

This leads us to the second assumption in our list. A central premise of Waluchow's common law constitutionalism is the claim that we can distinguish between mere "moral opinions" and "moral commitments": the former "describes moral views that have not been critically examined so as to achieve reflective equilibrium, and the latter those that have" (Waluchow 2007, p. 224). *True* moral commitments are those that resist after a careful reflection under an interpretive scheme. On Waluchow's account,

> [i]t's the commitments, not the beliefs, that are said to be true – although those who believe that moral sentences express propositions to which truth values can be assigned will hope that their beliefs share this property as well. Following Rawls, we can say that our moral opinions sometimes conflict with our moral commitments. (Waluchow 2007, p. 224)

I believe that the assertions 4 to 9 in our list follow from this claim. It is the distinction between commitments and beliefs which allows one to speak of a community's constitutional morality (i.e., the interlocking moral structure to which a community is committed). Given that many of these commitments are not explicitly enunciated, sometimes they are only visible after considerable interpretive work. As Robert Brandom has shown in his insightful philosophy of language, there are not only *acknowledged* commitments, but also "inferentially articulated conceptual contents," which remain implicit until they are thematized by participants in a rational discourse (Brandom 1994, p. 68).[13] A central point of Brandom's inferentialism is the claim that any social practice contains a constellation of commitments that must be inferentially articulated in order to be intelligible: "Undertaking a commitment to a claim with one content involves undertaking commitments to claims whose contents are (in the context of one's other commitments) its commitive-inferential consequences" (Brandom 1994, p. 194). The relationship among different commitments requires an explanation that goes beyond the explicit relations among enumerated propositions. In addition to formal-logical relations among these claims, there are *material inferences* between explicit and implicit commitments. To use a trivial example, "undertaking commitment to the claim that Pittsburgh is to the West of Philadelphia is one way of undertaking commitment to the claim that Philadelphia is to the East of Pittsburgh." Even if these commitments are not expressly acknowledged, "*they are commitments nonetheless*" (Brandom 1994, p. 194).

We can see how this Brandomian scheme fits perfectly into Waluchow's account of constitutional morality. What makes it possible to speak of "true commitments" of a community (in Waluchow's sense) is the complex *network* of inferences among explicit and inferentially articulated commitments. Waluchow provides a forceful case, therefore, for a plausible but apparently controversial claim, which is the assumption that a community (perhaps the whole community, or the institution with final authority to settle the law) "can be wrong about what its own constitutional morality requires." Waluchow explains his argument about "true commitments" with an example about the permission of same-sex and same-gender marriage in Canadian law, which illustrated this possibility in sensible way:

> When Court decisions are criticized for being out of sync with the moral views of citizens, the focus is almost always on some widespread moral *opinion* that is at odds with the court's ruling. The focus is almost never on the general principles and values to which most citizens are actually committed (. . .). When judicial recognition of same-sex marriage is criticized for being against the moral beliefs of Canadians, the reference is almost always to moral opinions. These are moral opinions that, upon reflection, flatly contradict fundamental beliefs, principles, values, and considered judgments that enjoy widespread, if not universal, currency within the community, and they introduce significant evaluative dissonance. They are also opinions that are inconsistent with any reasonable interpretation of the Charter and the many judicial decisions made in its name. (Waluchow 2007, p. 225)

One must consider, therefore, the inferential relations among commitments to assess the plausibility of a moral claim. The community's constitutional morality is constituted by these commitments to values, principles, and more specific norms, instead of the particular beliefs that one reaches through intuition, perception or

[13] I have argued in previous works that Dworkin's method of interpretation can be understood according to Brandom's inferentialist pragmatism, and that once we read it in this way, many objections to Dworkin's "protestant interpretation" disappear (Bustamante 2020, 2021, 2023). As I hope is clear in this chapter, I believe that Waluchow's common law constitutionalism can also be explained with Brandom's theory of the meaning of concepts. For an intriguing reading of Dworkin as a closet inferentialist, see Decat (2015).

moral insight. Once you take this point seriously, everything else in Waluchow's long list of claims becomes plausible, and it becomes easy to see that interpreters can identify *mistakes* about the community's constitutional morality even when this conclusion is at odds with the beliefs of the majority or the will of institutions with political authority. A judge's enforcement of her "own views of the community's constitutional morality" can be legitimate when it correctly identifies "erroneous beliefs of the community and its legislative representatives," as Waluchow has put it.

This is not an argument that Dworkin would resist. Dworkin's central assumption in *Law's Empire* is a strong commitment to a "right-wrong picture" of adjudication (Dworkin 1983, p. 289). He proposed a conception of objectivity that allowed one to distinguish between a *correct* judgment and a judgment *upheld* by the majority. The political value of integrity is Dworkin's test for this methodological account of objectivity. It allows one to distinguish between the attitudes of *deferring* to a community's judgment and *making a correct judgment* about the content of rights and obligations. Dworkin thinks that citizens, lawyers and judges have a political responsibility to make judgments about the concrete decisions that the community's most cherished moral commitments entail. They cannot acquit this responsibility without an account of the propriety conditions for these judgments, which "integrity" attempts to provide. The responsibility to decide legal cases is personal *only* in the sense that the judgments required to describe moral propositions are not a mere reproduction of the beliefs held by institutions or political authorities. They are judgments that all of us must make and that never claim authority in the strong sense of being final or supreme.

We reach, now, the only assertion that remains controversial between Dworkin and Waluchow, which is the third assertion in our original list: "judges have a responsibility to make first-order moral judgments about these (moral) truths." Before we analyze this claim, we should bear in mind that the disagreement is narrower that it might seem, as Waluchow acknowledges in the fragment below:

> They [the true commitments of a community's constitutional morality] are in some way tied to its constitutional law and practices. Following Dworkin, we might say it is "the political morality presupposed by the laws and institutions of the community." In drawing upon Dworkin, my intention is not to signal acceptance of the particular theory of interpretation he recommends for ascertaining the morality presupposed by or embedded in the law. For reasons that lie well beyond the scope of this investigation, I do not believe that an interpretation of a body of law must, as Dworkin claims, be a moral theory of that object to which the theorist personally subscribes. It can, instead, be what Julie Dickson aptly terms as an "indirectly evaluative" theory of the sort outlined and defended by Jules Coleman. It is a theory that invokes moral norms, not to justify but to explain why it is the way it is, to show its relationships with other areas of the law, and so on. (Waluchow 2007, p. 227)[14]

[14] Waluchow's quotes in the fragment are taken from Dworkin (1978, p. 126), Dickson (2007), and Coleman (2001).

The crucial part in this long quote is the fragment in which Waluchow expresses agreement with Dworkin about the claim that the political morality relevant in adjudication is that which is *presupposed* by the laws and institutions of a certain community. It is because of these communal commitments and presuppositions that Dworkin believes integrity is a political virtue in the first place. Integrity provides a way to make these multiple commitments "hang together" in an intelligible way.

But there comes a point in which Waluchow and Dworkin appear to disagree. *Contra* Dworkin, Waluchow argues that his project does not authorize judges to make first-order judgments to which the judge must personally subscribe. Judges should draw, instead, on "Raz's theory of detached normative statements and reasoning from a point of view." In other words, Waluchow is committed to the following claims:

1) any moral reasoning that takes place in the process of constitutional review can be undertaken from the perspective or point of view of the democratic community and its CCM commitments; and
2) this process can be undertaken by a judge without the unwarranted intrusion of her own first-order moral convictions (Waluchow 2018, pp. 122–123).

I believe that the disagreement between Dworkin and Waluchow on this point can be overcome without significant loss. Dworkin and Waluchow mean different things when the former supports (and the latter rejects) the claims that interpreters must make a "theory" and that this theory requires a "first-order" judgment to describe a particular moral norm. When Dworkin speaks of a theory, he means to refer to a *general description* that employs arguments that are not qualitatively different from those of the participants of the practice. Dworkin makes this point only because he rejects the possibility of a relevant distinction between first-order and second-order levels for the analysis of a given proposition about morality or law, inasmuch as the concepts (and sentences) that appear in these two levels must have the same meaning. In other words, there is no difference in kind between the arguments that one can employ in the first level of the practice or in the second level that allegedly reports or describes that practice, because any submission about the content of the practice will be assessed as "correct" or "incorrect" in the same way, regardless of the point of view in which the assessor stands. Furthermore, any theory of law, for Dworkin, should be constructed from within the practice, because it is made of arguments that may "fold back to the practice," instead of leaving it untouched. A theory fails to describe a practice correctly if it fails to explain the relations between the commitments of a practice and the entitlements these commitments imply.

It is only when we consider the distinction between "first-order" and "second-order" inquiry that we can see where the real disagreement between Waluchow and Dworkin lies. As Waluchow acknowledges, Raz thinks that "a detached legal statement is a statement of law, of what legal rights and duties people have, not a statement about people's beliefs, attitudes, or actions, not even about their beliefs, actions, or attitudes about the law" (Raz 2009a, p. 153). According to Waluchow, this means that

> the statement cannot be reduced to an external statement of the form "S believes that he ought to do x" or "The legal officials of legal system y have enacted law L, requiring x, and will therefore hold S accountable should he fail to do x." But neither does the statement carry the full normative force that a statement uttered from the internal point of view usually does. This is because it does not commit the speaker to acceptance of the normative point of view it expresses. (...) Rather, the aim is to inform others what they ought to do according to the law, and this information is conveyed from a point of view that is not necessarily of the speaker. (Waluchow 2018, p. 124)

In this passage, Waluchow appears to subscribe to Raz's idea that one can see *different things* depending on their "perspective" or point of view. The distinction allows for descriptions of a normative practice that appear different when they are made from the "point of view of the law," or the "point of view of the community's constitutional morality," or the "personal point of view" of the assessor. The distinction makes sense because the "first-order" description must be an explanation that is coherent with one's *beliefs* about what a particular norm requires. A good theorist, who examines the practice from a second-order perspective, must explain what the participants of legal practice accept as normative, because it is their acceptance or belief that makes the rule of recognition binding. The attitude of those who *adopt the point of view* of a normative system is an attitude of *acknowledging its normative force.* If this normative force depends on one's beliefs about a given norm, it is therefore dependent on a mental state. It is *because* of this putative dependence on mental states that it is important for Raz, Dickson, Hart and others to distinguish between the point of view of the *officials*, who *accept* a rule of recognition, and the point of view of the *theorists*, who describe the attitude of officials from a *detached* or theoretical point of view. But I do not think that this distinction matters (or must remain relevant) for theorists like Waluchow and Dworkin, since both argue that what is relevant to determine the content of the community's constitutional morality is this community's *true commitments*, instead of an authority's (or a group's) belief or other mental state. Once we take this pragmatic thought seriously, a major methodological turn can be made. The normative status of a norm becomes less mysterious, since a norm is the product of a group's commitments and the entitlements that derive from them.

The interpretive responsibilities of a judge who is called to make sense of the commitments of a community's constitutional morality is not determined by her motives or personal beliefs, but by the *norms* that determine the appropriateness of judgments and intentional actions. "Judging and acting – endorsing claims and maxims, committing ourselves as to what is or shall be true – is binding ourselves by norms. It is making ourselves subject to assessment according to the rules that articulate the *contents* of those commitments" (Brandom 2009, p. 33). The kind of theoretical responsibility that we must acquit to claim entitlement to our rational judgments, therefore, is a "*task* responsibility"—that is, a "responsibility to *do* something" (Brandom 2009, p. 35, emphasis in original). As Brandom proceeds, following Kant's insights in his *Critique of Pure Reason*, the specific aspect of this task responsibility "is the responsibility to *integrate* the judgment into a unity of apperception," i.e., to achieve a *synthesis* that integrates "new endorsements into the whole that comprises one's previous endorsements," which involves three things: first, a critical responsibility "to weed our materially incompatible commitments"; second, an ampliative responsibility "to extract material inferential consequences of each commitment"; and third, a justificatory responsibility to "be prepared to offer reasons for the commitments (both theoretical and practical) that one acknowledges" (Brandom 2009, p. 36). This latter justificatory responsibility, in turn, involves "citing prior commitments (or undertaking further commitments) that inferentially entitle one to those new commitments," aiming at "a whole constellation of commitments that is *consistent*" (Brandom 2009, p. 36, italics in original).

Once one grasps the idea that this interpretive responsibility is a task responsibility to articulate the consequences of these normative commitments (in case of Waluchow, of the commitments of the community), one no longer needs to assert, like Raz famously did, that for a law to be "capable of being authoritative" it must "be, or be presented as, *someone's view* on what the subjects ought to do" (Raz 1994, p. 221, italics added).

Raz seems to adopt, with that statement, an atomistic theory of the meaning of authoritative pronouncements. If you think that Raz is correct about this, you will end up accepting the view that Greenberg described as the "communication theory" of interpretation, i.e., the view that the content of the law is determined by a mental state (an intention) of the authority who enact it (Greenberg 2011b, p. 248). On this view, the primary determinant of the content of an enactment must be the intention of the legislature competent to enact a valid law. "The very idea of law-making institutions," says Raz, "is that of institutions which can make the law they intend to make. No alleged justification of law-making institutions which does not include that assumption can make sense" (Raz 2009b, p. 275). Put in another way, no theory of interpretation could be accepted without encompassing the "Authoritative Intention Thesis," which asserts that "to the extent that the law derives from deliberative law-making, its interpretation should reflect the intentions of its lawmaker" (Raz 2009b, p. 275).

This is not the position advocated by Dworkin, who seems to be more consistent with the view defended by Hans Kelsen in his Pure Theory of Law. Despite Kelsen's moral relativism, Kelsen shares with Dworkin an important reluctance to resort to intentions, desires, beliefs, or any other psychological states. Kelsen holds that the meaning that matters for legal cognition is not the subjective meaning that a norm promulgation may have for its author, but rather the objective meaning that is attributed by a superior norm in the hierarchical structure of norms (Kelsen 1992, p. 10). What makes an event a "legal act," says Kelsen, is the "objective" or "legal" sense that is attributed by a legal norm: "The specifically legal sense" of a legislative event "comes by way of a norm whose content refers to the event and confers legal meaning on it," so the act can be "interpreted (...) according to this norm" (Kelsen 1992, pp. 10–11). In a similar way, Dworkin thinks that legal interpretation is different from "conversational" interpretation because the former does not assign meaning "in light of the motives and purposes and concerns it supposes the speaker to have," attempting to report statements about an "intention" of that speaker (Dworkin 1986, p. 50). Legal interpretation is, instead, a form of "constructive" interpretation. Like conversational interpretation, constructive interpretation is "essentially concerned with purposes rather than causes" of the practices and norms being interpreted. Nonetheless, the relevant purposes for this kind of interpretation "are not (fundamentally) those of some author but of the interpreter" (Dworkin 1986, p. 52)—that is, purposes that the interpreter can legitimately *ascribe* to the object of their interpretation.

The assumption that the relevant purposes for constructive interpretation are those of the "interpreter" has led Dworkin's critics to object that a Dworkinian interpreter is free to impose upon the practice a set of independent values that are selected according to her own private assessment (Postema 1987, p. 301). Nevertheless, as I argued in length (Bustamante 2020, 2021), this objection fails because Dworkin presupposes that the interpreter can also be wrong when she endeavors to determine the content of the law, and he offers us a test to determine when that is the case. It must be possible to distinguish the content of the law from the content of any beliefs that the author or the interpreter might possess (Dworkin 1986, p. 83). Although "legal reasoning means bringing to bear on particular discrete legal problems (...) a vast network of principles of legal derivation or of political morality" (Dworkin 2006, p. 50), the relevant principles in any acceptable interpretive claim must be "principles embedded in our legal practice" (Dworkin 2006, p. 51). Like Kelsen, Dworkin assumes that the practice of interpretation is driven by law, because he thinks that "the history or shape of a practice or object constrains the available interpretations of it" (Dworkin 1986, p. 52), and that "the practice being interpreted sets the conditions of interpretation" (Dworkin 1986, p. 64).

Although Dworkin is considering legal interpretation while Waluchow is considering the interpretation of the norms of the community's constitutional morality, their shared assumption that what matters are the interpretive *commitments*, instead of mere beliefs, implies that they are treating constitutional reasoning in a similar way. Dworkin and Waluchow disagree about whether to call that interpretation an interpretation of "law," as Dworkin would put it (given his inflated concept of law that treats it as a branch of political morality), or an interpretation of the "community's constitutional morality," as Waluchow would describe it (given his legal positivist effort to clearly distinguish law and morality). But both agree that it is *appropriate* for a constitutional judge to employ these standards in constitutional adjudication, and both can be read as interpreting them according to the commitments implicit in the normative practice, instead of the beliefs (or intentions) of the judge or the interpreter at stake.

Waluchow correctly thinks that what a person believes about a particular aspect of the political morality that applies to her situation matters less than the commitments actually embedded in this political morality. It becomes, thus, far more important to determine the *implicit norms* to which an authority (or a community) *commits*, even if her (or its) personal view about what these commitments entail is inconsistent with these implicit norms. An authority is no less responsible for the commitive-inferential consequences of her deeds just because she is in a state of error. It may perfectly be the case that an authority endorses a norm that leads, in a particular case (say, a case about same-sex marriage), to conclusions she is not willing to accept (say, that same-sex marriage is lawful); when this is the case, it is the job of a critical interpreter to make that inconsistency explicit and hold that authority accountable. This works for law but should work also for political morality, or the community's constitutional morality. To reconstruct the commitments of a community's constitutional morality, one should make a responsible judgment about what these commitments entail. I believe there is an important difference between, on one side, Raz and, on the other side, Waluchow and Dworkin. Raz adopted a sharp distinction between "detached" and "engaged" statements because he thought that law is what officials acknowledge from the "engaged" point of view: the officials' personal opinions matter for correctly describing the law, but the legal theorists' do not. But neither Waluchow, nor Dworkin can consistently accept this view. For them, competent interpreters can reach similar conclusions regardless of their personal opinions or their interpretive positions (or points of view). In effect, it is hard to think of *inferential relations among commitments* (or between commitments and entitlements) that will change depending on whether they are undertaken from the point of view of the practitioner or the legal theorist. If to be "detached" is to be based on true commitments instead of mere opinions or untheorized impressions, then both points of view must be detached. And if to be "engaged" is to be based on one's own preferences, desires, beliefs, or other mental states, then none can be engaged. Inferential relations, even when we consider relations among implicit commitments, are *rational* relations (even though sometimes we might be using informal logic or material inferences, instead of formal logic). Their correctness does not depend on the mental states of the theorist or the participants of the practice. I believe that Dworkin was right, therefore, to drop the distinction between first-order descriptions, or descriptions of legal norms made by those who believe or internalize the normative force of a practice, and second-order, or detached, descriptions of those norms. To be correct, any person must describe *the same* inferential relations among commitments, which exist regardless of an interpreter's (or, perhaps, a whole community's) unreflective beliefs. If I am right, a similar point can be made about Waluchow's analysis of the community's constitutional morality. Perhaps Waluchow's insightful and sophisticated theory of the community's constitutional morality should drop that distinction too.[15]

[15] To repeat, I believe that Waluchow—like Dworkin—has reasons to accept the interpretation of his distinction between "true commitments" and "moral opinions" offered in this Appendix. As Waluchow acknowledged in the interview at the end of this volume, one of his main reasons (perhaps *the* main reason) to distinguish his jurisprudence from Dworkin's is that while Dworkin thinks one can interpret the law based on "paradigms" provisionally accepted by interpreters as fixing correct and incorrect ways to read legal material, Waluchow believes that at the foundation of a legal system lies a rule of recognition that is accepted as a matter of convention or social rule (Bustamante et al. 2024). Nonetheless, Waluchow (2007, p. 124) agrees with Dworkin (1978, p. 76) that there are no fixed standards in law—except, perhaps, for the rule of recognition. Even if you think that this disagreement about the rule of recognition is an important disagreement about the foundations of law, it is possible to argue that, when it comes to the interpretation (either of the valid norms of a legal system that incorporates moral principles amongst its validity criteria, or of the community's constitutional morality), both agree that the proper way to distinguish a correct from an incorrect decision is to discriminate between "true commitments" (or commitments inferentially

References

Brandom, Robert. 1994. *Making it Explicit*. Cambridge, MA: Harvard University Press.
———. 2009. *Reason in Philosophy*. Cambridge, MA: Harvard University Press.
Bustamante, Thomas. 2020. Revisiting the Idea of Protestant Interpretation: Towards Reconciliation Between Dworkin and Postema. In *Philosophy of Law as an Integral Part of Philosophy: Essays on the Jurisprudence of Gerald J. Postema*, ed. Thomas Bustamante and Thiago L. Decat, 113–139. Oxford: Hart Publishing.
———. 2021. Is Protestant Interpretation an Acceptable Attitude Towards Social Practices? An Analysis of Dworkin and Postema. *American Journal of Jurisprudence* 66: 1–25.
———. 2023. Fish Versus Dworkin: A Comparison Between Two Versions of Legal Pragmatism. In *New Essays on the Fish–Dworkin Debate*, ed. Thomas Bustamante and Margaret Martin, 259–291. Oxford: Hart Publishing.
Bustamante, Thomas, Saulo de Matos, and André L.S. Coelho, eds. 2024. Interview with Professor Wil Waluchow. In this volume.
Coleman, Jules L. 2001. *The Practice of Principle*. Oxford: Oxford University Press.
Decat, Thiago L. 2015. Inferentialist Pragmatism and Dworkin's Law as Integrity. *Erasmus Law Review*: 14–25.
Dickson, Julie. 2007. *Evaluation and Legal Theory*. Oxford: Hart Publishing.
Dworkin, Ronald. 1978. *Taking Rights Seriously*. 2nd printing. Cambridge, MA: Belknap Press.
———. 1983. My Reply to Stanley Fish (and Walter Benn Michaels): Please Don't Talk About Objectivity Any More. In *The Politics of Interpretation*, ed. W.J.T. Mitchell, 287–313. Chicago: University of Chicago Press.
———. 1984. A Reply by Ronald Dworkin. In *Ronald Dworkin & Contemporary Jurisprudence*, ed. M. Cohen, 247–300. London: Duckworth.
———. 1986. *Law's Empire*. Cambridge, MA: Belknap Press.
———. 2006. *Justice in Robes*. Cambridge, MA: Belknap Press.
———. 2011. *Justice for Hedgehogs*. Cambridge, MA: Belknap Press.
Gadamer, Hans-Georg. 2004. *Truth and Method*. Trans. Joel Weinsheimer and Donald Marshall. London: Continuum.

---

articulated, as I suggest) and mere "moral opinions" (or untheorized beliefs). Under the inferentialist interpretation of the notion of moral commitments, however, the theoretical disagreement between Dworkin and Waluchow about the grounds of law will not have an impact on the choice of the method of interpretation appropriate for constitutional adjudication. However, there is a relevant difference between Waluchow and Dworkin, on one side, and Raz and the exclusive positivists, on the other side, inasmuch as Raz's preemption thesis implies that the content of the law is *fixed* and that the primary way to interpret it is to appeal to the intention of the lawmaker, instead of reconstructing implicit norms (Raz 2009b, p. 275). Waluchow need not use Raz's distinction between different "points of view" to analyze our assertions about the law. Waluchow's insistence that judges should interpret the norms of CCM by making "detached" statements only makes sense because he is presupposing a Razian vocabulary (the distinction between detached and committed statements) (Raz 2009a, pp. 153–154). However, Raz employs this vocabulary (of "detached" statements) to mark the way that lawyers and scholars interpret the law, *not* the way that citizens and judges do it (Raz 2009a, p. 155). Dworkin does not make use of that distinction because Dworkin does not think that citizens and judges should interpret the law in a way that is different from that of scholars and lawyers (see, on Dworkin's "protestant" account of interpretation, Bustamante 2020, 2021). This does not mean that a judge should substitute the principles embedded in the law by their own convictions, only that the judge (like any other interpreter) has a *responsibility to make a critical judgment* about what these principles entail. Once again, Waluchow is closer to Dworkin than he is to Raz. In Waluchow's and Dworkin's theories, judges, citizens, lawyers, and theorists should describe the law and a community's constitutional morality in the same way. I believe that Waluchow and Dworkin are both right about this.

Greenberg, Mark. 2011a. The Standard Picture and Its Discontents. In *Oxford Studies in the Philosophy of Law*, ed. Leslie Green and Brian Leiter, vol. 1, 39–106. Oxford: Oxford University Press.
———. 2011b. Legislation as Communication? Legal Interpretation and the Study of Linguistic Communication. In *Philosophical Foundations of Language in the Law*, ed. Andrei Marmor and S. Soames, 217–256. Oxford: Oxford University Press.
Hart, H.L.A. 1994. *The Concept of Law*. 2nd ed. Oxford: Oxford University Press.
Himma, Kenneth E. 2002. Inclusive Legal Positivism. In *The Oxford Handbook of Jurisprudence and Philosophy of Law*, ed. Jules Coleman and Scott J. Shapiro, 124–165. Oxford: Oxford University Press.
Kelsen, Hans. 1992. *Introduction to the Problems of Legal Theory*. Trans Bonnie L. Paulson and Stanley L. Paulson. Oxford: Oxford University Press.
Macedo Junior, Ronaldo Porto. 2016. On How Law Is Not Like Chess – Dworkin and the Theory of Conceptual Types. In *Democratizing Constitutional Law: Perspectives on Legal Theory and the Legitimacy of Constitutionalism*, ed. Thomas Bustamante and Bernardo Fernandes, 293–324. Heidelberg: Springer.
Nye, Hillary. 2016. Staying Busy While Doing Nothing? Dworkin's Complicated Relationship with Pragmatism. *Canadian Journal of Law and Jurisprudence* 29: 71–95.
Patterson, Dennis. 1996. *Law and Truth*. Oxford: Oxford University Press.
Perry, Stephen. 1995. Interpretation and Methodology in Legal Theory. In *Law and Interpretation*, ed. Andrei Marmor, 97–135. Oxford: Oxford University Press.
Posner, Richard. 2003. *Law, Pragmatism and Democracy*. Cambridge, MA: Belknap Press.
Postema, Gerald J. 1987. Protestant Interpretation and Social Practices. *Law and Philosophy* 6: 283.
Raz, Joseph. 1994. *Ethics in the Public Domain*. Oxford: Oxford University Press.
———. 1999. *Engaging Reason*. Oxford: Oxford University Press.
———. 2009a. *The Authority of Law*. 2nd ed. Oxford: Oxford University Press.
———. 2009b. *Between Authority and Interpretation*. Oxford: Oxford University Press.
Ripstein, Arthur. 2007. Introduction: Anti-Archimedeanism. In *Ronald Dworkin*, ed. Arthur Ripstein, 1–21. Cambridge: Cambridge University Press.
Shapiro, Scott. 2011. *Legality*. Cambridge, MA: Harvard University Press.
Waldron, Jeremy. 1999. *Law and Disagreement*. Oxford: Oxford University Press.
Waluchow, W.J. 1985. Herculean Legal Positivism. *Oxford Journal of Legal Studies* 5: 187–210.
———. 1994. *Inclusive Legal Positivism*. Oxford: Oxford University Press.
———. 2007. *A Common Law Theory of Judicial Review: The Living Tree*. Cambridge: Cambridge University Press.
———. 2018. Normative Reasoning from a Point of View. In *Unpacking Normativity: Conceptual, Normative, and Descriptive Issues*, ed. Kenneth E. Himma, M. Jovanovic, and Bojan Spaíc, 119–134. Oxford: Hart Publishing.

Thomas Bustamante is Professor of Legal Theory and Philosophy of Law at the Federal University of Minas Gerais, Brazil, and Senior Research Productivity Fellow of the National Council for Scientific and Technological Development (CNPq), Brazil. He was a Global Research Fellow with a Fulbright Visiting Research Grant at the New York University, from 2020 to 2021, and a Research Fellow at King's College London, from 2022 to 2023, with a grant from CAPES Foundation. He holds a PhD from the Pontifical Catholic University, Rio de Janeiro. Some of his works in English appear in the *Canadian Journal of Law and Jurisprudence*, *Modern Law Review*, *Jurisprudence*, *Australian Journal of Legal Philosophy*, *American Journal of Compartive Law*, and *German Law Journal*. He has edited the books *New Essays on the Fish-Dworkin Debate* (with Margaret Martin, 2023), *Philosophy of Law as an Integral Part of Philosophy: Essays in the Jurisprudence of Gerald J Postema* (with Thiago L Decat, 2020), *Democratizing Constitutional Law: Perspectives on Legal Theory and the Legitimacy of Constitutionalism* (with Bernardo Fernandes, 2016), *Argument Types and Fallacies in Legal Argumentation* (with Christian Dahlman, 2015) and *On the Philosophy of Precedent* (with Carlos Bernal Pulido, 2012).

Lessons from Waluchow: Necessity, Desirability, and Intelligibility of (Weak) Judicial Discretion

Imer B. Flores

Abstract In my contribution to Wilfrid J. Waluchow's festschrift, I revisit some of his outstanding contributions to the field of legal philosophy and legal theory, including his living tree constitutionalism, which has its roots in his inclusive positivism. I agree with him that the controversial practice of judicial review is justifiable since it is neither merely compatible with our so called constitutional or liberal democracies, nor contingent, but necessary to further the community's constitutional morality and its true fundamental moral commitments. As Waluchow acknowledges: "Judges are not… being asked to decide on the basis of their own best judgments concerning the demands of moral truth. Rather they are being asked to decide on the basis of their best judgments as to the democratic community's best judgments concerning the demands of moral truth." Moreover, I disagree with him that there is: "No way of telling, among the various reasonable answers offered, which is right, or whose answer is best—or even better."

1 Introduction

> *Leave not a rack behind: We are such stuff/As Dreams are made on/and our little life/Is rounded with a sleep.*
>
> William Shakespeare, *The Tempest*, Act 4, Scene 1 (1917).

Acknowledging my own debts to W.J. Waluchow for the force and the grounds of his influence, as a legal philosopher and—most importantly—as a person, is the main aim of my contribution to his *festschrift*. And so, in what follows, my purpose is to pay homage to him, by revisiting both analytically and critically some of his outstanding contributions to the field of legal philosophy and theory—not only about his account on the nature of law and judicial discretion, *i.e.*, inclusive legal

I. B. Flores (✉)
National Autonomous University of Mexico (UNAM), Instituto de Investigaciones Jurídicas, Circuito Mario de La Cueva s/n, C.U., Coyoacán, Ciudad de México, CDMX, Mexico
e-mail: imer@unam.mx

T. Bustamante et al. (eds.), *Law, Morality and Judicial Reasoning*, Law and Philosophy Library 147, https://doi.org/10.1007/978-3-031-61879-6_9

positivism, but also of its relationship and justification of charter review, *i.e.*, living tree constitutionalism.

I agree with him that the controversial practice of judicial review is justifiable since it is neither merely compatible with our so called constitutional or liberal democracies, nor contingent, but necessary to further the community's constitutional morality and its true fundamental moral commitments. Let me point out a tension: this acknowledgment, *i.e.*, the necessity of a weak form of judicial review, is at odds with the endorsement of Hart's soft positivism and Waluchow's inclusive legal positivism, which consider that such references to morality are a mere contingency (Waluchow 2009a). For now, I will bracket this discussion to begin with a brief reference to the broader lessons learned—and to be learned—from the legal philosopher and most importantly from the person. In the following sections, I will summarise the discussion both on the nature of law and judicial discretion, on one side, and its relationship to the justification of charter review, on the other.

Waluchow began the "Acknowledgments" to his *Inclusive Legal Positivism*, by recognizing his "overwhelming debt" to H.L.A. Hart, who supervised his thesis, *i.e.*, "Adjudication and Discretion", and provided "the kind of guidance and encouragement of which doctoral students dreams are made" (Waluchow 1994, p. vi). Later, in a very personal introductory note to a symposium celebrating the 50th anniversary of the publication of Hart's *The Concept of Law* (Hart 1961/1994), he reiterated the "enormous debt of gratitude" to his supervisor and solidified his conviction that Herbert was a "truly remarkable human being" (Waluchow (2011b, p. 5). He not only recounted, in his own words, a story narrated by Nicola Lacey in her fascinating book about Hart's personal life, *i.e.*, the passage in which both Ronald Dworkin and Hart wanted to know each other's views and had Waluchow, somehow, as their intermediary (Lacey 2004, pp. 334–345), but also shared two further stories: one, on how Hart eventually replaced R.M. Hare, as his doctoral supervisor; and, the other, on how under a tight schedule, with Hart's help, he managed to finish his dissertation on time.

Waluchow insisted that there is much we can all learn from Hart, both as a legal philosopher and as a person. On the one hand, Hart's philosophy, philosophical approach, and his many contributions to legal philosophy and associated fields are and continue to be monumental. He indubitably "stands among the giants of 20th century philosophy of law" Waluchow (2011b, p. 9). Among the many lessons learned, he accentuates one, which I would like to highlight as one that I learned, directly from Waluchow—and so, indirectly from Hart—not only on how a word or even few words can mean so much, but also on how the context of utterance can make such a difference.

In Hart's voice: "[W]e must never take these [or any] words alone but consider whole sentences in which they play their characteristic role" Hart (1953/1983a, p. 26).[1] Furthermore, as Waluchow points out: "Hart suggested, we should always

[1] See also Hart (1953/1983a, p. 31): "[W]e should not... abstract words... from the sentences in which alone their full function can be seen".

bear in mind that one and the same word or sentence, used in one context, can play a very different role, and mean something quite different, in another" Waluchow (2011c, p. 365). In addition, Hart discerned three different recommendations in doing philosophy of law: (1) avoid the traditional, Aristotelian method of definition *per genus* and *differentia*; (2) evade any method of definition, if applied to singular words, because it is not likely to shed much light on a multi-faceted and somewhat puzzling phenomenon like law; and (3) keep in mind that one and the same word or string of words can be used to serve different functions or roles in different sentences. Briefly explained, "[W]e very much need to be sensitive to the *context of utterance* when attempting to build an understanding of a phenomenon like law by examining the words and concepts typically employed in its analysis and/or practice." As Waluchow clarified, we should always ask whether the assertions are made from what Hart famously referred as the "internal point of view" or the "external point of view" (Waluchow 2011c, p. 366).[2] Finally, he not only cautioned about "the importance of context of utterance and the attendant danger of attempting to understand words in isolation from the sentences in which they can be employed", but also "the importance of context and perspective when doing legal theory" (Waluchow (2011c, p. 367).

On the other hand, regarding Hart as a person, let me quote Waluchow at length (Waluchow 2011b, pp. 9–10):

> Herbert Hart was not only a talented, accomplished scholar. He was a kind, generous man who always made me feel like I counted both as a scholar and a person. When in his presence, I never once felt anything but complete support and understanding. Hart always conveyed his beliefs that my views on whatever issues we were discussing were worth considering even though he was the master and I the student. I also learned, from Hart—and in a different way, Hare—how a few words can mean so very much, one way or the other, to a person struggling to make his mark in the world. Had I not had the great fortune of receiving Hart's letter after my meeting with Hare, I might never had gone on in philosophy and enjoy whatever meager success I have had as an academic. Had I not been so lucky as to have a supervisor who was willing to drop everything to help me meet an urgent deadline, I might never have finished my dissertation. These are the thoughts I entertain when I remember my supervisor and the pivotal role he played in helping to make me the scholar and person I am today. These are the thoughts I endeavour to keep firmly in mind when, in dealing with my own graduate students, I struggle to meet the very high standard he set for me. Thank you, Herbert.

Although I was neither a formal student nor a supervisee of Wil, I completely relate to him and his words. Somehow, I am a first-hand witness (as an insider and participant) of the relationship with his students without being one—or at least without realizing so (as an outsider and observer). Hence, I can make *mutatis mutando* his words my own to refer to him as "a talented, accomplished scholar", "a kind, generous man", and "a truly remarkable human being", who, in trying to meet the very high standard that Hart set for him, has raised the bar even higher for

---

[2] See also: Hart (1961, pp. 86–88; 1994, pp. 89–91).

everyone else, by taking under his wings many graduate students and junior colleagues, included myself. *Noblesse obliges!*

2 The Nature of Law and Judicial Discretion: Inclusive Legal Positivism

> [T]he rule of recognition may incorporate as criteria of legal validity conformity with moral principles or substantive values.
> H.L.A. Hart (1994, 250)

Waluchow's *Inclusive Legal Positivism*, which is both the title of a book and of a very influential account on the nature of law, was originated in his doctoral dissertation. In his own voice: "I attempted to defend Hartian positivism, against Dworkin's powerful critique" (Waluchow (2011b, p. 4), which was intended to debunk it as "the ruling theory of law" (Dworkin 1977a/1978, p. vi). Waluchow claimed that Hart's positivism was not "restricted to content-neutral, "pedigree" tests of legal validity" and that Hart's rule of recognition "can easily accommodate conformity with a set of moral values and/or principles as necessary condition of legal validity, something that Hart himself acknowledged in a variety of places, and which he later confirmed in his *Postscript* to *The Concept of Law*" (Waluchow 2011b, p. 6).

For that purpose, Waluchow—in a footnote—first quotes Hart's celebrated Oliver Wendell Holmes Jr. lecture "Positivism and the Separation of Law and Morals": "Bentham indeed recognized, as Austin did not, that even the supreme legislative power *might* be subjected to legal restraints by a constitution and would not have denied that moral principles, like those of the fifth amendment, *might* form the content of such legal constitutional restraints" (Hart 1958, p. 599; emphasis added); later, Hart's recognized classic *The Concept of Law*: "In *some* systems [of law], as in the United States, the ultimate criteria of validity explicitly incorporate principles of justice or substantive moral values" (Hart 1961, p. 199/1994, p. 204; emphasis added); and, finally, the renowned *Postscript*: "[T]he rule of recognition *may* incorporate as criteria of legal validity conformity with moral principles or substantive values" Hart (1961/1994, p. 250; emphasis added).

The problem is that Hart's remarks—by using words like *may*, *might*, or *some*—fail to accommodate conformity with a set of moral values and/or principles as a necessary condition of legal validity. This argument, in my opinion, falls short of acknowledging anything other than a mere contingency. From my perspective, all legal systems—in one way or another—necessarily do incorporate, include, or even integrate references to morality, *i.e.*, to what humankind as a whole or at least to what a community considers to be encouraged and discouraged, by providing a justification for granting certain permissions or establishing such prohibitions. The fact that those references are sometimes complete and explicit and other times incomplete and implicit does not cancel such incorporation, inclusion or even integration.

Consider, for instance, the taking clause, which in the case of The United States of America's Constitution requires a "fair compensation", whereas in the Mexico's Constitution it merely states "compensation". Does the latter formulation allow for an "unfair compensation", or the compensation must be "fair" to amount as a true compensation, even if it did not expressly say so? Bear in mind that according to the Merriam-Webster dictionary the word *compensation* implies the "act of compensating, *i.e.*, the state of being compensated", and *compensate* has two main meanings: 1. "to provide something good as a balance against something bad or undesirable: to make up for some defect or weakness"; and 2. "to give money or something else of value to (someone) in return for something (such as work) or as payment for something lost, damaged, etc". In that sense, even if it does not explicitly say "fair" compensation, it must make up for the loss or damage suffered, in a proportionate way to the affectation (Flores 2009a, pp. 99–100).

In what follows, I would like to critically revisit Hart's influential views on judicial discretion (Hart 1961, pp. 138–44/1994, pp. 141–7, 252–4; 2013), through Waluchow's lenses in two of his early writings: (1) "Strong Discretion" (Waluchow 1983); and (2) "Hart, Legal Rules and Palm Tree Justice" (Waluchow 1985a). He began "Strong Discretion" by affirming (Waluchow 1983, p. 321):

> Most legal philosophers and scholars seem to follow Professor H.L.A. Hart in suggesting that judicial discretion is an unavoidable feature of legal systems; that there are "hard cases" where the law "runs out" and the judge must appeal to (e.g.) community standards of morality to decide the issues left unresolved by the law. Hart goes so far as to argue that recourse to this kind of discretion is not a necessary evil, but rather something which we should cherish. [...]

So judicial discretion is viewed by Hart as a highly desirable means of achieving flexibility and rationality in the law.

Immediately after, Waluchow said: "Dworkin disagrees." Before exploring the extent—or not—of the disagreement, let me bring to your attention not only to the lines that Waluchow quoted from Hart—in between the two parts reproduced above—but also its relevance to his thought, in general, and to his "living tree constitutionalism", in particular. In the quote, Hart—according to Waluchow—submits that viable legal systems must: (Hart 1961, p. 127/1994, p. 130)

> [C]ompromise between two social needs: the need for certain rules which can, over great areas of conduct, safely be applied by private individuals to themselves without fresh official guidance or weighing up of social issues, and the need to leave open, for later settlement by an informed official choice, issues which can only be properly appreciated and settled when they arise in a concrete case.

Later on, standing over the shoulders of Hart, Waluchow developed the following idea: "The living tree conception brings these two approaches together into a kind of common law understanding of Charters—one that seeks to combine both the relative fixity of entrenched written law and the relative adaptability [*i.e.*, flexibility] characteristic of the common law" (Waluchow 2007a, p. 183).[3] So far, it

[3] See also: Waluchow (2005, pp. 225–226) and Flores (2009b, pp. 45–46).

is clear that Hart not only "defended both the *necessity* and the *desirability* of judicial discretion" (Waluchow 1985a, p. 44), but also combined—as Waluchow and many other authors do—the needs for both fixity and flexibility.[4]

Thus, to what extent does Dworkin—or anyone else—disagree? As Waluchow acknowledges, Dworkin not only distinguished between *strong* and *weak* senses of discretion, but also identified three different senses of discretion: (1) as *judgment*[5]; (2) as *final authority*[6]; and (3) as *choice.*[7] Depending on the range of the standards and the kind of decisions they purport to control: "[If] the lieutenant had ordered the sergeant to take his five most experienced men on patrol", he does not have strong discretion, because that order purports to govern his decision, by requiring him to take the "five most experienced men on patrol". Whereas if the sergeant "has been told to pick any five members for patrol", he does have strong discretion, because the order does not purport to govern his decision, by allowing him to "pick any five members for patrol" (Dworkin 1977a/1978, p. 32). As Waluchow recognizes: "[T] here is no significant difference in saying that a standard purports to control a decision and that it actually does so." Really, "[t]he crucial question is whether the decision-maker is *entitled* to step beyond the relevant authoritative standards and to base his decision, in whole or in part, on non-authoritative standards. If the decision-maker is not entitled, his decision is *controlled* and he has no strong discretion" (Waluchow 1983, p. 329).

In short, if an authoritative standard that purports to control a decision succeeds in doing so, the decision-maker has no discretion in the strong sense. However, if it fails, then the decision-maker still has no discretion in the strong sense or at least is not entitled to step beyond the authoritative standards, although he acts as if he had discretion in the strong sense or exercises some form of it to base his decision retrospectively in what was a non-authoritative standard at that time. In Dworkin's voice: "[if a judge] makes new law and applies it retroactively in the case before him, then the losing party will be punished, not because he violated some duty he had, but rather a new duty created after the event" (Dworkin (1977a/1978, p. 84). What's more, Waluchow concedes: "Democratic theory loses in the process as well. If judges decide these "open" issues by weighing social aims which they think relevant and important, then they assume the role of the legislator—a role which ought, on

[4]See: Pound (1923/1946, p. 1; 1960, p. 23) and Cardozo (1921, 1924, p. 1). See also Flores (2009b, pp. 45–46).

[5]See: Dworkin (1977a/1978, p. 31): "Sometimes we use 'discretion' in a weak sense, simply to say that for some reason the standards an official must apply cannot be applied mechanically but demand the use of judgement."

[6]Dworkin (1977a/1978, p. 32): "Sometimes we use the term in a different weak sense, to say only that some official has final authority to make a decision and cannot be reviewed and reversed by any other official."

[7]Dworkin (1977a/1978, p. 32): "We use 'discretion' sometimes not merely to say that an official must use judgment in applying the standards set him by authority, or that no one will review that exercise if judgment, but to say that on some issue he is simply not bound by standards set by the authority in question."

traditional democratic theory, to be reserved for elected officials who, unlike the majority of judges, are responsible to the electorate. The judge should apply law, not make it" (Waluchow 1983, p. 322).[8]

Additionally, Dworkin is adamant in defending the one-right answer thesis (Flores 2015, pp. 181–185),[9] by arguing according to Waluchow that "neither mere uncertainty or disagreement on a legal question, nor the inability to demonstrate that one answer is right, entails that there is no right answer. It is just that an answer cannot be arrived at mechanically or easily, but requires the use of judgment, *i.e.*, *weak* discretion" (Waluchow 1983, p. 331). In other words, judges are neither entitled nor have strong discretion; even though sometimes they seem to exercise a strong discretion, it does not follow that they must do so, since they will be usurping a legislative function which corresponds to someone else. In conclusion, following Dworkin, "[S]trong discretion *need* not be exercised even if it is in fact sometimes exercised. Perhaps the judges should simply try a bit harder!" (Waluchow 1983, p. 336).

Let me clarify that Dworkin cannot—and in fact does not intend to—neglect that there are both strong and weak forms of discretion. His problem is with the characterization of judicial discretion in the strong sense as a matter of "choice". In short, he not only accepts judicial discretion, in the weaker sense, as "judgment" of pre-existing authoritative standards, but also rejects judicial discretion, in the stronger sense, as "choice" beyond them, *i.e.*, non-authoritative standards. The fact that those authoritative standards sometimes—or probably most of the time—are open textured and that other times their framers-drafters cannot anticipate all the fact-situations which will eventually emerge and seemingly left some issues unresolved is no reason to dismiss their authority or authoritativeness (Waluchow 2000). That is precisely the reason why, we can—as Dworkin does—agree with the necessity and desirability of judicial discretion, in the weak sense, and still disagree with the notion that the law "runs out", and so that the only option requires judicial discretion in the strong sense, as a matter of "choice". On the contrary, let me suggest that it is necessary "to interpret [law] and to interpret it is to show it in its best moral light" (Waluchow 2008b, p. 86).[10]

In what follows, I will suggest that the strong sense is neither necessary nor desirable, whereas the weak sense is necessary and desirable. For that purpose, let me turn to "Hart, Legal Rules and Palm Tree Justice",[11] where Waluchow defends

---

[8] See also: Bacon (1625/1994, p. 141): "Judges ought to remember that their office is *jus dicere*, and not *jus dare*; to interpret law, and not to make law, or give law."

[9] See also: Dworkin (1977b, p. 84): "[F]or all practical purposes, there will always be a right answer in the seamless web of our law"; and Dworkin (1977a/1978, p. 116): "The law may not be a seamless web; but the plaintiff is entitled to ask Hercules to treat it as if it were". For Waluchow's criticism of Dworkin's "Herculean Positivism", see: Waluchow (1985b).

[10] See: Flores (2013).

[11] By the by, the term "palm tree" seems to be pejorative, whereas "living tree" is not. There is nothing really against palm trees, which at the end are one form of living tree with roots (most commonly invisible underground), other than being too flexible and appearing simpler—a visible

both the necessity—due to the open texture of language—and desirability—due to the open-ended nature of aims—of judicial discretion. On the one hand, concerning the necessity of judicial discretion,[12] he starts by recalling that Hart not only contrasted two methods of communicating general standards of behavior: the inferior method of example and the superior method of language[13]; but also emphasized the "open texture of language" (Hart 1961, pp. 123, 124–5; 1994, pp. 126, 128):

> In all fields of experience, not only that of rules, there is a limit, inherent in the nature of language, to the guidance which general language can provide. There will indeed be plain cases constantly recurring in similar contexts to which general expressions are clearly applicable ('If anything is a vehicle a motor-car is one') but there will also be cases where it is not clear whether they apply or not. ('Does "vehicle" used here include bicycles, airplanes, roller skates?')...
>
> [...]
>
> [H]owever smoothly they work over the great mass of ordinary cases, will, at some point where their application is in question, prove indeterminate; they will have what has been termed an *open texture*... uncertainty at the borderline is the price to be paid for the use of general classifying terms in any form of communication concerning matters of fact.

Borrowing Hart's example of the rule prohibiting "vehicles" in the park, there are cases which fall into the "core of settled meaning", such as "fully operational motorcycles, Ford LTD's and Mac trucks are vehicles and are thus legally prohibited". However, there are certain things which do not fall within the "core" of the term "vehicle", such as "toy motorcars, motorized skateboards or "a shell of a car with a rusty engine, no gear box, a roof like a sieve, and several ties missing" [that] fall within what Hart terms the "penumbra of uncertainty", where there are respectable reasons both for and against their inclusion within the scope of the term" (Waluchow 1985a, p. 46). And so, according to Hart, we can choose either way, whereas for Dworkin it is still a matter of judgment, of the pre-existing authoritative standards, which interpretation is better, correct, or even the right one (Flores 2015).

According to Waluchow for penumbral cases: "Hart suggests, the rule's, and thus the law's, guidance runs out, and it is the judge who must choose whether to subsume the entity or fact-situation under the rule" (Waluchow 1985a, p. 46). Apparently, for Hart, if a specific rule's guidance runs out, the law's guidance runs out too, but that does not necessarily follow. It may follow either if law can be reduced to a specific rule (if that specific rule runs out, law will unavoidably run out as well) or if law can be reduced to a form of language (if language runs out, law will unavoidably run out as well) (Flores 2011, p. 156). Fortunately for us, law is more than any specific rule or a mere form of language, and as a complex institution, it does not run out; there is still much room to look for guidance, including as Hart pointed out, early, the "context of utterance" and, later, the "reference to purpose". In

trunk and few palms, with or without fruits, namely, coconuts—than other less flexible and more complex ones—with a visible trunk, branches, leaves, and even flowers or fruits. *Cfr.* Waluchow (2005, 2007a, 2007b, 2009b, and 2011a).

[12] Waluchow (1985a, b, p. 45): "it is necessary that judicial discretion exist in a legal system".

[13] *Cfr.* Waismann (1968).

short, the problem is that Hart jumps to the conclusion that it is a matter of choice, not of judgment, "even though it may not be arbitrary or irrational is in effect a choice" (Hart 1961, p. 124; 1994, p. 127), and will amount to the exercise of a strong legislative or quasi-legislative discretion (Waluchow 1985a, p. 47). For Dworkin, as Waluchow admits, it clearly does not follow from the thesis of open texture that judges have a strong legislative or quasi legislative discretion (Waluchow 1985a, p. 49).

On the other hand, considering the desirability of judicial discretion,[14] Waluchow reminds us that the argument begins "with the familiar premise that legislators cannot anticipate all the fact-situations to which the general rules they express might reasonably be thought to apply. Nevertheless they can, and probably do, anticipate certain clear and paradigm cases", such as the "operators of noisy automobiles taking Sunday drives through the public park. Their aim or intention is to prevent these occurrences by excluding such vehicles. But what of the *unanticipated* cases?" Waluchow (1985a, p. 53). In Hart's view, the aims and intentions are here indeterminate (Hart 1961, p. 126; 1994, p. 129):

> We have not settled, because we have not anticipated, the question which will be raised by the unenvisaged case when it occurs... When the unenvisaged case does arise, we confront the issues at stake and can then settle the question by choosing between the competing interests in the way which bests satisfies us. In doing so we shall have rendered more determinate our initial aim, and shall incidentally have settled a question as to the meaning, for the purposes of this rule, of a general word.

Although, we agree with Hart, as Waluchow puts it: "It is better... not be blindly predetermined and that the question of what is to be done be left to the informed discretion of the judges who can more fully appreciate and rationally settle it when it arises in a concrete case" (Waluchow 1985a, pp. 53–54). We disagree with him that: "[W]e should not cherish, even as an ideal, the conception of a rule so derailed that the question whether it applied or not to a particular case was always settled in advance, and never involved, at the point of application, a fresh choice between open alternatives" (Hart 1961, p. 125; 1994, p. 128). In a few words, the problem again is that Hart jumps to the conclusion that it is a matter of choice, not of judgment, and will amount—as already mentioned—to the exercise of a strong legislative or quasi-legislative discretion (Waluchow 1985a, p. 47). For Dworkin, as Waluchow would admit, it clearly does not follow from the thesis of open-ended nature of aims that a judge has strong legislative or quasi legislative discretion (Waluchow 1985a, p. 49).

Before moving to the following section, let me stress that Waluchow concludes this article by pointing out the vital differences between Hart's early "standard" position offered in both his Holmes' lecture and his *magna opera* Hart (1958, 1961/1994), and the later "altered" version presented in his entry for the *Encyclopedia of Philosophy* Hart (1967/1983b). In addition, Waluchow clarified from the start that his aim was not to show that Hart's "standard" view changed but that it should be changed in favor of the "altered" one (Waluchow 1985a, b, p. 42 fn 8).

[14] See Waluchow (1985a, p. 53): "judicial discretion is a highly desirable feature of legal systems".

On one side, following the "open texture of language", as well as the distinction between a "core of settled meaning" and the "penumbra of uncertainty", H.L.A. Hart pushed "formalism" to one vicious extreme and "rule skepticism", *i.e.*, "realism", to the other, and tried *a la* Aristotle to get hold of the virtuous middle for his position: determinacy in easy cases, which fall into the "core of settled meaning", and indeterminacy in hard cases, which fall into the "penumbra of uncertainty". On the other, following the criticisms of both Lon L. Fuller and Ronald Dworkin, the notion of "open texture" seems to have been replaced with the notion of "relative indeterminacy" (Waluchow 1985a, p. 68)[15] or "moderate indeterminacy" (Flores 2011). In Hart's voice (Hart 1967, p. 271/1983b, p. 106):

> The clear cases are those in which there is general agreement that they fall within the scope of a rule, and it is tempting to ascribe such agreement simply to the fact that there are necessarily such agreements in the shared conventions of language. But this would be an oversimplification because it does not allow for the special conventions of the legal use of words, which may diverge from their common use, or for the way in which the meaning of words may be clearly controlled by reference to the purpose of a statutory enactment which itself may be either explicitly stated or generally agreed.

Apropos Waluchow comments (Waluchow 1985a, pp. 68–69):

> So Hart (now) wishes to allow that the explicitly stated or generally agreed purpose of a rule can be used to determine whether a case clearly falls within its scope, and thus within the central element of settled law. On this account, even if the open texture of the terms used in the expression of a rule causes indeterminacy, this can sometimes be overcome by an appeal to other factors. If, for instance, it is clear that the obvious purpose of the rule would be satisfied only if the rule were taken not to apply in a penumbral case, then the rule *just might not* apply in that case. The law would provide full guidance despite open texture.

In fact, Hart seems to concede that "the meaning of words may clearly be controlled by reference to purpose"; this point was stressed originally by Fuller very early on, in his "Positivism and Fidelity to Law—A Reply to Professor Hart" (Fuller 1958, pp. 82–86): "[I]s it really ever possible to interpret a word in a statute without knowing the aim of the statute?" (Fuller 1958, pp. 82–86).[16] In his own words (Hart 1967, p. 271/ 1983b, p. 107):

> It is of crucial importance that cases for decision do not arise in a vacuum but in the course of the operation of a working body of rules, an operation in which a multiplicity of diverse considerations are continuously recognized as good reasons for a decision. These include a wide variety of individual and social interests, social and political aims, and standards of morality and justice; and they may be formulated in general terms as principles, policies, and standards. In some cases only one such consideration may be relevant, and it may determine decision as unambiguously as a determinate legal rule.

Notwithstanding, Hart's comeback in the "Postscript" regarding "judicial discretion" insists on judges having law-making powers and so "judicial legislation" (Hart 1961/ 1994, p. 272; emphasis in the original):

---

[15] *Cfr*. Hart (1983b, p. 104): "the relative indeterminacy of the rules or precedents to give effect to social aims, policies, and values."

[16] See also: Fuller (1949, pp. 625–626) and Flores (2016, pp. 421–422; and 2017, pp. 48–52).

> [I]n any legal system there will always be certain legally unregulated cases in which on some point no decision either way is dictated by the law and the law is accordingly partly indeterminate or incomplete. If in such cases the judge is to reach a decision and is not, as Bentham once advocated, to disclaim jurisdiction or to refer the points not regulated by the existing law to the legislature to decide, he must exercise his *discretion* and *make* law for the case instead of merely applying already pre-existing settled law. So in such legally unprovided-for or unregulated cases the judge both makes new law and applies the established law which both confers and constrains his law-making powers.

Hart further suggests—following Holmes—that such legislative powers are "interstitial" (Hart 1994, p. 273, emphasis in the original):

> It is important that the law-creating powers which I ascribe to the judge to regulate cases left partly unregulated by the law are different from those of the legislature: not only are the judge's powers subject to many constraints *narrowing his choice* from which a legislature may be quite free, but since the judge's power are exercised only to dispose of particular instant cases he cannot use these to introduce large-scale reforms or new codes. So his powers are *interstitial* as well as subject to many substantive constraints. None the less there will be points where the existing law fails to dictate any decision as the correct one, and to decide cases where this is so the judge must exercise his law-making powers.

Hart's insistence on the nature of such law-making powers as interstitial, but legislative still, gets him back over the shoulders of Holmes.[17] However, the fact of being interstitial does not cancel it being legislative. As you can imagine, my feeling is that by appealing to a form of discretion that equates "creative judicial activity" to "judicial legislation" or "judicial creation", Hart misses an important distinction, and we seem to be in danger of missing it too. The distinction that I have in mind—among judicial activities—is between "interpretative" and "inventive", which corresponds to a "weak" and "strong" forms of judicial discretion,[18] *i.e.*, between the weak discretion to interpret the existing law—and even implicit principles and aims or purposes—to be applied to the case at hand and the strong discretion to invent, *i.e.*, quasi-legislate or legislate, new law—or even to change the existing law.

After all, Hart acknowledged (Hart 1961/1994, p. 274):

> [J]udges do not just push away their law books and start to legislate without further guidance from the law. Very often, in deciding such cases, they cite some general principle or some general aim or purpose which some considerable relevant area of the existing law can be understood as exemplifying or advancing and which points towards a determinate answer for the instant hard case.

Reconsider Hart's "No vehicles in the park" example. Imagine that someday a boy, called Freddie, who only wants to learn how to ride his bicycle, comes into a park with it and is prevented from riding it by the park-keeper, who points out the

---

[17] Hart (1977/1983c, p. 128; quoting *Southern Pacific v. Jensen*, 244 U.S. 205, 221 (1917); Holmes, dissenting): "I recognize without hesitation that judges do and must legislate, but they can do so only interstitially; they are confined from 'molar to molecular motions'."

[18] See: Flores (2011, pp. 170–171). See also: Dworkin (1977a/1978, pp. 31–39 and 68–71; 1986, pp. 66–7; 2006, p. 15).

prohibition. Suppose that his mother, Mrs. Mercury, challenges the decision on his behalf and reaches a point where a judge with final authority must settle the dispute. The word "vehicles" is vague. Bicycles are typically included in vehicles, but it is unclear whether the prohibition incorporates bicycles or not. What is the judge expected to do? Is the judge expected to invent, quasi-legislate or legislate a (new) law or to change the (existing) law, acting as a legislator? Or is the judge expected to interpret the law, appealing not only to principles but also to aims and purposes? Alternately: Is the judge expected to exercise a strong legislative discretion to go either way? Or is the judge expected to exercise a weak interpretative discretion to remain guided in the quest for the solution to the case at hand? In my opinion, the judge is expected to exercise a weak interpretative discretion, appealing not only to principles but also to aims and purposes. In that sense, the prohibition can be said to be intended to protect the users of the park from certain forms of vehicles that might cause a danger to them. The question is whether a boy riding a bicycle endangers the rest of the park users or it is compatible with them. I believe that the judge will rule that the law is that a bicycle *per se* does not jeopardize them and, for that reason, the prohibition "No vehicles in the park" does not apply to bicycles (Flores 2011, pp. 171–172).

Taking the distinction seriously implies that judges, instead of exercising a strong inventive (or legislative) discretion pushing their law books aside, do—and if I may add must—exercise a weak interpretative discretion by appealing not only to principles but also to aims and purposes in the quest for further guidance. The problem I find with Hart's arguments —and his followers'—is that this "mean" position, *i.e.*, creative interpretation, in between the extremes represented by non-creative interpretation, *i.e.*, deductive, or mechanical application, and creative legislation, echoes his archenemy, as Hart himself acknowledged (Hart 1961/1994, pp. 274–275):

> This indeed is the very nucleus if the 'constructive interpretation' which is so prominent a feature of Dworkin' theory of adjudication. But though this procedure certainly defers, it does not eliminate the moment of judicial law-making, since in any hard case different principles supporting competing analogies may present themselves and a judge will often have to choose between them, relying like a conscientious legislator, on his sense of what it is best and not on any already established order of priorities prescribed for him by law. Only if for all such cases there was always to be found in the existing law some unique set of higher-order principles assigning relative weights or priorities to such competing lower-order principles, would the moment for judicial law-making be not merely deferred but eliminated.

As Waluchow advanced, Hart did not change his "standard" view on the subject-matter, but I concur with him that it should be changed in favor of the "altered" one. Anyway, regardless of changing his view or not, I am convinced that "there is good reason for abandoning [the standard view] in favour of [the] modified position" (Waluchow 1985a, p. 70). Especially, since the strong judicial discretion is incompatible with Waluchow's justification of charter review which embodies a form of weak judicial discretion.

3 The Justification of Charter Review: Living Tree Constitutionalism

> Human nature is not a machine to be built after a model, and set to do exactly the work prescribed for it, but a tree, which requires to grow and develop itself on all sides, according to the tendency of the inward forces which make it a living thing.

John Stuart Mill (1859/ 1989, p. 60).

As already advanced, I am fully convinced that the practice of judicial review is justifiable since it is neither merely compatible with our so called constitutional or liberal democracies, nor contingent, but necessary to further the community's constitutional morality and its true fundamental moral commitments. In this regard, Waluchow offers one of the best justifications and exemplifies it with the living tree metaphor.[19]

Waluchow began his article "Constitutions as Living Trees: An Idiot Defends" by setting the stage, advancing that he aims to defend the existence of Bills or Charters of Rights and the practices of judicial review to which they normally give rise against a variety of objections that have been made in both popular and academic discourse. In the process, he addressed the arguments of his strongest critic, namely Jeremy Waldron, who is prominent in providing the core of the case against Charters and their enforcement by judges, as well as arguing for the "dignity of legislation" and the "circumstances of politics" (Waluchow 2005, p. 207).[20]

In a nutshell, while advocates, such as Ronald Dworkin, Samuel Freeman, and John Rawls, among others, argue that the role that Charters play is one of providing a (more or less) stable, fixed point of agreement on and pre-commitment to moral limits to government power, *i.e.*, moral rights upon which valid government action may not infringe; Waldron challenged (a) the very *intelligibility* of this fixed point conception of Charters; (b) the moral and political *desirability* of attempting to have them play the assigned role; and (c) the various *arguments* and *analogies* put forward in defense of (b) (Waluchow 2005, p. 208).

As we will see, instead of attempting to discover such a fixed point, Waluchow advances that Charters represent a "mixture of only very modest precommitment combined with a considerable measure of humility. The latter stems from recognition that we do not in fact have all the answers when it comes to moral rights, and that we should do all we can to ensure that our moral short sightedness does not, in the circumstances of politics, lead to morally questionable government action" (Waluchow 2005, p. 210).

According to Waluchow, Waldron thinks that there is a "deep inconsistency" in the very idea of Charters: on the one hand, considering people as responsible moral

---

[19] See: Waluchow (2007a). For the original sketch of the arguments, see: Waluchow (2005) and for the summary of the book, see: Waluchow (2007b). Along with others, I had the opportunity of commenting it in a book symposium published in *Problema* 3, see: Flores (2009b), which included a reply to his critics, *vid.* also Waluchow (2009b).

[20] *Cfr.* Waldron (1999a, b, 2006).

agents fully capable of pursuing their own conceptions of the good life on an ongoing basis and participating in democratic politics, by electing accountable legislators, empowered to make decisions on their behalf; on the other hand, viewing them as predators, unable to constrain themselves and hence to exercise their rights responsibly without undermining the rights of others.

In sum, Waldron contests not only the intelligibility and desirability of Charter constraint of democratic power and the saving grace of judges, who, according to him, are neither elected nor accountable, but also the suitability of the metaphor of Ulysses tying himself to the mast to avoid the enchanting music and singing voice of the sirens, luring him to shipwreck into the cliff. Although, as he points out: "[E]ven if there is an objectively right answer to the question of what rights we have, still people disagree implacably about what the right answer is" (Waldron 1999a, p. 244)[21]; and so, as Waluchow puts it (Waluchow 2005, p. 217):

> Yet if we cannot agree on the rights we have, let alone what these entail for the questions of law and public policy which Charters being to the fore, then it is sheer folly to believe that we—and this includes judges—could ever agree on what a Charter's provisions mean and on the limits they supposedly impose on legislative and executive power. And if we cannot agree on the limits established by a Charter, we can hardly pre-commit to them. We cannot tie ourselves to the mast of entrenched moral rights, if we cannot locate the mast, let alone agree on what it might look like.

In Waldron's words: "My theme in all this is reasonable disagreement, but I cannot restrain myself from saying that anyone who thinks a narrative like this is appropriately modeled by the story of Ulysses and the sirens is an idiot" (Waldron 1999a, p. 268). Notwithstanding, Waluchow insists not only on the desirability—and even necessity—of charters, judges, and rights, but also on the intelligibility of the Ulysses' metaphor, despite both the existence of deep disagreements about many concrete implications of Charter rights and the fact of running the risk of being labelled as an idiot himself.

Waluchow comes aptly with an alternative conception to cope with the sheer fact of our pervasive reasonable disagreements: "Only an idiot would think that we can intelligibly pre-commit to limits upon which we cannot agree in advance. At best we can pre-commit to a practice which licenses other people, viz., judges, to make our

[21] See: Waluchow (2013, pp. 203–204): "Even if there is a truth of the matter with respect to the important questions of political morality that concern us in liberal democracies, to a very large extent, it seems, that truth is epistemically inaccessible to us. And if it's epistemically inaccessible to us, we have no way of discovering which, among the various reasonable answers offered to the questions posed, are correct or more justified. No way of telling who has it right or whose answer is best—or even better." *Cfr.* Dworkin (2011, p. 91): "But the default thesis is patently, mistaken, because it confuses two different positions—uncertainty and indeterminacy—that it is essential to distinguish… But in all these respects indeterminacy differs from uncertainty. "I am uncertain whether the proposition in question is true or false" is plainly consistent with "it is one or the other," but "The proposition in question is neither true nor false" is not. Once uncertainty is taken into account, in some such way, then the default thesis of indeterminacy collapses, because if one of these alternatives—uncertainty—holds by default, then indeterminacy, which is very different, cannot."

decisions for us on issues and questions upon which we ourselves cannot reach agreement" (Waluchow 2005, pp. 220–221). For that purpose, he opts—as we already pointed out—for the living tree metaphor, which I have traced all the way back to John Stuart Mill's *On Liberty*,[22] but had not been popularized until recent years.[23]

Nevertheless, Waluchow recalls that in *Edwards v. Attorney-General of Canada*,[24] which is a landmark Canadian constitutional law case, decided by the Judicial Committee of the United Kingdom's Privy Council in 1929 and now commonly referred to as "The Persons Case", Lord Sankey acknowledged[25]:

> The British North America Act planted in Canada *a living tree capable of growth and expansion within its natural limits*. The object of the Act was to grant a Constitution to Canada. "Like all written constitutions it has been subject to development through usage and convention". [...]
>
> Their Lordships do not conceive it to be the duty of this Board—it is certainly not their desire—to cut down the provisions of the Act by a narrow and technical construction, but rather to give it a large and liberal interpretation so that the Dominion to a great extent, but *within certain limits*, may be mistress in her own house.

Immediately after, Waluchow proceeded to flesh out the metaphor by suggesting that a Charter need not be viewed as attempting to establish definite and stable fixed points of agreement and pre-commitment, but as planting a "living tree", which provides both the necessary fixity to serve its guidance function, and flexibility to adapt—or even adjust—it in the future, *i.e.*, it is to some extent stable, and so to some extent capable of growth and expansion within its natural limits: "Flexibility must be balanced with certainty. The future must, to the extent foreseeably possible, be accommodated to the present."[26] The institutional or structural design will require, practically by definition, that someone establishes certain limits, but that does not necessarily mean the abandonment of "the rule of law by providing its judges with unbridled discretion" (Waluchow 2005, p. 229).

As Waluchow acknowledges: Dworkin's theory of constitutional law and interpretation has met many similar objections, *i.e.*, that his "moral reading" grants judges unbridled power to decide constitutional cases according to their own moral lights, but these criticisms "either ignore or seriously underplay the dimension of "fit" in

---

[22] See: Mill (1859/1989, p. 60): "Human nature is not a machine to be built after a model, and set to do exactly the work prescribed for it, but a tree, which requires to grow and develop itself on all sides, according to the tendency of the inward forces which make it a living thing."

[23] On the notion of a constitution as a living entity, *vid.* Beard (1936) and *vid.* also Ackerman (2007), Balkin (2011), Flores (2009b, 2017), Kavanagh (2003), Rehnquist (1976), Sager (1990) and Waluchow (2007a).

[24] *Edwards v. Canada* (Att'y Gral.), [1930] A.C. 124.

[25] *Ibid.*, 136 (quoting Robert Borden) (the emphasis is mine). See: Waluchow (2005, p. 222) and for a more detailed discussion of "The Persons Case", see also: Waluchow (2011a, pp. 105–109).

[26] Waluchow (2011a, p. 1017) (quoting *Law Soc'y of Upper Can. v. Skapinker*, [1984] S.C.R. 357 (Can.)).

Dworkin's account" (Waluchow 2005, pp. 229–230, fn 53). In Dworkin's voice (Dworkin 1996, p. 10)[27]:

> [C]onstitutional interpretation is disciplined, under the moral reading... Judges may not read their own convictions into the Constitution. They may not read the abstract moral clauses as expressing any particular moral judgment, no matter how much that judgment appeals to them, unless they find it consistent in principle with the structural design of the Constitution as a whole, and also with the dominant lines of past constitutional interpretation by other judges. They must regard themselves as partners with other officials, past and future, who together elaborate a coherent constitutional morality, and they must take care to see that what they contribute fits with the rest. (I have elsewhere said that judges are like authors jointly creating a chain novel in which each writes a chapter that makes sense as a whole.)

Following Dworkin, Waluchow advances that he will develop a conception of a "community's constitutional morality", which avoids both extremes, on one side, too much fixity to the extent that one is ruled by the "dead hand of the past", and, on the other, too much flexibility to the extent that law neither provides certainty nor serves its guidance function. What's more, he encouraged substituting the "hubristic message"—suggesting that we do know which moral rights count, why they count, and the many complex ways they count in the myriad circumstances of politics—with a more "humble message" (Waluchow 2005, pp. 235–236):

> We do *not* know, with certainty, which moral rights count, why they count, and in what ways and to what degree they count in the myriad circumstances of politics. What we do know, however, is the following. We know that the constellation of moral rights chosen for inclusion in our Charter constitutes, at least for the time being, a *reasonable* answer to the question of which moral rights deserve constitutional protection against governmental power. We further know that a reasonable answer to the question of why we should choose these and not some other collection of rights is that the chosen set contributes, in ways consistent with (though certainly not determined by) the demands of reason and morality, to the workings of a reasonably free and democratic society which aspires to respect its members as rights bearers deserving of equal concern and respect. We further know that we are somewhat in the dark concerning the many concrete questions of rights which will inevitably, and in unforeseen ways, come to the fore when government power is exercised, principally, though not exclusively, through the introduction of general legislation. Although we do not know in advance what these questions will be or how they should be answered, we commit ourselves to asking them, and to acting on the answers arrived at by the relevant Court(s) in whose hands we agree to place the decision.

Afterwards, Waluchow presents the case for judicial review. As he had already advanced, Waldron's critique is based on the premise that there is "disagreement all the way down", but it cannot go all the way down: "Something must be presupposed, something must be given before we can begin to reason about the world and what we can know of it" (Waluchow 2005, p. 241).[28] Certainly, "There is considerable

[27] See: Dworkin (1985, p. 158; 1986, 228).

[28] See also: Waluchow (2008a, p. 69): "But sometimes these disagreements are not as deep as might appear at first blush. A society that differs in many of its surface moral opinions is often one in which there is considerably more agreement than initially meets the eye—even if these are agreements that are "incompletely theorized," and even if they emerge only after an attempt has been made to reconcile conflicting moral views." *Cfr.* Sunstein (1996).

plausibility in the suggestion that we should turn to judges to help us avoid the injustice and lack of wisdom of permitting unfettered stable or transient majorities to determine whether the government acts they support unjustifiably infringe important minority interests and rights, contestable as these might be" (Waluchow 2005, p. 239). Finally, he concludes that living trees have fixed roots, but whose branches can develop over time, reconciling our self-image as self-governing, autonomous rights holders who, unfortunately, do not have all the answers (Waluchow 2005, p. 247; 2007b, p. 139).

Since we—as individuals—do not have all the answers, we must turn to someone or something else, such as judges or courts, and the community's constitutional morality (CCM). Waluchow develops this idea in *A Common Law Theory of Judicial Review. The Living Tree* and in a chapter following its publication Waluchow (2007a, pp. 226–227; 2008a, pp. 76–77). He not only distinguishes between two conceptions of morality, one as "positive morality" and the other as "critical morality", but also adds two further conceptions, one as "personal morality" and the other as "community's morality" (a form of "political morality") (Waluchow 2008a, pp. 65–67; 67–70). In doing so, he recalled first the popular complaint: "Judges engaged in judicial review under a bill of rights are granted far too much licence to impose their own subjective moral views on the community and its democratic representatives" Waluchow (2008a, p. 67). And, secondly, he made explicit: "In saying that judicial review results in a judge substituting her own personal morality for those of the community and / or its representatives, one implies that there is a morality (or at the very least a set of moral beliefs) that can be ascribed to the community and which the judge's decision displaces" (Waluchow 2008a, pp. 67–68).

He introduces a further distinction between mere *moral opinions* and *true moral commitments* and, with a little help from "something like" John Rawls' "reflective equilibrium", and insists that there is an *ongoing* "requirement of reflective equilibrium" (RRE), which is a necessary condition of responsible moral decision making (Waluchow 2008a, pp. 72–73).[29] This is due to two important facts: "(a) that our moral opinions almost never square exactly with our true moral commitments; and (b) that the latter are not always consistent with one another and can sometimes change over time as new facts and circumstances are brought to light" (Waluchow 2008a, p. 73).

Furthermore, he reiterates: "[A] community's constitutional morality is not the personal morality of any particular person or institution. Nor is it the morality decreed by God, inherent in the fabric of the universe, or discernible via the exercise of pure practical reason. Rather, it consists of the moral norms and convictions to which the community has actually committed itself" (Waluchow 2008a, p. 77).[30] In

---

[29] See: Rawls (1971, pp. 20–21, 48–51; and 1999, pp. 18–19, 42–45).

[30] See: Waluchow (2011a, p. 1036): "CCM is not the impoverished positive morality... That is, is not a function of simple consensus on some moral question... Neither is it the personal morality, consisting of a set of general norms and particular moral judgments and opinions attributable to any

that sense, "In ruling against a government action, (for example, a statute or judicial ruling) that has the support of popular moral opinion, judges may not be acting undemocratically because they might, in fact, be *enforcing*, not *thwarting*, the community's very own constitutional morality" (Waluchow 2008a, p. 80). Waluchow concludes by turning the tables on the critics: "Judicial review may not only be consistent with democracy, it may well be, in the circumstances in which we find ourselves, one of its requirements" (Waluchow 2008a, p. 92).

In an article engaging with David Strauss's book (Strauss 2010), which embraces both living tree constitutionalism and purposive interpretation, Waluchow suggests that it does not deal adequately with the "apparent undemocratic nature of living tree constitutionalism and, in particular, the practices of charter review and interpretation with which it has come to be associated" (Waluchow 2011a, p. 1004). In that sense, he reiterates that the living tree constitutionalism need not to conflict with the fundamental principles of democracy, and recaps the democratic challenge comes in two distinct forms (Waluchow 2011a, p. 1029):

> First, there is the dead-hand concern ... that an entrenched constitutional charter ties the people now to strictly to decisions made by the people then. This will be referred as "the intergenerational problem." Second, there is the no less worrisome concern that, in adopting a constitutional charter, we assign unelected, [un]accountable judges unbridled discretion in the task of interpreting and applying what are, in effect open ended provisions. It assigns judges, not the people *then*, let alone the people *now*, the essentially unrestrained task of answering our most fundamental moral and political questions for us. Let this be called "the discretion problem."

Waluchow indicates that living constitutionalism provides a successful answer to the first prong of the dilemma, *i.e.*, "the intergenerational problem",[31] but concedes that it is not clear whether and how it dealt with the second one, *i.e.*, "the discretion problem".[32] He proceeds to recapitulate that living constitutionalism revolves around four basic claims:

---

specific person or institution... Nor is the morality decreed by God, inherent in the fabric of the universe or residing in Plato's world of forms. Rather, it is a kind of community-based, positive morality consisting of the fundamental moral norms and convictions to which the community has actually committed itself and which have, in one way or another, acquired some kind of formal constitutional recognition. It is the political morality actually embedded in—or endorsed or expressed by—a community's constitutional practices". See also Waluchow (2013, p. 205; [2015, 34]): "CCM is not the personal morality of any particular person or institution... Nor is the morality decreed by God, inherent in the fabric of the universe or residing in Plato's world of forms. Rather, it is a kind of community-based, positive morality consisting of the fundamental moral norms and convictions to which the community has actually committed itself and which have, in one way or another, acquired some kind of formal legal [constitutional] recognition. It is the political morality actually embedded in—or endorsed or expressed by—a community's legal [constitutional] practices".

[31] See Waluchow (2011a, p. 1028): "Instead of being slaves to a king or despot, we become slaves to previous generations and their specific moral and political views."

[32] See Waluchow (2011a, p. 1031): "Instead of being slaves to previous generations with their own distinctive... perspectives on certain important moral and political questions, we now seem to be slaves to democratically unaccountable philosophers kings, who drape themselves in judicial robes

- [A] constitution is an instrument with abstract moral provisions that can grow and adapt to its ever-changing environment—moral, social, and political—without losing its identity and guidance function;
- [A] constitution's abstract provisions *should* be allowed to grow and adapt to its—or their—environment(s);
- [T]his process can take place through genuine constitutional interpretation, not construction or formal amendment; and
- [T]his growth process facilitated by interpretation can occur legitimately.

Bear in mind that Waluchow believes that though this process of determining the contours of the living constitution both can be and is undertaken by actors outside of courts, the leading players are invariably the judges who are called on to provide authoritative answers to constitutional questions in highly controversial cases (Waluchow 2011a, p. 1002).[33] I concur with him that it is not necessary "to transform the judicial task into something significantly different from the role judges have traditionally been thought to serve: namely, making a good faith attempt to engage in the impartial application of binding legal standards created by way of democratically respectable processes, that is, to play the role they are often called on to play in countless every day, run-of-the-mill legal cases." Additionally, judges in charter cases are "seeking to hold the democratic community to its own constitutionally grounded, stable, and reflective moral commitments, and if, in addition to this, that set of commitments can often be discovered through a kind of morally neutral, impartial reasoning, then the sting of the democratic challenge can largely be avoided." What's more (Waluchow 2011a, pp. 1038–1039):

> Judges are not being asked to decide on the basis of their own best, discretionary judgments concerning the demands of Platonic moral truth. They are being asked to decide on the basis of what is, in effect, their own best judgments as to the democratic community's best judgments concerning the demands of Platonic moral truth. Judges can be said, in such circumstances, to be doing nothing more contentious than trying their best to apply, in a fair, impartial manner, standards that originate from an entirely legitimate source—namely, the community's own fundamental moral commitments.

Certainly, "Judges should and creatively develop or construct the norms of CCM in an incremental, case-by-case way, in much the same manner as common law judges" (Waluchow 2011a, p. 1040; 2013, p. 209). Moreover, this methodology is neither exclusive to common law jurisdictions nor implies strong discretion.[34] Allow me to clarify. If judges are forced to engage in the strong discretionary creation of norms, not their neutral and impartial application in a weaker discretionary form, it will

and set about issuing sober moral pronouncements from the bench, all the while making it appear as though they are doing nothing more than interpreting norms created and endorsed by others with the acknowledge authority to do so."

[33] See: Rawls (1993/1996, pp. 235–240) and Dworkin (1985, pp. 33–71).

[34] See: Flores (2009b, pp. 54–62). See also: Scalia (1997, p. 8): "[T]he common law grew in a peculiar fashion—rather like a Scrabble board. No rule of decision previously announced could be *erased*, but qualifications could be *added* to it."

amount to an exercise of discretion as a matter of choice, not of judgement, which indeed renders it vulnerable to the democratic challenge. However, if judges exercise discretion in a weak form, as a matter of judgement, not choice, *i.e.*, as a matter of interpretation, not invention, they are not vulnerable to such challenge, since they will be enforcing the pre-existing law, neither creating nor reforming the existing one.

As we have already seen, Waluchow defends both the necessity—due to the open texture of language—and desirability—due to the open-ended nature of aims—of judicial discretion. Moreover, by appealing to Rawls's idea of public reason, he tilts—or at least seems to tilt—the balance in favour of judgement, *i.e.*, weak discretion: "The discretionary decisions judges are sometimes called on to make will be consistent with democratic principles because they appeal to reasons that no reasonable dissenter within the democratic community could object to, given the duty of civility to which all members of a democratic community who find themselves in a state of reasonable moral pluralism are committed" (Waluchow 2011a, p. 1043).[35] Moreover, "[J]udges, in deciding cases under the moral provisions of a bill of rights, are, in fact, helping to shape and render more determinate the very content of constitutional morality. Legal judgments under those provisions are not to be starkly contrasted with or separated from judgments of the community's constitutional morality" (Waluchow 2008a, p. 83).

However, Waluchow seems to concede that given the facts of reasonable pluralism, many of us will inevitably disagree with the moral bases upon which the judges' decisions are made. Yet, "[T]he principal role of a judge is not to adjudicate on the basis of his or her own convictions in regard to issues of political morality ... but to hold the community to its own fundamental moral commitments on such matters" (Waluchow 2013, p. 205). Furthermore, he adds: "[T]he role of the judge is to engage—or at the very least make a good faith attempt to engage—in the impartial, neutral application of binding legal standards" (Waluchow 2013, p. 207). Hence, "Judges are not ... being asked to decide on the basis of *their own* best judgments concerning the demands of moral truth. Rather they are being asked to decide on the basis of their best judgments as to the *democratic community's* best judgments concerning the demands of moral truth." As Waluchow acknowledges: On the one hand, "Judges can be said, in such circumstances, to be doing nothing more contentious than doing their best to *apply* ... standards that originate from an entirely legitimate source, namely, the community's own fundamental moral beliefs and commitments". And, on the other, "[t]hat the norms of CCM can be largely discovered via a process of reasoning that can plausibly be described as 'impartial'

[35] See also: Waluchow (2011a, p. 1044). "Judges who make a decision after a sincere attempt to offer justification in terms of CCM or, failing that, in terms of a CCM construction justified by way of some reasonable balance of relevant public reasons, need not be viewed as an alien force compelling democratic citizens to act independently of their deepest convictions. Rather, the decision should be viewed by each and every member of the democratic community as an exercise of public power to which none of them, reasonable dissenters included, can reasonably object, given their joint commitment to the duty of civility."

and 'morally neutral' is also, of course, a highly contentious claim" (Waluchow 2013, p. 208).

Notwithstanding, Waluchow—following both Ronald Dworkin and Joseph Raz—argues that it is truly possible to respond to these contentious claims (Waluchow 2015, pp. 25–26). How come? To put interpretations in their best moral light by appealing to first-order moral judgements, judges need not to do it from their own perspective, but from the democratic community's point of view[36]:

> [I]n pursuing what Dworkin calls "constructive interpretation" of constitutional rights, judges need not aim to put objects of their interpretations in their best moral light, *as viewed from the perspective of the judges' own*, first-order moral judgments. Rather, following Raz, we can say that judges both can and characteristically attempt to do so *from the perspective of the democratic community and its first-order moral judgments.*

On one side, he finally accepts that "interpreters must exercise *judgment* in fashioning their interpretive theories. Dworkin goes so far as to suggest that in a mature legal system there almost always will be a best constitutional theory, and judges (and legislators) can sensibly be charged with the duty to try their best to discern and implement its requirements in making their authoritative decisions" (Waluchow 2015, pp. 28–29).[37] On the other, certainly, following Raz's addition of a third alternative to the internal (committed) and external (detached) points of view distinction, namely the internal but detached normative statements and perspectives, Waluchow affirms: "An instructive way of viewing Dworkin's fit condition... is to see that constructive interpretation be undertaken, not from the point of view of the interpreter and her own first-order moral beliefs, but from the point of view of a particular community with its own distinctive history of decisions and commitments" (Waluchow 2015, p. 43).

In my opinion, it is plausible that the interpreters' best judgement be detached from their own first-order moral beliefs and, hence, morally neutral. However, their decision, as any authoritative statement, by appealing to the best judgement of the community's constitutional morality and its first-order moral beliefs, although detached from their own, cannot be completely detached; it must be committed to something, namely, the community's constitutional morality. Waluchow sums up his paper (Waluchow 2015, pp. 49–50):

> After arguing that constructive interpretation, which necessarily aims to place its object in its best moral light, can be undertaken from a point of view other than that of the interpreter [*i.e.*, from the perspective of the community], I went on to argue for the following claims: (1) Constitutional interpretation and review can be undertaken from the point of view of the democratic community and its CCM commitments; (2) This process can be undertaken by a judge without the deliberate intrusion of her own, first-order moral convictions; (3) When undertaken from this point of view, constitutional interpretation and review can be rendered consistent with democracy; and (4) This I so even when these activities require a good deal of substantive moral reasoning and argument on the part of judges.

---

[36] See: Dworkin (1986, pp. 52–53) and Raz (1979, pp. 153–157).

[37] See also: Dworkin (1977a, b/1978, pp. 286–290).

4 Conclusion

-She thinks I was an idiot to trust you. A lot of people seem to think that actually.
-I am about to stock into a room with the most murderous woman in the world, who's already has tried to kill me twice, that I know of. Who is an idiot?
-I suppose we should say goodbye, one idiot to another.
Exchange between Jaime Lannister and Tyrion Lannister,
The Game of Thrones, Season 7, Episode 7 (2017).

To conclude, I would like to make explicit that I am still critic of Waluchow's inclusive legal positivism (cfr. Dickson 2001, Giudice 2015), but since I fully endorse his living tree constitutionalism, I also can be labelled as an idiot. And so, my contribution can be read as "A homage from one idiot to another". Finally, allow me to share a personal anecdote. In 2011, I was honoured and humbled by the invitation to deliver a keynote address dedicated to honouring the 50th anniversary of H.L.A. Hart's *The Concept of Law*, as part of "*Primeras Jornadas Internacionales de Filosofía del Derecho*", hosted by *Universidad Francisco Marroquín*, in Guatemala. To finalize my remarks, I decided to quote some lines from the personal introductory note that Waluchow had just submitted, to be included in the volume that Jorge Fabra and myself were editing for *Problema.* While I was reading it out loud, my voice started to break, but I managed to close my speech. Since Juan Vega had to comment on my address, as I descended from the stage, our paths crossed on his way up. At the same time of congratulating me, he was also asking:—"Are you okay?"—"Yes."—"Were you about to cry?"—"Y-e-s. . ." With tears in my eyes, I shared my insight: "I've just realized how fortunate we are. W.J. Waluchow is the H.L.A. Hart for many of us in our generation". Thank you, Wil, my good friend, and great inspiration! Cheers!

Acknowledgments I want to thank: Thomas Bustamante, for an exhaustive revision and edition of my chapter; Alexia Michelle Araujo, Antonio Rojas Benítez, Rene Hernández, Edgardo Ocampo, and Rubén Rivera, for helpful research assistance; Matthew Bifano, Víctor Castañeda, Kenneth E. Himma, and Yanara Suenaga, for comments and critiques on the previous versions; a couple of anonymous reviewers, for their observations and suggestions; and, finally, Wilfrid J. Waluchow, for providing "The stuff that dreams are made of".[38]

References

Ackerman, Bruce. 2007. The living constitution. *Harvard Law Review* 120: 1737.
Bacon, F. 1625/1994. Essays. London: Everyman.
Balkin, Jack. 2011. *Living Originalism.* Cambridge: Harvard University Press.
Beard, Charles A. 1936. The living constitution. *Annals of the Aeicab Association of Political Science* 185: 29.

[38] *The Maltese Falcon* (John Huston, 1941 film, screen play based upon the novel by Dashiell Hammett, 1930). *Cfr.* Carly Simon, "The Stuff that Dreams are Made of" (1987 song).

Cardozo, Benjamin. 1921. *The nature of the judicial process*. New Haven: Yale University Press.

———. 1924. *The growth of the law*. New Haven: Yale University Press.

Dickson, Julie. 2001. *Evaluation and legal theory*. Oxford: Hart Publishing.

Dworkin, Ronald. 1977a. *Taking rights seriously*. Cambridge: Harvard University Press. (there is 2nd ed. with a "Reply to Critics": 1978).

———. 1977b. No right answer? In *Law, morality and society: Essays in honour of H.L.A. Hart*, ed. P.S. Hacker and J. Raz. Oxford: Oxford University Press.

———. 1985. *A matter of principle*. Cambridge: Harvard University Press.

———. 1986. *Law's empire*. Cambridge: Harvard University Press.

———. 1996. *Freedom's law. The moral reading of the American constitution*. Cambridge: Harvard University Press.

———. 2006. *Justice in robes*. Cambridge: Harvard University Press.

———. 2011. *Justice for Hedgehogs*. Cambridge: Harvard university press.

Flores, Imer B. 2009a. Legisprudence: The role and rationality of legislators—*Vis-à-Vis* judges—Towards the realization of justice. *Mexican Law Review* 1 (2): 91.

———. 2009b. The living tree constitutionalism: Fixity and flexibility. *Problema. Anuario de Filosofía y Teoría del Derecho* 3: 37.

———. 2011. H.L.A. Hart's moderate indeterminacy thesis reconsidered: In between Scylla and Charybdis? *Problema. Anuario de Filosofía y Teoría del Derecho* 5: 147.

———. 2013. The problem about the nature of law *Vis-à-Vis* legal rationality revisited: Towards an integrative jurisprudence. In *The philosophical foundations of the nature of law*, ed. Wil Waluchow and Stefan Sciaraffa, 101–127. Oxford: Oxford University Press.

———. 2015. The legacy of Ronald Dworkin (1931-2013): A legal theory and methodology for hedgehogs, Hercules, and one right answers. *Problema. Anuario de Filosofía y Teoría del Derecho* 9: 157.

———. 2016. Intelligent or unintelligent fidelity?. In *book review symposium* on *fidelity to our imperfect constitution*: Six views and a response. *Constitutional Commentary* 31 (3): 407.

———. 2017. Constitutional interpretation, intelligent Fidelity, and (Im)perfection: On James E. Fleming's *Fidelity to our imperfect constitution*. *Problema. Anuario de Filosofía y Teoría del Derecho* 11: 31.

Fuller, Lon L. 1949. The case of the Speluncean explorers. *Harvard Law Review* 62: 616. (reprinted in 1999. *Harvard Law Review* 112: 18.

———. 1958. Positivism and Fidelity to law —A reply to professor Hart. *Harvard Law Review* 71: 630.

Giudice, Michael. 2015. *Understanding the nature of law. A case for constructive conceptual explanation*. Cheltenham: Edward Elgar.

Hart, H.L.A. 1958. Positivism and the separation of law and morals. *Harvard Law Review* 71: 593.

———. 1961. *The concept of law*. Oxford: Oxford University Press. (there is a 2nd ed. with a "Postscript": 1994).

———. 1983a. Definition and theory in jurisprudence. In *Essays in jurisprudence and philosophy*, 21–48. Oxford: Oxford University Press. (originally published: 1953).

———. 1983b. Problems of the philosophy of law. In *Essays in jurisprudence and philosophy*, 88–119. Oxford: Oxford University Press. (originally published: 1967).

———. 1983c. American jurisprudence through English eyes: The nightmare and the Noble dream, 123-144. In *Essays in jurisprudence and philosophy*. Oxford: Oxford University Press. (originally published: 1977).

———. 2013. Discretion. *Harvard Law Review* 127: 652.

Kavanagh, Aileen. 2003. The idea of a living constitution. *Canadian Journal of Law and Jurisprudence* 16: 55.

Lacey, Nicola. 2004. *A life of H.L.A. Hart: The nightmare and the Noble dream*. Oxford: Oxford University Press.

Mill, John S. 1989. On liberty. In *On liberty and other writings*, ed. Stefan Collini. Cambridge: Cambridge University Press. (originally published 1859).

Pound, Roscoe. 1946. *Interpretations of legal history*. Cambridge: Harvard University Press. (original published: New York: Macmillan Company, 1923).
———. 1960. *Law finding through experience and reason*. Athens: University of Georgia Press.
Rawls, John. 1971. *A theory of justice*. Cambridge: Harvard University Press. (there is 2nd ed. rev: 1999).
———. 1993. *Political liberalism*. New York: Columbia University Press. (there is 2nd ed. rev. "with a "New Introduction" and the "Reply to Habermas": 1996).
Raz, Joseph. 1979. *The Authority of law*. Oxford: Oxford University Press.
Rehnquist, W.H. 1976. The notion of a living constitution. *Texas Law Review* 54: 693.
Sager, Lawrence. 1990. The incorrigible constitution. *New York Law Review* 65: 893.
Scalia, Antonin. 1997. Common-law courts in a civil-law system: The role of United States Federal Courts in interpreting the constitution and Laws. In *A matter of interpretation. Federal Courts and the law*, 3–48. Princeton: Princeton University Press.
Shakespeare, William. 1917. *The tempest*. New Haven: Yale University Press. (originally written 1610-1611).
Strauss, David A. 2010. *The living constitution*. Oxford: Oxford University Press.
Sunstein, Cass. 1996. *Legal reasoning and political conflict*. Cambridge: Harvard University Press.
Waismann, F. 1968. Verifiability. In *Logic and language*, ed. A. Flew. Oxford: Blackwell.
Waldron, Jeremy. 1999a. *Law and Disagreement*. Oxford: Oxford University Press.
———. 1999b. *The dignity of legislation*. Oxford: Oxford University Press.
———. 2006. The Core of the case against judicial review. *The Yale Law Journal* 115: 1346.
Waluchow, W.J. 1983. Strong discretion. *The Philosophical Quarterly* 33 (133): 321.
———. 1985a. Hart, legal rules and palm tree justice. *Law and Philosophy* 4: 41.
———. 1985b. Herculean Positivism. *Oxford Journal of Legal Studies* 3: 187.
———. 1994. *Inclusive Legal Positivism*. Oxford: Oxford University Press.
———. 2000. Authority and the practical difference thesis: A defense of inclusive legal positivism. *Legal Theory* 6: 45.
———. 2005. Constitutions as living trees: An idiot defends. *Canadian Journal of Law and Jurisprudence* 18: 207.
———. 2007a. *A common law theory of judicial review. The living tree*. Cambridge: Cambridge University Press.
———. 2007b. A common law theory of judicial review. *Problema. Anuario de Filosofía y Teoría del Derecho* 1: 117.
———. 2008a. Constitutional morality and bills of rights. In *Expounding the constitution. Essays in constitutional theory*, ed. Grant Huscroft, 65–92. Cambridge: Cambridge University Press.
———. 2008b. Legality, morality, and the guidance function of law. In *The legacy of H.L.a. Hart: Legal, political and moral philosophy*, ed. Matthew Kramer et al., 85–100. Oxford: Oxford University Press.
———. 2009a. Four concepts of validity. Reflections on inclusive and exclusive positivism. In *The rule of recognition and the U.S. constitution*, ed. Matthew D. Adler and Kenneth Einar Himma, 123–144. Oxford: Oxford University Press.
———. 2009b. A living tree constitutionalist replies. *Problema. Anuario de Filosofía y Teoría del Derecho* 3: 147.
———. 2011a. Democracy and the living tree constitution. *Drake Law Review* 59: 1001.
———. 2011b. H.L.A. Hart: Supervisor, Mentor, friend, inspiration. *Problema. Anuario de Filosofía y Teoría del Derecho* 5: 3.
———. 2011c. Lessons from Hart. *Problema. Anuario de Filosofía y Teoría del Derecho* 5: 363.
———. 2013. On the neutrality of charter reasoning. In *Neutrality and theory of law*, ed. Jordi Ferrer Beltrán et al., 203–224. Dordrecht: Springer.
———. 2015. Constitutional rights and the possibility of detached constructive interpretation. *Problema. Anuario de Filosofía y Teoría del Derecho* 9: 23.

Cases

Edwards v. Canada (Att'y Gral.), [1930] A.C. 124 (UK)
The Law Soc'y of Upper Canada v. Skapinker, [1984] S.C.R. 357 (Can.)

Imer B. Flores is Professor-Researcher at Institute for Legal Research (*Instituto de Investigaciones Jurídicas*) and at Law School (Facultad de Derecho) of the National Autonomous University of Mexico (UNAM). He is co-founder of *Problema. Anuario de Filosofía y Teoría del Derecho.* He has a LL.B. and a Ph.D in Law from UNAM and a LL.M. from Harvard Law School, Harvard University. He is also a member of the Mexican Academy of Sciences (AMC) and of the National System of Researchers (SNI) of Mexico's National Council of Humanities, Science and Technology (CONAHCYT).

Fixed and Non-fixed Meaning in Constitutional Interpretation: Waluchow's Answer to Humpty Dumpty's Paradox

Saulo de Matos and Ricardo Dib Taxi

Abstract This chapter discusses the concept of interpretation in Waluchow's book *A Common Law Theory of Judicial Review: The Living Tree* as a standpoint for a reorientation of the idea of charter review. In Waluchow's argument, the problems usually regarded as inherent to constitutionalism and to the judicial entrenchment of a charter of rights are strongly reoriented as soon as we abandon an image of fundamental rights as fixed limits. The chapter is divided into two parts. The first part presents the conception of interpretation as a conversational model—that is, the idea that interpreters are bound to a plain meaning that has already been given, either by literal comprehension or a conventional reading, and need only be enforced by the interpreter. It then summarizes the methods of interpretation at hand, since this conversational model is acknowledged as correct. In the second part, the chapter presents the non-fixed meaning conception of interpretation and discusses which elements are necessary for it to take place. The chapter concludes by raising some epistemological problems of the common law theory of constitutional interpretation—particularly the fact that it depends on some basic intuitions of the interpreter regarding a community's constitutional morality.

1 Introduction: Humpty Dumpty's Paradox

In this chapter, we will focus on some aspects of the debate about legal interpretation in constitutional law: namely, two models that answer the so-called Humpty Dumpty's paradox. This debate is part of what is conventionally called constitutionalism. *Constitutionalism* is a term that derives from *constitution*, which, in a minimal sense, consists of a set of norms (rules, principles, or values) that create, structure, and often set the limits of governmental power or authority (Waluchow 2007, p. 19). It is possible to say that any modern State has a constitution in this weak sense, since, even in extreme cases of absolutist governments, there must be at least one norm

S. de Matos (✉) · R. D. Taxi
Federal University of Pará, Faculdade de Direito, Campus Universitário, Belém, Brazil
e-mail: saulodematos@ufpa.br; ricardoadt@ufpa.br

T. Bustamante et al. (eds.), *Law, Morality and Judicial Reasoning*, Law and Philosophy Library 147, https://doi.org/10.1007/978-3-031-61879-6_10

through which people can identify who is the sovereign. A constitution, in these terms, is very similar to what Hart (1994, pp. 79–91) has conventionally called "secondary legal rules." Thus, in this weak sense, even England has a constitution, however unwritten.

The idea of constitutionalism, however, goes beyond the mere notion of a constitution itself. Authors linked to constitutionalism defend the idea that a government can and should be limited in its powers by norms and that its authority or legitimacy depends on the degree of observance of these limitations. It was through this idea, theoretically founded by thinkers such as John Locke and Thomas Jefferson, that the shiny project of refounding the European republics could develop, putting an end to the *ancien régime*. In the background of this idea, we have the fundamental right of any citizen participating in the political community to demand justification for the exercise of governmental power, and, in turn, we have the notion that a government must be conceived as a rational entity capable of understanding the needs and interests of its citizens and acting in accordance with the general will of the political community, beginning in a democratic public space and based on the value of autonomy and respect for fundamental political rights such as freedom of expression, voting, and association.

When thinking about constitutionalism according to this definition, three questions immediately emerge. For each of them, we propose a different paradox.

The first is the question of whether a government can, in fact, be limited by political or legal rights, considering (in the wake of the Benthanian conception) that rights are the product of an act of the government itself. Would it be possible to speak of self-limitation? Under the influence of the ordinary philosophy of language, the analytical theory of law presents an explanation for this self-limitation through the idea of secondary rules that, like the rules that determine the meaning of words in ordinary language, are publicly constituted through social practices recognized by agents and linking everyone who participates in the social practice in question, without depending on a particular individual in order to be considered valid (Hart 1994, p. 201). Self-limitation is therefore possible, at least in theory.

How can we guarantee, however, that such self-limitation does not ultimately become an imposition of a social, libertarian, or socialist ideology? This is the first paradox, referred to here as Marx's paradox, present in the article "On the Jewish Question" by Karl Marx:

> It is puzzling enough that a people who is just beginning to liberate itself, to tear down all barriers between its various sections, and to stablish a political Community, that such people solemnly proclaims (Declaration of 1791) the rights of egoistic man separated from his fellow men and from the community [...]. This fact becomes still more puzzling when we see that the political emancipators go so far as to reduce citizenship, and the political Community, to a mere means for maintaining these so-called rights of man, that, therefore, the *citoyen* is declared to be the servant of egotistic *homme*, that the sphere in which man acts as a communal being is degraded to a level below the sphere in which he acts as a partial being. (Marx 1977, p. 366)

Thus, for Marx, every attempt at self-limitation of governmental power through a political bill or charter of rights is paradoxical, insofar as it consists of an act of strengthening the depoliticized human being and, at the same time, a self-depoliticization of politics (Menke 2015, pp. 7–12). In other words, declarations of fundamental human rights are the first and last political act. Marx's paradox reveals, in this sense, the difficulty in identifying limits to political power without letting such limits become fetters, made by any particular group in society to definitively imprison the other members of the political community.

A second question refers to how the constraints on a government should be designed so that each new government does not change its own limits and thus render such constraints innocuous. One mechanism, frequently proposed by constitutionalism, is the creation of a constitutional entrenchment of rights, which makes procedures to amend constitutional norms difficult, therefore guaranteeing the system greater stability. This idea is usually translated in reference to an excerpt from Homer's *Odyssey*, in which Ulysses must pass through a sea full of mermaids who can bewitch sailors through their song, taking them to the bottom of the ocean. Ulysses, therefore, asks the sailors to tie him to a ship's mast so that he can hear the sirens' song but not let himself be taken to the bottom of the sea.

The Ulysses paradox is related to the ties created by such entrenchments, referring to the difficulty in justifying the democratic legitimacy of such clauses in relation to future generations who will not have participated in the public debates about the deliberative construction of constitutional norms. If this is done, we will, in a way, be equating the view of the other members of the political community, who did not participate in the deliberation process of drafting a constitution.

Finally, a third issue is associated with the idea that written rules allow greater certainty and predictability about which rules should be considered valid and, therefore, limit governmental power. In the case of a written constitution, the question becomes one of who should have the power to interpret it and how to limit the power of this interpreter. Lewis Carroll effectively demonstrates this concern in his take on the famous fable of Humpty Dumpty:

> "There's glory for you!"
>
> "I don't know what you mean by 'glory,'" Alice said.
>
> Humpty Dumpty smiled contemptuously. "Of course you don't—till I tell you. I meant 'there's a nice knock-down argument for you!'"
>
> "But 'glory' doesn't mean 'a nice knock-down argument,'" Alice objected.
>
> "When I use a word," Humpty Dumpty said, in rather a scornful tone, "it means just what I choose it to mean—neither more nor less."
>
> "The question is," said Alice, "whether you can make words mean so many different things."
>
> "The question is," said Humpty Dumpty, "which is to be master—that's all."
>
> Alice was too much puzzled to say anything, so after a minute Humpty Dumpty began again. "They've a temper, some of them—particularly verbs: they're the proudest—adjectives you can do anything with, but not verbs—however I can manage the whole lot of them! Impenetrability! That's what I say!"
>
> "Would you tell me please," said Alice, "what that means?"
>
> "Now you talk like a reasonable child," said Humpty Dumpty, looking very much pleased.

> "I meant by 'impenetrability' that we've had enough of that subject, and it would be just as well if you'd mention what you mean to do next, as I suppose you don't mean to stop here all the rest of your life."
>
> "That's a great deal to make one word mean," Alice said in a thoughtful tone.
>
> "When I make a word do a lot of work like that," said Humpty Dumpty, "I always pay it extra." (Carroll 1991, p. 364)

Humpty Dumpty's paradox, as the problem will be labelled here, consists of the fact that the translation of constitutional norms into written language brings new problems to constitutionalism, insofar as it creates the need to limit the power of the interpreter, who cannot have unlimited power to interpret constitutional clauses yet must be able to respond to the social conflicts that often arise after the promulgation of a constitution, based on the constitution itself (Waluchow 2007, p. 39).

In what follows, the text will present two answers to Humpty Dumpty's paradox—namely, the problem of how to determine the content of legal propositions in constitutional law. Wil Waluchow's work *A Common Law Theory of Judicial Review: The Living Tree* is an attempt to respond to this paradox. This chapter seeks to reconstruct the background of the debate between theories of fixed meaning and theories of non-fixed meaning in order to identify the main problems that each of these theories must address when building a reasonable proposal about constitutional interpretation. First, theories of fixed meaning will be presented, along with their main characteristics and how such theories can now be thought from a Gricean model. The main difficulties faced by such theories will be discussed, in particular, the problem of fiction. Subsequently, theories of non-fixed meaning will be presented and discussed in their advantages to theories of fixed meaning. The fundamental problems of such theories will be explained—in particular, the need to deal with intuition. Finally, the chapter discusses Waluchow's answer to Humpty Dumpty's paradox on the basis of a theory of democracy.

2 Semantic Theories of Fixed Meaning: Textualism and Intentionalism

One of the ways to solve Humpty Dumpty's paradox is to propose a theory of meaning, according to which the meaning of a text or term depends on the correct identification of a fact: either the intention of the sender of the message or the literal meaning of the text that is communicated. In this case, the interpreter has no way of changing the meaning of a term even arbitrarily, insofar as it is pre-defined by a past act or given fact. In the case of constitutionalism and theories of interpretation of the law, such semantic theories are called theories of fixed meaning because they are based on the assumption that constitutional propositions can be identified through a simple reference to the literal meaning of constitutional provisions or the intention of the authors of a constitution (Waluchow 2007; Dworkin 1986).

Such theories have great appeal in the tradition of political liberalism because they seem to fit common sense about the nature of law as an instrument for mediating social conflicts through conventions, presupposed by the act of creating legislative diplomas. Thus, the adjudicative bodies would have as their main function identifying the parameters for the mediation of social conflicts, established, in a democratic way, by the legislative power. Despite this image being counterfactual—given that contemporary democracies admit numerous delegations of powers to the administrative and judicial spheres, which do not have the same form of legitimation as the legislative body—it is an extremely attractive model, as it establishes a control of the interpretive power of the magistrates, as well as certainty and predictability for citizens.

2.1 Textualism and Intentionalism

The fixed-meaning model acknowledges at least two theories of constitutional interpretation: textualism and intentionalism. Each defends a specific factor as a determining factor for the identification of the content of a legal proposition.

Intentional theories of law are based on a connection between intention and meaning. For these theories, there is no meaning without attribution of intention. The lyrics "Eu te amo," written on the sands of Mosqueiro Beach by the waters of the Bay of the Sun, have no meaning. They only have meaning when we attribute to them the intention of an author—for example, a couple in love who, walking along the beach, writes such letters in the sand. For intentionalists, the meaning of a legal text is determined by the communicative intent of the authority that enacted the text. Every act of interpreting a legal text, therefore, needs to seek the communicative intention of the legislator to be valid.

On the other hand, textualist theories do not focus on legislators but on the addressees of legal texts. Considering the rule of law parameter (for example, transparency and predictability), such theories argue that the task of interpretation, performed by adjudicative bodies, is to determine the meaning of legal texts based on what citizens can, normally and in a justified way, presume from the terms and texts. Addressees are normally justified in attaching a certain meaning to terms present in legislative acts, provided that they recognize standard cases of use of such terms in ordinary language. One option for such identification would be to look for such lexical patterns in dictionaries accepted by the political community. However, given the difficulty in certain complex cases and the fact that legislative acts have a series of indexical terms, the interpreter must usually appeal to the standard meaning, enriched by the context of the term's use.

In non-pathological cases, there will be no serious divergence between textualists and intentionalists, since legislators normally base themselves on expressions available to the understanding of ordinary citizens (Poscher 2015). In this sense, any theory of constitutional interpretation, according to this model, must adopt the assumption that the objective of the interpretation of legislative acts is, in the first instance, to identify the legislator's intention when enacting them, and this must be done as a collection of directives that the legislator intends to communicate when elaborating and promulgating the diploma in question. If, however, there is incompatibility between the legislator's intention and the ordinary meaning of the term, textualists defend the primacy of the latter, while intentionalists defend the precedence of the former.

2.2 *Linguistic Pragmatism As a Basis for Theories of Fixed Meaning*

At the same time, it is common for jurists to believe that they do not need any semantic theory to determine the meaning of legal texts. It is enough, as stated above, to look for the communicative intention of the legislative authority or the lexical meaning of legal terms, which can be identified without recourse to a specific theory of language. This view is false for one simple reason: people have all sorts of intentions when speaking or expressing themselves. As in ordinary language, the interpreter needs explanatory principles to differentiate between the various types of intention and then decide which should prevail in the legal case. Therefore, a theory, in the sense of a set of basic propositions and explanatory principles, is necessary.

The contemporary theory most accepted by those who appeal to a semantic theory of fixed meaning seems to be a form of linguistic pragmatism, inspired by the work of Paul Grice. This is because, based on linguistic pragmatism, it is possible to seek to overcome the following difficulties in the interpretation of legal texts (Neale 2012):

a) The difficulty of identifying the intention of something that is not an individual—that is, the intention of a social practice;
b) Difficulties in distinguishing between what is involved in having an intention and having a communicative intention, and, consequently, failures to understand the differences involving the types of causes of expectations and limitations with respect to the formation of true intentions and the factors that come from the epistemological point of view used as evidence to determine communicative intentions;
c) The difference between the linguistic meaning of an expression X and how X is ordinarily understood in a certain occasion or text;
d) The difficulty of determining the implications of an expression X, present in a given piece of legislation;
e) The difficulty of determining which parts of what the legislator intends to communicate should be considered decisive for the content of the law;
f) Differences between metaphysical questions about what is determined from the constitutive point of view, a law (questions about the objective of the law), and the epistemological question about its cognition (method questions);
g) Problems related to differentiating between (i) the meaning of statement X, (ii) how X is being used to say or assert something, (iii) what the law prescribes,

(iv) what the law means, (v) what the law implies, and (vi) what the legislator intended.

In this sense, starting with the last point, a Gricean semantic theory makes it possible to differentiate between (i) what a sentence X *means*, (ii) what a certain person S *says* when producing X on a certain occasion or text, and (iii) what S *means* when producing X on a certain occasion or text. When I say "I'm tired," the meaning of that sentence is stable regardless of indexical terms. "Meaning" signifies, in this context, something in a certain way. I can mean something directly or indirectly. When I say "I'm tired" in the context of a late-night party, this could mean that I am literally (directly) exhausted or, indirectly, that I would like to go home. Therefore, by using the expression "I'm tired," I can mean more than one thing, and, moreover, I expect that my interlocutor will understand the fact that I have used one meaning to imply another. In other words, I expect my recipient to infer from the fact that I say "I'm tired" that I want to communicate that I would like to go home. This differentiation between saying and implying is difficult in many contexts, but it is extremely useful for understanding acts of communication and as a theory of language for the interpretation of legal documents, such as a contract.

In this context, two questions need to be answered by any adequate theory of interpretation based on a fixed-meaning model: (a) What is involved in an audience forming a hypothesis about what I am saying?; and (b) What is involved in hearing and then forming a hypothesis about what I am implying? If *S* wants to mean *p* in a certain circumstance by employing a certain expression, we can say that *S* is performing a certain act of meaning and that *S* is engaged in communicative behavior. Interpretation is the formulation of a certain hypothesis about what *S* means by using a certain expression. Therefore, we can say that interpretation, in this bias, always includes the identification of a certain mental state that the sender had at the moment of producing a certain act of meaning.

2.3 Fictions in the Theories of Fixed Meaning

The adoption of the semantic theory of linguistic pragmatism as a basis for determining the meaning of legal texts seems to lead to the following image about the nature of law (Neale 2012):

(a) The enactment of normative diplomas by the legislator is the method developed by modern democracies to communicate to citizens, administrative bodies, and arbitrators their solutions to certain social conflicts;
(b) Such pieces of legislation make a difference in relation to the set of legal rights of citizens;
(c) The use of ordinary language is considered the most efficient method to express the directives of the legislator—furthermore, the most efficient, stable, public, and equitable way to use ordinary language is through written documents that are accessible to all;

(d) There is a presumption of the supremacy of the legislator, and members of the judiciary must act as agents in charge of confirming this supremacy when solving social conflicts through the correct identification of their intentions.

We will not discuss all of the assumptions of this standard image in detail.[1] It is important, for the purposes of this chapter, that the model above, for the reception of Grice's theory by constitutionalism, presupposes the "legal fiction" of the state of mind of the legislator, such as the mental state or intention of an interlocutor in a conversation between two or more people.

Here we use "legal fiction" in the same sense as Kelsen. Legal fiction is any concept, used by legal thought, to create a false antecedent to support a legal conclusion and promote a specific political objective. It works with the linguistic device of *als ob* ("as if"). For example, in *The Pure Theory of Law*, Kelsen (1960) states that the idea of a gap in the legal system is a legal fiction, given that, according to him, the logical point of view is that the legal system has no gaps. Such fiction is used by legal dogmatics to allow the adjudicative body powers to create legal rights not provided by the legal system and, at the same time, limit this constructive power to exceptional cases, or to cases in which there are gaps in the law.

Another legal fiction indicated by Kelsen (1960) is that of attribution (*Zuschreibung*) of will to collective entities or to people without the legal capacity to perform a specific legal action. Legal dogmatic creates the fiction, in the form of the antecedent of a legal argument, that a collective or individual entity has or has not performed a specific action, in order to apply the legal sanction corresponding to the so-called representative of that collective or individual entity. A subspecies of this type of legal fiction concerning the attribution of will is the fiction of the identity of will (*Fiktion der Willensidentität*), in which the will of the representative is in no way linked to the will of the represented, as in the case of the representation of the people in a modern parliament through parliamentarians; even so, the representative claims to act in the will of the represented (Kelsen 1960, p. 302). Kelsen claims that this is an artifice used exclusively to fictitiously strengthen the democratic authority of a legislature.

In the case of the reception of linguistic pragmatism of a Gricean matrix through contemporary legal theory, the problem is in item (d), in which there is, in Kelsenian terms, the legal fiction of the legislator's intention as a determinant for the identification of valid law. In the case of an interlocutor in an ordinary conversation, the communicative intention exists in the form of a psychological fact. On the contrary, in the case of a legislature with several members, there is no analogous psychological entity. Legal texts do not have a single author. Sometimes, no member of the legislature that enacted the normative piece has read every word of the legal text.

Furthermore, even if we could find a consensus on a certain meaning of the terms present in a legislative instrument, there would still be debate as to whether, from the point of view of political theory, we can understand the legislature as "they/them"

[1] For further discussion, see Greenberg (2011), pp. 217–264; Kyritsis (2017).

and not "they," "him/her," or "that." In this sense, we would need, again, a legal fiction of the legislator's institutional intention.

3 Theories of Non-fixed Meaning: Legal Constructivism

An alternative to solving Humpty Dumpty's paradox is the abandonment of the legal fiction of the legislator's intention in the form of a psychological fact and the adoption of a semantic theory of non-fixed meaning—that is, a theory that does not assume that the task of the interpreter of a legislative diploma is to find a pre-fixed meaning, but rather to contribute (along with the legislator) to developing the most adequate meaning for the solution of social conflicts. In this case, as Waluchow (2007) points out, the content of constitutional rights needs to be identified based on non-fixed points or factors, such as values, theories, principles, or purposes. As opposed to fixed factors, this type of semantic theory is sensitive to the context of the application of the law, being able to adapt to contemporary circumstances, trends, and beliefs, in addition to defending that its authority is based on the justice and sovereignty of "people-now" (Waluchow 2007, p. 55).

The meaning of a term will be determined by the role that it plays within a certain theory. In this sense, it escapes the problems of the legal fiction of the legislator's intention, insofar as the meaning of a term is not naturalized in the form of a psychological fact. On the contrary, its meaning depends on the political theory that justifies the role of a constitution and judicial review in the midst of democratic regimes.

3.1 Theory-Theory

We have already discussed that all attribution of meaning needs to explain how, in the midst of several facts or factors of a linguistic act, a hypothesis about the meaning of an expression can be adequately constructed. Thus, even if the conception of democratic legitimacy, the pillar of this type of theory, can be accepted, it is still necessary to understand how the attribution of meaning or determination of the content of the law will be done.

First, we cannot say that constructivist semantic theories do not consider intent as an important factor in identifying valid legal rights. Insofar as law is normally seen as an institutional fact, any attempt to justify valid legal propositions must include an appeal to the intention of those who participated in the collective action of lawmaking, under penalty of arbitrariness in the attribution of meaning in practice. Hence, the classic debate between textualists and intentionalists is no longer a debate about which intention should have primacy—that of members of the legislature at the time of the act or that of members of the political community—but a debate about how to give objective intentions or reasonable purposes to the legislator in order to promote a morally legitimate government. Thus, the key element of constitutional interpretation becomes which "theory" is better able to explain the current phenomena of constitutional interpretation, as in the case of Waluchow's common law theory.

What does it mean to consider "theory" the key element for semantic theory? Of course, "theory" is a controversial concept. However, we can say that "theory" in the context of a semantic theory means that the meaning of a proposition or concept will be determined on the basis of the role of that concept in relation to the other concepts and principles in the background of a certain theory. In other words, the interpreter must identify the content of the law by appealing to a theory in the form of a set of commitments assumed and claimed by a given social practice. The meaning of a specific set of propositions needs to be determined through the role they play in theories. In the case of a set of legal propositions or legal concepts, the meaning will be determined by the analysis of social facts (*explanandum*) in the light of the explanatory principles of the specific domain of law (*explanans*), thus seeking to specify which implicit and explicit commitments are being used in the context of determining conceptual content (Eleftheriadis, 2011).

3.2 *Intuitions in Theories of Non-fixed Meaning*

As stated above, theories of non-fixed meaning must appeal to factors of social practice in order to input the meaning on the basis of explanatory principles. This type of theory can be compared with cases in which we need to represent the interests of certain people with no temporary capacity to act rationally. This is the case, for example, when we need to define whether a very elderly patient with a serious condition should undergo certain medical procedures, such as, resuscitation, which can cause acute pain to their already weakened bones. Bioethics is full of such examples. In these cases, we need to represent what would be the rational action to be adopted based on biological and social facts related to the case and explanatory principles of rational action. The same seems to be true for theories of non-fixed meaning, with the only difference being that, in this case, we do not have to consider the possible intention of an individual, but of a collectivity. In this way, just as we can consult family members to make the best decision about a patient's interest, we can consider speeches by legislators, meeting briefings, and other material. However, there is not, in this case, the fiction that legislators have a single intention in the form of a specific mental state of someone participating in a conversation.

Given that this type of theory depends on an inferential model of the inductive type to determine the meaning of propositions—that is, that the content of constitutional law is determined through inferences, based on inductions linked to the conceptual role in a given theory—there are three central problems with this type of theory (Margolis and Laurence 2000):

(a) The concept of theory: There is disagreement in the social sciences about the explicative principles (*explanans*) that should be considered valid for an adequate theory. Theories of non-fixed meaning seem to presuppose a nonexistent consensus on this matter.

(b) The error problem: It is possible to think of cases in which two theories assign different and contradictory roles to the same concept or legal proposition. In this case, a legal right could be considered valid under one theory and invalid under another. How does one determine which theory should prevail?

(c) The problem of intuition: A possible solution to the error problem is to propose the existence of a set of inductively accepted convictions in the background of social practices, something close to Wittgenstein's concept of form of life or a community's constitutional morality (Waluchow 2007, p. 233). In this case, however, it seems that the theory in question comes to depend on intuitions, in the sense of non-theorized judgments, about more basic convictions about institutional morality and about the mechanisms of construction and change of social reality.

We do not consider intuition per se to be a problem for social theories. However, it can become a pathology, limiting the correct understanding of social practice, insofar as it is based on mere common sense, not being subject to argumentative reasoning and not taking into consideration evidence or experimentation in the field of social sciences which could prove the intuition wrong. The great challenge of theories of this type seems to be how to submit such intuitions about our form of life to rational control through institutional arrangements and the virtue of judges.

4 Waluchow's Answer to Humpty Dumpty's Paradox

A central thesis of Waluchow's theory of constitutional interpretation consists of defending the idea that an adequate answer to Humpty Dumpty's paradox depends on a theory of democracy. Therefore, in order to know how judges should interpret constitutional provisions, it is necessary to consider three more fundamental issues: "(a) What role is a Charter supposed to play in a constitutional democracy? (b) Is a Charter (...) a good thing to have in a constitutional democracy (and if so why?)? (c) Is judicial review on the basis of a Charter (...) a good thing to have in a constitutional democracy (and if so, what form should it take?)?" (Waluchow 2007, p. 128).

> Waluchow has a popular answer to this question that consists of making it obvious: (a) there are "objective" truths, concerning, for example, political morality, what the framers intended, or the Charter's plain and original meaning, which an impartial, morally neutral judiciary is capable of discerning and drawing upon in making Charter decision; and (2) Charters aspire to entrench the rights these truths describes or establish, as fixed points of agreement in and precommitment to moral limits on government power. (Waluchow 2007, p. 180)

In this sense, judges have the obligation to apply the law, instead of creating it by their own will. Although vagueness is part of every interpretation attitude, legal texts have a core meaning that must be protected and enforced. To deny it is to open the way to arbitrariness.

We shall not be confused by the power of rhetorical arguments that try to exaggerate the role of discretion in legal interpretation. In modern democracies, the power to create the law is given to the legislative branch, whose members are the rightful representatives of the people.

When the meaning of a rule is not clear in a given situation, the role of the interpreter is to make their best effort to grasp that meaning, instead of pretending that it does not exist. There are, of course, different ways in which this interpretation can occur. For some, the role of constitutional interpretation is to recover the original meaning as it was conceptualized by a country's founders. For others, the conventional meaning in legal practice is the right one.

When we apply this idea to the interpretation of a charter of rights, things become significantly more complicated. Although the meaning of legal norms is fixed, those norms can be altered anytime by the legislative will, following the necessary changes that a community must endeavor to develop itself. With a charter of rights, things operate differently. If constitutionalism literally means "the idea that powers of government both can and ought to be limited" (Waluchow 2007, p. 21), the charter functions to entrench these limitations and make it resistant to the circumstances of politics.

The alleged passivism of this conception could be answered by pointing out that interpreting is different from creating. Ever since the theological tradition of hermeneutics, to interpret is to discover the meaning of a text. People depend on that activity, and the interpreter cannot betray their role by transforming the meaning of a norm according to their own best judgment of a case.

Despite the differences, what these methods have in common is the idea that the meaning is already fixed and need only be found. Waluchow argues that three factors are usually seen as decisive when identifying the content of constitutional law on the basis of a fixed view: meaning, intention, and precedents (Waluchow 2007, p. 53). Through these factors, we are then able to establish fixed points that courts should discover in order to know the intention or purpose of legislation. Textualists and intentionalists, for different reasons, tend to agree with this idea (Poscher 2015).

From an epistemological point of view, these methods of interpretation based on a conversational model of the relation between legislators and courts are impossible, above all because there is no collective legislative intention in the same rich psychological sense as an individual speaker (Greenberg 2011). Therefore, the fiction of a conversation or communication between legislators and courts is a difficult case for the following reasons. In the case of a speaker in ordinary conversation, communicative intentions exist as a matter of psychological fact. In the case of constitutional interpretation, by contrast, there is no analogous psychological entity. Furthermore, it is hard to believe that a majority of legislators share overlapping communicative intentions, and this idea would necessarily not treat legislature as a unity.

From the fact that it is theoretically impossible and practically undesirable to believe that the content of constitutional rights can be determined through fixed points or factors, (above all, facts about collective legislative intention), it follows, according to Waluchow (2007), that the content of constitutional law must be identified on the basis of non-fixed points or factors, such as values, theories, principles, or goals. In opposite to fixed factors, this family of factors is sensible to the context of their application, being able to grow and adapt to "contemporary circumstances, trends, and beliefs and whose current and continued authority rests on its justice or on factors like the consent, commitment, or sovereignty of the people-*now*" (Waluchow 2007, p. 55). At the same time, it is assumed that non-fixed points are able to provide the relative stability and entrenchment that are necessary for constitutionalism.

Waluchow (2007, p. 55) calls the "living tree" every theory that spurns appeals to fixed points—that is to say, constructivist theories of constitutional interpretation. However, legal constructions create a kind of a double bind: on the one hand, it seems inevitable for the law to appeal to non-fixed points or factors in order to justify valid legal propositions; on the other hand, these constructions shift the full burden of legitimacy to the judge or whomever has to construct (that is, to amend) the law, especially in a constitutional law domain (Poscher 2015). Waluchow's common law methodology for constitutional interpretation is part of this tradition of constructivist theories. Consequently, it has to answer two basic question: (a) Which theory of democratic legitimation should be accepted on the background of a living tree theory?; and (b) What kind of non-fixed factors should determine the interpretation of constitutional provisions?

4.1 Constitutional Democracy

A theory of constitutional interpretation in democratic societies, built as a theory of meaning of constitutional provisions, has as its counterpart a model of the relationship between political actors (especially), legislation, and courts. In rejecting a fixed-view model of constitutional interpretation, Waluchow simultaneously argues against the standard view or standard conception of the relationship between legislatures and courts, according to which we should regard it as a kind of communication or conversation on the basis of a pragmatic philosophy of language (Greenberg 2011). In a non-pathological case, legislators will usually rely on expressions to convey their intentions that an average speaker would have chosen in the same circumstance, and the role of the courts consists of finding this intention or common meaning in order to justify valid constitutional propositions (Poscher 2015). It is not the case that this model is the natural one, but it is the more legitimate one in democratic societies.

Therefore, in order to establish the living tree theory of meaning for constitutional law, Waluchow has to draw a new picture of the kind of democratic association that exists between legislators and courts. The alternative picture consists of a kind of partnership or shared-authority model, which can be regarded as a theory of constitutional democracy, inspired by Rawls's approach. Accordingly, the legitimacy of a legislator's or court's decision regarding constitutional provisions depends on a correct grasp of a community's constitutional morality, other things being equal. Waluchow outlines his idea in the following sense:

> (a) that the rights to which a Charter refers are best viewed as rights of political morality established within what we'll call the "community's constitutional morality"; (b) that the community can be wrong about what its own constitutional morality requires; (c) that judge's views about what that morality requires in a particular case might, on the other hand, be correct, or at least better; (d) that when this is so, judges can be required by the Charter—by law—to enforce their own views of the community's constitutional morality against the erroneous beliefs of the community and its legislative representatives; (e) that when judges fulfill this duty, it is almost always misleading to view them as imposing *their own* subjective moral views; and finally, (f) that in enforcing their views about the rights of their community's constitutional morality recognized in a Charter, judges are in fact respecting, not violating, democratic principle. (Waluchow 2007, pp. 219–220)

Thus, Waluchow seems to follow Kant's difference between private and public reason. Accordingly, in the domain of law and rights, we are dealing not with strictly moral laws, but with obligatory laws for which there can be an external lawgiver. Consequently, it is possible for Waluchow to state a kind of morality that can be clearly distinguished from our personal morality or personal moral judgments: "It is one thing to say that our legal fate hinges on the judge's own personal morality and quite another to say that it hinges on her own personal views about what the community's constitutional morality requires" (Waluchow 2007, p. 231). Individual actions and institutions are therefore justified in different domains. The moral duties of a legal office under civil conditions are independent moral reasons that require the holders of these offices to modify their moral horizons.

A central concept for justifying judgments on institutional issues is, according to Waluchow, a community's constitutional morality. This is a type of general institutional morality that, in contrast to personal morality, is built on the basis of a particular group and institutional actions, especially through a constitutional charter and its rule of recognition: "it consists of the moral norms and convictions to which the community, via its various social forms and practices, has committed itself and that have in some way or other been drawn into the law via the rule of recognition and the law it validates. It is the morality actually embedded in social and legal practices, in the way in which principles of corrective justice are embedded in our tort law" (Waluchow 2007, p. 227). In this sense, it has to do with principles that apply to the realization of certain institutional acts in a certain time and place in accordance with a system of general institutional rules. These principles are distinct from personal moral principles due to the fact that they are created through the roles, offices, and powers that exist only in what is called the "civil condition."

Finally, in order for such a picture of democracy to be plausible, it is important to assume the fact of an irreducible pluralism of moral views. Instead of creating a form of moral disagreement all the way down (Waldron 1999), Waluchow (2007, pp. 228–229) appeals to the idea of an overlapping consensus. That is to say, from the fact of pluralism, it follows that constitutional justification should be able to be reasonably endorsed by people who disagree with one another. He embraces a form of optimistic epistemology in the domain of moral reasoning, assuming that, despite our moral disagreement, there is a bedrock formed by a body of incompletely theorized principles on the foundation of our civil condition, which can provide answers to questions concerning fundamental rights. Thus, court decisions on constitutional issues should provide citizens with methods of cooperation for realizing their community's constitutional morality, which is always underdetermined.

4.2 Critical Remarks

Even if we assume that a non-fixed view about constitutional interpretation can provide a model for a democratic relationship between legislators and courts on the basis of a constitutional conception of democracy, we still have to face the problem of which factors can determine the content of constitutional law—for we cannot simply appeal to meaning, intention, or precedents as descriptive facts related to the intention of a legislator.

From the perspective of methods of interpretation, the difference between theories of constitutional interpretation consists of how much weight is given to each of the key factors (meaning, intention, precedent, or theory). For example, contemporary intentionalists believe that the content of constitutional law (connected with legal utterance) is determined by the communicative intentions of the authority, whereas contemporary textualists stress that the meaning of constitutional provisions must be identified through an analysis of the meaning that can be justified in connecting with a legal utterance (Poscher 2015).

How about the living tree family? It is, of course, not the case that constructivist or living tree theories of constitutional interpretation do not consider meaning, intention, or precedent as part of their methods. Because law is usually regarded as an institutional social fact, every attempt to justify valid legal propositions must include appeals to the meaning or intention of the constitutional text. In this sense, from the perspective of living tree theories, the debate about whether courts should adopt textualist or intentionalist approaches to constitutional interpretation is less about which one will do a better job at revealing linguistic or intended meaning, and more about how to interpret constitutional charters (via the imputation of either objective intentions or reasonable purposes to the legislature) in order to promote morally legitimate government (Fallon 2019, p. 32). Therefore, a key element of constitutional interpretation is "theory," as in the case of a common law theory of judicial review or Dworkin's law as integrity (Waluchow 2007, p. 65).

As stated above, to consider "theory" a key element of constitutional interpretation is to define a specific set of propositions through the role they play in theories. Because of its constructivism, Waluchow's common law theory of constitutional interpretation is based on an inferential inductive model structure—that is to say, the content of constitutional law is determined through inferences based on inductions about the conceptual role in given theories. It appears, therefore, that Waluchow's common law theory faces the three problems identified above: the concept of theory, error problem, and intuition.

One possible response to the questions above consists of insisting that there is a kind of community constitutional morality as a bedrock of constitutional law, or a kind of consensual paradigm regarding legal science (Kuhn 2011). However, the appeal to institutional morality appears not to be informative enough, for it depends on at least some intuitions, in the sense of non-theorized judgements about institutional morality and the mechanisms of construction and change of social reality. In fact, these intuitions can be tested using an inductive methodology that may provide some answers to our critical remarks. Nevertheless, because inductive reasoning is always defective, it is likely the case that the error and paradigm problems will reoccur.

In this context, considering the possibility of a type of agreement on constitutional morality, we need more evidence and experimentation in order to acknowledge that there is an overlapping consensus about basic standards in our society (for example, concerning abortion or same-sex marriage), or at least that some basic principles and rights are necessary for preserving our human dignity and democratic system or can be inferred by our constitutional institutional design. Without a dialogue with the social sciences, Waluchow's constitutional theory cannot provide an adequate answer to this problem, but it certainly gives us some fruitful directions to explore.

At the end of his chapter (within this anthology) about the similarities between Waluchow's inclusive legal positivism and Dworkin's theory of law as integrity, Thomas Bustamante discusses the role of inference in Waluchow's theory regarding the case of same-sex marriage. Although Waluchow hastens to avoid the kind of "first-order moral judgments" that Dworkin considers to be an indispensable part of legal adjudication, Bustamante argues that, correctly understood, such interpretive judgments are an inevitable part of the inferences that must be made when dealing with a community's constitutional morality. Quoting Robert Brandom and the distinction between acknowledged and inferentially articulated commitments, Bustamante shows that this movement of going beyond opinions and toward a presupposed commitment is an inferential movement for which the interpreter "should make a responsible judgment about what these commitments entail" (Bustamante 2024).

Bustamante's reading is undoubtedly provocative, and we are not sure whether Waluchow would agree with it. Nevertheless, this interpretive movement seems to be much better suited than a presupposition of interpretive conventions that disregard distinct dimensions of social plurality.

5 Conclusion

We have sought to demonstrate that the two main currents of constitutional interpretation can culminate in serious pathologies. On the one hand, theories of fixed meaning, based on linguistic pragmatics of the conversational type, depend on a legal fiction of a legislator's intention. On the other hand, theories of non-fixed meaning, based on determining the meaning of a term with reference to its role in a theory from an inferential model of the inductive type, depend on intuitions with shared convictions of participants in the social practice.

At the same time, this chapter sheds light on Waluchow's constitutional interpretation by stressing its epistemological arguments against a fixed view of charters and judicial control, and stressing its central epistemological and linguistic theses on how we should justify the content of constitutional provisions in a non-fixed view. Accordingly, "theory"—in contrast to "meaning," "intention," and "precedents"—should be regarded as key factor in identifying true constitutional propositions. Therefore, the meaning of a constitutional proposition is identified with reference to other constitutional propositions and the respective roles they play within a given theory.

Our final remarks are directed at the role of intuition in Waluchow's theory. It seems to be the case that an appeal to a community's constitutional morality (and its overlapping consensus on the basis of an inductive methodology of constitutional interpretation) depends strongly on non-theorized judgments or intuitions. This seems unavoidable unless constitutional theory can enter into dialogue with social sciences, which may provide evidence about social reality.

References

Bustamante, Thomas. 2024. Waluchow and Dworkin's disagreement on legal theory, precedent, and adjudication: A family affair. In this volume.

Carroll, Lewis. 1991. *Through the looking-glass and what Alice found there*. Urbana: Project Gutenberg. https://www.gutenberg.org/files/12/12-h/12-h.htm#link2HCH0006.

Dworkin, Ronald. 1986. *Law's empire*. Cambridge: Belknap Press.

Eleftheriadis, Pavlos. 2011. Descriptive jurisprudence. *PRO* 5: 117–145.

Fallon, Richard H. 2019. The statutory interpretation muddle. Draft of Legal Theory Workshop presented at the UCLA Law School.

Greenberg, Mark. 2011. Legislation as communication? Legal interpretation and the study of linguistic communication. In *Philosophical foundations of language in the law*, ed. Andrei Marmor and Scott Soames, 217–264. Oxford: Oxford University Press.

Hart, H.L.A. 1994. *The concept of law*. 2nd ed. Oxford: Oxford University Press.

Kelsen, Hans. 1960. *Reine Rechtslehre*. 2nd ed. Wien: Verlag Österreich.

Kuhn, Thomas S. 2011. *A estrutura das revoluções científicas*. São Paulo: Perspectiva.

Kyritsis, Dimitrios. 2017. *Shared authority*. Oxford: HART Publishing.

Margolis, Eric, and Stephen Laurence. 2000. *Concepts: Core readings*. Cambridge: MIT Press.

Marx, Karl. 1977. Zur Judenfrage. In *MEW/Marx–Engels–Werke Band 1*. Berlin: Dietz.

Menke, Christoph. 2015. *Kritik der Rechte*. Berlin: Suhrkamp.

Neale, Stephen. 2012. Convergentism & the nature of law. Draft of paper presented at the Oslo Workshop on the Pragmatics of Legal Language.

Poscher, Ralf. 2015. Hermeneutics, jurisprudence and law. In *The Routledge companion to hermeneutics*, ed. Jeff Malpas and Hans-Helmuth Gander. London: Routledge.

Waldron, Jeremy. 1999. *Law and disagreement*. Oxford: Oxford University Press.

Waluchow, Wilfrid J. 2007. *A common law theory of judicial review: The living tree*. Cambridge: Cambridge University Press.

Saulo de Matos is Professor of Philosophy of Law at the Federal University of Pará, Brazil. He holds a PhD from University of Gottingen, Germany, and a Master's degree from the University of Heidelberg, Germany. His doctoral dissertation on the legal and political idea of popular sovereignty in modernity ("*Zum normativen Begriff der Volkssouveränität*") was published in Germany by Nomos Verlag in 2015. He was visiting scholar at University of California in Los Angeles (2013) and University of Gottingen (2017).

Ricardo Dib Taxi is Professor of Philosophy of Law and Tort Law at the Federal University of Pará, Brazil, and Professor of the Master and PhD Program in Human Rights of the same University. He holds a PhD from Federal University of Para, with a visiting period at Birkbeck College- University of London (between June 2014 and May 2015). He also coordinates a research group on Law and Narrative.

Waluchow's Theory of Constitutional Interpretation from a Rhetorical-Argumentative Point of View

Katharina Stevens

Abstract This chapter argues that the theory of judicial interpretation standing behind Wil Waluchow's philosophy of judicial review can best be understood with the tools of rhetorical argumentation theory. Waluchow directs supreme court judges to use a common law approach when they decide constitutional cases, but he is aware that constitutional precedent will not always be sufficient to determine the required decision in a case. If this happens, judges should turn to their Community's Constitutional Morality (CCM) and decide according to it. CCM is determined by analyzing the moral commitments a community has made through its legal and political actions and formulating them into a coherent whole. I argue that the construction of CCM follows the same process as the construction of idealized audiences which are utilized in rhetorical branches of argumentation theory to evaluate reasoning. I then go on to develop the rhetorical theory of judicial reasoning that, I believe, should stand behind Waluchow's approach to judicial review.

1 Introduction

One of Wil Waluchow's important contributions to the philosophy of law has been his well-known defense of judicial review as not only compatible with democracy but, if it is done right, an important element in the truly democratic self-governance of a community. This defense was most prominently presented in his book *A Common Law Theory of Judicial Review: The Living Tree* (Waluchow 2007). Waluchow's strategy for defending judicial review is not to show that the practice will *never* undermine democratic self-governance. Waluchow acknowledges that constitutionally guaranteed rights are often formulated in vague language that allows for many interpretations. He agrees that it is undemocratic to allow a handful of unelected judges to declare democratically enacted law invalid because it conflicts with their own, subjectively preferred interpretation of these rights. And he realizes

K. Stevens (✉)
University of Lethbridge, Department of Philosophy, University Hall, Lethbridge, AB, Canada
e-mail: katharina.stevens@uleth.ca

T. Bustamante et al. (eds.), *Law, Morality and Judicial Reasoning*, Law and Philosophy Library 147, https://doi.org/10.1007/978-3-031-61879-6_11

that judicial review can amount to just that. And so he accepts that judicial review can be undemocratic if it is understood and implemented in the wrong way.

Instead of defending judicial review whatever shape it may take, he develops a normative account of constitutional interpretation that, if followed, is meant to transform an anti-majoritarian and potentially undemocratic practice into one that realizes the "authentic" will of the democratic community and thereby becomes neither undemocratic nor truly anti-majoritarian. Waluchow advocates for a common-law method of interpreting the constitution and argues that, where this method provides judges with discretion, they should decide according to the community's constitutional morality (CCM). CCM is the set of moral commitments that the community has made through their prior legal and political decisions, brought into coherence through a process of reflective equilibrium. By using this method of constitutional interpretation, judges can aim to realize the will of the democratic community even during judicial review. However, this is a refined, coherent version of this will that would emerge after sober, self-reflective, reasonable deliberation. In other words: they create outcomes that reflect a will of the majority that is much less likely to be tyranny-of-the-majority-tyrannical than the majority's will that includes rash decisions and opinion fueled by fear, hate or hype.

One of the criticisms most often faced by Waluchow's theory of constitutional interpretation is that CCM is in fact not determinate enough to decide all (or even most) of the question judges face during judicial review. And if CCM is too sparse to deliver clear answers, then Waluchow's attempt at using it to allow judges to bring judicial review and democratic values into agreement must fail: Whenever CCM gives out, judges have to rely on their own opinions again, and the democratic worry returns (Alexander 2009; Brand-Ballard 2008; Miller 2007; Stoljar 2009; Struchiner and Shecaira 2009).

Waluchow has dedicated several papers to showing how judges can reason constructively about CCM without thereby falling back into employing their own moral opinions to answer questions of constitutional interpretation (e.g. Waluchow 2008, 2013, 2015). Through this, he has argued that CCM will be able to offer determinate guidance considerably more often than his critics feared. In this paper, I want to contribute to the task of alleviating the critic's worries over judges' ability to make judicial review democratically legitimate by following Waluchow's method of interpretation from another angle. One assumption that Waluchow's critics must make if their criticism is to be successful in undermining Waluchow's theory is that the democratic value of judges' reasoning with CCM depends on its results. They need to assume that using CCM gives the outcome of judicial review democratic legitimacy only in those cases where judicial decisions are determinably guided by it to correctly mirror the decision that the constitutional community would make if their reasoning was coherent and authentic. Otherwise, for example if using CCM generated democratic legitimacy for procedural reasons, CCM sometimes running out would not rob decisions made through reasoning with it of their democratic legitimacy. And in fact, I think that Waluchow's (2008, 2013, 2015) answers to his critics can be used to show more than just that CCM is more often determinate than it appeared. They can be used to expand his theory about CCM in a way that allows judges using Waluchow's method of interpretation to engage in judicial review in a democratically legitimate way because of the way in which they relate to the democratic community whose constitution they are interpreting. As a result, their decisions can then have democratic legitimacy based on the process by which they are generated—not just because they have the right content. As a result, using Waluchow's method of interpretation can allow judges to make democratically legitimate decisions even if they make mistakes in their reasoning about CCM, as long as those mistakes are honest mistakes.[1]

Elsewhere I (2019) claimed that Waluchow's suggestion that judges use CCM as a tool for constructing constitutional interpretations is strongly related to the role that idealized audiences play in rhetorical argumentation theory. In this paper, I want to expand on this idea. I argue that the argumentative-rhetorical lens through which I suggest interpreting Waluchow's theory shows that judges can preserve democratic legitimacy by making their decisions through arguments whose validity they measure by the adherence of an audience consisting of the CCM-accepting democratic community. When judges construct justifications for their constitutional answers that are meant to be valid according to the standards of an audience who accepts CCM, they acknowledge that audience's prerogative to determine not only what the correct answers are, but also what kinds of premises, reasons and types of argument may be used to derive answers. In other words: The rhetorical-argumentative lens on Waluchow's theory of constitutional interpretation reveals that judges who follow Waluchow's theory of interpretation do not only imbue their decisions with democratic legitimacy if they accomplish answers in harmony with the citizenry's existing moral commitments. Rather, choosing to follow Waluchow's method of constitutional interpretation allows them to act in service to the democratic community to which they belong as just one member, offering arguments to an audience that consists of the democratic community and is, at the same time, also the measuring stick by which the validity of these arguments is determined. The democratic legitimacy of the judge's answers then does not derive only from their content, but comes also from the process through which the judges arrived at them, and from the relationship in which the judges see themselves with the democratic community.

This paper will be organized as follows: First, I will provide an overview over Waluchow's theory of constitutional interpretation, the objection I am going to

[1]Importantly, as I understand it, Waluchow is aware that the democratic worry persists if judges interpret the constitution by using interpretative methods other than the one he suggests—and that therefore the democratic worry persists where judges have discretion over how to interpret the constitution. Critics that point out that real judges who have the authority to engage in judicial review do not *de facto* use the interpretive method that Waluchow describes, and are therefore *de facto* engaging in an undemocratic practice, talk past him: Obviously *no* theory of interpretation could deal with the democratic worry unless it is implemented. Blaming that on the theory is like claiming that the can-opener does not work because *not* using it resulted in an unopened can. Waluchow's responses to his critics concentrate on showing that judges engaged in the good-faith application of his theory can avoid undermining democracy—and I will follow him in this. I thank one reviewer for pointing out that a critic may be tempted to fault Waluchow's interpretive theory for the reality that not all judges make use of it.

concentrate on in this paper, and Waluchow's own answers to it. Then I will introduce the basic building blocks of the rhetorical theory of argumentation. Finally, I will show how viewing Waluchow's theory through the lens of rhetorical argumentation theory strengthens his account.

2 Waluchow's Common Law Theory of Judicial Review—A Quick Overview

Waluchow develops his theory of constitutional interpretation in answer to a much-discussed problem: Allowing unelected judges to strike down, undercut or modify law enacted by a democratically elected legislature because they think it to be in conflict with a constitutionally entrenched fundamental right seems to be contrary to the ideal of democratic decision-making.

2.1 Setting the Scene: The Discussion Before Waluchow

The democratic worry is based on a straight-forward argument. Democratic systems are supposed to acknowledge and respect each eligible[2] citizen's right to equal participation in political decision making. This is typically realized through majoritarian decision-making mechanisms. The majoritarian element is important because, as Waldron (e.g. 2006) puts it in his argument against judicial review, majoritarian decision making is unbiased and gives each person the most influence it can while at the same time giving every person equal influence. Therefore decisions that are reached via this process can reasonably be counted as expressions of the "will of the people" and are therefore legitimized.[3] Judicial review, by contrast, undercuts this inherently respectful decision-making mechanism by diverting power away from the democratic community and into the hands of a few individuals empowered to vet and potentially reject the results of the democratic process (Waldron 1993, 2004, 2006).

Of course, arguments in favor of judicial review exist, and had existed before Waluchow entered the discussion. What Waluchow calls the "standard case" for judicial review justifies the counter-majoritarian nature of judicial review by citing the danger of the "tyranny of the majority".[4] The argument goes like this: A process

---

[2]Eligibility requires, e.g. to be of voting age.

[3]For a contractarian version of this argument, that is also accepted by proponents of judicial review, see, e.g. Freeman (1990).

[4]This standard case as Waluchow (2007) describes it is a combination of several different arguments made by several authors, among them Freeman (e.g. 1990) and Dworkin (e.g. 1996), but does not pretend to represent any of them in detail. In addition, Waluchow later argues that Dworkin's theory can be read as being extremely close to his own (Waluchow 2015).

that realizes the right to equal participation in political decision making through majority voting does not prevent unjust decisions. In fact, it does not even prevent decisions that undermine the equal opportunity of all citizens to participate in political decision making, or decisions that result in denying some members of the community other kinds of basic rights necessary for a life with dignity. Minorities—community members who have characteristics that set them apart from the majority—are especially vulnerable to such decisions because their small numbers make it unlikely that they will be able to utilize the majoritarian decision-making process in their favor. To prevent the worst infringements on the rights of minorities, certain limits to the kind of decisions that majorities can make are needed. Charters or bills of rights, enforced through judicial review, provide those limits. They allow communities to determine, in a moment of calm collection, those rights that have to be taken off the table of everyday democratic decision making. Avoiding the tyranny of the majority justifies the counter-majoritarian effects of judicial review.

Waluchow does not think that this argument is without merit. He agrees that there is a real danger that majority-based decision making can result in serious rights infringements, and he points out that it is not even necessary to assume that this will happen out of ill-will or bigotry. After all, people have a hard time imagining the consequences that their decisions may have on those who lead significantly different lives, and they find it difficult to correctly assess the significance of harms that they have never experienced (Waluchow 2007). Nonetheless, Waluchow follows Waldron in rejecting the "standard case" as it stands. As Waldron (1993, 2004, 2006) points out, the rights that are typically included in bills and charters of rights are worded vaguely for a reason. People can usually agree on the importance of certain rights in the abstract. However, there is almost always substantial, good faith disagreement about their exact meaning, the kinds of cases they apply to, the weight they have when compared to other rights they may come in conflict with etc. So, while there might be a truth about the exact meaning of rights, it would be hubris for any group of people to claim that they know it with enough certainty to coercively impose their decisions on everybody else. But this is exactly what judicial review, in the conception of the "standard case", does. The standard case assumes that when they created the bill or charter of rights, the People determined the most important, basic rights once and for all. When judges, in the course of judicial review, engage in constitutional interpretation, then they either simply identify and enforce these pre-determined, immutable rights as they find them or they somehow determine their "real" meaning. But this view of what judges do is deeply disrespectful to the current people of a presumably democratic country. Why should they accept that either the framing generation or a small number of judges determines the exact meaning of those abstract rights? Waluchow agrees with Waldron that what these rights mean should be determined by the current democratically organized community. This leaves him with the tension of acknowledging both the worry about the tyranny of the majority and the worry about the illegitimacy of giving a small group of individuals the power to resolve good-faith disagreement about the specific meaning of constitutional provisions.

2.2 *Waluchow's Common Law Constitutionalism and CCM*

Waluchow's project is to resolve this tension by offering judges a method of constitutional interpretation that significantly reduces the risk of the tyranny of the majority without undermining the community's ability to democratically self-govern. The core of this method is the use of common-law reasoning to slowly weave the moral rights-commitments that a country's democratically organized community makes through democratic processes into a constitutional doctrine capable of providing the basis for deciding constitutional cases.

2.2.1 The Common Law Method

The common law is a part of the law that is built, maintained and revised through precedent. Specifically, it develops through setting, distinguishing, extending and overruling precedent decisions—legal decisions that create authoritative reasons to repeat the decision if a later case arises to which the precedent case applies. A precedent applies to a present case if the present case shares all those factors with the precedent case that were legally relevant to the precedent decision. To *follow* an applicable precedent is to repeat the precedent decision in the present case. An applicable precedent must be followed if a present case shares *all* legally relevant factors with the precedent case. However, if the present case has some additional factors that are not shared with the precedent case and that speak against making the decision, then the precedent can either be *distinguished* or *extended*. To distinguish a precedent means to cite the legally relevant difference between the precedent and the present case as a justification for not repeating the precedent decision. To extend a precedent means to repeat the precedent decision in spite of the legally relevant difference. Precedents can also be extended to cases to which they do not technically apply because the present case does not share *all* the legally relevant factors of the precedent (persuasive precedents). Individual common-law decisions slowly turn very specific authoritative reasons stemming from single precedents into lines of precedent that provide broader common-law principles.

Waluchow advocates for a common-law method of applying and developing constitutional law because it provides a balance of both stability and flexibility. The individual judge is bound by the common law where she must follow precedent but, at the same time, she is afforded small discretionary decisions where she can either distinguish or extend. New content enters the common law through these discretionary decisions. Therefore, the common law usually develops slowly and incrementally through small, discretionary aspects of decisions that are otherwise bound by the authoritative reasons provided by precedents and common law principles. This is also how Waluchow wants constitutional law to develop around the constitutional text; slowly and through small, discretionary steps that give no individual judge too much power at any single time.

2.2.2 CCM

Still, Waluchow acknowledges, all these small discretions add up over time and create constitutional law around the text. Therefore, if judges want to avoid undermining the democratic self-governance of their community, they need a way to bind the discretionary aspects of constitutional interpretation and decision making to the community's democratic will. Waluchow shows how this is possible by introducing the idea of a *Community's Constitutional Morality* (CCM). CCM is neither the *true* morality of moral realism (whatever that may be) nor is it the set of positive moral opinions that the majority in a country at this moment may endorse. Rather, CCM is identified by taking the majority's mere moral opinions and bringing them into coherence through the Rawlsian method of reflective equilibrium. This method resolves, for example, inconsistencies between abstract moral principles (commitment to non-discrimination on the basis of sex) and object-level moral judgements (the judgement that wearing short skirts makes women partially guilty for their own rape). It distinguishes *mere* moral opinions from authentic moral commitments, discarding the former while forming the latter into a coherent system.[5] However, not all of the resulting moral theory is CCM. Rather, CCM is that subset of this theory that has some kind of legal and constitutional pedigree in that its principles and judgements are endorsed in legal and political materials produced through the democratic processes of the country (Waluchow 2007). CCM is therefore a coherent version of the majority's positive morality as it is incorporated into the law. It can be considered the moral theory to which the democratically organized community of a country has committed itself through their democratic actions. According to Waluchow, judges can use CCM to determine how the community would resolve constitutional cases that leave some space for discretion, assuming that the community decided these cases based on its authentic moral commitments instead of, e.g., irrational fears (Waluchow 2007, 2008). By deciding cases according to CCM, judges use their discretion to introduce the morality of the democratically organized community into constitutional law, not their own morality.

[5]Waluchow (2007) argues that our express wishes and opinions can be inauthentic if they are causally connected to impairments of our ability to make judgements coherent with our overall web of moral and factual beliefs. As an example, he offers the case in which an otherwise responsible adult drunkenly demands that their friends let them drive their car home themselves. The drunk person's judgement is impaired by alcohol, and their express wish does not cohere with their other moral and factual beliefs about the preciousness of human life, the effects of alcohol on driving ability etc. Therefore, it is legitimate to judge their express wish to drive as inauthentic. Waluchow believes that just like individuals, communities too can suffer from impaired judgement—e.g. when they are swayed by irrational fears or hate (e.g. after a terrorist attack), or when they are trying to make judgements under conditions of inadequate information (e.g. about the experiences of a minority group). Under these circumstances, communities might make judgements that are incoherent with moral or factual ideas that they have committed themselves to (e.g. the inviolability of certain human rights).

2.3 Waluchow on Accessing and Constructing CCM

Waluchow's attempt to resolve the tension caused by the democratic worry and the fear of the tyranny of the majority was subjected to several criticisms. Among them, the most troubling are those that question whether even the good-faith use of Waluchow's interpretive theory can provide decisions made during judicial review with democratic legitimacy: Critics doubt CCM's ability to provide effective and reliable constraint for judicial reasoning and, based on this, judges' ability to use CCM in order to imbue their decisions with democratic legitimacy (Alexander 2009; Brand-Ballard 2008; Miller 2007; Stoljar 2009; Struchiner and Shecaira 2009). The worry was formulated in a number of different ways, two of which Waluchow picked out as especially pertinent and anwered in a number of later papers.

First, he faced the claim that judges who use CCM need to engage in their own reasoning about the likely content of CCM and its normative implications for their specific case. Thereby, they cannot help but to insert their own thinking into their decisions, which re-animates the democratic worry.

Waluchow answers this objection by arguing that judges who reason through the lens of CCM do in fact engage in their own reasoning, but not from their own point of view. Instead, they take the Razian (1979) *detached point of view*, which allows them to reason about what someone accepting CCM should do given the commitments of CCM, instead of what *they themselves* should do, given their own commitments (Waluchow 2015). This is accomplishable by reasoning *as if* they accepted CCM instead of their own moral commitments. The effect is that, while judges do enter the results of their own reasoning into their decisions, they do not enter their own moral commitments.[6]

Second, Waluchow had to answer the objection that CCM would run out, unable to deliver a determinate answer to every question that a judge may have to confront when engaged in judicial review. Waluchow (2013, 2014) acknowledges that sometimes, a case may pose a question that CCM cannot provide a definite answer to, but only a range of acceptable answers. This may happen, for example, because the democratic community is itself deeply divided so that there is no coherent set of principles with a democratic pedigree that can provide a determinative answer. When this is the case, judges will have to engage in a kind of CCM-construction (albeit a bounded one because of the limits provided by clearly unacceptable answers): Because they must make a decision, and because this decision will enter both constitutional law and CCM, they have no choice but to contribute to the content of both.

---

[6] As, e.g. Bustamante points out in his chapter in this collection, Waluchow's theory here is very similar to Dworkin's as it is expressed, e.g. in *Law's Empire* (1986). It would be possible to understand Waluchow's idea of taking the commitments a community has made historically and discerning from them their authentic commitments regarding a new case or problem as a version of Dworkin's claim that a judge should preserve a community's *integrity* when engaged in adjudication.

However, Waluchow argues that even if this happens, it is still possible to preserve some of the democratic pedigree of the decision by limiting the reasons that judges use while constructing CCM to *public reasons* as he, following Rawls (e.g. 1996), understands them: Reasons that any reasonable member of the community—no matter their other moral commitments—could accept *as reasons*, even if they would consider them outweighed by other, non-public reasons that they personally accept. By combining reasons provided by CCM with reasons that any reasonable community-member would have to acknowledge as having the status of reasons, an otherwise underdetermined question may, in the end, be given an answer (Waluchow 2013, 2014). And this answer would have to be accepted as legitimate by any reasonable community-member. This is because any given community-member could be expected to acknowledge that the reasons which in her mind outweigh the public reasons given by the judge could not legitimately be used in judicial review without disrespecting the equal standing of some other community-member who could reasonably reject that they count as reasons at all.[7] She would therefore have to accept the content of the resulting decision as democratically legitimate because it is based only on reasons that either have a clear democratic pedigree (CCM) or cannot be denied the status of reasons by any reasonable person belonging to the democratically organized community (public reasons).

Through answering these two objections, Waluchow shows that CCM can provide judges with guidance that is much more reliable than the critics thought at feeding the authentic moral commitments of the democratically organized community into the content of the constitutional law. As a result, the constitutional law is slowly constructed as an expression of the authentic moral theory that can be found in the background of the everyday, democratic political and legal decision made by the community (Waluchow 2010). Therefore, it mirrors a product of democratic decision making faithfully, just that this product is one that has been subjected to a process of amelioration which reduces the risk of decisions that will be tyrannical. This means that Waluchow shows that the *product* of judicial review is, in many more cases than the critics thought, in harmony with the democratic will of the community.

However, I believe that Waluchow's answers to his critics can be developed to do more than that. They also provide an opportunity to show that Waluchow's method of constitutional interpretation suffuses the process of judicial review with a democratic spirit, guiding judges to see themselves as servants to the democratic will of the community to which they belong as only *one* member instead of its watchdogs.

[7]Waluchow is somewhat unclear about what should happen if a judge should come to the conclusion that she and her colleagues on the court cannot identify a determinate answer even when they add public reasons to CCM. He argues that judges should not automatically defer to the legislature whenever it is controversial which answer CCM + public reasons provides because this will be controversial in many cases: Most of the time, someone will disagree with the court about which answer CCM + public reasons give. However, this is different from the case where the judges find themselves at a loss after having engaged in a good faith effort to determine this answer. I assume that in these rare cases, deference to the legislature would be appropriate.

Even when judges fail in their attempt to apply CCM correctly and therefore do not produce a decision that reflects the authentic democratic will, the way in which they reason nonetheless introduces some democratic legitimacy into their decision. I argue that this legitimacy is procedural, rather than based on substantial outcomes. As I see it, Waluchow's own writings show that he has this effect in mind (e.g. Waluchow 2013). I therefore hope that when I now propose to re-frame his theory from an argumentative-rhetorical point of view, I will not only show where this democratic spirit comes from, but also create a version of Waluchow's theory that is very much in keeping with his project, even if it involves a slight revision. However, before I can proceed with my argument, I first have to introduce some key-concepts of rhetorical argumentation theory.

3 Rhetorical Argumentation Theory

"Rhetoric" tends to have a bad reputation as being concerned chiefly with persuasion at the cost of reason. And indeed, rhetorical theories of argumentation evaluate arguments by determining whether they are capable of gaining the assent of the addressed audience. They describe reasoning and arguing as ways to solve problems, answer questions or resolve disagreements. Arguments are good or bad to the degree that they succeed in doing so, relative to the audience to which they are addressed (which might, in some cases, be the arguer or reasoner herself) (Aikin 2011; Crosswhite 1996; Perelman and Olbrechts-Tyteca 1969; Tindale 1999, 2004). Standards for argument evaluation are also audience-dependent, in that whether something counts as a reason depends on whether the intended audience accepts that it is a reason (Aikin 2011; Crosswhite 1996; Tindale 2004). In other words: Reasoning and argumentation aim at gaining the assent of an audience, and an argument is cogent or valid if it is apt at doing so, which can be determined by measuring it against those standards of argument goodness and definitions of what counts as a reason that are accepted by the target audience.

Unsurprisingly, the rhetorical theory of argumentation has been subjected to serious objections, maybe the most important of which is that it allows the cogency of an argument to vary with the foolishness of the audience (e.g. Aikin 2011; Johnson 2000). Any argument, so the criticism goes, no matter how bad it would appear to the majority of reasoners, or even the argument's author herself, will be valid in the theory's eye if it is constructed for an audience that is gullible, naïve, uneducated or thick enough to fall for it.

And in fact, at first sight, the rhetorical theory of argument seems to encourage the immoral practice of persuading audiences via arguments that the arguer herself considers to be weak or even invalid, as long as they are effective.

However, rhetorical argumentation theory's aim is not to assist arguers in winning arguments at all costs, but rather to develop an understanding of argumentative goodness that acknowledges the centrality of the audience. So in order to deal with the potentially devastating objection outlined above, rhetorical argumentation theorists have introduced the concept of an idealized audience, the most important and famous version of which is Perelman and Olbrechts-Tyteca's *universal audience* (Perelman and Olbrechts-Tyteca 1969). The universal audience is free from the idiosyncratic failings that may make it possible to persuade a particular audience with arguments that others would recognize as bad. Its members do not have false or contradictory beliefs, nor biases that can be exploited, nor can their inability to concentrate or remember the meaning with which a term was used earlier be used against them, etc.[8]

As may be clear from this description alone, the universal audience is also not real. Rather, it is an imagined audience that the arguer should direct her arguments to, and it serves as a less relativistic measurement for argument quality: A valid argument is the argument that cannot only gain the adherence of its particular target audience but also that of the universal audience. The function of the universal audience is, at the very least, to exclude intentionally deceptive arguing from being recognized as "good" by the theory. This is because the members of the universal audience, as constructed by the arguer, would not fall for tricks or accept false premises that the arguer knows about. So arguments in which the arguer uses what she believes to be fallacies or falsehoods cannot be good arguments, no matter how effective they are with regard to the addressed, particular audience: Directing their arguments to the universal audience, in addition to the actual audience, keeps the arguer honest.

The idea of the universal audience is one of the most controversial aspects of Perelman and Olbrecht-Tyteca's work. The extensive discussion surrounding it has produced many different interpretations of how it should be understood. Among them, Crosswhite's (1996) and Tindale's (1999, 2015) method for constructing the universal audience is most relevant for comparison with Waluchow's theory of CCM.

Both authors emphasize Perelman's claim that the universal audience is to be derived from real, particular audiences. This happens either by removing what the arguer perceives as the particular audience's actual deficits like their false beliefs and their shortcoming in reasoning-ability. Or it happens by including more and more members in the addressed audience so that an arguer's argument must be imagined as being scrutinized by more and more different people, making the discovery of flaws more and more likely. What this comes down to is that the universal audience is an ameliorated version of the particular, actual audience and constructed by an

[8] I suspect that readers of this chapter may be more familiar with Habermas' dialectical theory of argument than the rhetorical theories I rely on here, simply because of Habermas' presence in political and legal philosophy. For them, it might be helpful to think of the universal audience as fulfilling a similar function as the ideal speech situation (Habermas 1980). However, I find a rhetorical, rather than a dialectical approach more helpful in this context. This is because rhetorical theorists often take the idea of a speaker, addressing an audience, as the foundation of their theorizing. By contrast, dialectical theories tend to treat the dialectical engagement of at least two speakers as foundational. Judges, especially when engaged in judicial review, are to me closer to the speaker addressing an audience than the arguer addressing an interlocutor.

arguer intending to address the particular audience from which it is derived. As a result, the universal audience changes with the particular audience, but also with the arguer's understanding of the audience and her beliefs about what is a fallacy, and which premises that the audience accepts are or are not acceptable.

It follows that according to Tindale and Crosswhite's interpretation, the universal audience is not a static representation of an entity with direct access to truth and capable of flawless reasoning. Rather, it is a changing, idealized version of actual audiences. Further, Crosswhite points out that the construction of the universal audience itself is never finished and always open to criticism. Because the construction of the universal audience by an arguer aims at a representation of what is universally reasonable in a particular audience, it is always possible that the arguer finds herself corrected by others. Therefore, she always has to imagine two universal audiences: The one she can picture, based on her amelioration of a real audience, and the one she cannot picture, the *undefined* universal audience, that may at any moment manifest itself in an actual, particular interlocutor who presents a criticism of her construction of the universal audience and convinces her to change it (Crosswhite 1996).

This reference to an unknowable, undefined universal audience that may at any moment criticize the author's construction of universality serves the important function of acknowledging the limitedness of the human mind in identifying the standards of reasonableness: Arguers can only ever *aim* at the assent of the universal audience because they can only ever aim at constructing the universal audience in a way that would not be criticized by the undefined universal audience. It also ties the arguer back to the particular audience: The arguer remains unable to conclusively reject the particular audience's judgement of her arguments on the basis that their rejection of them is based on the idiosyncrasies that the universal audience lacks. This is because the undefined universal audience may reveal itself in this judgement, showing the arguer that his construction of the universal audience was flawed.

It is important to take note that the rhetorical theory of argumentation as I presented it here limits the set of arguments that can count as good, cogent or convincing from two directions: On the one hand, the requirement that the argument would convince the universal audience prevents the arguer from exploiting her audience's idiosyncratic failings, like false beliefs, inconsistencies in their belief system or a tendency to fall for certain fallacies. On the other, that argument goodness is measured by the argument's ability to gain the actual, particular audience's adherence makes it so that some arguments which the majority of audiences and the arguer would consider cogent and convincing might still be bad arguments when presented to that particular audience. For example, the argument may use premises or a kind of inference that the audience could not be expected to accept or even understand. Telling a 3 year old that they should eat a certain food because it contains amino acids that will help them with protein synthesis is not making a good argument—unless we are dealing with a truly exceptional 3 year old.

However, this does not mean that arguers are reduced to the use of premises that are already salient to their particular audience, or even ones that their particular audience has already reflectively endorsed. Rather, as Tindale shows, arguers have to use premises that are available in their audience's *cognitive environment* (Tindale 1992). The cognitive environment can be explained by comparing it to a visual environment. Wherever a seeing person is, there will be certain aspects of her visual environment that she is already directing attention to. In a park, she might already be looking at the pretty flowers and the inviting park bench. But she might not yet have noticed the trash can that she can use to get rid of her candy wrappers, even though it is visible, half-hidden behind some shrubbery, making it easy for others to direct her attention to it. Similarly, there may be premises that a particular audience is not thinking about just now, or has in fact never reflectively endorsed, but that can be easily brought back into memory or that are only one or two quick inferential steps away. Arguers can make use of these premises, sometimes even without having to perform these inferential steps for the audience. For example, an arguer who knows that her audience has in the past shown themselves committed to allowing either all or none of their children to have candy or stay up later may, even if she suspects that her audience never consciously thought about the meaning of equality, rely on premises about the importance of equality when arguing about some other treatment that the children should receive.

4 Waluchow's CCM Reasoning Through the Lens of Rhetorical Argumentation Theory

Above, I explained the method Waluchow wants judges to use who find that they have discretion while performing judicial review. I can summarize it here in three steps plus one supplementary step in cases of doubt:

First, judges should use a method of reflective equilibrium to determine the current, authentic moral commitments of the community governed by the constitution which are somehow connected to the law, discarding as mere opinions those aspects that cannot be integrated into a coherent whole. This forms CCM.

Second, judges should construct a point of view which accepts these and only these commitments (this is what Waluchow identifies with the Razian detached point of view).

Third, judges should determine which decision would be acceptable from this perspective. Where judges realize that there would be disagreement among the community's members about the content of CCM, or where CCM is not enough to fully determine an answer to the question that has arisen, they can integrate a supplementary step. This step consists in the attempt to constructively develop CCM in a way that no reasonable community member could call unreasonable by using only public reasons.

4.1 Reasoning with CCM Understood As Rhetorical Argumentation

Seeing these three steps next to my short explanation of idealized audiences in rhetorical argumentation theory reveals that the construction of CCM can be understood as the construction of an idealized audience that falls short of a fully universal audience in very specific, deliberate ways, and with a special emphasis on equipping the resulting audience with a specific set of beliefs, namely those that the democratic community has committed itself to. I argue that doing so enhances Waluchow's theory without compromising his principal ideas.

Like the construction of a universal audience, Waluchow's construction of CCM starts with a particular audience—the community that is governed by the constitution in question. From it, the judge derives an idealized version through a process meant to discard problematic aspects of the audience's actual perspective. However, the audience that a judge would construct as accepting Waluchow's CCM is less fully idealized than the universal audience. This is because Waluchow requires judges to integrate even beliefs that the judge herself finds gravely mistaken into CCM, as long as those beliefs can survive the process of reflective equilibrium. For example, even a pro-life judge would, in Canada, be unable to construct the Canadian community's CCM as reflecting the pro-life view, no matter how morally repugnant she might think abortion to be. The judge would therefore have to accept that an idealized democratic Canadian audience would consider reproductive rights to include access to abortion. This is so because the method of reflective equilibrium as Waluchow envisions it does not prioritize the belief-system of the reasoner/arguer/judge like constructions of the universal audience do. Rather, it aims at the internal coherence of the resulting CCM. This makes sense because Waluchow's goal is not to guide the judge to finding the *correct* answer to their question about constitutional interpretation from the point of view of abstract, platonic morality. Rather, Waluchow wants the judge to use their discretion in the service of realizing the authentic commitments of the democratically organized community: Constructing an idealized audience via Waluchow's CCM therefore must aim at constructing the idealized democratic audience instead of the universal audience.

I also believe that the use of CCM is parallel to the use of an idealized audience in rhetorical argumentation theory. Walcuhow asks judges to find answers to their question of constitutional interpretation through the perspective of someone (the democratic constitutional community) who accepts CCM. Thereby, Waluchow's judge excludes premises and kinds of inferences that she herself may accept, but that are not included in, or follow from, CCM. Like the rhetorical arguer, she is constrained from two sides: She may only use what the constitutional community accepts, and she may only use those aspects of it that withstand the test of the reflective equilibrium. Further, Waluchow's idea that judges can make democratically legitimate decisions by relying on the community's true commitments as they deduce them from the community's democratically determined actions mirrors Tindale's tool of an audience's cognitive environment. And so does the introduction of the possibility of constructing CCM through the use of public reasons: Both the possibility to deducing true commitments from the community's actions and the ability of using public reasons in order to construct CCM releases judges from the restriction to only use premises that the members of the democratic community already reflectively accept. However, it holds them bound to the restriction that only what is already in the community's cognitive field of vision is available. This brings into reach those insights into the nature of CCM that are not yet salient to the community, but which can be constructed through inferential steps warranted by the community's own commitments. It is important to note, at this point, that Waluchow refuses to give more than a general description of what reasons count as public reasons. From the point of view of rhetorical argumentation theory this refusal to provide a determinate definition is not a flaw, but a boon of his theory. Those reasons count as public reasons that have the status of being reasons based on the minimal concept of reasonableness about which an overlapping consensus exist in the constitutional community. Waluchow can then be interpreted as committed to the rhetorical idea that even what counts as a reason is audience-dependent.

4.2 A Change in Judicial Self-perception

In sum, then, there are striking parallels between rhetorical argumentation theory's use of ideal audiences and Waluchow's use of CCM. Importantly, however, the move of framing Waluchow's theory of constitutional interpretation as one that asks judges to engage in rhetorical argumentative reasoning is not just a change in vocabulary. It contains an important shift, a shift that I believe is beneficial and want to encourage: A judge who moves from seeing herself deciding constitutional cases while using CCM as a reasoning tool to seeing herself as constructing arguments for an idealized audience consisting of the democratic community of which she is only *one* member thereby also changes her self-perception. She stops conceptualizing herself as a decision maker aimed at making the right decision. Instead, she thinks of herself as an arguer aiming to construct a convincing argument whose ultimate cogency will depend on the assent of her audience—the idealized version of the democratic community. The difference is perhaps easiest to express by saying that judges under the first self-conceptualization write opinions in order to *explain* their decisions, which assumes that the decisions are correct and the audience need to be shown why. Judges under the second self-conceptualization write opinions to *argue* for their decisions, which assumes that the decisions are reasonable attempts at correctness and the audience is the yardstick by which this correctness is measured.

Waluchow's interpretive method, as I frame it, then does not simply yield results that mirror the outcomes of democratic decision making. It also causes a shift in judicial self-perception that imbues judicial review as a process with a democratic spirit: Judges see themselves as quite literally as public *servants* to the democratic community, to which they belong as only one member, and submit the correctness of their decision to the measure of that community's assent.

4.3 What the Rhetorical Theory of Argumentation Suggests for the Development of Waluchow's Theory of CCM

In my estimation, Waluchow's work on his theory of CCM after the appearance of his 2007 book has developed the theory in beneficial ways that open the possibility of interpreting it in the terms of rhetorical argumentation theory. However, I think that there is still the possibility to worry that even if judges take their ideal CCM audience as the yardstick by which to measure the validity of their constitutional arguments and decisions, CCM itself remains their own work, unchecked by the democratic will of the community. This leaves judges with the ability to automatically reject criticisms of their decisions by simply claiming that these criticisms a based in the mere opinions, sorted out by the process of amelioration towards CCM and therefore unable to support a serious objection.

I believe that rhetorical argumentation theory provides the necessary theoretical tool to develop the theory of CCM in a way that can deal with this worry. The reader may remember that I spent some time explaining Crosswhite's concept of the undefined universal audience and the ever-present possibility that it might at any moment become embodied by a member of the particular audience. This audience member may criticize the arguer's construction of the universal audience, prompting them to revise their idea of reasonability and thereby the yardstick by which they themselves measure the validity of their arguments. I believe that Waluchow's theory of CCM needs to integrate a similar element. Waluchow's normative theory of interpretation should require judges to pay attention to the reactions that their decisions engender in political, public, even academic discourse and to remain on the look-out for reasons to believe that their construction of CCM was flawed or has become outdated. Where judges find such reasons, they should be required to adjust their theory of CCM for later decisions and, if necessary, to revisit an issue they might have already considered settled. Only then does the normative theory of interpretation Waluchow suggests tie judges' construction of CCM—the idealized audience of the democratic community—back to the actual constitutional community. This then completes the re-conceptualization of judges engaged in judicial review as serving their democratic community, creating a process of judicial review that is imbued with a democratic spirit through and through instead of just aiming at outcomes that mirror outcomes with democratic pedigree.

While Waluchow has not, so far, discussed such an element in great detail, he has mentioned the possibility of a dialogue between the courts and the legislature approvingly in his 2007 book, when he cited Hogg and Bushell (p. 146 ff). Hogg and Bushell (1997) argue that the Canadian court-system stands in a dialogue with the Canadian legislature because the specific way in which the constitution is set up enables the legislature to issue a response to most decisions made in the course of judicial review. The most powerful instrument for making such responses is section 33, the override clause, which allows the legislature to enact a statute "notwithstanding" its (perceived) conflict with a constitutional right. In addition, there are less powerful instruments that give the legislature the ability to realize its objective by amending the rejected legislation.

Waluchow can also point to the Canadian Supreme Court's history, should he wish to integrate an element parallel to the undefined universal audience into his theory. The SCC has re-considered older decisions when community members bring issues before the court again, such as when they repeated their discussion of the constitutionality of a statute forbidding physician assisted death.[9] Because such things have already happened, it would not require much argument to justify integrating a requirement for the court to be open to re-hearing cases on already decided issues into Waluchow's theory. As a result, members of the constitutional community would be given the chance to correct their court's idea of what CCM is, completing Waluchow's project of democratizing judicial review.

References

Aikin, S.F. 2011. The rhetorical theory of argument is self-defeating. *Cogency* 3: 79–92.
Alexander, L. 2009. Waluchow's living tree constitutionalism. *Law and Philosophy* 29: 93–99.
Brand-Ballard, J. 2008. Review essay: A common law theory of judicial review by W.J. Waluchow. *Notre Dame Philosophical Reviews*. http://ndpr.nd.edu/review.cfm?id=14605.
Carter v. Canada (Attorney General), 2015 SCC 5, [2015] 1 S.C.R. 331.
Crosswhite, J. 1996. *The rhetoric of reason: Writing and the attractions of argument*. Wisconsin: University of Wisconsin Press.
Dworkin, R. 1986. *Law's empire*. Cambridge: Belknapp Press.
———. 1996. *Freedom's law: The moral reading of the American constitution*. Oxford: Oxford University Press.
Freeman, S. 1990. Constitutional democracy and the legitimacy of judicial review. *Law and Philosophy* 9: 327–370. https://doi.org/10.1007/BF00212703.
Habermas, J. 1980. Discourse ethics: Notes on philosophical justification. In *Moral consciousness and communicative action*. Cambridge: MIT Press.
Hogg, P.W., and A.A. Bushell. 1997. The charter dialogue between courts and legislatures (or perhaps the charter of rights isn't such a bad thing after all). *Osgoode Hall Law Journal (1960)* 35: 75.
Johnson, R. 2000. *Manifest rationality*. Mahwah: Routledge.
Miller, B. 2007. Review essay: A common law theory *the*. *American Journal of Jurisprudence* 52. http://ssrn.com/abstract=1093365.
Perelman, C., and L. Olbrechts-Tyteca. 1969. *The new rhetoric: A treatise on argumentation*. Notre Dame: University of Notre Dame Press.
Rawls, J. 1996. *Political liberalism*. New York: Columbia University Press.
Raz, J. 1979. *The authority of law: Essays on law and morality*. Oxford: Clarendon Press.
Rodriguez v. British Columbia (Attorney General), [1993] 3 S.C.R. 519.
Stoljar, N. 2009. Waluchow on moral opinions and moral commitments. *Problema* 3.
Struchiner, N., and F. Shecaira. 2009. Trying to fix roots in quicksand: Some difficulties with Waluchow's conception of the true community morality. *Problema* 3: 134–145.
Tindale, C.W. 1992. Audiences, relevance, and cognitive environments. *Argumentation* 6: 177–188. https://doi.org/10.1007/BF00154324.

[9] See the decisions *Rodriguez v. British Columbia* (1993) and *Carter v. Canada* (2015).

———. 1999. *Acts of arguing: A rhetorical modal of argument*. Albany: State University of New York Press.
———. 2004. *Rhetorical Argumentation*. Thousand Oaks: Sage.
———. 2015. *The philosophy of argument and audience reception*. Cambridge: Cambridge University Press.
Waldron, J. 1993. A right-based critique of constitutional rights. *Oxford Journal of Legal Studies* 13: 18–51. https://doi.org/10.1093/ojls/13.1.18.
———. 2004. *Law and disagreement*. Oxford: Oxford University Press.
———. 2006. The Core of the case against judicial review. *The Yale Law Journal* 115: 1346–1406. https://doi.org/10.2307/20455656.
Waluchow, W. 2007. *A common law theory of judicial review*. New York: Cambridge University Press.
———. 2008. Constitutional morality and bills of rights. In *Expounding the constitution*, ed. G. Huscroft, 65–92. Cambridge: Cambridge University Press.
———. 2010. Constitutional morality and judicial review. In *Constitutional topography: Values and constitutions*, ed. A. Sajo and R. Uitz, 3–20. The Hague: Eleven International Publishing.
———. 2013. On the neutrality of charter reasoning. In *Neutrality and theory of law*, ed. J. Ferrer Beltran, J.J. Mareso, and D.M. Papayannis, 203–224. Dordrecht: Springer.
———. 2014. Democracy and living constitutionalism. In *Courts, interpretation and the rule of law*, ed. K.E. Himma and M.A. Jovanovic, 73–88. The Hague: Eleven International Publishing.
———. 2015. Constitutional rights and the possibility of detached constructive interpretation. *Problema* 9: 23–52.

Katharina Stevens is Associate Professor of Philosophy at the University of Lethbridge, Canada. She holds a Ph.D in Philosophy from McMaster University and a MA in Philosophy from the University of Windsor, Canada. She has published works in peer reviewed journals such as *Topoi*, *Argumentation and Advocacy*, *Legal Theory*, *Informal Logic*, and *Argumentation*.

Waluchow on Reasoning with the Morality of the Community

Fábio Perin Shecaira

Abstract This chapter discusses Wil Waluchow's recent work on the legitimacy of judicial review. More specifically, the chapter assesses Waluchow's claim that judicial review under bills of rights can be a democratically legitimate practice so long as judges base their interpretation of constitutional rights on the "community's constitutional morality". Judges, according to Waluchow, must take care to respect the community's constitutional philosophy instead of imposing their own political views on the community. The chapter recognizes the merits of Waluchow's views but also indicates some ways in which they should be developed and supplemented. For these purposes, the chapter relies on a distinction (proposed by Joseph Raz and elaborated by John Gardner) between reasoning about the law and reasoning with the law. The chapter proposes an analogous distinction between reasoning about and reasoning with the constitutional morality of the community.

1 The Democratic Legitimacy of Constitutional Review

Wil Waluchow has argued that judicial review of legislation under bills of rights is, or at least can be, a democratically legitimate practice. Even though judges in constitutional courts are typically unelected and bills of rights are filled with vague notions (dignity, equality, freedom, due process, etc.), it is not necessarily undemocratic for judges to strike down legislation that they consider to be in conflict with constitutional rights. According to Waluchow, judges may legitimately enforce vaguely worded constitutional rights so long as they ground their interpretation of such rights on the fundamental convictions of the community whose interests are at stake. Judges should not impose their personal moral philosophies upon the community but should let themselves be guided by the philosophy of that very community. What matters is how the community understands the relevant notions—

F. P. Shecaira (✉)
Federal University of Rio de Janeiro, Faculdade Nacional de Direito, Rio de Janeiro, Brazil
e-mail: fabioperin@direito.ufrj.br

T. Bustamante et al. (eds.), *Law, Morality and Judicial Reasoning*, Law and Philosophy Library 147, https://doi.org/10.1007/978-3-031-61879-6_12

dignity, equality, freedom, due process, etc.—not how individual judges would like them to be understood.

So, according to Waluchow, in interpreting and applying constitutional rights, judges should seek to enforce a "kind of community-based, positive morality consisting of the fundamental moral norms and convictions to which the democratic community has actually committed itself and which have acquired some kind of formal, constitutional recognition" (Waluchow 2018, p. 121). Judicial review of legislation under bills of rights is legitimate so long as it reflects and enforces the *community's constitutional morality* (or CCM).

The nature of CCM and its importance to judicial review are major topics in Waluchow's important book, *A Common Law Theory of Judicial Review: The Living Tree* (2007). Recently, Waluchow has returned to these topics in order to address objections formulated by different authors. One of these objections—perhaps the most significant one—is the argument that CCM does not offer much in the way of guidance for judges in industrialized and culturally complex societies like Canada, the US, Brazil, etc.[1] "The community", a term implying unity and homogeneity, is, in fact, often in deep disagreement about the meaning and scope of fundamental rights. How can judges rely on CCM to interpret the concept of *freedom*, say, when "the community" is actually a diverse group of people made up of liberals, libertarians, communitarians, socialists, etc.? In any truly diverse community, judges will end up choosing, among the possible alternatives, the conception of freedom that they, the judges, find most attractive. But that does not seem very democratic.

Let us call this argument the "Objection from Diversity". Waluchow has an interesting answer to give to this objection. Indeed, the purpose of the present chapter is to analyze Waluchow's recent attempt to refute the Objection from Diversity in a recent paper titled "Normative Reasoning from a Point of View" (2018). My critical comments will appear in Sect. 3, after some preliminary remarks in Sect. 2. The point of Sect. 2 is to introduce some general concepts from argumentation theory that should help us to assess Waluchow's views.

2 Reasoning with the Law

Waluchow acknowledges that CCM may lack the consistency or homogeneity necessary to guide and constrain judges in constitutional cases. But he insists that this does not negate the legitimacy of constitutional review. Waluchow's argument is neatly summarized in the following passage:

> So even when a judge must engage in contentious moral reasoning in choosing from among alternatives the norms of CCM appear to leave open, we may still sensibly view her as reasoning and choosing from a detached perspective, ie. from a point of view defined by the substantive constraints imposed by the community's prior moral commitments. *She is still*

[1] This objection is formulated, for instance, by Struchiner and Shecaira (2009).

> *working from these premises* regardless of whether she might have preferred (morally) to work from very different ones. (Waluchow 2018, p. 129; emphasis added)

The final sentence in this passage may remind one of the influential distinction proposed by Joseph Raz (1995) and elaborated by John Gardner (2012) between two types of legal reasoning, namely, reasoning *about* the law and reasoning *with* (or according to) the law.[2] The first type of legal reasoning involves the straightforward application of an already-valid legal norm to the facts of a legal case. In more technical terms, it is the type of reasoning that has only valid legal norms as major or operative premises. For example:

Argument 1

1. Anyone who enters a public park with a vehicle is liable to pay a fine of $100 (a valid legal norm);
2. John entered a public park with his car (facts of the case);
3. So, John is liable to pay a fine of $100 (ruling).

Reasoning with (or according to) the law, on the other hand, is more complex than that. As Gardner puts it, it is the kind of reasoning that has "already-valid legal norms among its major or operative premises, but combines them non-redundantly in the same argument with moral or other merit-based premises" (Gardner 2012, p. 39). Below is one of Gardner's examples, slightly modified for my purposes.[3] Notice that the ruling is not based simply on the application of a legal norm to the facts of the case but, more circuitously, on the interaction of norms of different kinds:

Argument 2

1. The Civil Rights Act of 1964 gives everyone the legal right not to be discriminated against in respect of employment on the ground of his or her sex (a valid legal norm);
2. Denying a woman a job on the ground of her pregnancy is morally on a par with discriminating against her on the ground of her sex (a moral norm);
3. So, women have a legal right not to be denied a job on the ground of their pregnancies (a new legal norm);
4. Now, this woman P has been denied a job by D on the ground of her pregnancy (facts of the case);
5. So, D owes P a job (ruling).

Argument 2 is more complex than Argument 1 in more than one way. While Argument 1 contains only of one inference (from 1 and 2 to 3), Argument 2 is a composite of two inferences (from 1 and 2 to 3, and from 3 and 4 to 5).[4] But that is not the difference between Arguments 1 and 2 that is most relevant to this paper. More significant is the fact that Argument 2 does not rely exclusively on premises

---

[2] I discuss the importance (and the limitations) of the distinction in Shecaira (2014).

[3] For the original argument, see Gardner (2012, pp. 39–40).

[4] Notice also that the first of these two inferences is non-deductive, which arguably makes its evaluation less straightforward.

expressing already-valid legal norms, but also on a premise expressing a moral norm not yet sanctioned by positive law, namely, premise 2. The existing legal norm about discrimination on the ground of sex (premise 1) does quite not reach the case of P, who has been discriminated against on the ground of pregnancy. To justify a conclusion in favor of P, the arguing judge affirms a connection of a moral nature between the two kinds of discrimination. She then constructs a new legal norm (premise 3), which is something she is authorized to do on the assumption that judges have law-making powers.[5] As Gardner might put it, there is more than one norm "operating" in Argument 2, and they are not all norms of positive law.

For jurists who are suspicious about judicial discretion at every level, Argument 1 is an example of the ideal type of legal argument. But even the most severe critic of judicial discretion must acknowledge that reasoning with the law is a common feature of legal adjudication. Indeed, I would argue that is an unavoidable aspect of adjudication. Whenever positive law is indeterminate or requires revision (e.g. because there is social pressure for its reach to be altered, as in the case of P versus D), then legal reasoning will involve the combination of legal premises with moral or other non-legal premises that are needed to fill in the law's gaps or help redraw its limits.[6] It seems to me that this is also the kind of reasoning that Waluchow has in mind when acknowledging the existence of constitutional cases where judges will have to "work from the premises" of CCM. They will take these premises as starting points but will need to resort to moral considerations about how to resolve occasional inconsistencies in CCM.

To be clear, Waluchow himself does not rely on Gardner's definition of reasoning with the law. What I am proposing is that Waluchow's understanding of reasoning "from the premises of CCM" is analogous to Gardner's understanding of reasoning with the law (even though the legal premises in Gardner's examples are derived from statute or precedent, not from CCM[7]). These are structurally similar ways of reasoning because they impose similar constraints on a judge's ability to choose her own premises.

Here is another one of Gardner's examples of reasoning with the law (again, slightly modified for my purposes[8]). It is particularly germane to our discussion because it shows how moral considerations may be used in order to resolve inconsistencies within the law (or within CCM, as the case may be):

Argument 3

[5] The law-making power of a judge tends to be more restricted than that of legislators, although that is something that varies according, inter alia, to the nature of the local doctrine of stare decisis.

[6] At any rate, this is how legal positivists (Waluchow being one of them) tend to think: all law is positive law; and positive law is not capable of solving every legal question that might reach the courts. Positive law is often vague, ambiguous, contradictory, etc.

[7] In any case, the distinction between positive law and CCM is not very sharp. As Waluchow puts it, CCM is a positive morality that has received some kind of formal, constitutional recognition (e.g., by being referred to in constitutional precedent).

[8] See Gardner (2012, p. 187).

1. Tortfeasors are liable to pay full reparative damages to those whom they tortiously injure (a valid legal norm);
2. Jones tortiously injured Smith to the tune of $100 (fact of the case);
3. But the tort was also the breach of a contract between Jones and Smith, and the contract provided for maximum reparative damages of $50 for any breach (also a fact of the case);
4. Contracts and the limits on damages they set are legally binding as between parties to the contract (a valid legal norm);
5. And it is unjust to let someone avoid a legally binding contractual limit on damages by instead suing the other contracting party in tort (a moral norm);
6. So, Jones is liable to pay Smith only $50 in reparative damages (ruling).

In this argument, a moral norm (premise 5) is brought in to resolve a conflict between valid and applicable legal norms (premises 1 and 4). This, I surmise, is roughly the sort of exercise in which any judge will have to engage when trying to enforce constitutional rights on the basis of CCM in a divided community. That is to say, this is the sort of exercise that the judge will have to undertake whenever there is a need to decide which of two (or more) competing conceptions of the relevant rights ought to be enforced.[9] Although limited to the conceptions endorsed by the community (personally she may support none of them), the judge will have to exercise independent judgment about which conception is preferable (at least in the sense of being the least wrongheaded or least suboptimal). In other words, she will have to construct an argument that combines CCM-based premises with other kinds of premises as to which of the conflicting CCM norms is preferable for the community, in the sense of being, e.g., more just or more humane or more useful.

3 Reasoning with the Morality of the Community

So, I submit that a helpful way to interpret Waluchow's reply to the Objection from Diversity is this. Constitutional review will not always be based on straightforward reasoning *about* the law or about the positive morality of the community. Sometimes it will be based on reasoning *with* the law or *with* the positive morality of the community. This is not an uncommon form of legal reasoning; in fact, judges engage in it routinely, within and outside the domain of constitutional law. How could they not, if positive law and positive morality are so often indeterminate?

But a problem remains. The definition of reasoning with the law proposed by Gardner is vulnerable to the criticism that it is overbroad.[10] Reasoning that combines legal norms with non-legal norms does not come only in the relatively uncontroversial forms exemplified by Arguments 2 and 3. There are arguments

[9] I am assuming that conflicts between CCM norms cannot be resolved by means of any simple maxim such as *lex posterior derogat priori*.

[10] Or so I argue in Shecaira (2014).

that fit the general definition of reasoning with the law but that many would not regard as involving the exercise of a normal and legitimate amount of discretion. Taking the case of *Lochner v. New York* as a loose source of inspiration, let us consider the following argument:

Argument 4

1. The liberty of the individual is to be protected against state interference (a valid legal norm stating a constitutional right);
2. The liberty of the individual encompasses the right to purchase or sell labor (a morally contentious definition of the scope of the right);
3. So, the liberty of the individual to purchase or sell labor is to be protected against state interference (a new legal norm);
4. So, the liberty of bakery employees to agree to work for more than 60 h a week or 10 h a day is to be protected against state interference (ruling).

According to Gardner's definition, this should count as reasoning with the law. It combines legal and moral premises in an attempt to determine the scope of the constitutional right to liberty. But it is hard to avoid the sense that, in Argument 4, the law is exercising very little constraint—arguably less than is necessary for democratic legitimacy. The arguer takes a notoriously ambiguous concept, that of *liberty*, and glibly asserts that it encompasses the (apparently unlimited) right to purchase and sell labor. That may be a case of reasoning with (a modicum of) the law, but it is still a highly discretionary kind of reasoning that is apt to worry critics of constitutional review.

In fact, going back to Argument 3, one might now want to argue that it, too, is marked by a problematic glibness. The conflict of norms is resolved in that argument by means of a questionable moral claim: "it is unjust to let someone avoid a legally binding contractual limit on damages by instead suing the other contracting party in tort". But what if the tort was premeditated? Is it not also unjust to allow someone to use a contract as a means to avoid making full compensation for harm they intended to inflict? The conflict of norms was settled very quickly in Argument 3, and there are grounds for contending that Argument 3, albeit a case of reasoning with the law, is not the kind of reasoning that we want judges to engage in—at least not when constitutional rights are at stake.

Glib resolutions of conflicts of norms are common and worrisome to constitutional lawyers. It is precisely this worry that explains the popularity of attempts to structure and render more objective the process of balancing constitutional rights; think, for instance, of the so-called "proportionality test" in its various forms. Imagine that a judge were trying to reason her way through a conflict within CCM. For example, she might have to choose between alternative interpretations of the concept *liberty* that are endorsed by different groups within the community and are equally compatible with existing constitutional doctrine. How should a judge reason with these norms of CCM? How could she attempt to settle the conflict without making herself vulnerable to the sort of criticism attracted by the likes of the *Lochner* decision?

I will not limit myself here to pointing out the problem. Some brief suggestions for mitigating it promptly come to mind, and we might take the opportunity to ask if Waluchow would want to endorse any of the following propositions:

1) For the sake of clarity, conflicts within CCM should be adjudicated by application of some explicit and systematic method (as opposed to being adjudicated on the basis of judicial intuition). It is important for an author like Waluchow, involved as he is in a project about the legitimacy of judicial review, to propose a particular method for the resolution of conflicts between (conceptions of) constitutional rights. An obvious candidate would be, to repeat, the proportionality test, given its promise of providing structure and transparency to constitutional reasoning. It should be emphasized, however, that the proportionality test is not to be valued as a means of significantly reducing judicial discretion but, more realistically, as a means of exposing the assumptions that a judge brings to bear in her assessment of the relative importance of the conflicting (conceptions of) rights.
2) To minimize the chance that judges will make personal and idiosyncratic judgements about the relative importance of different conceptions of rights, conflicts within CCM could be adjudicated by application of criteria that do not violate the duty to argue on the basis of "public reasons" (in more or less the Rawlsian sense).[11] This second suggestion, in contrast to the previous one, is put forward in the hope that it may serve to limit judicial discretion in at least one sense. Religious considerations, for instance, are notoriously problematic for public reasoning, just like any other consideration that would not be endorsed by all reasonable members of the community. Limits on judicial discretion with respect to possible grounds for a decision are significant from the point of view of democratic legitimacy, even if such limits do not necessarily reduce judicial discretion with respect to the variety of possible rulings (e.g. a judge impeded from grounding a conservative ruling on religious considerations may still find suitably secular reasons for the same decision).[12]
3) In light of the idea that democratic nations form a wider community with fundamentally shared values, conflicts within CCM could be adjudicated in the same way as they have been adjudicated by the courts of other democratic nations in similar cases. This suggestion may serve to limit discretion with respect to the outcomes themselves, at least when there is a clear consensus among democratic nations with respect to the matter under contention. When there is no such consensus, any reference to the laws of foreign countries could be vulnerable to the charge of cherry-picking.

[11] The ideal of public reason is often attacked for being overly rigid, rationalistic and even undemocratic. For a more positive take on public reason, see Shecaira and Struchiner (2019).

[12] It should be noted that Waluchow has often expressed sympathy for such Rawlsian concepts as *public reason* and *reflective equilibrium*. My suggestion that Waluchow should use Rawlsian ideas to supplement his work may thus sound odd. The oddness disappears, however, if we consider that there is some disagreement between us about to how to use Rawlsian ideas in connection with CCM. In particular, I have objected to Waluchow's use of the device of reflective equilibrium as a means of reducing judicial discretion with respect to rulings (as distinct from the grounds thereof). See Struchiner and Shecaira (2009).

Of course, this list is not exhaustive. All foregoing suggestions have to do with the adjudication of conflicts within CCM; i.e. with the appropriate way to reason with inconsistent premises derived from the morality of the community. It is also important to try to devise instructions to help judges identify CCM norms prior to balancing; i.e. instructions that could help to minimize errors in the preliminary process of deriving the relevant premises from CCM.[13] In sketching out these suggestions, my purpose has not been to solve the problems left open by Waluchow's work but simply to illustrate the point that the democratic legitimacy of constitutional review requires more than the general idea that judges should reason "with" or "from" CCM norms. This idea is a sensible one, but it ought to be complemented by more definite suggestions about how judges should use premises drawn from CCM. Referring to these premises and glibly adjudicating conflicts between them is not what we expect of judges in constitutional cases. It is not enough to start from the right premises. As the discussion around *Lochner* has shown, the right premises must still be handled with democratic care.

4 Conclusion

This chapter is not unsympathetic to Waluchow's general project. I agree with the idea that judicial attention to CCM is a promising way to improve the democratic status of constitutional review. This is an important point, since judicial review of legislation is a practice that many constitutional systems currently authorize and will probably continue to authorize in the decades to come. That being the case, it is expected that scholars engage in discussion about how to improve the practice.

On the other hand, this chapter is critical insofar as it emphasizes questions in need of response. How exactly are judges to adjudicate the frequent conflicts between the norms of CCM? Can a judge who simply picks one of the conflicting norms on the basis of intuition be described as arguing *with* or *from* the norms of CCM in any significant sense? Can the relevant norm be selected in such a way that judges will be genuinely limited in their exercise of discretion? I suppose that the readers of Waluchow's work will be interested to see how he would respond to these questions.

Acknowledgements I am grateful to two anonymous referees for comments on a draft of this chapter. Wil Waluchow was my doctoral supervisor from 2009 to 2012 at McMaster University. I am deeply indebted to him for his guidance and kindness over the years. It is an honor to contribute a chapter to a volume dedicated to his outstanding scholarship.

[13] One such suggestion could be that constitutional courts ought to encourage members of the community to participate in legal debate by submitting *amicus curiae* briefs or attending public hearings.

References

Gardner, John. 2012. *Law as a leap of faith. Essays on law in general.* Oxford: Oxford University Press.
Raz, Joseph. 1995. *Ethics in the public domain. Essays in the morality of law and politics.* Oxford: Clarendon Press.
Shecaira, Fábio Perin. 2014. Gardner on legal reasoning. *Law and Philosophy* 33 (6): 747–772.
Shecaira, Fábio Perin, and Noel Struchiner. 2019. Audience diversity and the rhetorical value of public reason. *Rechtstheorie* 50: 1–16.
Struchiner, Noel, and Fábio Perin Shecaira. 2009. Trying to fix roots in quicksand: Some difficulties with Waluchow's conception of the true community morality. *Problema* 3: 133–145.
Waluchow, W.J. 2007. *A common law theory of judicial review: The living tree.* New York: Cambridge University Press.
———. 2018. Normative reasoning from a point of view. In *Unpacking normativity: Conceptual, normative, and descriptive issues*, ed. Kenneth Himma et al. Oxford: Hart.

Fábio Perin Shecaira is Professor of Legal Theory, Faculty of Law of the Federal University of Rio de Janeiro (since 2012). He has a PhD in Philosophy from McMaster University (2012) and has been a Visiting Researcher at Harvard Law School (2011). He has published in English in journals like *History of Philosophy Quarterly*, *Australian Journal of Legal Philosophy*, *Law and Philosophy*, *Informal Logic*, *Ratio Juris* and *Argumentation*.

Part III
Constitutional Morality Applied

Reconciliation and the Living Tree Metaphor

Michael Giudice and Xavier Scott

Abstract The 'living tree' metaphor has become a central way of understanding constitutional interpretation in Canada. It also serves as the foundation of Wil Waluchow's important work on a 'common law' conception of constitutionalism. Yet despite the clear normative appeal of the metaphor, for a progressive and adaptive constitutional order, we believe it has some significant moral, political, and legal presumptions and limits. We argue that such limits and presumptions become apparent when examining Canada's commitment to reconciliation between settler institutions and Indigenous peoples, which reveal the metaphor to be more of an obstacle than an aid to reconciliation. We suggest we are likely better off suspending use of the metaphor (and its associated constitutional constraints) and must instead look for alternative constitutional perspectives. In particular, Indigenous conceptions of nation-to-nation partnerships and Two Row Wampum diplomacy provide valuable sources for rethinking settler-Indigenous relations in Canada.

1 Introduction

The 'living tree' has become something of an iconic metaphor in Canadian constitutional law, serving as a high-order principle for courts in interpreting constitutional provisions of various kinds. The metaphor was first introduced in the well-known 'Persons case', declaring the Canadian constitution open to incremental change and growth over time via judicial interpretation.[1] The normative appeal of the metaphor of course lies in its aspiration for a progressive society and commitment to adapt constitutional law to evolving social and political conditions. Yet, like many metaphors, its apparent benefits risk overshadowing its hidden costs, in this instance, of a

[1] *Edwards v. Canada* [1930] A.C. 124.

M. Giudice (✉) · X. Scott
York University, Department of Philosophy, Faculty of Liberal Arts and Professional Studies, Toronto, ON, Canada
e-mail: giudice@yorku.ca; xscott@yorku.ca

T. Bustamante et al. (eds.), *Law, Morality and Judicial Reasoning*, Law and Philosophy Library 147, https://doi.org/10.1007/978-3-031-61879-6_13

primarily moral and political nature. The vast majority of criticisms of living tree constitutional interpretation focus on democratic and separation of powers arguments, namely, that it is undemocratic for unelected, unaccountable judges to be making law (and especially law of the highest order, constitutional law), which is within the sole purview of democratic institutions such as legislatures. This will not be our line of critique. Instead, we shall subject the living tree metaphor to sustained scrutiny from the perspective of reconciliation with Indigenous peoples in Canada, and argue that the metaphor, and the commitments it represents, bind Canadian constitutional law to certain fixed structures and practices in particular, and a European and colonial past in general. Taking a nation-to-nation relationship and the Two Row Wampum as the foundation of reconciliation, we aim to show that the living tree metaphor, despite its positive connotations, may ultimately serve as an additional obstacle to reconciliation in Canadian law and politics. As we shall explain, reconciliation likely requires abandoning—or at the very least suspending endorsement of—the metaphor and its associated legal and political constraints. In its place we shall suggest that a forest, of multiple legal orders, and with new formative moments, might be a better metaphor for understanding the character and goals of reconciliation.

The chapter is divided into the following parts. In Sect. 2 we briefly trace the history of the metaphor and situate its understanding in an ongoing debate between living tree and fixed view conceptions of constitutionalism, with a special focus on Wil Waluchow's defence of a 'common law' conception of constitutionalism. In Sect. 3 we identify key presumptions and limits to application of the living tree conception of constitutionalism in Canada. In Sect. 4, freed from the presumptions and limits of the living tree conception, we present competing ways of understanding the character and goals of reconciliation between State institutions and Indigenous peoples in Canada. In Sect. 5, we examine Wampum diplomacy and the different approaches to law and political society advocated by a number of Indigenous scholars. Finally, in Sect. 6 we conclude with some observations about the need for the kind of work involved in assessing dominant metaphors and concepts in Western legal orders where reconciliation with Indigenous peoples must be taken seriously and meaningfully pursued.

2 Living Tree and Fixed Views of Constitutionalism

In 1928 the Supreme Court of Canada (SCC) unanimously ruled that women were excluded from the class of 'qualified persons' under the Constitution for the purpose of serving as Senators.[2] The SCC reached its decision in part by referring to Roman law and early English decisions, which did not consider women fit for any public

[2] *Reference Re Meaning of the Word "Persons" in Section 24 of the British North America Act, 1867* [1928] S.C.R. 276.

office. However, at the time the SCC was not in fact the highest court in Canada, as Canada was still largely a colony. There was therefore an opportunity for five women (the 'Famous Five')[3] to appeal the SCC's decision to the Judicial Committee of the Privy Council of England, which subsequently reversed the SCC's decision. In his opinion for the Privy Council Lord Sankey wrote:

> The British North America Act planted in Canada a living tree capable of growth and expansion within its natural limits. . .Their Lordships do not conceive it to be the duty of this Board—it is certainly not their desire—to cut down the provisions of the Act by a narrow and technical construction, but rather to give it a large and liberal interpretation so that the Dominion [of Canada] to a great extent, but within certain fixed limits, may be mistress in her own house, as the provinces to a great extent, but within certain fixed limits, are mistresses in theirs.[4]

Lord Sankey noted that Canada was itself a living and growing society, moving towards greater inclusion and equality.[5] Therefore, he argued, interpretation of its constitution ought to grow and adapt to the changing values of society, rather than be fixed according to the views of its authors. Since women had gained the right to vote a decade earlier and the term 'persons', while perhaps not originally intended to include women, could reasonably be interpreted as including them, Lord Sankey decided that women were therefore eligible to serve as senators under Canadian constitutional law. The rest is, as they say, history. The idea of the living tree, and the understanding that the constitution ought to be given a "large and liberal interpretation", especially in the *Charter* era, are now firmly in place in judicial practice in Canada.[6] As Grant Huscroft remarks, "Lord Sankey is not often discussed these days, but there is no doubt that his metaphor is the inspiration for the dominant school of thought on Charter interpretation – progressive interpretation" (Huscroft 2004, p. 415).

The living tree metaphor has not only become a central way of understanding constitutional interpretation in Canada. It also serves as the core idea for one of the most sustained defences of the *Charter of Rights and Freedoms* and judicial review

---

[3]The Famous Five were a group of suffragists from Alberta. Led by Judge Emily Murphy, they became famous for their success in arguing the 'Persons Case'. The other members included Nellie McClung, Louise McKinney, Henrietta Edwards, and Irene Parlby.

[4]*Edwards v. Canada* [1930] A.C. 124, at 136-7.

[5]For example, in *Edwards* the Privy Council notes the "continuous process of evolution" being undergone by the many communities under the British system of government and that Canada ought not to be judged according to standards used in communities that are in a different "stage of social, political, and economic development". Further, the primary reason for the Privy Council's decision rested on the need to provide a Constitution to Canada—"a responsible and developing state". Moreover, Lord Sankey notes that from 1916 until 1922, various statutes were passed to allow women the right to vote and sit as Members of Parliament in both the Provinces' and Dominion's legislative bodies.

[6]See, e.g., *Hunter v. Southam* [1984] 2 S.C.R. 145, at 155; *A.G. Quebec v. Blaikie* [1979] 2. S.C.R. 1016, at 1029; *Law Society of Upper Canada v. Shapinker* [1984] 1 S.C.R. 357, at 365; *Reference re Same-Sex Marriage* [2004] 3 S.C.R. 698, at para 22; *Reference re Securities Act* [2011] S.C.C. 66, at para 56.

in Canada. In *A Common Law Theory of Judicial Review: The Living Tree* (Waluchow 2007), Wil Waluchow develops a "common law" conception of charters of rights and argues how the practice of judicial review, despite objections, is defensible, perhaps even required, on democratic grounds. The common law conception is meant to reframe debate and urges both critics and advocates alike to rethink their popular understanding of charters of rights as commitments to "fixed points of agreement" to which later governments are bound. Against this understanding, Waluchow argues that charters of rights ought to be understood not as sets of fixed, unalterable standards, but rather as statements of fundamental commitments of political morality whose significance and implications can only be fully appreciated as they are developed incrementally over time, on a case by case (i.e., common law) basis. Waluchow offers an array of arguments showing why charters of rights are indeed valuable, and why judges—and not legislatures or other bodies—are better situated to interpret and protect such rights.

A key part of Waluchow's account is the difference between living tree approaches to constitutional interpretation and fixed view doctrines, which hold that constitutions ought to be interpreted according to their original meaning or intention.[7] Had the Privy Council in *Edwards* adopted a fixed view approach to legal interpretation, the Famous Five of course would have lost their claim to allow women to serve in the Senate. Yet such fixed view doctrines, while providing some certainty and stability, are not without their problems. As Waluchow observes, for example, an intergenerational problem will inevitably arise if a fixed view of constitutional interpretation is adopted: "[h]ow can one group of people justifiably place entrenched constitutional impediments of a decidedly moral nature in the way of a second group of people who might live in radically different circumstances and perhaps with radically different moral views?" (Waluchow 2023). Living tree approaches solve this problem by inviting judges to "recognize that constitutions can grow and adapt to ever-changing circumstances without losing their identity or their legitimacy" (Waluchow 2023).

Waluchow defends the living tree approach through careful analysis of the practice of judicial review of *Charter* rights in Canada and the system of common law interpretation according to precedent, whereby the law is not seen as fixed for all time but develops gradually as new issues arise:

> Charters need not be seen as embodying a naive confidence in our judgments about which rights count, how they are to be interpreted, and which political actions (including legislative acts) are consistent with fundamental rights. Charters can and should be viewed as representing a *concession* to our inability fully to understand both the nature of fundamental rights and how these might be infringed by government action - and this includes, paradigmatically, government actions premised on the relatively blunt instrument of binding general legislation (Waluchow 2005, p. 228, original emphasis).

[7]For a helpful overview of different types of fixed views, see Waluchow (2007, pp. 52–73).

Determining such infringements, Waluchow maintains, is often done on a case-by-case basis, where decisions develop the law and understanding of *Charter* rights in a piecemeal, incremental fashion.[8]

The connection between the living tree approach and judicial review has invited criticism that the living tree approach is undemocratic and puts too much power into the hands of judges. Jeremy Waldron, for example, has persistently opposed the practice of judicial review on precisely these grounds, maintaining that a democratic society ought to update its laws to reflect its moral commitments, should it wish to do so, through the legislative process and not courts.[9] Part of his worry is that judges can use judicial review to alter any law they disagree with on personal or ideological grounds and overturn laws passed by elected representatives. In response, Waluchow argues that the living tree interpretation of constitutions does not open the law to any and all changes a judge might wish to make. He notes:

> And just as the traditional rules of precedent combine respect for the (albeit limited) wisdom and authority of previous decision makers (legislative and judicial) with an awareness of the need to allow adaptation in the face of changing views, and new or unforeseen circumstances, so too must constitutional interpreters respect the wisdom and authority of previous interpreters, while allowing the constitution to adapt so as to respond to changing views, and new or unforeseen circumstances. *Living constitutional interpretation, though flexible and adaptive, is no less constrained and disciplined than reasoning under common law* (Waluchow 2023, emphasis added).

So, on the one hand, the living tree conception is promoted as a means to keep our constitutional protections up-to-date with contemporary ideas of morality and changing circumstances. However, on the other hand, it maintains a commitment to a given legal history to keep constitutional practice and interpretation from becoming a system whereby unelected judges rule according to their own arbitrary preferences.

The debate between Waluchow and Waldron is much richer than what we have presented here, but for our purposes its brief rehearsal is sufficient to begin to unpack some key presumptions and limits to the living tree conception of constitutionalism. In doing so, we aim not so much to challenge the living tree conception of constitutionalism in the abstract, but more so its application in particular contexts, and in this instance, the context of reconciliation in Canada between settler governments and Indigenous peoples.

3 Presumptions and Limits of the Living Tree Conception

In this section we identify key presumptions and limits of the application of the living tree conception of constitutionalism. In each instance we identify the presumptions and limits then show how they work to the detriment of the

---

[8] See also Kavanagh (2003, p. 55).

[9] See, for example, Waldron (1999).

understandings of Indigenous peoples and goals of reconciliation in Canada. This account will serve to demonstrate why, we believe, we ought to abandon—or at least suspend endorsement of—the living tree conception as the best way to understand and practice constitutionalism in Canada. The account will also help to set up exploration, based on Indigenous perspectives, of an alternative conception of constitutionalism in the remaining sections.

3.1 Presumption 1. Acceptable Versus Unacceptable Growth

Defenders of the living tree approach, such as Waluchow, have something of a more challenging task than fixed view proponents, since they must presume and navigate a boundary between (i) change and development of constitutional law through judicial interpretation which is compatible with existing practice and commitments and (ii) change and development which is not. Is there a way of formulating a standard to delineate the boundary, or will the boundary itself need determination on a case-by-case basis? Fixed view doctrines permit no such change, and therefore face no such challenge (though of course, what might be an easier approach on some grounds may not necessarily be the correct approach, as Waluchow might point out).

To address this challenge Waluchow introduces the idea of a 'community's constitutional morality': a community's true moral commitments, which might very well differ from prevailing but ultimately misguided moral opinions (Waluchow 2007, pp. 233–238).[10] The idea of a community's constitutional morality draws inspiration from John Rawls's notion of a reflective equilibrium, which moves between general moral principles and considered moral judgments, and which in Rawls's hands presents a powerful tool for thinking about political morality and constitutional morality in particular. We do not aim to challenge Waluchow's account of a community's constitutional morality, but do observe that it leaves intact the key question identified above—how might courts be guided in determining, and how might the rest of us tell, whether particular change and growth falls within the limits permitted by the living tree approach? This question, we submit, takes on increased significance when viewed in combination with the second presumption identified next, where some moral growth and development might be needed but might require more than the incremental kind of change provided by living tree or common law constitutionalism.

Yet wherever that boundary might lie, we can note that Indigenous peoples have not fared very well under Canada's living tree constitution, which does seem to permit courts quite a bit of discretion in when to develop the law and when not to. John Borrows, for example, has perhaps done more than most to show that, despite large, liberal, and progressive interpretations given to *Charter* rights, Indigenous rights have been "frozen" in time by the courts, restricted to protecting

[10] See also Waluchow (2008).

practices, customs, and traditions as they existed pre-contact with Europeans (Borrows 1997–1998).[11] And even when Indigenous peoples have tried to avail themselves of specific *Charter* rights, they have met little success. For a recent illustration, consider the SCC case, *Ktunaxa Nation v. British Columbia*, in which the Ktunaxa Nation argued that their *Charter* right to freedom of religion ought to extend to protection of land considered to be sacred.[12] At issue in the case was the construction of an overnight ski resort on traditional Ktunaxa grounds (Qat'muk), which the Ktunaxa sincerely believed would drive Grizzly Bear Spirit from the land. In rejecting the claim, the majority explained:

> The Ktunaxa must show that the Minister's decision to approve the development interferes either with their freedom to believe in Grizzly Bear Spirit or their freedom to manifest that belief. But the Minister's decision does neither of those things. This case is not concerned with either the freedom to hold a religious belief or to manifest that belief. The claim is rather that s. 2 (a) of the Charter protects the presence of Grizzly Bear Spirit in Qat'muk. This is a *novel* claim and invites this Court to extend s. 2 (a) beyond the scope recognized in our law... We would decline this invitation. The state's duty under s. 2(a) is not to protect the object of beliefs, such as Grizzly Bear Spirit. Rather, the state's duty is to protect everyone's freedom to hold such beliefs and to manifest them in worship and practice or by teaching and dissemination (emphasis added).[13]

Justice Moldaver, while ultimately concurring, nonetheless disagreed with the rest of the majority that the Ktunaxa's right to freedom of religion had not been infringed. He maintained instead that freedom of religion ought to be understood to include more than just its original Judeo-Christian meanings:

> As this Court stated in *R. v. Big M Drug Mart Ltd.*,... the interpretation of freedom of religion must be a "generous rather than a legalistic one, aimed at fulfilling the purpose of the guarantee and securing for individuals the full benefit of the Charter's protection"... The connection to the physical world, specifically to land, is a central feature of Indigenous religions... In many Indigenous religions, land is not only the site of spiritual practices in the sense that a church, mosque or holy site might be; land may itself be sacred, in the sense that it is where the divine manifests itself. Unlike in Judeo-Christian faiths for example, where the divine is considered to be supernatural, the spiritual realm in the Indigenous context is inextricably linked to the physical world. For Indigenous religions, state action that impacts land can therefore sever the connection to the divine, rendering beliefs and practices devoid of their spiritual significance. Where state action has this effect on an Indigenous religion, it interferes with a believer's ability to act in accordance with his or her religious beliefs and practices... To ensure that all religions are afforded the same level of protection under s. 2

---

[11] See also Borrows (2016) ch. 4. It is worth noting that Borrows is actually an advocate of living tree constitutional interpretation; he argues that it has simply not been applied consistently in Canada. While we agree with him on this level, as we argue throughout this chapter, we are skeptical that the kind of changes needed to properly respect Indigenous rights of all kinds can be accomplished through the courts, without significant, new constitutional moments happening first.

[12] *Ktunaxa Nation v. British Columbia (Forests, Lands, and Natural Resource Operations)* [2017] S.C.C. 54.

[13] *Ktunaxa*, paras 70 and 71. [emphasis added].

> (a), courts must be alive to the unique characteristics of each religion, and the distinct ways in which state action may interfere with that religion's beliefs or practices.[14]

As Justice Moldaver argued, there was an opportunity in this case to grow and develop the *Charter* right to freedom of religion, in a way which is more inclusive and accommodating of Indigenous beliefs, values, and practices, but his colleagues saw this as an unacceptable change. We do not mean to take sides in this case, or pronounce that the majority made a mistake, but only wish to show that a living tree approach might be unable to determine when to expand and grow the law and when not to, as the disagreement between Justice Moldaver and the rest of the majority shows in *Ktunaxa*. It might permit courts too much by way of discretion, and it would be difficult to deny that in Canada, at least, such discretion has rarely been exercised to the advantage of Indigenous peoples.

3.2 Presumption 2. Pre-condition of Moral Justification

Adoption and justification of a living tree conception, with its piecemeal, incremental approach to development of constitutional provisions and rights, as the morally and politically correct approach to interpretation, also presumes that some basic pre-condition of moral justification in society has already been met. Only if such a pre-condition is met does it make sense to work on development, progress, and the refinement of existing commitments. But if such a pre-condition is not met, i.e., the society is not at a level where we can say that its basic laws and institutions are sufficiently just such that the only work remaining to be done is of a developmental or refinement kind, then something like a new beginning, with new constitutional moments, is instead required.

Early on in *A Common Law Theory of Judicial Review* Waluchow acknowledges this presumption:

> The modern Charter societies with which we are herein concerned are, as we have noted, in this way "healthy." Despite their many flaws, those who live within such societies generally believe them to be of sufficient value to warrant continued allegiance and acceptance.... [O] f course there will be those—for example, some Aboriginal and Quebec Separatist groups in Canada—who have a strong preference for an entirely new system whose fundamental rules and character would be different. But few, even among these groups, believe the society in which they currently exist to be so unjustified, so unjust or corrupt, as to warrant rejection altogether (Waluchow 2007, p. 44).

To repeat, we do not wish to challenge the general account of living tree constitutionalism which Waluchow presents.[15] We do, however, believe its application in

[14] *Ktunaxa*, paras 121, 127, 128.

[15] Indeed, in societies where the pre-condition of moral justification is met, we see nothing wrong with adopting the living tree conception of constitutionalism. To avoid possible misunderstanding, we should also note that in those societies where this pre-condition is not met, we are not suggesting that a fixed view conception of constitutionalism is therefore better. Instead, in all such societies

the Canadian context is far from problem-free. Observing some longstanding issues, Douglas Sanderson writes:

> First Nation people face poorer outcomes in terms of health, education, wealth and social status when compared to their settler counterparts. More specifically, First Nation communities are statistically more prone to teen suicide, experience higher rates of crime, suffer an endemic lack of housing and clean water, and have little access to education beyond the primary years. First Nation people are overrepresented in prisons and underrepresented in the economy (Sanderson 2014, pp. 524–526, author's notes omitted).

These are indeed significant failings, and as we will show as well, only scratch the surface. Ongoing forms of colonialism provide additional reasons to doubt that Canada has treated Indigenous peoples in a just manner, and some of the injustice is so deeply entrenched in the Canadian constitutional structure that it may in fact require a new "system whose fundamental rules and character would be different". If this is so, then the living tree conception might mask rather than address the work that needs to be done.

3.3 *Presumption 3. A Comprehensive and Supreme Canadian Legal System*

In writing about the definition and characterization of Indigenous rights by Canadian state courts, Gordon Christie identifies the following problem:

> ....the truly puzzling aspect of all this is how it could be that grounds for rights that *predate* the Crown (and for peoples who suffer the direct impacts of colonialism, wrought by the Crown) come to be treated such that they must fit within the conceptual system of the laws of the state (Christie 2019, p. 79, original emphasis).

Christie is of course noting that even with recognition of Indigenous rights by Canadian courts, and the recognition and affirmation of Indigenous rights in the *Constitution Act, 1982*,[16] such rights are recognized squarely within, and therefore are validated by, the Canadian legal system (from which it follows, in turn, that their definition and interpretation fall to organs of the Canadian legal system, i.e., its courts; more on this below). His observation is therefore helpful for seeing another presumption underlying the living tree conception of constitutionalism in Canada: that Canada's constitution, as the source of supreme and comprehensive legal authority in Canada, began when it was planted in 1867. The presumption, plainly stated, is that with the *British North America Act*, 1867, Canadian constitutional authority was not only born but comprehensively assumed. As a European (in this

---

where the pre-condition of moral justification is not met we need to look beyond constitutional interpretation altogether and pursue new constitutional orders.

[16] *Constitution Act, 1982*, chapter 11 (U.K.), Schedule B. Section 35(1) reads: "The existing aboriginal and treaty rights of the aboriginal peoples of Canada are hereby recognized and affirmed."

instance, British) project of colonization, the context is important here. The United Kingdom presumed and imposed a particular model of law—established in post-Westphalian Europe—that centralizes power in the state and which claims comprehensive and supreme power over all peoples within a given territory. On this model and understanding of law, Indigenous rights can and do have legal validity within the Canadian legal system, but only in virtue of the say so of the centralized, Canadian legal system, as Christie observes.

3.4 Presumption 4. *Terra Nullius*

Closely related to Presumption 3, but worth separate attention, is the presumption of *terra nullius*, the idea that land not under the control of a (European) sovereign is 'unowned' and therefore open for discovery, possession and colonization. Land is needed to found a new territorial state and, since dispossession is considered an unjust means to establish a state, some legal justification is required for any new acquisition of territory. The problems with the doctrine of *terra nullius* are many and worthy of sustained investigation, but for our purposes we need only observe that the presumption that Indigenous peoples did not occupy lands in North America, with distinct practices and forms of governments, prior to the arrival of Europeans, is patently false.[17] For this reason, it is in turn false to presume that North America was simply fertile and unoccupied ground, in 1492 or 1867, on which a new, comprehensive and supreme legal system could be planted without obstruction. It is doubtful that the gradual approach to development of law advocated by the living tree conception of constitutionalism is able to outgrow this beginning.[18]

3.5 Limit 1. Sections 91 to 95 of the *British North America Act, 1867* and the *Constitution Act, 1982*

We ought to ask what "growth and expansion within natural limits" might mean in the Canadian context, and especially with respect to recognition of Indigenous traditions and authority. Part of the limits, no doubt, are fixed by sections 91 to 95 of the *British North America Act*, 1867, and the *Constitution Act*, 1982, which carefully divide—without remainder—the respective jurisdictions of the federal and provincial governments in Canada. Indeed, it is the fixity of certain parts of the Constitution, as natural limits, which Lord Sankey also observed in *Edwards*:

[17] See, for example, Asch (2002). See also Borch (2001).

[18] For discussion of several ways in which the living tree metaphor is distorting, see Mills (2017, pp. 228–229).

> It must be remembered, too, that their Lordships are not here considering the question of the legislative competence either of the Dominion or its provinces which arises under ss. 91 and 92 of the Act providing for the distribution of legislative powers and assigning to the Dominion and its provinces their respective spheres of Government. . . Their Lordships are concerned with the interpretation of an Imperial Act, but an Imperial Act which creates a constitution for a new country.[19]

Here Lord Sankey is noting that while some parts of the Constitution of Canada are able to grow and expand, others, such as the division of powers, are settled. No jurisdiction or constitutional authority was recognized for Indigenous peoples at the time of confederation in 1867, and while Aboriginal rights were recognized and affirmed in 1982 with the *Constitution Act,* 1982, no associated amendments to sections 91 to 95 were made to recognize Indigenous governments alongside the federal and provincial governments. As things continue to stand, under Canadian constitutional law only federal and provincial governments have constitutional authority.[20]

This division of authority, and perhaps more significantly the delegated and subordinate status of Indigenous rights, is roundly rejected by many Indigenous communities and scholars. For example, on the status of Aboriginal rights in Canada, Dale Turner writes:

> Aboriginal rights, as constitutional rights, are still developing in law; that said, one important principle is now embedded in Canadian law and politics: the meaning and content of Aboriginal rights is expressed in the legal and political discourses of the Canadian state, and therefore Aboriginal rights exist or have legitimacy only *within* the Canadian state... But many Aboriginal peoples do not understand their rights in terms that are amenable to the state's legal and political discourses. This is because many Aboriginal peoples do not perceive the political relationship as one of subservience; that is, they do not view their rights as somehow legitimated by the Canadian state. Rather, many Aboriginal peoples understand the political relationship as one of 'nation to nation' (Turner 2006, pp. 3–4, original emphasis).

Below we will explore more fully the obstacle which the Canadian state poses to Indigenous claims of self-governance and sovereign status, in the form of its commitment to a certain view of the nature of law and legal system.

3.6 Limit 2. Court-Centrism

Another key limit to application of the living tree conception of constitutionalism in Canada, which helps to explain how it restrains growth and expansion of constitutional law, is recognition that the living tree conception is a court-centric view, presuming that courts are well-, perhaps best-placed, to accomplish the moral growth

---

[19] *Edwards*, 138.

[20] S.91.24 of the Constitution Acts, 1867 and 1982 identifies 'Indians, and Lands reserved for the Indians' as exclusively under the jurisdiction of the federal government. See Dodek (2016, p. 74).

society needs in its constitutional law, and perhaps also that the work of courts *alone* is sufficient to carry out the requisite development. However, recalling Presumption 2, this takes for granted that the existing sources of law are sufficiently robust for the required moral and political growth, such that all that remains is interpretation or application of existing constitutional rights and provisions. But in a society which might not yet qualify as sufficiently just, it is likely that interpretation and application by courts presumes too much, and what is really needed is creation, up stream, of new sources of law and institutional arrangements. Courts, in other words, with their incremental approach to improving law through judicial interpretation, might not only be too slow in achieving the required change, but also, and more importantly, quite possibly *incapable* of achieving the degree or kind of change required to transform Canadian society from unjust to reasonably just in its relations with Indigenous peoples. Most worrisome, a constitutional self-image of a living tree might falsely re-assure a society that the courts are on top of things, with the work of developing and growing constitutional law well in hand. The progressive character of the metaphor holds out the promise that Canada's current constitutional norms are capable of achieving reconciliation through incremental change. Once again, Indigenous perspectives provide an important source of doubt. As Patricia Monture-Angus has observed, Canadian courts might be institutionally unable to appreciate key dimensions of Indigenous rights claims, since such courts, provincial and federal, are simply not in the business of questioning their own authority to adjudicate such disputes: "[t]here is an insurmountable problem in taking Aboriginal claims to territory before the courts. Courts owe their creation to the fact of Canadian sovereignty. They cannot question that sovereignty because, to find it wanting would in fact dis-establish their own legitimacy" (Monture-Angus 1999, p. 65 [internal notes omitted]). Similarly, in commenting on the SCC's decision in *Sparrow*, a key case in Aboriginal rights law in Canada,[21] and in which the court noted that the sovereignty of the Crown was beyond question ("never any doubt"), Christie remarks:

> This stance indicated the presence of some sort of barrier (at least in the minds of the judges) beyond which Canadian law apparently could not venture—its imagination could not reach out to the task of questioning matters of state legitimacy. Furthermore, this seemed linked to a deep reluctance on the part of the judiciary to examine historical and political context, reflected in its narrow approach to matters of Crown-Aboriginal relations (Christie (2019, p. 12).[22]

And along the same lines, though with a focus on interpretation of treaty relationships in Canada, Aaron Mills writes:

> The structural relation of settler supremacy that characterizes Canada-Indigenous relationships means that even if somehow the Supreme Court of Canada could get the doctrine right, inequality between Indigenous and settler peoples would persist. Yet the overarching theme of this book is treaty *remedies*. It will be clear by now that I think that's the wrong frame for

[21] *R. v. Sparrow*, [1990] 1 S.C.R. 1075.

[22] See also Christie (2019, p. 77).

> thinking about changing treaty relationships today because it assumes too much, namely that the courts have a leading role to play in reorganizing treaty relationships. The courts are an institution internal to Canada's constitutional order and, as creations by and under its authority, are by definition incapable of taking up the very issue at stake in treaty: the coordination of distinct constitutional orders (Mills 2017, pp. 223–224 [internal notes omitted, original emphasis]).

We will return later to the idea of 'distinct constitutional orders', but it is important to take stock at this point. The presumptions and limits we have surfaced in this section are not the only important presumptions and limits to the living tree conception of constitutionalism (others will be investigated below), but they seem to us especially foundational and critical. They establish, among other things, that while the living tree metaphor might be useful for understanding how we might want to allow our constitutional ideals to grow and adapt, its rootedness in the history and identity of a given legal culture, and its use in the hands of state courts, likely make it an inappropriate framework and associated understanding for addressing the issue of reconciliation between State institutions and Indigenous peoples in Canada. It is to this claim that we now turn.

4 The Character of Reconciliation

Reconciliation in the Canadian context is simultaneously a moral and political aspiration as well as part of a legal settlement. It marks official recognition that the relationship between Canadian settlers and Indigenous peoples needs mending, after years of racism and colonization which continue in many forms to the present day.[23] For a helpful statement of the character and goals of reconciliation, at least from the perspective of the Canadian state, the Department of Justice begins its 'Principles Respecting the Government of Canada's Relationship with Indigenous Peoples' by noting:

> The Government of Canada is committed to achieving reconciliation with Indigenous peoples through a renewed, nation-to-nation, government-to-government, and Inuit-Crown relationship based on recognition of rights, respect, co-operation, and partnership as the foundation for transformative change.
>
> Indigenous peoples have a special constitutional relationship with the Crown. This relationship, including existing Aboriginal and treaty rights, is recognized and affirmed in section 35 of the Constitution Act, 1982. Section 35 contains a full box of rights, and holds the promise that Indigenous nations will become partners in Confederation on the basis of a fair and just reconciliation between Indigenous peoples and the Crown.
>
> The Government recognizes that Indigenous self-government and laws are critical to Canada's future, and that Indigenous perspectives and rights must be incorporated in all aspects of this relationship. In doing so, we will continue the process of decolonization and hasten the end of its legacy wherever it remains in our laws and policies (Department of Justice Canada 2018).

[23] See Truth and Reconciliation Commission of Canada (2015).

Of particular interest in the Department of Justice's statement is what might count as 'transformative change', and especially its ambivalence about the precise form that reconciliation will take. At times it indicates that reconciliation will be on the basis of a nation-to-nation relationship and at other times that it will be a process that takes place within Canada, between 'partners in confederation' through the 'incorporation' of Indigenous peoples into all aspects of Canadian society (and in which section 35 already contains a 'full box of rights'). These are two very different understandings, as we will proceed to show.

While greater recognition of Indigenous rights, in the *Constitution Act*, 1982, and over the last 50 years in the courts, might be positive steps, they are profoundly limited steps, as Indigenous scholars routinely point out.[24] For example, remarking on the federal government's response to the 1996 Report of the Royal Commission on Aboriginal Peoples, Glen Sean Coulthard writes:

> The stated purpose of the federal government's position is to clearly establish the terms under which Aboriginal governments might negotiate 'practical' governing arrangements in relation to their own communities and with other governments and jurisdictions. In setting out these terms, however, the state unilaterally curtails the jurisdictional authority made available to Aboriginal nations through the so-called 'negotiation' process... One should recognize a familiar pattern here. Instead of proceeding with negotiations based on the principle of Indigenous self-determination, Canada's policy framework is grounded in the assumption that Aboriginal rights are subordinately positioned within the ultimate sovereign authority of the Crown (Coulthard 2014, p. 123).

As Coulthard goes on to explain, "colonial powers will only recognize the collective rights and identities of Indigenous peoples insofar as this recognition does not throw into question the background legal, political, and economic framework of the colonial relationship itself" (Coulthard 2014, p. 41 [author's notes omitted]).[25] Returning to the Department of Justice's statement, subordination within and dependency upon the existing Canadian legal system likely fall well short of what might count as 'transformative change', since these fail to respect the perspectives of peoples who do not see themselves as subordinate, enjoying only delegated authority where provided by the pleasure of the Crown.[26]

There is therefore an unresolved issue in the concept of reconciliation, at least in the Canadian context. Is reconciliation meant to be a process and objective internal to existing Canadian constitutional law, or must it be a process and objective between Canadian state institutions and sovereign, independent First Nations? The former understanding sees reconciliation as taking place between 'partners in Confederation', which sees First Nations as distinct societies but still within Canada, similar to Quebec's status within Canada. The latter understanding, however, sees reconciliation between Canadian state institutions and First Nations as more akin to

[24] See Turner (2006, p. 28) and Christie (2019).

[25] See also Nadasdy (2017, pp. 12–15).

[26] See Turner (2006).

an international process and objective, between equally sovereign and independent nations. It is this understanding that we wish to explore further.

The living tree metaphor rooted Canadian jurisprudence in a European legal tradition whose principles were often designed to deny legal recognition to Indigenous peoples around the world.

While the post-Westphalian state system was ostensibly created to overcome the challenges posed by diverse religious groups across European states, a number of scholars have noted the ways in which this system was explicitly arranged to deny sovereignty to First Nations peoples.[27] As Pat Moloney points out, Thomas Hobbes bases the idea of a pre-legal order, in which all manner of deceit and violence are 'just', on the First Nations peoples of the Americas (Moloney 2011). Indeed, Hobbes makes the sovereign state—that great leviathan—the mechanism by which the brutal life of the state of nature can be brought to an end. He imputes a lack of sovereignty to the First Nations peoples of the Americas and thereby implicitly puts them beyond the protections of even international law.[28] This not only allows the sovereign states of Europe to colonize them, but makes such colonization a blessing and the sole means by which to establish law and put an end to the anarchy of the state of nature.

In contrast to the sovereignty doctrine and its associated presumptions espoused by Hobbes, Leroy Little Bear, a Blackfoot researcher, argues that colonialism "tries to maintain a singular social order by means of force and law, suppressing the diversity of worldviews.... Typically, this proposition creates oppression and discrimination" (Little Bear 2000, p. 77). In contrast to the unitary nature of European sovereign states, Little Bear notes the 'spider-web of relations' that characterize First Nations societies. One consequence of this approach to understanding law is that social sanctions are diffused throughout society, such that: "It is as though everybody is a 'cop' and nobody is a 'cop'" (Little Bear 2000, p. 84). However, this is a major departure from the dangerous state of affairs that Hobbes describes as existing in the state of nature. The social diffusion of law creates powerful social pressure to act according to social virtues that are woven into the various cultures of First Nations peoples. According to Little Bear: "Law is not something that is separate and unto itself. Law is the culture, and culture is the law" (Little Bear 2000, p. 83). Sanderson notes that First Nations peoples originally intended to induct European settlers into this 'web of relations' through wampum or pipe ceremonies and that British settlers recognized the importance of these ceremonies for their survival in North America for the first three centuries after contact (Sanderson 2013).

A form of legal order that elides the unitary system of law that exists in the Western European tradition may strike some legal theorists as a complete departure

[27] Antony Anghie argues that the constitution and development of international law stem from the colonial encounter and that sovereignty doctrine, an evolving and central component to international law, was in fact forged as a tool to manage the colonial encounter between Europe and its exterior. See Anghie (2004). See also Scott (2018).

[28] See Hobbes (1968, pp. 187–188).

from having law at all. One might argue that societies in which 'the culture is the law' are in fact pre-legal societies, which lack the secondary rules of adjudication, change and recognition that H.L.A. Hart identified as defining a legal system (Hart 2012, chapters 5 and 6). Indeed, many Western states consider supremacy to be a core feature of legal systems. For example, a constitutional crisis recently arose in Europe when Poland's Supreme Court ruled that parts of the EU constitution (particularly those related to the supremacy of EU law) were inconsistent with the Constitution of the Republic of Poland. Commenting on this development, Luxembourg's Minister of Foreign Affairs, Jean Asselborn, commented: "The primacy of European law is essential for the integration of Europe and living together in Europe. If this principle is broken, Europe as we know it, as it has been built with the Rome treaties, will cease to exist" (Siebold and Ptak 2021). Legal supremacy, from this perspective, is a necessary feature of legal systems if they are to provide the reassuring sense of order that Hobbes lauds as the primary virtue of sovereign states. Moreover, the unified cultural identity of Europe is here tied to the legal framework that grants EU law supremacy over that of member states.

The living tree conception of constitutionalism fits quite well with the presumption that single state legal systems, which claim supreme and comprehensive authority over their territories, are the paradigmatic form of law. Within such systems of law, there is room for growth and expansion as state courts interpret and apply law, but the institutional structure of supreme and comprehensive authority over all subjects and matters within the state territory, and the authority of state courts to adjudicate any disputes, including those over the rights of various groups, remain fixed. In slightly different terms, incremental change to the content of law is compatible with claims of comprehensive and supreme authority, but transformative change, which would alter the very identity, perhaps structure of a comprehensive and supreme legal system, is not. Comprehensive and supreme authority, on this view, is not only part of the nature of law, but necessary for social order.

But must law everywhere and always be organized in the form of a single, overarching legal system which governs supremely and comprehensively over all those in its territory? Probably not. Christie articulates the difference between unitary and pluralistic constitutional designs particularly well:

> At the heart of all this are two distinct perspectives on the world around us: *that of the Crown and its courts*—that Indigenous peoples are *already* subsumed within the nation state of Canada, the only details being how this subsumption will be finalized in a new "just and fair" arrangement—and *that of Indigenous peoples*—that the project of colonialism is not complete, and that before an internal "just and fair" arrangement can be imagined, first the matter of the existence of *continuing* multiple independent legal and political authorities must be acknowledged and addressed (Christie 2019, p. 126 [original emphasis]).[29]

In Canada we might even be witnessing some notable developments which suggest more pluralistic models of relationships between state and Indigenous peoples are not just possible but becoming actual. Framework agreements, letters of

[29] See also Nadasdy (2017, pp. 72–73).

understanding, and reconciliation protocols are remarkable for just this reason, as they are characterized and accepted by provincial, federal, and Indigenous governments precisely as 'nation-to-nation' or 'true partnerships' standing outside conventional sources of law.[30] As such, they are not best characterized as delegated or subordinate sources of law, but represent the potential for extra-systemic recognition of Indigenous authority. Two features stand out about these developments. First, they recognize Indigenous governments as nations or partners, existing on a horizontal level with provincial and federal governments. This is a departure from the division of powers, reserved exclusively for the provinces and federal government, contained in sections 91 to 95 of the *Constitution Acts*, 1867 and 1982. Second, they are not judicial decisions, i.e., not mere interpretation or application of existing law. Instead, they have more of a creative status, bringing into existence new sources of (potentially constitutional) law. At the risk of stretching the metaphor too far, framework agreements, letters of understanding, and reconciliation protocols, with their creative and extra-systemic status, represent not a new branch to the existing tree that is the Canadian constitution, but something more radical—more transformative, at least potentially—which are new trees entirely, planted alongside and co-existing with state law and altering its status with respect to Indigenous law. Whether they and the model of law they represent flourish remains to be seen.

5 Two Row Wampum and Reconciliation

It is important to note that ideas and principles for conceiving of multiple, co-existing independent legal orders already exist, so the kind of difference Christie articulates above is not one which requires starting from scratch. Wampum belts have been used by Indigenous peoples on Turtle Island to record agreements amongst themselves, as well as with settlers. For example, the 'Gäsweñta' or 'Two Row Wampum' was an agreement between the Haudenosaunee and the Dutch to peaceably share the land. Key principles to this treaty were the principles of equal authority and non-interference. In fact, according to Chief Irving Powless Jr., when the treaty was being negotiated, the Dutch had specifically asked that the Haudenosaunee refer to them as 'father', while the Haudenosaunee would be referred to as 'son' (Powless Jr. 2000). This was rejected by the representatives of the five nations because it would have granted the Dutch more authority than the Haudenosaunee. Instead, they proposed the term 'brother' to show the equality on which the treaty would be based. Further, when the Dutch brought out a paper treaty to ratify the agreement, the representatives of the five nations said that they were welcome to record the agreement on paper if they wished. However, the

[30]For discussion of these developments, see Giudice (2020, ch 4). See also Christie 2019, pp. 342–343, fn 3).

Haudenosaunee would follow their own custom of recording the agreement using a wampum belt of purple and white quahog shell beads.

The Two Row Wampum agreement is important to our argument here in a number of respects. First and most importantly, it establishes two systems of government and makes non-interference in one another's affairs the basis of peace. It recognizes, as a principle of law, that two peoples can agree to share a territory in a spirit of cooperation, without either subordinating the other to their ways of doing things, or somehow "validating" each other's law. Had settlers adhered to these principles, instead of attempting to plant a new and independent constitutional order, we might have a living tree*s* metaphor that emphasizes how the strength of the forest comes from a diversity of trees. Second, since the Two Row Wampum agreement was negotiated at a time when settlers lacked the knowledge or numbers to forcibly colonize North America, it also marks a time when the power relationship between First Nations peoples and European settlers was reversed. Sanderson describes the situation in which the original treaties were signed in the following way:

> Too often today we forget that from the late 1490s (the arrival of John Cabot) until the earliest decades of the 1800s, international diplomacy on Turtle Island was conducted according to Indigenous—not European—protocols. These diplomatic protocols, known as wampum diplomacy, involved the exchange of belts and strings of beads called wampum in a complex set of customs, interactions and expectations that governed the relations between nation-states. Wampum were not merely gifts: the exchange of wampum signalled intention and certified agreements. Wampum served as mnemonic devices that, in their beaded patterns, encoded the contours of commitments between parties.
>
> The language of Indigenous international diplomacy is tied directly to the land and the various 'other than human beings'—animals, plants, trees, rocks, insects—that inhabited Turtle Island, bound together in an all-pervasive ecology. Indigenous nations regarded themselves as part of these landscapes, and divided themselves into family clans based on animal totems in order to represent their place in the geography and spirit of the land. This set of relationships between Indigenous communities and the land and animals around them was known as the *web of relations*. When Europeans arrived in Turtle Island, the presumption of First Nations was that these newcomers would have to be welcomed and brought into the existing order of things—that with help, the Europeans would eventually find their own place in the web of relations on Turtle Island (Sanderson 2013, original emphasis).

As Sanderson recounts, for three centuries this was the prevailing understanding and relationship between Indigenous peoples and settlers, though things eventually changed markedly as power dynamics shifted. Among other objectives, it is this original relationship that reconciliation is meant to restore—a nation to nation relationship. It also requires, as we have tried to argue, suspension of commitment to living tree or common law constitutionalism, which presumes the right structure and set of rights are already in place, needing only incremental improvement from the courts as time passes. Instead, what are required are new (or perhaps renewed) constitutional moments which create genuine constitutional pluralism of the kind Sanderson, Christie, Turner, and others envisage.

6 Conceptual Reconciliation

We have no doubt left several questions unanswered for each question we did address. While we have tried to show the limits and costs of the living tree metaphor for understanding and approaching issues of reconciliation between settler institutions and Indigenous peoples in Canada, we have not offered any final, once-and-for-all conclusions about where we might go with the metaphor. Should we simply abandon it altogether, for now, perhaps only adopting it again once some basic moral and political pre-conditions have been met? Should we simply complicate the metaphor by thinking of several trees, perhaps as a small forest, to alert attention to the possibility and need for recognition of several, independent but coordinated legal orders, in which Indigenous governments sit alongside as genuine partners with provincial and federal governments? Would such a pluralistic understanding also encompass the need for new institutions, perhaps a new court (of equal standing with the SCC) that will handle disputes over Indigenous rights, claims, and self-government, but created in a way led by Indigenous peoples with special attention to Indigenous practices and understandings? And how would such new institutions, and new sources of law (in the form of, e.g., framework agreements, letters of understanding, and reconciliation protocols) figure into wider projects of reconciliation, which must address a whole host of issues arising from, among others, land claims, residential schools, clean water, and over-representation in prisons?

We should also note that we are far from offering the most sustained, rigorous, and insightful account of the contradictions, tensions, and puzzles which emerge from examination of the relations between existing Canadian constitutional law and rights of Indigenous peoples in Canada.[31] We have instead focused narrowly on a British-introduced and Canadian-accepted metaphor, that of the living tree, as our point of departure. This was necessary but also deliberate, as we saw in the metaphor an instance of what Isaiah Berlin warns of: pervertible metaphors, apparently positive but capable of causing much misunderstanding, misdirection of efforts, and "misery and frustration" (Berlin 1999). Metaphors, and the concepts they are couched in, shape the way we think about and act in the world, and if we are not careful and mindful, our metaphors and concepts can act as obstacles to our moral and political objectives. While certainly not the whole picture, such conceptual harms constitute one of the many dimensions of Canada's colonial history and ongoing relationship with Indigenous peoples. We would like to conclude with a few thoughts on what could be called conceptual reconciliation, and what we see as two major obstacles to its achievement.

The first obstacle is general and methodological. In the philosophy of law, like many other fields in philosophy, conceptual analysis is still a predominant approach to answering questions about the nature of law. While there are variations, the general method should be familiar. To identify the character and features of a particular concept, the linguistic intuitions of a particular group are tested, typically

[31] See again Borrows (1997–1998), Christie (2019), Nadasdy (2017) and Monture-Angus (1999).

by a priori means (e.g., thought experiments). This process is repeated with increasing precision, until the concept is refined. The identity of the group performing the analysis of course matters, and unfortunately, in the field of philosophy of law, it should be no surprise that it is a European, settler group's view which swamps the field. The range of concepts to be refined has also been fixed, for nearly two centuries, by the dominant group. This makes it urgent to take up Indigenous legal theory, which we believe offers the kind of insights and challenges for truly transformative change. Core concepts in legal theory, such as authority, wrongdoing, dispute resolution, sovereignty, and contract, to name just a few, no longer look the same once viewed through the lens of Indigenous perspectives.[32] Indeed, it is difficult to think about these concepts in the same way once settler and Indigenous perspectives have been equally considered. This possibility requires, however, moving beyond conceptual analysis to conceptual comparison and often conceptual revision.

Yet we also do not want to give the impression that it is simply a matter of renovating existing settler concepts to take account of Indigenous perspectives. Some concepts might need to go altogether, and the concept (or metaphor) of a single living tree, at least in the current Canadian context, might be a prime example (we will mention another one shortly). Settler legal philosophy will also need to broaden its list of concepts to consider, to include some that are quite unfamiliar but central to Indigenous ways of thinking. We believe these include but are not restricted to relatedness or connection, land (and we do not mean land as real estate), spirit, creation, and the sacred (Ignace and Ignace 2017). Understanding these concepts cannot be done alone, but will require developing the skills to listen to and learn from Indigenous perspectives.

The second obstacle is more specific, and resides in the dominant role the particular concept of legal system plays in understanding law. As we stated, conceptual reconciliation does not mean that all existing settler concepts simply take on new or additional meanings. Some might have to go altogether, and we believe the settler concept of legal system is one of them, at least in particular contexts. To be specific, by legal system we mean the idea that all laws are found in special kinds of unities, which make general claims of comprehensiveness over all of social life and supremacy over other kinds of norms (religious, moral, etc.). In analytical legal theory the idea of legal system is central and has been declared as the key idea to distinguishing law from other kinds of norms or normative orders (Raz 1975). The trouble, however, is that the concept of legal system recommends a very specific (and a very dangerous) way for one legal order to relate to others, namely by claiming supremacy over those other legal orders. In Canada these dangers have materialized. From confederation in 1867 up until the present day claims of comprehensiveness and supremacy of the legal system of the Canadian state over Indigenous peoples and their legal orders are all too easy to see. To give just a couple of examples, in 1876 the *Indian Act* attributed no validity to Indigenous legal

[32] See, e.g., Nadasdy (2017).

orders whatsoever. Even in 1982 with the constitutional entrenchment of Aboriginal rights and treaty rights, Indigenous legal orders still only exist as delegated or recognized by virtue of the Canadian state.

As we saw above, Indigenous scholars such as Turner, Coulthard, and Christie have pointed out that such understandings will not do. It is therefore a top priority for non-Indigenous scholars, such as ourselves, to question the necessity of the concept of legal system (and related concepts and metaphors such as the living tree); listen to Indigenous peoples and learn from Indigenous scholarship; and be open to alternative visions of how different legal orders might relate to each other.

There is one last thought to share, and this is about the concept of partnership. Some might view the expressions of a 'nation-to-nation' or 'government-to-government' partnership as mere rhetoric or symbolic statements; certainly, their continued use without concrete steps to realize such a relationship or partnership can become tiresome. But we find value in these expressions, not only as an aspiration to be articulated and pursued together by Indigenous and settler peoples, but also for the profound questions they raise, for example, about what a partnership is, its varieties, and what particular kinds of partnership nations might need or expect to have with each other. Among these questions we have become increasingly stuck on one: what kinds of practices, self-conceptions, or characters make for being a good partner? And as descendants of newcomers on Turtle Island, our thoughts have become grounded in trying to identify and develop measures for self-improvement as a partner. We think of these as part of the pre-conditions of truth, reconciliation, healing, and partnership. There is a lot of work to do, since there is a lot of self-improvement that needs to happen to come to grips with the past and present, and to construct a genuinely shared vision for the future. Overcoming the two obstacles we mentioned and pursuing conceptual reconciliation might be a small, narrowly focused beginning, but it is no less important or necessary for that reason. From a settler perspective, we have a responsibility to listen and see when our concepts (and metaphors) are getting in the way of becoming good partners.

References

Anghie, Antony. 2004. *Imperialism, sovereignty and the making of international law*. Cambridge: Cambridge University Press.

Asch, Michael. 2002. From Terra nullius to affirmation: Reconciling aboriginal rights with the Canadian constitution. *Canadian Journal of Law and Society* 17: 23–39.

Berlin, Isaiah. 1999. The purpose of philosophy. In *Concepts and categories*, ed. H. Hardy, 1–11. London: Pimlico.

Borch, Merete. 2001. Rethinking the origins of Terra nullius. *Australian Historical Studies* 32: 222–239.

Borrows, John. 1997–1998. Frozen rights in Canada: Constitutional interpretation and the trickster. *American Indian Law Review* 22: 37–64.

———. 2016. *Freedom and indigenous constitutionalism*. Toronto: University of Toronto Press. ch. 4.

Christie, Gordon. 2019. *Canadian law and indigenous self-determination*. Toronto: University of Toronto Press.

Coulthard, Glen Sean. 2014. *Red skin, white masks*. Minneapolis: University of Minnesota Press.

Department of Justice Canada. 2018. Principles: Respecting the Government of Canada's relationship with indigenous peoples. https://www.justice.gc.ca/eng/csj-sjc/principles-principes.html. Accessed 21 April 2022.

Dodek, Adam. 2016. *The Canadian constitution*. 2nd ed, 74. Toronto: Dundurn Press.

Giudice, Michael. 2020. *The social construction of law*. Cheltenham: Edward Elgar.

Hart, H.L.A. 2012. *The concept of law*. 3rd ed. Oxford: Oxford University Press. chapters 5 and 6.

Hobbes, Thomas. 1968. In *Leviathan*, ed. C.B. Macpherson. New York: Penguin.

Huscroft, Grant. 2004. A constitutional 'work in Progress'? The charter and the limits of progressive interpretation. In *Constitutionalism in the charter era*, ed. Grant Huscroft and Ian Brodie, 413–438. Markham: LexisNexis. 415.

Ignace, Marianne, and Ronald E. Ignace. 2017. *Secwépemc people, land, and Laws*. Montreal: McGill-Queen's University Press.

Kavanagh, Aileen. 2003. The idea of a living constitution. *Canadian Journal of Law and Jurisprudence* 16: 55–89.

Little Bear, Leroy. 2000. Jagged worldviews colliding. In *Reclaiming indigenous voice and vision*, ed. Marie Battiste, 77–85. Vancouver: UBC Press.

Mills, Aaron. 2017. What is a treaty? On contract and mutual aid. In *The right relationship*, ed. John Borrows and Michael Coyle, 208–247. Toronto: University of Toronto Press. 228-9.

Moloney, Pat. 2011. Hobbes, savagery, and international anarchy. *American Political Science Review* 105 (1): 189–204.

Monture-Angus, Patricia. 1999. *Journeying forward: Dreaming first nations' Independence*. Halifax: Fernwood Publishing.

Nadasdy, Paul. 2017. *Sovereignty's entailments*. Toronto: University of Toronto Press.

Powless, Irving, Jr. 2000. Treaty making. In *Treaty of Canandaigua 1794: 200 years of treaty relations between the Iroquois confederacy and the United States*, ed. G.P. Jemison and A.M. Schein, 15–34. Santa Fe: Clear Light Publishers.

Raz, Joseph. 1975. The institutional nature of law. *Modern Law Review* 38: 489–503.

Sanderson, Douglas. 2013. 'Toward an Aboriginal grand strategy', *Global Brief*. https://globalbrief.ca/2013/06/toward-an-aboriginal-grand-strategy/. Accessed 18 March 2022.

———. 2014. Overlapping consensus, legislative reform and the *Indian act*. *Queen's Law Journal* 39: 511–550.

Scott, Xavier. 2018. Repairing broken relations by repairing broken treaties: Theorizing postcolonial states in settler colonies. *Studies in Social Justice* 12: 388–405.

Siebold, Sabine, and Alicja Ptak. 8 October 2021. 'You are playing with fire': EU faces crisis over Polish court ruling. Reuters. https://www.reuters.com/article/us-poland-eu-idCAKBN2GY10K. Accessed 26 April 2022.

Truth and Reconciliation Commission of Canada. 2015. *Honouring the truth, reconciling for the future: Summary of the final report of the truth and reconciliation commission of Canada*. Montreal: McGill-Queen's University Press.

Turner, Dale. 2006. *This is not a peace pipe*. Toronto: University of Toronto Press.

Waldron, Jeremy. 1999. *Law and disagreement*. Oxford: Oxford University Press.

Waluchow, Wil. 2005. Constitutions as living trees: An idiot defends. *Canadian Journal of Law and Jurisprudence* 18: 207–247.

———. 2007. *A common law theory of judicial review: The living tree*. Cambridge: Cambridge University Press.

———. 2008. Constitutional morality and bills of rights. In *Expounding the constitution*, ed. Grant Huscroft, 65–92. Cambridge: Cambridge University Press.

———. 2023. Constitutionalism. In *The Stanford encyclopedia of philosophy*, ed. Edward N. Zalta. Stanford: Stanford University. Spring 2018 Edition. https://plato.stanford.edu/archives/spr2018/entries/constitutionalism/. Accessed 25 April 2022.

Cases Cited

A.G. Quebec v. Blaikie [1979] 2. S.C.R. 1016.
Edwards v. Canada [1930] A.C. 124.
Hunter v. Southam [1984] 2 S.C.R. 145.
Ktunaxa Nation v. British Columbia (Forests, Lands, and Natural Resource Operations) [2017] S.C.C. 54.
Law Society of Upper Canada v. Shapinker [1984] 1 S.C.R. 357.
R. v. Sparrow [1990] 1 S.C.R. 1075.
Reference Re Meaning of the Word "Persons" in Section 24 of the British North America Act, 1867 [1928] S.C.R. 276.
Reference re Same-Sex Marriage [2004] 3 S.C.R. 698.
Reference re Securities Act [2011] S.C.C. 66.

Michael Giudice is Professor in the Department of Philosophy, York University, Canada. BA (philosophy and law in society, University of New Brunswick), MA, PhD (philosophy, McMaster University). He specializes in general jurisprudence, legal pluralism, constitutional law, methodology, and associated areas in political theory. His recent books include Social Construction of Law (Edward Elgar, 2020), and with Keith Culver, The Unsteady State (Cambridge University Press, 2017).

Xavier Scott is Instructor in the Department of Philosophy, York University, Canada. BA (philosophy and political science, Brock University), MA, PhD (social and political thought, York University). He specializes in social and political thought with a focus on the role of culture and religion in politics and law. His recent publications include 'From Crusades to Colonization: Violence in Religious and Secular Political Theory' (Journal of the Council for Research on Religion, 2019) and 'Repairing Broken Relations by Repairing Broken Treaties: Theorizing Post-Colonial States in Settler Colonies,' (Studies in Social Justice, 2018).

Global Justice, Indigenous Knowledge, and the Epistemic Merits of Institutionally Embodied Moral Intuitions

Jorge Sanchez Perez

Abstract Wil Waluchow's notion of Community's Constitutional Morality (CCM) was developed as a tool for the identification of moral norms and considered judgments that are in some way tied to a community's constitutional law and practices. In this paper I first argue that even though the tool was conceived under a state-based paradigm, it also works on a global scale. Then, I show how by relying on this tool we can achieve two important and clearly differentiable goals. The first goal relates to efforts regarding the construction of global theories of justice. By using Waluchow's CCM we can overcome what I call the problem of adjudication among different existing moral intuitions. That is, the need to choose between different and competing fundamental moral commitments that ought to guide our moral deliberations. Instead, by using CCM, we can identify Embodied Moral Intuitions that hold an epistemic advantage over Personal Moral Intuitions, which are commonly used to ground normative projects. The second goal relates to contemporary efforts to decolonize our perspectives about justice, domestic and global. By relying on Waluchow's notion of CCM, the reality that Indigenous knowledge, despite it not having been properly acknowledged in most philosophical academic debates, is already a part of our debates about global justice becomes undeniable and a call for action to further expand our understanding of global political morality.

1 Introduction

In this chapter I engage with the work of Wil Waluchow and show how his body of work not only is compatible with forward-looking research agendas in philosophy, but it also forces us to engage with such agendas in a meaningful way. On this occasion, I not only want to show my respect and admiration for his work but also

J. S. Perez (✉)
University of Alberta, Department of Philosophy, Edmonton, AB, Canada
e-mail: jsanchezperez@ualberta.ca

T. Bustamante et al. (eds.), *Law, Morality and Judicial Reasoning*, Law and Philosophy Library 147, https://doi.org/10.1007/978-3-031-61879-6_14

the possibilities that his research in legal philosophy opens to other fields such as moral and political philosophy.

In Sect. 2 I introduce the readers to the view of a Community's Constitutional Morality (CCM), which I call Waluchow's insight. This insight establishes that social norms surrounding or giving existence to political and social institutions give us something to point at when discussing issues connected to law and morality. In this section, I identify and acknowledge that Waluchow's work is shaped under debates focused on the notion of the state. However, I point out the fact that if we switch the focus of our inquiries towards the question of political communities, of which states are but an example, his work can easily be extrapolated to a global scenario.

In Sect. 3 I proceed to develop my relational account of political communities. I define them as *communities of practices among members where those practices are mediated by institutions that partake in the effort to implement some form of respect of social norms to regulate relevant moral and political affairs.* I justify this definition and advocate the compatibility of this definition with a Hartian jurisprudential tradition. In Sect. 4, I introduce the reader to a global political community and its current commitments. I provide evidence for the claim that Indigenous knowledge is already part of the political morality of the global political community. This political morality is a social fact that, following Waluchow's insights, contains a set of moral norms and considered judgments that we can properly attribute to the community.

Section 5 is where I engage with the notion of Institutionally Embodied Moral Intuitions. I explain how they have merits that give us reasons to choose them over personal intuitions from different authors in efforts to construct moral theories. I highlight the challenge of adjudication as a problem that, as we stand, presents severe problems to personal moral intuitions competing with one another. One of my main claims is that by identifying an object already accepted by a large number of the members of the global political community, I am able to rely on a social fact instead of the intuitions of any one individual.

The final section contains some closing remarks about this chapter and the work of Wil Waluchow. I explain how, by relying on his work, I am able to point out to a global political morality that includes Indigenous knowledge as a social fact. Putting it in those terms, and whether any specific agent acts in accordance with such a political morality or not, it becomes impossible to deny the existence of such a political morality and those views. Given that it becomes mandatory for us to incorporate reasons in favour or against Indigenous knowledge in our current moral deliberations, I highlight how Waluchow's work gives us an important method to promote and engage with forward-looking agendas that can make the discipline more inclusive and open for future generations of scholars.

2 A Community's Constitutional Morality: Waluchow's Insight

Two of Wil Waluchow's most notable contributions to the field of philosophy are his account of the limits of the law as presented in *Inclusive Legal Positivism* (1994), and his defense of judicial review as a possible democratic institution in *A Common Law Theory of Judicial Review: The Living Tree* (2007). Although both works are canonical in their own ways, in this chapter I will focus more on the implications or insights that we can take from Waluchow's view on Constitutional law and that we can extrapolate to other fields of philosophy such as moral and political philosophy, and in particular to debates about global justice. In this section I first introduce the readers to Waluchow's CCM. I then move on to present a lingering question that his account leaves unanswered: *what is a political community?* By addressing this question, I open the door to extrapolate Waluchow's reasoning from the domestic sphere to the global one.

One of the most important features of Waluchow's attempt to justify the democratic credentials of the practice of judicial review,[1] the possibility of a court challenging a law under constitutional parameters, is the identification of two pairs of contrasting concepts. The first pair consists of personal morality versus community morality. By personal morality, Waluchow means the subjective moral views of individual agents or the things they are morally committed to and that they would prefer to see endorsed by their community and the legal system they are a part of (2007, p. 220). Against this, Waluchow contrasts the community's morality, which unlike the morality of a single individual agent, is attributable to the community as a whole (2007, p. 220).

The second set of contrasting concepts that Waluchow presents are moral opinions versus true moral commitments (2007, p. 223). The former, following Rawls, are described as "moral views that have not been critically examined so as to achieve reflective equilibrium," that is, as views wherein principles and judgments are not necessarily consistent with one another (Rawls 1999, p. 18). On the other hand, the latter are those moral views that a moral agent has truly committed themselves to follow. In calling these an agent's true moral commitments, one does not assert or imply that they are "true" in the sense of being objectively morally[2] true, only that the agent is truly committed to them (Waluchow 2007, p. 224).

---

[1] Waluchow uses the term "Charter" to refer to "any written constitutional instrument, or part thereof, that specifies what appear to be moral rights against which government actions are to be measured in assessing their legal force, effect, or validity" (Waluchow 2007, p. 10). I will follow his terminology in this chapter.

[2] Something being "objectively morally true" could be interpreted in at least two different ways. The first one could be something like metaphysical objectivity, or something that corresponds to a true moral element of the world. In this sense, we could be in the face of something being objectively morally true because it captures that which is moral in the world. A correspondence theory of truth could be an acceptable way to understand this. Another way to understand something to be objectively morally true could be to claim that such a thing is objectively true in virtue of epistemic

A final step in Waluchow's project is identifying a possible *place* where those community commitments can be found. This *place* is the realm of legal and political practices of a community. This realm includes, but is not necessarily limited to, charters, judicial decisions, legislative choices, and the practices of various political institutions as they adjudicate questions about law and morality in their political community.

Waluchow defines CCM as "the set of moral norms and considered judgments properly attributable to the community as a whole representing its true commitments, but with the following additional property: they are in some way tied to its constitutional law and practices" (2007, p. 227). It is plausible to view Waluchow as tangentially following the Dworkinian idea that there is something like a "political morality presupposed by the laws and institutions of the community" (Dworkin 1978, p. 126). Unlike Dworkin, however, Waluchow does not assert that the identifying moral principles or political morality presupposed by a social system implies the endorsement of that political morality (Waluchow 2007, p. 227; Stoljar 2009, p. 116). In other words, Dworkin's notion of political morality involves the necessary connection of such political morality with the best possible justification from a moral point of view. Waluchow's does not.

Waluchow's view of political morality aims to describe or point at *something* within a society that can be said to inform certain existing legal and political practices carried out by institutions within that community. Thus, allowing for the possibility of identifying *something* relevant without assessing whether that *thing* is good or not. This process is in line with what Julie Dickson calls "indirectly evaluative" propositions. In her view, to call something a moral principle of a community or to identify a political morality within a community is to attribute "some evaluative property to that feature of the law" this does not "entail a directly evaluative proposition that the feature of the law is good (or bad)" (Dickson 2001, p. 53).

Regarding this point, you will see a different interpretation of Waluchow's work by Professor Thomas Bustamante in his collaboration for this volume. There, Bustamante argues that Waluchow and Dworkin both share a similar inferentialist method of constitutional interpretation. For Bustamante, Dworkin's concept of law as integrity is on the same camp as the inclusive legal positivist tradition that Waluchow represents. Perhaps the difference Bustamante's and my interpretations comes from our approach to integrity in Dworkin's work.

As Marmor properly notices, integrity for Dworkin is an element that works as a paradigm within non-ideal circumstances (Marmor 2019, p. 19). To put integrity in those terms means to recognize the Rawlsian distinction between ideal and non-ideal

merits. In other words, this second way of understanding objectivity is about the possibility of properly supporting a given claim under an argumentative framework. Waluchow's claim seems to be about the first kind of objectivity without engaging with the latter. I thank Professor Thomas Bustamante for highlighting the need to further clarifying this point in a previous draft. For a lengthier discussion of objectivity and the law see Postema (2001), Raz (1999, chapter 6) and Marmor (1995).

theory (Rawls 2001; Simmons 2010; Stemplowska and Swift 2012). Broadly speaking, ideal theory tells us what the goal is, while non-ideal theory tells us how to correct things to get us to the goal. In that sense, the former deals with regulative elements and the latter with corrective ones. Following that, it is possible to understand integrity as a tool for the correction of a moral wrong via the proper interpretation of certain legal claims. Integrity then can be further understood as a moral commitment on itself that is justified by some other, this time ideal, commitment such as dignity, equality, or freedom. For a Dworkinian judge, the personal commitment to ideal and non-ideal seems unavoidable due to the methodological claims Dworkin makes.

In the case of Waluchow, what seems to be at stake is not so much a commitment to correct or guide precedents towards the ideal via the non-ideal. Instead, mainly the identification of the ideal claims that guide the lives of certain communities. This, of course, does not necessarily mean that rectification cannot be part of the efforts of a Waluchowian judge, it just means that that is not the only thing they do, unlike the Dworkinian judge. And when this rectification happens, it does not follow necessarily from the judge's personal commitment to some non-ideal or ideal claim. A Waluchowian judge can, when needed, apply reflective equilibrium to determine what CCM requires. Another case where a Waluchowian judge might have to apply some form of correction might be in cases of legal indeterminacy such as those when the law does not provide a clear answer to an issue of adjudication. In those cases, the judge could arrive at an answer that is compatible with the CCM in *the right way* (Waluchow 2021, p. 57).

For Waluchow, the right way would imply that the judge exercises this capacity in a legitimate way and this would involved that decision is: 1. not arbitrary; 2. impartial and neutral in surveying the alternatives; 3. one that gives equal consideration to the interests of all affected parties; 4. based on a general principle (or set of principles) that extends by its terms to cases beyond the one being decided; 5. based on sound reasoning (empirical and logical); 6. offered from the point of view of the community's legal system and its CCM; 7. respectful of what Rawls calls the duty of civility, and 8. dedicated to process not result (Waluchow 2021, pp. 64–65).

In this paradigm, a Dworkinian judge will always aim at correcting a state of affairs towards the ideal goal that underlies his personal commitment to integrity, facing an impossible challenge when a right answer is not possible. A Waluchowian judge, on the other hand, will identify those ideal goals of the community and act to correct those gaps if or when they appear, without necessarily embracing them.

Although an important and rich analysis could be further explored in this area, that is a debate that I will leave for another time. For now I want to point at the fact that all of Waluchow's views about the democratic credentials of judicial review and his account of a CCM are part of a larger debate regarding the possibility of a state to remain democratic while limiting the effects or validity of certain laws passed by its legal officials (Waldron 1999, 2006). That is, Waluchow's views are framed under a traditional view of the state as the center of debates about law and morality. In other words, the focus of his position is that which focuses on the political community commonly known as the state. However, I consider that if we answer the question "What is a political community?" we can make progress towards seeing how his framework and insights can be extrapolated towards a larger, global, scale.

3 Political Communities As Communities of Practices

Without a doubt, the state seems like a fundamental point of reference for theoretical considerations about politics or about legality (Raz 2014). Yet, to reduce every form of political community to a state seems problematic in the sense that it is equivalent of denying the existence of other forms of political organization throughout history. The Greek Polis, the Roman Republic, or the Incan Tahuantinsuyo, all clearly forms of political communities but hardly a state in the sense of the European phenomena that appeared between the fifteenth and sixteenth century in Europe (Sanchez-Perez 2020, pp. 128–129). Perhaps a step back is necessary to make sense of the social phenomena known as political communities. This step is one of abstraction and it allows us to consider a broader picture of what is at stake when considering if something is a political community or not.

For the next couple of paragraphs, I want the reader to bear with me in considering our current social reality. To do that, a good idea is to look at the world as it is presented to us today. When paying attention, the entire globe is subject to common issues and challenges that affect us all beyond the framework or constrains of a single state. Considering issues such as the Covid19 pandemic of 2020, the reality of climate change, or the economic crashes 2008, 2010, and so on and so forth, we have good reasons to think that the global society is linked in important and meaningful ways. Given this reality, it would also be hard to argue against the existence of a coherent set of rules and practices that guide, for better or worse, things like the global economy. These rules and practices, also known as social norms, work as "the foundation of the global market, and the global market sustains the human population at its seven-billion size" (Wenar 2016, p. 116).

In other words, a set of social norms that allows for human exchanges, commercial and others, can be identified and so can its effects in many of the interactions we have across the globe. Examples of the products of those social norms, which I will refer here as institutions, that exist in virtue of these rules and practices are the World Bank, the International Monetary Fund, the World Trade Organization, and the World Health Organization. These institutions are not the only ones in existence globally, nor necessarily the most important. However, they are useful examples of institutions that deal with property, possession of goods, and health across the globe that have been in place for several decades, if not longer, and whose practices and activities give us a point of reference for analysis. Just as in the case of Waluchow's insight regarding the CCM, the social norms surrounding or giving existence to these institutions give us something to point at when discussing issues connected to law and morality.

As evidence suggests, going back to the issue of political communities, *social norms* and *institutions* play a fundamental role in meaningful areas of our lives. For that reason, I suggest that we focus our conceptualization of political communities around those two concepts instead of an reducing them to the state. This level of abstraction, I think, can better clarify what we are after when considering the question "what is a political community?" and connected issues regarding the identification of a community. Together, these two concepts serve me to articulate a broad relational definition of political communities as *a set of practices among members where those practices are mediated by institutions that partake in the effort to implement some form of respect of social norms to regulate relevant moral and political affairs*. By relevant moral and political affairs, I mean those about the organization of social life, such as sharing the burdens that come with sustaining society and the benefits that society produces or guarantees.

This conceptualization of political communities seems to be compatible with HLA Hart's views of social norms and societies. To clarify that, it is important that I first introduce what Hart understands by social norms, which in his view are defined in opposition to habits. First, unlike social norms, deviation from a habit does not draw criticism from oneself or from other group members. Social norms, on the other hand, carry with them pressure for conformity via criticism, including self-criticism. Second, in the case of social norms, "deviation from the standard is generally accepted as a good reason for making" the criticism (1994, p. 55). Finally, unlike a habit, some group members "must look upon the behaviour in question as a general standard" (1994, p. 56) for the whole group. These differences leave us with two aspects to consider: (a) the external aspect of group behaviour, which is a quality of both habits and social rules; and (b) the internal aspect, which is a reflective critical attitude towards the rule that informs the criticisms towards the deviation from the standard which is characteristic of the social norms alone (1994, pp. 55–57).

On the other hand, institutions can be conceived as the set of social entities that claim jurisdiction over certain groups, pointing the community members to the standards for action—i.e., social norms—of such political community. Furthermore, institutions tend to claim jurisdiction over individual members and communities on specific relevant issues. Examples of institutions that fit this description are the judiciary or the parliament of any country. The judiciary seems to allow for systemic relationships in what we commonly call a legal system, while parliament would do the same in what we usually call a representative system of democracy. As a reminder, I can mention that Hart talks about institutions in several parts of The Concept of Law (Hart 1994, pp. 167, 199, 214, 239, 240, etc.). Following this, it seems entirely possible to conceive social institutions as entities that bridge, or mediate obligations or privileges derived from social norms between the different group members, as being compatible with the Hartian tradition.

Based on the previous points, I conceive a political community in terms of the relationships between members of a group, social norms, and the institutions that mediate between them. In this sense, the institutions point the members of the group in the direction of the standards for action when issues relevant for moral and political consideration arise and where those institutions could claim jurisdiction. I will use the example of the USA to show how this relationship-based approach to political community can work with states. It seems relatively intuitive to assert that the country currently known as the USA is a political community. But it seems complicated to argue that the USA's political community is only its legal system, or only its judiciary, or only its legislative branch, or only its executive branch, or only the sum of its citizens. Instead, it seems more likely that the USA's political community is the group of individuals who engage in certain common social practices that are mediated by different institutions, some mentioned above, aimed at regulating relevant and moral political affairs of the group that we commonly identified with its citizenry. This relational definition of political community allows me to identify three elements—members, social norms, and institutions—when looking at different social phenomena.

In the same vein, my account of political communities can be applied to Indigenous communities currently existing in other countries. For example, the Inuit community. Clearly, this community has members, norms that have their own ways of being implemented, and institutions that mediate between the members. Yet, this political community clearly exists within or in parallel to other political communities. Those other political communities with whom the Inuit community overlaps are the USA, Canada, Greenland, and Russian communities. Making sense of this reality of complex interactions between and among political communities can further show that states are not necessarily the best point of departure for all of our analysis.

Going back to the main thread of argumentation here, I consider it important to remember that Hart does not seem to conceive social norms in a vacuum but as part of a social set of interactions. For him, the law is a social phenomenon—among many—that regulates human life in society (1994, p. v). We can contrast this with a contemporary of Hart, Hans Kelsen, for whom the law is better understood as a logical system of norms meant to regulate human behavior (Kelsen 1967, p. 4). This comparison shows that, for Hart, social norms do not affect single humans creating individually binding obligations. Instead, they are part of the social fabric of relationships. Furthermore, many social norms are mediated by institutions that allow and inform the interactions of the members of society.[3]

By understanding institutions as the entities that mediate between individuals' obligations, we can overcome the need to presuppose some form of pre-existing joint commitment as a way to understand societies as authors such as Margaret Gilbert

[3] Jorge Fabra's approach to political communities in terms of norm-compliance is worth mentioning. He refers to political communities as "relevant entities that have a prominent role in our theoretical and practical reasoning due to the pressing demands they impose on their subjects" (2019, p. 8) and as "groups that exert intense forms of social pressure to effectively secure compliance with sets of rules that regulate important politico-moral domains" (2019, pp. 80–81). I consider that there is substantial compatibility between Fabra's views and my own, most likely due to the fact that we are both drawing from a Hartian tradition. However, unlike Fabra, I consider that focusing on social norms and the institutions that help mediate between them and the members of the community might give us a clearer picture of the social phenomena under discussion.

have suggested (1989, 2000, 2014, 2018). Furthermore, institutions in this sense can be adequately described as entities that guide those members who look upon them to help conduct their lives. If we consider institutions this way, we are one step closer to adequately identifying a political community when looking for one. What comes after is determining the content of those social norms and what they are supposed to regulate. That is, the relevant moral and political affairs of such a community.

As a point of clarification, my account of political communities does not claim that social norms are always respected or that institutions are always capable of mediating between practices, members, or other institutions linked to the social system. It just points out that one can identify certain political communities by identifying the existence of certain institutions and the social norms they point at when addressing interactions among themselves and members of the political community. With that conceptual tool at hand, we can see how, if Waluchow's insights are about identifying moral commitments within a political community, this analysis needn't be reduced or limited to only the state. If we look for social norms and institutions at the global level, we can probably find the same points of reference that Waluchow talks about when looking at the state.

In the next section I will proceed to identify a global political community and the social norms that at the core regulate meaningful relationships among members of that community. In other words, which norms at the global scale can be equivalent to those identified by Waluchow's CCM when discussing the issue at the state or domestic level. I will also show how Indigenous knowledge is already part of the conversation when it comes to global political morality.

4 The Global Political Community and Its Commitment to Indigenous Knowledge

In Sect. 2 I claimed that three elements are relevant for identifying a political community (1) members, (2) social norms, and (3) institutions. Furthermore, I established that a political community is such because it focuses on relevant moral and political affairs. The issues at stake for a political community are those about the organization of social life, such as sharing the burdens that come with sustaining society and the benefits that society produces. Within this category, issues such as labour, finances, health, other basic entitlements by members within the group, and membership determination are considered part of a possibly much longer list. Following that, a political community can be identified by paying attention to different institutions constantly at play in the world. I will briefly introduce, in the following paragraphs, two key institutions and show how they satisfy the conditions of articulating obligations derived from social norms among members of a global community.

The first one is the International Labour Organization (ILO), with its 187 member states. This organization's goal is to set the international standards for labour in a way that promotes opportunities "for women and men to obtain decent and productive work in conditions of freedom, equity, security and dignity" (International Labour Organization 2019, p. 7). To pursue this goal, the organization can apply sanctions to those who violate the organization's standards. A relevant feature of the organization is article 33 of its constitution. This article establishes that if a member of the organization fails to comply with the recommendations made to them, the ILO can recommend actions towards securing compliance with its decisions. This institution satisfies the condition of serving to provide mediation between community members and their obligations. By engaging in the implementation of social norms in the form of labour standards, this institution provides a great example of the kind of institution regulating a relevant aspect of social life at a global scale that is inexorably linked to the production or sustaining of society.

The previously introduced institution is contained within or structurally connected to the United Nations (UN), another institution that was created in the aftermath of World War II (WWII) to maintain international peace and security. Currently, almost every country and many international organizations are connected in one way or another to the UN.[4] This institution has its own set of rules and regulations that enable it to articulate obligations at a global scale to secure its goals. It can easily be considered the most comprehensive global institution in the entirety of human history. Perhaps two of the institution's most important practices are the gathering of the general assembly and the meetings of the security council. In the first one, every member state can participate and discuss world peace and security issues, while in the second one, the security council members can participate and dictate measures to secure peace and security at the international level. One of the essential prerogatives possessed by the UN's security council is the faculty to authorize military forces against entities deemed to be violating the Charter of the United Nations. When it comes to obligations and sanctions across the world, it would be hard to identify a more heavily endowed institution.

As it stands, it is easy to identify a set of members, norms, and institutions in the previous two examples. What follows then, following what I have called Waluchow's insight, is the identification of set of moral norms and considered judgments properly attributable to the global political community and that are in some way or form tied to its legal or political practices. Here I want the reader to remember that when talking about a commitment of the community, we are talking about it in descriptive terms and without necessarily assessing the moral correctness of that commitment. That is, I am not yet looking for the moral justification or for a way to argue in favour of any particular moral commitment in place. What is at stake is the identification of social norms that can give us a clear image of what the

[4]It is important to remember that WWII involved most countries on the planet, and the violence resulted in the death of up to 80 million people and the destruction of entire nations. One of the most critical features of WWII was the violence that certain states enacted against their citizens. It is therefore worth noting that the UN allows for individual citizens to complain about states' human rights violations. See Art. 1 of the Optional Protocol to the International Covenant on Civil and Political Rights.

political morality of the global political community looks like at this point in time. In other words, what is stake here is the identification of a social fact.

Here I want to point at two important legal and political documents that shed light in the search of the current political morality of the community. The first one is the Earth Charter and the second is the United Nations Declaration on the Rights of Indigenous Peoples. The Earth Charter, an international declaration of fundamental values and principles made public in 2000 and endorsed by The United Nations Educational, Scientific and Cultural Organization (UNESCO) establishes in its first article that the charter recognizes that all beings are interdependent, and every form of life has value regardless of its worth to human beings. This declaration makes an important move from an *anthropocentric* view towards a *cosmocentric* one.

Anthropocentrism can be roughly understood as an approach where everything in the universe is arranged to produce and serve humans (Rolston 1988, p. 197) or as "the unjustified privileging of human beings, as such, at the expense of other forms of life" (Curry 2018, p. 67). In contrast, cosmocentrism is an approach usually attributed to Indigenous peoples from different parts of the world where it is assumed that human existence is part of a more extensive system of interactions, where each action affects the whole system (Jarandilla Nuñez 2019, p. 423). Based on that, humans "should not consider themselves as superior to other living beings in the world, who also have different ways of organizing and contributing to the systems of life on earth" (Jarandilla Nuñez 2019, p. 424). The idea here is that humanity's intrinsic value cannot be seen as a way of justification of rule over the rest of beings in existence. Instead, the environment and everything in it has intrinsic value, and humans share that value.

The Earth Charter serves as a good example to show the inclusion of Indigenous views and knowledge into the global political morality currently in place. Yet, it is not the only piece of evidence to support my claim. The United Nations Declaration on the Rights of Indigenous Peoples (UNDRIP), adopted in 2007, is another ground-breaking legal and political source that helped further the incorporation of Indigenous worldviews into discussions about global justice. In the preamble of the UNDRIP, the General Assembly of the United Nations formally recognized that "respect for Indigenous knowledge, cultures and traditional practices contributes to sustainable and equitable development and proper management of the environment", while in article 29 of that same document the General Assembly acknowledged that "Indigenous peoples have the right to the conservation and protection of the environment and the productive capacity of their lands or territories and resources."

These two documents are not the only ones I could mention and analyze here to show a set of norms that show that the global political community and its members have incorporated Indigenous knowledge into them.[5] But together they provide

[5] Other important global sources that provide further evidence for my claim are the Indigenous and Tribal Peoples Convention, 1989 from the International Labour Organization; art. 8 of the Convention on Biological Diversity, which establishes that each party "subject to its national legislation, respect, preserve and maintain knowledge, innovations and practices of indigenous and local communities embodying traditional lifestyles relevant for the conservation and sustainable use of

strong evidence that such knowledge has made its way into the morality of the global political community.

As I established in Sect. 2, the relational definition of political communities that I use here does not deny nor contradict the possibility of political communities existing within other political communities. This allows me to identify the political morality of any political community within the global one. An example of this is the indigenous Andean concept of Sumak Kawsay, which has become a "centerpiece of ascendant indigenous movements and endogenous development in the Andean countries and have encouraged a pan-Latin American Perspective" (Zimmerer 2012, p. 601). This approach makes sense of a worldview where the fundamental moral commitment is not to humans' well-being but of humans' living-well. The key difference here is that although human value and status are recognized, this does not exclude the possibility of recognizing a similar value in other beings in existence.

Sumak Kawsay made its way into chapter 7 of the Constitution of Ecuador as a regulative concept applying to all individual duties and rights, and as a way of formally recognizing nature as a subject of rights. Although it is the first constitutional charter in the world to engage in this kind of challenge to an anthropocentric view, other countries have started to follow its example. On December 21 of 2010, the Bolivian government passed the law N° 71 under the title *Law of the Rights of Mother Earth*. This central piece of legislation recognizes nature's status as a subject of rights.

Another example of Indigenous knowledge informing the morality of a political community within the global political community is one from Māori philosophy. According to Tuari Stewart, this kind of Philosophy "is found in Māori discourses about the relationship between people, things, the environment and the world" (Stewart 2021, p. 2). These discourses are in turn grounded on three epistemological pillars (1) everything in existence is related; (2) all things are living; and (3) worlds regarded as "unseen" in Western terms can be mediated by the human (Stewart 2021, p. 55). Under this *relational* framework lies the recognition, or basic normative commitment, that each creature in existence has a *mauri* (life force) that "joins all beings (...) into one interdependent whole, each part depending for its well-being upon the health of each other part and of the whole itself." (Patterson 1998, p. 70).

Two essential bills that rely on this political morality were passed in recent years by New Zealand authorities. The first one is the Te Urewera Act of 2014, where the mostly forested area in the North of New Zealand known as Te Urewera was declared a legal entity. In article 11, the bill recognizes that Te Urewera is "a legal

---

biological diversity and promote their wider application with the approval and involvement of the holders of such knowledge, innovations and practices and encourage the equitable sharing of the benefits arising from the utilization of such knowledge, innovations and practices"; and art. 30 of the Convention on the Rights of the Child which states that "In those States in which ethnic, religious or linguistic minorities or persons of indigenous origin exist, a child belonging to such a minority or who is indigenous shall not be denied the right, in community with other members of his or her group, to enjoy his or her own culture, to profess and practise his or her own religion, or to use his or her own language;" among others.

entity, and has all the rights, powers, duties, and liabilities of a legal person". The second one is the Te Awa Tupua (Whanganui River Claims Settlement) Act of 2017, where in the same vein as in the previous decision, the New Zealand Parliament declared in article 12 that "Te Awa Tupua is an indivisible and living whole, comprising the Whanganui River from the mountains to the sea, incorporating all its physical and metaphysical elements;" and in article 14 that "Te Awa Tupua is a legal person and has all the rights, powers, duties, and liabilities of a legal person".

What I have shown so far is that at the global and domestic scale, clear examples to commitments that include Indigenous knowledge are part of a political morality that we can point at. The implications of this are various and important. In one sense it could be argued that the move from anthropocentric views to cosmocentric ones might need to be framed under a general move from human dignity towards something like the dignity of being. To properly argue and expand upon this would take me further away from the main topic of this chapter. For that reason, I will not discuss the implications of this possible argumentative move here. What I want to focus on for now are the benefits of using this descriptive approach towards a global political morality and how it can provide us a more appealing ground to construct the parameters for a global theory of justice than personal intuitions.

5 Institutionally Embodied Intuitions

Following Waluchow's insight that it is possible to identify the political morality of a community without necessarily endorsing it, I have shown that a commitment towards Indigenous knowledge in different shapes and forms is already part of the global political morality. To which extent and in which form is yet to discussed and it is not the focus of this paper. This commitment, however, does not provide enough grounds to support such a political morality, since to this point I have only committed myself to an exercise of identification and not one of justification. The question that arises now is *which merits does this political morality that includes Indigenous knowledge has, as starting point, over other possibilities if and when a global theory of justice is constructed?* To answer that in this section I will argue for the benefits of Institutionally Embodied Intuitions over Personal Intuitions. I will start showing what I mean by Personal Intuitions and the two important problems we might face when adopting them as points of departure for the construction of something like a global theory of justice.

Intuitions continue to play an important role in philosophical considerations. Yet, they are not without criticism. In his brief essay *When Philosophers Shoot From the Hip*, James Rachel claims that, when prompted to address current events, the following is true of philosophers:

> Sometimes they do what we might think philosophers ought to do: challenge the prevailing orthodoxy, calling into question the assumptions that people unthinkingly make. But just as often they function as orthodoxy's most sophisticated defenders, assuming that the existing

social consensus must be right, and articulating its theoretical "justification." (Rachel 1992, p. 801).

Rachels' assessment of the kind of answers provided by philosophers when faced with pressing issues serves as a good reminder that philosophers are people, too. They can articulate views that endorse or oppose the commonly held beliefs of other members of society. They are subject to the same prejudicial opinions as other members of the community.

Perhaps one of the clearest examples of a problematic social belief in the 1970s was the belief that killing was always worse than letting a patient die.[6] This position, upheld by the American Medical Association at the time, was challenged by Rachel in his essay *Active and Passive Euthanasia* (1975). He highlighted that letting a person die could lead to a slow and painful process, whereas helping somebody die could be quick and painless (1975, p. 78), thus putting tension on the idea that letting a person die was the obvious morally correct answer. Peter Singer adequately notes that in both of those essays, "Rachels rejected the idea that the role of moral philosophers is to take our common moral intuitions as data and seek to develop the theory that best fits those intuitions" (Singer 2005, p. 333). Singer, however, goes further in his critique of unquestioning reliance on intuitions. Based on a variety of answers in a *trolley problem* experiment, Singer raised doubts about the value of moral intuitions in moral reasoning. In the first scenario, person X can save five at the expense of one if X pulls a lever. In the second scenario, person X can save five at the expense of one, but here instead of pulling a lever, X must push a person from a bridge. Researchers discovered that the subjects involved were more willing to pull the lever than they were to push the other person off the bridge (Singer 2005, pp. 337, 347–348).

Based on that evidence, something like the intuition that there is no moral difference between pulling a lever and pushing a person, at least for Singer, can be discarded. Furthermore, for him, this experiment highlights the fact that people are more reluctant to enact direct violence against an individual than to move a switch or a lever even if the latter leads to similar or even worse consequences. Singer uses these cases to raise awareness about the possible connection between emotions, which could be linked to biological traits, and intuitions, thus making moral intuitions a problematic grounding for the construction of moral principles and theories. Singer concludes that this challenging (possible) relationship between emotions and intuitions puts theories that rely on intuitions on a shaky footing insofar as they lack rational grounds to support them.

The list of theories that rely on intuitions includes Rawls' theory of justice, which relies on the method of reflective equilibrium which Singer (2005, p. 345) claims "has always struck" him as dubious. For Singer, Rawls' project is grounded on the misconceived "analogy between the role of a normative moral theory and a scientific theory" (Singer 2005, p. 345). This, for Singer, is the case because the purpose of a

[6] Although it is possible to claim that this is also an issue today in the cases of physician assisted suicide.

scientific theory is to explain the existence of data in the world, while a normative ethical theory's purpose is to answer to the question of "what we ought to do?", and a possible answer to this last question is to reject all ordinary moral judgments. This answer, for Singer, is not even considered as a possibility within the model of reflective equilibrium. Singer's point is that "the model of reflective equilibrium, at least as presented in A Theory of Justice, appears to rule out such an answer, because it assumes that our moral intuitions are some kind of data from which we can learn what we ought to do" (Singer 2005, p. 346). Following that, and even if I disagree with some of Singer's conclusions, it seems possible to accept that it is problematic to accept intuitions as hard facts of the world without the possibility of challenging them.

Although I think that Rawls' use of intuitions is not fairly described by Singer, it is not my goal to defend reflective equilibrium against Singer's attacks in this work. Instead, I want to engage with the more nuanced and real possibility that individual intuitions might present us with a challenge of adjudication. For the sake of clarity, I will accept Sandberg and Juth's distinction between *practical* and *theoretical* intuitions. The former can be, broadly, understood as "automatic or pre-reflective judgments about what is right and wrong in particular scenarios," while the latter are "intuitions about abstract moral principles or ideas, or about what makes actions moral or immoral generally and what morality is about" (Sandberg and Juth 2011, p. 213). An example of practical intuitions could be the famous preamble of the United States of America declaration of independence "We hold these truths to be *self-evident,*[7] that all men are created equal." In contrast, an example of theoretical intuitions might be Kant's commonly known formula of the kingdom of ends, which states that one must "act according to the maxims of a member of a merely possible kingdom of ends legislating in it universally" (Kant 2005, p. 96). Both types of intuitions, I claim, face the same challenge.

When faced with the need to choose some moral element as starting point for a theory of global justice, given its universal or global nature, the need for generalizable intuitions and not ad-hoc answers to concrete situations becomes more obvious. For that reason, theoretical intuitions become the clear choice. Three examples of theoretical intuitions used as starting points by authors working on theories of justice come to mind. The first one is Nussbaum's Social Contract account which is grounded on the "the intuitive idea of a life that is worthy of the dignity of the human being" (Nussbaum 2006, p. 70); the second one is Rousseau's Social Contract model, where individuals must build societies around the intuitively true claim that freedom, or to be as "free as before" society existed (Rousseau 1913, p. 12), is to be guaranteed in any given social model. The final one is Gauthier (1986, p. 8), for whom *interest of the self* is what drives any Social Contract. Which of these intuitions is better than the other one?

There is no shortage of defenses of each those theories and the starting points they endorse for moral theorization, nor are those the only possible options in front of us

[7] The italics are mine.

when discussing moral reasoning. Intuitions are something that philosophers never seem to run out of. And each of them could—and many have been—justified in different and philosophically relevant ways. However, despite those efforts of justification, there is no solution in sight for what I call *the problem of adjudication among intuitions*. At least not one that could satisfy everyone. This challenge of adjudication poses difficult issues to which I will not here attempt to provide a solution.

Wittgenstein said that "if a man could write a book on Ethics which really was a book on Ethics, this book would, with an explosion, destroy all the other books in the world" (Wittgenstein 1965, p. 7). Although I do not share Wittgenstein's pessimism about the possibility of eventually developing a proper or correct ethical theory, I do think that we are nowhere near achieving that objective—i.e., identifying a moral theory that would *destroy all other moral theories*. So instead of pursuing this ambitious goal, I instead propose we start out theorizations with the identification and assessment of the set of moral norms and considered judgments properly attributable to the global political community. That is, with a social fact that can be pointed at when discussing issues related to a society.

By assessing the commitments revealed in the decisions and practices of global institutions, instead of relying on my own personal intuitions, or those of other philosophers who have engaged with issues of morality or justice in general, we can avoid the problem of adjudication among intuitions. Identifying these commitments will lead us to determine a set of what I call *the institutionally embodied moral intuitions of global institutions*. It is important to note, just as I have established in the previous sections discussing Waluchow's work, that it does not follow from the fact that one can identify these institutionally embodied moral intuitions in certain global institutions and their practices that such intuitions are sound or valid, morally speaking. However, their identification does provide us with an object largely accepted by members of the global political community. This object, unlike personal intuitions, has been filtered and discussed at length by a large number of members of the global political community and it shapes the behaviour of the institutions and the members that together make the social realm what it is.

By identifying an object already accepted by a large number of the members of the global political community, I am able to rely on a social fact instead of the intuitions of any one individual. A starting point of moral theorization derived from global institutions' practices provides us with a sensible starting point in developing a theory, the validity of which can be attributed to its capacity to provide us with what Rawls called a "public basis of justification." That is, something that large segments of a community could accept as some shared "fundamental ideas implicit in the public political culture in the hope of developing a political conception that can gain free and reasoned agreement in judgement" (Rawls 2005, pp. 100–101). Thus, I can avoid the previously established challenge of adjudication in favour of a more promising challenge of identifying elements within the political morality of a political community, which, as it stands today, involves Indigenous knowledge in a significative and meaningful way.

6 Final Remarks

If the reader accepts, as I think they should, the evidence that I have provided for the fact that a commitment to Indigenous knowledge is already part of the global political morality, at least two options become apparent. The first one is to accept the current political morality and construct our moral theorization around it, in a way that respects the pre-established commitments to Indigenous knowledge and what this implies in our interactions towards nature and other beings. The second one is to reject this described political morality as a point of departure for theorization. This last option forces those who reject it, as long as they are truly committed to engage in rational and reasonable debates and discussions, to provide us with reasons about why they would reject Indigenous knowledge and its implications from being part of our moral theorizations.

Whatever option those engaging in debates about global justice and moral theorization choose, by relying on Waluchow's insight that social norms surrounding or giving existence to political and social institutions give us something to point at when discussing issues connected to law and morality. It becomes possible to affirm that Indigenous knowledge is a reality that cannot be denied and needs to be included in our debates. Wil Waluchow's work on legal and political philosophy has important ramifications beyond the realm of the state. By taking his work and acknowledging the Hartian tradition that informs it to its most abstract and fundamental commitments, we can see implications that can resonate with forward-looking research agendas. These agendas, like mine, will forever be indebted to Wil Waluchow's capacity to provide us with a philosophical body of work ready to expand, include, and be open to what reality demands from us. Having had firsthand access to Wil Waluchow's views, comments, and insights, I will always regard myself as fortunate.

Acknowledgments I want to thank Wil Waluchow for his comments on different drafts of this paper. I also want to thank Leanne Woodward, Ben Nelson, Matt Grellette, Jorge Fabra, and Thomas Bustamante for their comments regarding different sections of this chapter. Finally, I want to thank all the participants of the philosophy colloquium series at Simon Fraser University for their input and suggestions when I presented sections of this paper.

References

Curry, Patrick. 2018. *Ecological ethics: An introduction*. New York: Polity.
Dickson, Julie. 2001. *Evaluation and legal theory*. Portland: Hart Publishing.
Dworkin, Ronald. 1978. *Taking rights seriously*. Cambridge: Harvard University Press.
Fabra-Zamora, Jorge. 2019. *Normative political communities: Foundations for a Hartian theory of state and non-state law*. Hamilton: McMaster University. October.
Gauthier, David. 1986. *Morals by agreement*. New York: Clarendon Press.
Gilbert, Margaret. 1989. *On social facts*. New Jersey: Princeton University Press.

———. 2000. *Sociality and plural subject theory: New essays in plural subject theory*. New York: Rowman & Littlefield.

———. 2014. *Joint commitments: How we make the social world*. New York: New York University Press.

———. 2018. *Rights and demands: A foundational inquiry*. Oxford: Oxford University Press.

Hart, H.L.A. 1994. *The concept of law*. New York: Oxford University Press.

International Labour Organization. 2019. Rules of the game: An introduction to the standards-related work of the International Labour Organization. In *Rules of the game*. Geneva: International Labour Organization.

Jarandilla Nuñez, Alan. 2019. Mother earth and climate justice. In *Routledge handbook of climate justice*, ed. Tahseen Jafry, 420–430. New York: Routledge.

Kant, Immanuel. 2005. *Groundwork for the metaphysical of morals*. Trans. Lara Denis. Mississauga: Broadview Editions.

Kelsen, Hans. 1967. *Pure theory of law*. Trans Max Knight. Los Angeles: University of California Press.

Marmor, Andrei. 1995. Three concepts of objectivity. In *Law and interpretation*, ed. A. Marmor, 177–201. Oxford: Oxford University Press.

———. 2019. Integrity in Law's Empire. Cornell Law School research paper No. 19–28. 9.

Nussbaum, Martha. 2006. *Frontiers of justice*. Cambridge: Harvard University Press.

Patterson, John. 1998. Respecting nature: A Maori perspective. *Worldviews*: 69–78.

Postema, Gerald. 2001. Objectivity fit for law. In *Objectivity in law and morality*, ed. B. Leiter, 99–143. Cambridge: Cambridge University Press.

Rachel, James. 1975. Active and passive euthanasia. *New England Journal of Medicine*: 78–80.

———. 1992. When philosophers shoot from the hip. *Journal of Clinical Epidemiology* 45 (7): 799–801.

Rawls, John. 1999. *A theory of justice: Revised edition*. Cambridge: Harvard University Press.

———. 2001. *Justice as fairness: A Restament*. Cambridge: Harvard University Press.

———. 2005. *Political liberalism: Expanded edition*. New York: Columbia University Press.

Raz, Joseph. 1999. *Engaging reason*. Oxford: Oxford University Press.

———. 2014. Why the state. In *King's College London Dickson poon School of law: Legal studies research paper series, paper no. 2014–38*, 24. London: King's College London.

Rolston, Holmes. 1988. *Environmental ethics: Duties to and values in the natural world*. Philadelphia: Temple University Press.

Rousseau, Jean Jacques. 1913. *The social contract - discourses*. London: Everymans Library.

Sanchez-Perez, Jorge. 2020. ¿Justicia para quién? Repensando el Uso del Estado-nación Como Marco Para la Teorización en la Filosofía Práctica. In *Las Transformaciones del Derecho en la Globalización*, ed. Jorge and Fabra-Zamora, 125–136. Mexico: Universidad Autónoma de México Instituto de Investigaciones Jurídicas.

Sandberg, Joakin, and Niklas Juth. 2011. Ethics and intuitions: A reply to Singer. *The Journal of Ethics*: 209–226.

Simmons, A. John. 2010. Ideal and nonideal theory. *Philosophy & Public Affairs* 38 (1): 5–36.

Singer, Peter. 2005. Ethics and intuitions. *The Journal of Ethics*: 331–352.

Stemplowska, Zofia, and Adam Swift. 2012. Ideal and nonideal theory. In *The Oxford handbook of political philosophy*, ed. David Estlund, 373–390. Oxford: Oxford University Press.

Stewart, Georgina Tuari. 2021. *Maori Philosophy*. London: Bloomsberry Academic.

Stoljar, Natalie. 2009. Waluchow on moral opinions and moral commitments. *Problema: Anuario de Filosofia y Teoria del Derecho*: 101–132.

Waldron, Jeremy. 1999. *Law and Disagreement*. Oxford: Oxford University Press.

———. 2006. The Core of the case against judicial review. *The Yale Law Journal*: 1346–1406.

Waluchow, Wil. 1994. *Inclusive Legal Positivism*. Oxford: Oxford University Press.

———. 2007. *A common law theory of judicial review*. Cambridge: Cambridge University Press.

———. 2021. The misconceived quest for the elusive right answer or dedication to a process, not a result. In *Constitutionalism: Old dilemmas, new insights*, ed. Alejandro Linares Cantillo,

Camilo Valdivieso-León, and Santiago García-Jaramillo, 54–70. Oxford: Oxford University Press.
Wenar, Leif. 2016. *Blood oil: Tyrants, violence, and the rules that run the world*. Oxford: Oxford University Press.
Wittgenstein, Ludwig. 1965. A lecture on ethics. *The Philosophical Review* 74 (1): 3–12.
Zimmerer, Karl S. 2012. The indigenous Andean concept of "Kawsay", the politics of knowledge and development, and the borderlands of environmental sustainability in Latin America. *PMLA (Modern Language Association)*: 600–606.

Jorge Sanchez Perez is an Assistant Professor of the Department of Philosophy at the University of Alberta. He previously held a postdoctoral fellowship at Simon Fraser University as part of the Extending New Narratives in the History of Philosophy project. He obtained his Ph.D. under the direction of Wil Waluchow at McMaster University. His research focuses on social epistemology, legal and political philosophy, Indigenous philosophy, and Latin American philosophy. He is currently working on questions regarding the identification of political communities, the limits of Western moral and epistemological paradigms, legal philosophy, and broader issues connected to methodological approaches to Indigenous philosophy.

The Common Law Methodology in Barren Soil: Prospective Judicial Precedents and Abstract Judicial Review

Breno Baía Magalhães

Abstract Waluchow argues that the common law methodology allows the interpretative construction of constitutional commitments to be incremental and bottom-up, since political decisions on constitutional rights would be guaranteed by agreements lacking a complete theorization. In deciding a case, a legal rule will be settled and later clarified or expanded by further cases or by legislative intervention. Thus, the actions of Congress and the Court will not be mutually exclusive but shared and cooperative. Behind these theoretical arguments, I singled out some features of institutional design which are necessary for this hypothesis to work, namely: (a) the development of a system of non-prospective and principle-oriented precedents; and (b) either a system of weak judicial review or a system of strong judicial review based on a model where a higher court decides cases focusing on actual facts rather than on abstract propositions. I argue that this methodology will not find fertile ground in the practice of constitutional courts whose precedents are constructed to operate as immutable rules imposed from top to bottom, and where constitutional rights cases are settled by an abstract form of judicial review.

1 Introduction and Context

As Sunstein and Vermeule (2003, pp. 885–951) have warned us, any theoretical construct in the field of constitutional theory must account for the problems concerning the institutional design of the legal system in which this theory is applied, given the intimate relationship between constitutional law and the functioning of political institutions. Although Waluchow's central thesis on the nature of Charter

B. B. Magalhães (✉)
Federal University of Pará, Faculdade de Direito, Campus Universitário, Belém, Brazil
e-mail: brenobaia@ufpa.br

T. Bustamante et al. (eds.), *Law, Morality and Judicial Reasoning*, Law and Philosophy Library 147, https://doi.org/10.1007/978-3-031-61879-6_15

rights is primarily moral,[1] its effectiveness and explanatory power seem to depend on elements related to the institutional design of a constitutional tradition.[2]

Although this assertion does not imply the need to dispute the main ideas of *A Common Law Theory of Judicial Review: The Living Tree*, it requires one to assess whether these ideas can be extended to a constitutional setting that differs from its original context. My aim in this chapter, therefore, is not to employ Professor Waluchow's theory to justify or explain the practice of the Brazilian constitutional experience, but rather to determine whether the *Common Law* methodology demands a specific institutional design to function properly. For this reason, it is important to emphasize that this contribution does not focus exclusively on the missed potentialities of a methodology poorly applied by some supreme or constitutional courts.[3]

Waluchow argues that the entrenchment of constitutional rights through charters would not entail, per definition, serious problems for popular self-government; on the contrary, it would be an important and necessary measure for a polity, as it would allow, on the one hand, a certain level of certainty and guidance for state action and would entail, on the other hand, an open space for accommodations arising from unforeseeable circumstances of politics and the need to create new rules (Waluchow 2009, p. 182).

To answer the traditional criticisms of judicial review, especially those addressing the fact that judges will be in charge of developing constitutional standards, Waluchow argues that the common law methodology allows the interpretative construction of constitutional commitments to be approached in an incremental and bottom-up way, since political decisions on constitutional rights would be guaranteed by agreements lacking a complete theorization. In deciding a given case, a legal rule will be settled and later clarified and expanded by judicial cases or by legislative intervention.[4] Congress, in turn, retains the capacity to respond to this decision, either to endorse its judicial reasoning or to challenge it and change its constitutional meaning. Waluchow sustains, therefore, that the activities of the legislature and the judiciary are not mutually exclusive, but instead collaborative and cooperative.[5]

---

[1] "Charter is best viewed as a device for dealing with our epistemic limitations in respect to the effects of government action on moral rights" (Waluchow 2009, p. 11).

[2] This is especially because the author considers his theory to be relevant to any democratic country that operates, for example, through a strong judicial review (nullification of the statute created by a parliamentary body) (Waluchow 2009, p. 12).

[3] As suggested by Waluchow, "we cannot blame the charters for failure or misapplication by the Judiciary of some of its provisions, those are distinct issues" (Waluchow 2009, p. 13).

[4] "An earlier precedent-setting case establishes a rule, the *ratio decidendi*, that is open to modification by later courts" (Waluchow 2009, p. 182).

[5] "[T]hese reasons are more than sufficient to warrant the conclusion that, in the end, we are very well served by a Charter understood as the common law model supposes—as one developed and applied by judges in partnership with other government bodies such as legislatures" (Waluchow 2009, p. 269).

On the background of these theoretical arguments, I intend to specify the features of institutional design necessary for Waluchow's argument to work, namely: (a) the development of a system of non-prospective and principled (or analogical) precedents, and (b) a system of judicial review that is either a weak form of judicial review or a strong form of judicial review in which a higher court decides cases based on actual facts instead of abstract legal considerations.

Based on my analysis of these requirements, I will argue in this chapter that the common law methodology does not find fertile ground in which to grow in constitutional experiences whose precedents are formulated to operate as immutable rules imposed from top to bottom and in which most constitutional rights cases are settled by an abstract form of judicial review.

2 A Bottom-Up Common Law Methodology

The model of constitutional precedents advanced by Waluchow follows a Razian and Hartian framework of legal reasoning, in which courts create a legal rule according to the factual elements brought by the plaintiff; hence, the legal provision of the given charter to be interpreted does not in itself contain a resolution or response to the legal dispute at hand (Waluchow 2009, pp. 199–200). By this account, some retroactivity and moderate prospectivity are essential to understanding this kind of precedent interpretation. In addition, more than one legal rule can be drawn from the judicial decision that serves as a guide when other analogous issues reach the lower courts. Courts and legislatures develop this judicial legal rule, taking turns to refine and improve the precedential rule (Waluchow 2009, p. 197).

Based on the assumption that all legal traditions deal with "precedents"[6] as a normative judicial category and that not all common lawyers subscribe to Waluchow's methodology,[7] it seems safe to say that the methodology mentioned above is but one of many potential readings on how to work with precedents, a particular kind of theory that facilitates the organic development of the "living tree" analogy.[8]

On the other hand, legal systems that regard precedents as a general legal norm that is capable of fulfilling various functions in adjudicative practice can hardly be successful instances of the metaphor of the living tree. Legal and constitutional traditions that establish a system of binding precedent from the top down, in order to simultaneously fulfill the functions of guaranteeing a complete legal predictability

[6] MacCormick and Summers (1997).

[7] This is especially true of Schauer (1991), who will serve as the basis for the idea that precedents must operate as rules. I do not argue that Schauer's sophisticated theory resembles this vulgar Brazilian reading of precedents, but it seems to be the case that his arguments are a helpful counterpoint to Waluchow's view of judicial precedents.

[8] It is true that coupling living constitutionalism with common law methodology allows one to avoid turning the former into the arbitrary exercise of political power (Waluchow 2010, p. 1033).

and triggering a decrease of caseload in higher courts, take on quite a different feature from the one suggested by Waluchow. Equality, predictability, and legal certainty are deontological or consequentialist justifications to follow precedents and may well inform political decisions to design procedural rules that adjust prior judicial decisions to implement these justifications (Duxbury 2008, pp. 150–180).

In such cases, precedents are treated as entrenched rules. When deciding a case, courts attempt to establish rules with prospective and stable effects. They purport to settle in advance any and all cases that will reach the judiciary on the same subject matter. The judicial rule is enacted at the highest degree of abstraction possible, with a view to covering as many future factual grounds as possible, favoring the assertion of canonical formulations for easy and quick consultation and subverting the logic of continuously building a legal rule from the bottom up.

The function of the higher courts in this particular setting is to canonically set up legal rules in a prospective and definitive manner to prevent the reemergence in the judiciary of the legal issue "settled" by the authoritative precedent. The precedent, in this model, is regarded not as the point of departure for constitutional deliberation, but instead as a point where the meaning of a constitutional text will be fixed. In other words, the constitutional precedent is an inorganic body inside the tree that blocks the natural flow of the sap.[9]

This argument assumes that there are several kinds of models of judicial precedents established through a combination of institutional design (judicial structure) and procedural rules affecting their binding nature and force (Bankowski et al. 1997, pp. 497–498). The rule-stating model, for example, ascribes an almost absolute binding force to the precedent that can only be overruled, distinguished, and interpreted by the court that fixed it in the first place.

This rule-stating model of judicial precedents induces interpretation-related problems based on original meaning and intention because the main concern of the lower courts will always be extracting the correct intentions and understandings of the higher court that produced the precedent, which in turn will always be the only legitimate institution to "rectify" the interpretation that eventually diverged from its original intention. That is, the tree dies slowly because the precedent is not regarded as something organic but as a legal rule that carries inside it predetermined and immutable contents. In Brazil, the Constitutional Complaint (*Reclamação Constitucional*),[10] a legal remedy that aims to strike down any judicial decision

---

[9] For a living constitutionalist advocate (in accordance with Waluchow), constitutional norms establish provisions that can grow and adapt to their environment without losing their identity and guiding function; those standards should also be allowed to grow and adapt (Waluchow 2010, p. 1029).

[10] *Brazilian Civil Procedure Code Article 988. An interested party or the Public Prosecutor's Office may file a Complaint: (...) III—to guarantee compliance with a binding precedent and with a decision of the Federal Supreme Court in concentrated. (...) § 4 The cases broached in items III and IV include the wrongful application of the legal interpretation and failure to apply it to corresponding cases.*

that does not follow the binding legal thesis formulated by the Supreme Court, is a good example of the consequences of this version of constitutional precedent.

Waluchow (2009, p. 199) is aware that extracting the *ratio decidendi* from a case is not an easy task, but for the successful extraction of a legal rule capable of stablishing a precedent, subsequent courts and the legislature should have a minimum degree of certainty as to their location and content. Thus, the organization and presentation of the opinion of the Supreme Court are important factors for the operationalization of a common law methodology.

Courts that are concerned with formulating prospective precedents give little or no attention to the justifications that support the construction of the rule of law and present their constitutional interpretation in an often dispersed manner, especially when the Supreme Court does not adopt a deliberative *per curiam* fashion of opinions.[11] As a consequence, precedents lose their incremental constructive aspects, since the lower courts (and the higher court itself) have incentives to occasionally rebuild the grounds, or substantive justifications (Schauer 1991, pp. 94–95), that underlie the forward-looking rules once formulated. The most important element in every precedent is the definition of a rule, similar to a legislative body crafting a statue, and not the development of substantive justifications that are rooted in political morality.

This kind of judicial reasoning weakens the epistemological advantages of the judiciary when it comes to making the best decisions based on a rational construction of a community's constitutional morality (CCM).[12] It hinges, moreover, on how the court introduces its interpretations to its audience.

A written opinion that combines the opinions of all of the justices that sit on the court, but that are only coincident in the final legal outcome,[13] does not make optimal use of the judicial vantage point in the political structure of the State. Under these conditions, the constitutional interpretation will be achieved by the mere aggregation of results and not by a deep and well-performed interpretation of the constitutional morality of the community. The advantages of constitutionalizing a Charter of Rights cannot be the accidental construction of a prospective rule by a court whose process of constitutional adjudication is inconsistent, inaccessible, or, at least, confusing to the public and to the other political branches.

One might argue that this would indeed be a valuable feature of deciding and setting a constitutional precedent, instead of a fatal flaw. The creation of a canonical

[11] Conrado Mendes argues that a deliberative written decision is one that is able to translate the ethical commitments of deliberation in a piece of judicial opinion in a way that is not only understandable for all audiences, but is also "aware of its fallibility and of the inevitable continuity of deliberation in the public sphere and in possible future cases" (2013, p. 110).

[12] "Judges are not philosopher-kings with a pipeline to moral truth. But they may well be in a very good position to determine the requirements of a community's true moral commitments and authentic wishes" (Waluchow 2009, p. 226).

[13] da Silva (2013, pp. 557–584), inspired by the Brazilian supreme court deliberation style, demonstrates that internal rules and practices may affect the legitimacy of judicial review by hindering deliberation.

rule without a strong and deep justification or coherent constitutional interpretation allows a wider margin for the legislature's role in responding to a judicial pronouncement, precisely because the court did not commit itself to any broad or complex theory on the meaning of the constitutional text.[14]

However, the cooperative and incremental argument must be able to guarantee a differentiated form of action for the judicial and the legislative branches on several levels, not only in the chronological aspect—that is, on who is able to give and when the final word on the subject of the controversy will be issued. This suggests that the above paragraph is a superficial reading of Sunstein's argument for "incompletely theorized agreements"; this is partly because he never denied or neglected the importance of clear arguments and coherent grounds mobilized by a Supreme Court in controversial constitutional matters,[15] only that its formulation in a broad and complex form of authority will be made and established over time, and only after its settlement in the judiciary and in social debates. A court committed to the *Common Law* methodology (though humble in building its grounds) and which it knows will be revisited and contested, refined, or repealed, cannot renounce the scrutiny of its peers, especially that of Congress.

If a court decides to strike down as unconstitutional the ill treatment of animals perpetrated by cultural practices (like rodeos) but cannot cohesively and coherently formulate the constitutional reason for this, and it sets out in a legally binding rule only the immediate outcome of its decision (the prohibition of the mistreatment of animals in any case), Congress will not have much difficulty in pulling out of its hat any given, but equally powerful, constitutional argument or justification to overturn the judicial decision, without there being a cooperative action in the construction or increment of the constitutional morality of the community.

The example, unfortunately, is not hypothetical. In 2016, the Brazilian Federal Supreme Court declared that a state's legal regulation of practices called *vaquejadas*[16] was unconstitutional. The majority of the court agreed on the characterization of the practice as "cruelty" under the constitution,[17] but they disagreed on

[14] Incompletely theorized agreements (ITA) may be a representation of this sort of constitutional adjudication style. As Sunstein puts it, "concrete outcomes are backed not by abstract theories but by unambitious reasoning on which people can converge from diverse foundations" (1999, p. 13).

[15] "None of these points suggests that incompletely theorized agreements always deserve celebration. The virtues of such agreements are partial. Some incompletely theorized agreements are unjust. If an agreement is more fully theorized, it will provide greater notice to affected parties. Moreover, fuller theorization—in the form of wider and deeper inquiry into the grounds for judgment—may be valuable or even necessary to prevent inconsistency, bias, or self-interest" (Sunstein 1996, pp. 43–44).

[16] The *vaquejada* is a sport in which two *vaqueiros* on horseback pursue a bull, seeking to pin it between the two horses and direct it to a goal (often consisting of chalk marks), where the animal is then knocked over.

[17] Constituição da República Federativa do Brasil, Art. 225, §1°, VII: In order to ensure the effectiveness of this right, it is incumbent upon the Government to—protect the fauna and the flora, with prohibition, in the manner prescribed by law, of all practices which represent a risk to their ecological function, cause the extinction of species or subject animals to cruelty.

the constitutional grounds and on the substantive justification underlying the ban. Some of the justices argued that cultural practices could not carry out acts of animal cruelty, since they would constitute violations of the right to a healthy and balanced environment for future generations. On the other hand, other justices attributed to non-human animals the moral right of not being subjected to cruel practices—even though dissimilar to a constitutional legal right, animal moral rights were a protection attributed to them regardless of the consequences for the environment. The losing minority argued that the constitution protects culture and sports as constitutional rights, the exact case of the *vaquejada*, a traditional sport of Brazil's northeast region.

In the end, it is unclear whether animals have "constitutional moral rights"; what the government obligations are that stem from moral rights in contrast to constitutional rights ascribed to human animals; whether protection against animal cruelty is based on an obligation to keep the environment balanced or on the need to protect the autonomous interests of non-human animals; and what the proper balance should be between culture, sport, and practices that may cause harm to animals. All of these concerns were regarded, in the court's reasoning, as constitutionally protected principles.

A year later, the National Congress passed a constitutional amendment (CA 96/2017) establishing that sports practices registered as Brazilian cultural heritage are not to be considered cruel if regulated by statutes that guarantee the minimum welfare of the animal. During legislative debates, legislators were aware of the court's decision, but at no time did they debate the constitutional grounds or justifications to overcome the court's binding precedent. They were only concerned with what they knew for sure: the outcome of the ruling (prohibiting *vaquejada*) and the decision to disregard the confusing judicial reasoning.

3 A Judicial Review Based on the Factual Violation of Constitutional Rights

Waluchow advocates for judicial review as a constructive form of the division of labor between judges and legislators, treating it as an essential feature of the common law methodology.[18] The expansion of the branches of this leafy tree is only possible by the casuistry of the demands that reach the courts as controversies about constitutional rights (Waluchow 2009, p. 261). The Canadian model of judicial review is unique and began, in practical terms, a trend of weak judicial review in Commonwealth countries (Gardbaum 2010, p. 97) that not only proposed the suspension of

[18] "Charters do not, in fact, need to presuppose that we all agree on right answers to questions about the meaning and implications (...)—and that judicial review is a quite sensible institutional mechanism for dealing with this particular feature of the circumstances of politics—and with the equally important circumstances of rule making" (Waluchow 2009, p. 217).

judicial decisions upholding the invalidation of a statute[19] but also allowed Parliament to disagree with the interpretive result reached by the Supreme Court by means of reasonableness.[20]

It is therefore a model of judicial review favorable to the *Common Law* methodology, which is not necessarily replicated in other constitutional designs, especially those adopting a model of constitutional or supreme courts that monopolize the declaration of unconstitutionality on the basis of an abstract procedure—that is to say, in which any controversy referred to the court is not necessarily the breach of a constitutional right of a particular person but the guarantee of the formal compatibility of a statute with the constitution.[21] In these instances, constitutional rights cases ruled on by courts are contingent because the judicial controversy falls on the constitutionality of a statute that affects a subset of constitutional rules in the abstract.

This model of judicial review can be found in Brazil and in many European countries that "have broad jurisdiction and open rules of access that allow (and often require) them to decide abstract constitutional questions in the absence of a concrete dispute" (Vanberg 2005, p. 10). However, the Brazilian case is more problematic because victims of constitutional rights violations do not have access to a direct judicial remedy to the court.

The argument is reinforced by comparative studies that propose the lack of a direct link between judicial review and optimal rights protection (Sadurski 2002, pp. 275–299). Waluchow stands for judicial review as a necessary institution for the improvement of constitutional rights, given the particularities in which courts operate with arguments about political philosophy.[22] Nevertheless, a theory of judicial review must be tested by the actual outcomes it produces (Sadurski 2002, p. 278). A successful link between weak judicial review and rights protection may explain the success of the Canadian case, but that does not mean that the common law theory will operate as smoothly in other constitutional,[23] political, or doctrinal settings.

It is safe to say that Waluchow is concerned not only with the practical results of the judicial ruling but also with the judicial provision of coherent and sound reasons. This means that it is not sufficient for a court to uphold an outcome that matches our desired ideological rights articulation.[24] In addition, a court must act for the right reasons and through the means articulated by the proposed theory. Thus, the success

---

[19] Section 33 of the Canadian Charter of Rights and Freedoms.

[20] Section 01 of the Canadian Charter of Rights and Freedoms.

[21] This problematic issue was first identified, but not developed, by Mendes (2007, p. 474).

[22] "I put forward only tentatively the suggestion that judicial review may provide a superior kind of public deliberation about issues of constitutional morality" (Waluchow 2009, p. 269).

[23] Tushnet (1999, p. 129) calls into question, for example, the advantages of maintaining a system of judicial review based on the judicial supremacy of rights protection in the US.

[24] We borrowed from Sadurski the expression "rights articulation," meaning the "specifications of the preferred application of a general constitutional right to a concrete issue" (2002, p. 282).

of the common law theory of judicial review in a given country's setting must be concerned with the way that the constitutional interpretation of the Supreme Court impacts rights protection.

As Shapiro and Sweet (2002, p. 345) argue, both models of judicial review put forward arguments to defend their primacy over each other based on interpretations of the distinction between law and politics. The argument for an abstract review is that courts do not review the content or political importance of a legal statute but the act of enactment of said statute alone (Habermas 1998, p. 243). The main purpose of abstract review is to enforce the separation of powers (Shapiro and Sweet 2002, p. 367) and solve competence conflicts in federalist countries (Cruz Villalon 1987, pp. 53–57). This rationale for abstract judicial review entails a clear division between it and a judicial review based on actual facts and on constitutional rights violations. In the latter (concrete judicial review), courts do not declare the nullification of policy aspects of a statute but of a specific application in which an individual right was violated. The court will not be forced to develop constitutional arguments for or against a broad policy adopted by the other political branches, and the scope of review will be much narrower (i.e., constitutional rights rules as applied in a specific set of facts).

On the other hand, the abstract model of review magnifies the scope of review, which can blur the distinction between law and politics. In general, abstract review does not concern litigation—that is, a case in which one of the disputing parties alleges damage enforced by an unconstitutional legal rule (Shapiro and Sweet 2002, p. 344).

In many jurisdictions, a minority of legislators may have the power to initiate the judicial review of a statute under any constitutional rule, which allows legislators and constitutional judges to interact with each other directly (Sweet 2000, p. 51). This model of review can be a powerful weapon for opposition parties (Vanberg 1998, p. 300),[25] especially because the short-term effect of a court decision will be the nullification of the statute, not its disapplication in cases in which its interpretations lead to a constitutional rights violation. The court may also function as a third legislative chamber for the legislative minority dealing with political losses over important partisan interests.[26]

Abstract models of judicial review operate on a very thin line between the legal and technical analysis of the compatibility of a statute with a constitutional text; in the jurisdiction assessed in this chapter (Brazil), this happens to be a provision that

---

[25] The rationale for an abstract judicial review from the perspective of a constitutional designer may be to ensure that they will be able to challenge government action once the constitutional lawmaking process is finished and, in the case of any future electoral loss of constitutional drafters, thus lowering the risk of constitutional-making for the latter (Ginsburg 2002, p. 53).

[26] That was the case in Brazil when the Workers Party (*Partido dos Trabalhadores*) was not in power and was not a majority force in Congress. With every political loss in congress, an abstract case was referred to the supreme court to rule on, mainly, political grounds (Taylor and Da Ros 2008, p. 825).

contains a constitutional right and the judicial reassessment of political justifications, opportunity, and convenience of public policies created by Congress.

Concrete review, on the other hand, should be narrower because the court has a specific fact situation that calls for the concrete decision of the case and provides more information regarding its practical effects on rights protection. Constitutional review, to reiterate, is not limited by the evaluation of the statute on its face and/or in light of its political purpose (Ginsburg 2002, p. 69), but will instead be performed in the context of its actual implications for the interests of persons in question. Legal systems that have abstract review may experience, therefore, a more prominent judicialization of politics than systems that do not, because the former harnesses the struggle between congressional majority and minority over policy outcomes to a particular end: "the progressive development of constitutional constraints on law--making" (Sweet 2000, 51).[27]

The Brazilian case provides a striking example of an abstract model of judicial review. In the Brazilian system, there are specific remedies for the direct access of political parties to the Supreme Court, and there is often no specific constitutional remedy that protects individual constitutional rights in the Supreme Court.[28] Thus, cases brought to the Supreme Court through the abstract route do not depend on the incidence of a concrete violation of a right of one or more specific persons; to obtain from the Supreme Court an interpretation of a constitutional provision, it suffices to argue that there is formal or material incompatibility with said constitutional rule.

Although issues pertaining to the protection of constitutional rights reach the court through abstract review, the lack of factual elements typical of a particular case prevents the court from formulating a clear or specific rule about pressing issues of constitutional jurisdiction.[29] Similarly, a system of abstract and prospective precedents reinforces the need for the court to decide cases with the greatest vagueness and least specificity. Although it enables the court to arrive at a decision in a timely manner, it offers in return few incentives for the continued engagement in a debate about the content of the community's constitutional morality. We know, clearly, the voting score obtained to invalidate the challenged statute, and we know the practical

[27] Ginsburg (2003) argues that the judicial review model adopted in new democracies, especially in cases of multiparty constituent assemblies, can follow an institutional design of abstract, open, and facilitated access review that guarantees electoral losers the ability to challenge a government action that disturbs the constitutional bargains.

[28] The German or Italian constitutional complaint, for example, operate alongside remedies of abstract review.

[29] In a thought-provoking piece, Shapiro and Sweet argue that US courts do engage in abstract review, regardless of the differences that sets them apart from their European counterparts. Some examples include preliminary injunctions and declaratory judgments. Other examples include judgments on overbreadth and vagueness in cases arising under the First Amendment, cases in which the Supreme Court will strike down as null and void a statute per se, irrespective of its application in a concrete situation. On the other hand, a government, in its defense of the supposed unconstitutional statute, must demonstrate a compelling argument for why it was drafted with less restrictive breadth so that it may not create a "chilling effect" (Shapiro and Sweet 2002).

result of the ruling, but we know little or nothing about the constitutional reasoning behind the decision.

In the absence of an actual and factual application of a congressional rule that has wrongly affected the rights of a group or person, the court cannot do much beyond speculating on and revising the justifications and objectives to be fulfilled by the statute, whose outcome will be the preservation (or not) of the legislative text in the legal order. This means that controversial government policies should be scrutinized in the early stages of implementation, and the court will not be able to envisage all possible factual hypotheses of unconstitutional statute applications. A statute may, for example, be brought before the court the same day it has come into force. Such a model of judicial review weakens, it seems to me, the argument of cooperation and the dialogical manner for the construction of Charter rights.

In 2017, the Brazilian Supreme Court declared the constitutionality of a 2014 federal law that created racial quotas for Black people in public office. According to the opinion of the justice that conducted the unanimity, the legitimacy of quotas for Black people holding public office is based on the constitutional right of equality. Therefore, racial quotas are a mandatory public policy for the realization of the right to equality as recognition, as they would be a necessary measure capable of combating institutional and structural racism in Brazil.

The court's decision was made in the context of abstract judicial review and is binding for the entire judiciary. Even if we do not question the need for a public policy that ameliorates the racial inequality that plagues public positions in Brazilian public administration, the decision that upheld the compatibility of a public policy with the constitution does not mean that the application of this now "constitutional" statute may not violate constitutional rights in specific factual situations.

Moreover, by "constitutionalizing" a transitory public policy whose main purpose is to reduce racial inequality, the court embraces as a higher law the political presumption that this particular public policy is the most efficient way to guarantee constitutional racial equality, even though the court does not have enough information and experience to confirm its results, which, unfortunately, have been mixed.[30] In other words, the court will eventually state that a suboptimal policy must be implemented as a constitutional right or a positive obligation, thus narrowing the space for political debate about more efficient policies.

The metaphor of dialogue as an inherent position in common law methodology is essential to Waluchow's argument (2009, p. 270),[31] as all political branches must act

[30] This public policy has had mixed results in its attempt to increase the number of Black judges and Black college professors in public universities. See Neto (2020). Per Mello and de Resende, "As five years have now gone by since the passage of this legislation, it seems safe to say that the goal of expanding racial/color diversity in federal civil service will not be achieved through public examinations for teaching careers. Moreover, meeting this goal becomes progressively harder, given the present scenario of resurgence of meritocratic discourses that question the legitimacy of affirmative actions for Afro-Brazilians" (2020, p. 8).

[31] On the contrary, they can each be seen to contribute, in their own unique ways, from their own unique perspectives, and within their unique contexts of decision, to the achievement of a morally

in concert for the development of the constitutional morality of a community. For example, a dialogue facilitated by judicial precedents will be incorporated and reinterpreted through congressional standards.[32] However, to speak about dialogue as a theoretical element is to characterize it and define it conceptually, not only in a descriptive way, but as a normative element that demands that constitutional rights must necessarily go through the joint development of all branches.

The scope of dialogical theory encompasses two premises: the absence of claims about hierarchy and the construction of possible rationalities that arise from interactions among the agents involved in political, legal, or communication processes. Conrado Hubner Mendes (2011) argues that dialogue suggests equality, mutual respect, and reciprocity.

Therefore, the relationship established between the participants in a dialogue is always horizontal and not hierarchical. Currently, democratic and constitutional theories have embraced a dialogical ideal originally developed in the field of political and moral philosophy. Its sources are, to name a few, communitarianism, republicanism, and the postmodern criticism of liberalism and modernity. This theoretical approach does not imply abandoning liberal rationality but reinterprets it as a "communicative rationality" that acts as a dialogue or discourse oriented towards understanding. Thus, the focus of dialogue theories is on the benefits of deliberation as a rational exchange of arguments from the point of view of the legitimacy of the outcomes (Torres Pérez 2009, pp. 103–106). Adapting from Aida Torres (2009, pp. 112–117), there are three reasons to argue for dialogical approaches: (a) better-reasoned interpretive outcomes; (b) participation and engagement; and (c) respect for political pluralism.

The dialogue metaphor in Canada is useful in discussing the justification, legitimacy, and operationalization of judicial enforcement of the compatibility of laws in a traditional parliamentary country in which the insertion of a Charter of Rights has generated procedural solutions unknown by classical judicial review models to establish the middle ground between judicial supremacy and parliamentary sovereignty.

Dialogue[33] as a metaphor in Canada is sometimes mentioned in an empirical fashion (demonstrating that Parliament has not been silent in the face of the judicial

sensitive and enlightened rule of law. (. . .), some have taken up this idea and suggested that judicial review sets the stage for a "dialogue" between the courts and the legislature (Waluchow 2009, p. 270).

[32] "[T]heir roles can be seen to be complementary and mutually supportive, not antagonistic. The one (the judges) is able to supplement the efforts of the other (the legislators). Each group, by making a good-faith effort to fulfill its role in dealing sensibly with the circumstances of rule making, can help contribute to an overall effort to secure the various benefits made possible by the rule of law" (Waluchow 2009, p. 262).

[33] Gardbaum (2010, p. 181) disagrees with the characterization of commonwealth models of judicial review as dialogic. Initially, all constitutional systems provide, to some extent, that constitutional rights may be limited by infraconstitutional legislation. Furthermore, almost all constitutional systems maintain some kind of interaction between institutions, and such interactions could be seen as dialogical in nature. Thus, the dialogue metaphor would be over-inclusive. Emmett

declarations of unconstitutionality based on the Charter)[34] and sometimes in a normative fashion[35] (arguing that the insertion of both the Charter and the notwithstanding clause have changed the political attitudes of Parliament and of the Supreme Court, in the sense that the content of rights will now be constructed, necessarily, through interactions between all the branches).

In both cases, the interaction between the branches is seen as dialogical (MacFarlane 2012, pp. 97–98). Classical studies of dialogue in Canada employ the metaphor of dialogue to argue that the Canadian Parliament has not remained silent after judicial statements about the constitutionality (or lack thereof) of statutes affecting constitutional Charter rights (Hogg and Bushell 1997), but also that such interactions should not necessarily occur as a crucial way to further develop the constitutional morality of a community, but as a contingency or a fortunate accident. I argue that the notion of dialogue within a model of common law judicial review is not limited to its potentialities or contingencies (that is, the fact that there is a post-judicial legislative response); rather, I postulate the idea of dialogue as the only way to obtain a shared construction of constitutional meaning.

MacFarlane also prefers to move away from dialogical metaphors when categorizing commonwealth countries and prefers to call them "models of weak judicial review" (2012, p. 100). The author suggests that the change is due to the impossibility of reconciling the normative and prescriptive approaches to institutional innovations in Canadian commonwealth countries.

[34]The main representatives of this empirical or descriptive argument are Hogg and Bushell (1997, p. 80), who, in a series of articles, have analyzed the behavior of Parliament after court rulings on the incompatibility of statutes with the Charter. They found that, in most cases, Parliament passed or altered statutes that were subject to judicial review, which could mean that the final word on policy matters would always be democratic. They considered the parliamentary attitude of continuous "responses" to be dialogical. In subsequent articles, they have reiterated that the sole focus of their argument was the adjustment of political choices that involved Charter rights and not a more complex and normative debate about constitutional interpretation (Thornton 1999, p. 534). This reply was directed at Manfredi and Kelly (1999), who accused the authors of putting forward a thin definition of dialogue. In a more recent manifestation, Hogg et al. (2007, p. 27) reaffirmed the empirical focus of their approach and explained that dialogue is the legislative continuity, and not a normative theory of how parliament should behave.

[35]Janet Hiebert (2002, p. 45) is one of the main representatives of this normative aspect, as she posits that the Canadian Charter has contributed, in political terms, to a reinterpretation of their respective constitutional roles. Courts and Parliament now jointly share the responsibility of interpreting and constructing the content of the Charter rights, even though each institution offers different interpretive contributions (their vantage points are not identical). The relational approach requires that the contributions of both institutions be thought of with a degree of modesty and with respect for the opposite interpretation. Respect, in turn, is characterized as the measure of the sincere effort to understand the reasons and motivations that led the other branch to a contrary understanding (Hiebert 2002, p. 52). The contribution of Hiebert's relational approach is not limited to the procedural aspects of a legislative response to judicial rulings, but it formulates a normative notion of building rights through shared political responsibility, to be carried out from parliamentary debates to responses to judicial review. It is worth noting that the author rejects the dialogue metaphor (she prefers the term "relational"), precisely because, in her view, dialogue would be restricted to the empirical aspect (Hiebert 2002, p. 50).

Much more suitable to the idea of the methodology discussed is a model of judicial review that offers incentives so that a legislature can, in due time, act in the interpretive construction of constitutional meaning. As argued by Sweet, concrete judicial review is a more costly way of challenging a statute, because it may take years and a handful of prior decisions made by ordinary judges before it reaches the Supreme Court; however, this time delay may be an important vehicle for dialogue between judges and the legislative branch. When the time comes for the Supreme Court to issue its "final" judicial decision, the constitutional conflict about constitutional rights may be sufficiently well informed, fed by arguments and relevant political debates.

Judicial review models such as the Brazilian on, on the other hand, do not prevent what I will call a "weak dialogue"—that is, the subsequent legislative response of judicial rulings by contingency with insufficient institutional incentives for a continuous or prolific debate on the meanings of the constitutional text. This hinders the development of an optimal functioning of the common law theory and weakens the arguments for judicial review as a way of creating more responsible and rights-aware legislators (Sadurski 2002, p. 286).

The Supreme Court rules on the text of a statute in the abstract, regardless of a factual context or a clear violation of a personal interest (Fallon Jr. 2019, pp. 77–78). It formulates an abstract, prospective precedent to serve as a fixed and definitive normative guide, without further justifications or argumentative grounds for structuring the rule.[36] Congress, ignoring or having difficulty understanding the court's ruling, then creates a new statute opposing the judicial outcome, without the sap of that interaction being able to traverse the body of the tree and create new, important branches—the picture in such cases is of a branch that falls to the ground and is replaced by another.

4 Conclusion

If it is difficult to argue against the normative and descriptive force of Waluchow's thesis for judicial review in countries inserted in the common law tradition, the same cannot be said about its transposition to cases of legal orders that adopt a static and proposition of judicial precedents formed through abstract judicial reasoning. Thus,

[36]The new Brazilian civil procedure code created a new normative category: the legal thesis (*tese jurídica*). This normative category would function as the synthesis of a court's ruling, which would have prospective binding effects on the whole judiciary. To make it clear, the legal thesis is not the *ratio decidendi*, but one part of the decision that operates procedural effects in Brazilian law. The Supreme Court has published these theses in its rulings. Formulated in abstract and generic language, the legal theses are similar to statutes, down to the debates among the justices on their exact wording. The theses do not, therefore, exclude the setting of the *Ementas* (summary of the leading justice's opinion) nor the publication of the full judgment (combining the opinions of all the justices).

the success and effectiveness of the common law theory thesis depends on institutional and practical aspects of a specific constitutional experience. The Brazilian case, as it currently stands, presents insurmountable challenges to Waluchow's thesis, as its legal and constitutional rules create a model of judicial precedent understood as a fixed and prospective rule, and its system of abstract judicial review favors the emergence of a weak version of dialogue between the judiciary and the legislature. On the other hand, Waluchow's model is only effective if judicial precedents are seen as legal principles to be developed over time through the interaction between the judicial and legislative branches, carried out by procedures that enable a concrete judicial review, and followed by judicial reasoning presented, albeit in a humble way, as coherent and substantive.

While keeping the original thesis intact to explain the North American practice, such conclusions indicate that the argument of the joint construction of political obligations guided by the constitutional morality of a community may not fit all comparative constitutional experiences. Thus, I argue that researchers interested in continuing Waluchow's thesis and applying it in other regions must address the following problems: (1) its adjustment to and compatibility with countries that combine (or don't) concrete judicial review with strong abstract review; (2) the place and functions of theories of dialogue as contingent or normative elements of the practice of fundamental rights in the analyzed constitutional order; and (3) how local perceptions of judicial precedents, which can be understood as fixed legal rules, affect the analogy of the living tree.

References

Bankowski, Zenon, D. Neil MacCormick, Lech Morawski, and Alfonso Ruiz Miguel. 1997. Rationales for precedent. In *Interpreting precedents: A comparative study*, ed. Neil MacCormick and Robert S. Summers, 497–498. Boston: Dartmouth Publishing.

Mendes, Conrado Hübner. 2011. *Direitos fundamentais, separação de poderes e deliberação*. São Paulo: Saraiva.

Cruz Villalon, Pedro. 1987. *La formacion del sistema Europeo de control de constitucionalidad (1918–1939)*. Madrid: Centro de Estúdios Constitucionales.

da Silva, Virgílio Afonso. 2013. Deciding without deliberating. *International Journal of Constitutional Law* 11: 557–584.

Duxbury, Neil. 2008. *The nature and authority of precedent*. Cambridge: Cambridge University Press.

Fallon Jr Richard, H. 2019. *The nature of constitutional rights: the invention and logic of strict judicial scrutiny*. Cambridge: Cambridge University Press.

Gardbaum, Stephen. 2010. Reassessing the new commonwealth model of constitutionalism. *International Journal of Constitutional Law* 8: 167–206.

Ginsburg, Tom. 2002. Economic analysis and the design of constitutional courts. *Theoretical Inquiries in Law* 3: 49–85.

———. 2003. *Judicial review in new democracies: Constitutional courts in Asian cases*. Cambridge: Cambridge University Press.

Habermas, Jürgen. 1998. *Between facts and norms*. Cambridge: MIT Press.

Hiebert, Janet. 2002. *Charter conflicts: What is the Parliament's role?* Montreal: McGill University Press.
Hogg, Peter, and Allison Bushell. 1997. The charter dialogue between courts and legislatures (or perhaps the charter of rights isn't such a bad thing after all). *Osgoode Law Journal* 35: 75–124.
Hogg, Peter, Allison Thornton, and Wade K. Wright. 2007. Charter dialogue revisited—Or much ado about metaphors. *Osgoode Hall Law Journal* 45: 1–65.
MacCormick, D. Neil, and Robert Summers, eds. 1997. *Interpreting precedents*. Boston: Dartmouth Publishing.
MacFarlane, Emmet. 2012. Conceptual precision and parliamentary systems of rights: Disambiguating "dialogue.". *Review of Constitutional Studies* 17: 73–100.
Manfredi, Christopher P., and James B. Kelly. 1999. Six degrees of dialogue: A response to Hogg and Bushell. *Osgoode Hall Law Journal* 37: 513–527.
Mello, Luiz, and Ubiratan Pereira de Resende. 2020. Concursos Públicos Federais para Docentes e Ações Afirmativas para Candidatos Negros. *Cad. Pesquisa.* 50: 8–29.
Mendes, Conrado Hübner. 2007. Book review: Common law theory of judicial review: The living tree, by Wil Waluchow. *Cambridge Law Journal* 66: 471–474.
———. 2013. *Constitutional courts and deliberative democracy*. Oxford: Oxford University Press.
Neto, Adalberto. 2020. CNJ vê limitação das cotas e cria força-tarefa para ter mais juízes negros. *UOL*, 12/07/2020, https://noticias.uol.com.br/cotidiano/ultimas-noticias/2020/07/12/cnj-ve-limitacao-das-cotas-e-cria-forca-tarefa-para-ter-mais-juizes-negros.htm
Sadurski, Wojciech. 2002. Judicial review and the protection of constitutional rights. *Oxford Journal of Legal Studies* 22: 275–299.
Schauer, Frederick. 1991. *Playing by the rules*. Oxford: Oxford University Press.
Shapiro, Martin, and Alec Stone Sweet. 2002. Abstract and concrete review in the United States. In *On law, politics, and judicialization*, 147–375. Oxford: Oxford University Press.
Sunstein, Cass. 1996. *Legal reasoning and political conflict*. Oxford: Oxford University Press.
———. 1999. *One case at a time: Judicial minimalism on the supreme court*. Cambridge: Harvard University Press.
Sunstein, Cass, and Adrian Vermeule. 2003. Interpretation and institutions. *Michigan Law Review* 101: 885–951.
Sweet, Alex Stone. 2000. *Governing with judges*. Oxford: Oxford University Press.
Taylor, Matthew, and Luciano Da Ros. 2008. Os partidos dentro e fora do poder: a judicialização como resultado contingente da estratégia política. *Dados* 51: 825–864.
Thornton, Alison. 1999. Reply to "six degrees of dialogue.". *Osgood Hall Law Journal* 37: 529–536.
Torres Pérez, Aida. 2009. *Conflicts of rights in the European Union*. Oxford: Oxford University Press.
Tushnet, Mark. 1999. *Taking the constitution away from the courts*. Cambridge: Harvard University Press.
Vanberg, Georg. 1998. Abstract judicial review, legislative bargaining, and policy compromise. *Journal of Theoretical Politics* 10: 300–326.
———. 2005. *The politics of constitutional review in Germany*. Cambridge: Cambridge University Press.
Waluchow, Wilfrid J. 2009. *A common law theory of judicial review: The living tree*. Cambridge: Cambridge University Press.
———. 2010. Democracy and the living tree constitution. *Drake Law Review* 59: 1001–1046.

Breno Baía Magalhães is Professor of Constitutional Law at the Federal University of Pará, in Brazil. He holds a B.A., a M.Phil, and a Ph.D in Law, all from the Federal University of Pará. He has been a Visiting Scholar from the Washington College of Law, at the American University. He received an Honorable Mention in the CAPES Prize for the Best Doctoral Dissertation in Law in Brazil (2016).

Democracy and Adjudication in Latin America: A Critical Analysis of Wil Waluchow's Common Law Theory of Judicial Review

Francisco Tarcísio Rocha Gomes Júnior

Abstract After recognizing the importance of a sound theory of adjudication in constitutional law, this chapter raises questions about Waluchow's common law theory of judicial review in Latin American constitutionalism. Despite most nations providing a progressivist constitutional protection of rights, one can find on this continent a conservative concentration of powers. Under this circumstance, the scope of a constitutional court (or a supreme court) is better understood under Gargarella's model of deliberative democracy. Judicial activism should be avoided and the courts seen as engineers of public debates over institutional dialogues. The common law theory of judicial review can play a role in regulating the democratic process and aid judges in adjudication, yet three elements should be developed within this theory. The first is the new dimension of democratic challenge. The recognition of new rights in such a conservative division of powers makes the power of courts stronger than that imagined by Waluchow. The second is the necessity of a new theory of rights wherein we could account for the importance of not only individual but also social and Indigenous rights. The third is the need for a theory of judicial self-restraint for the defense and construction of a community's constitutional morality.

1 Introduction

Candido Portinari's painting *Dead Child*, from 1944, effectively represents the suffering of those fleeing the drought in northeastern Brazil. The lack of public policies for social development in the region forced the local population to flee to urban areas in search of better living conditions.

This painting also represents a reality that is recurrent among of Latin American peoples. Although it is a region that produces significant wealth, great social inequality results in high rates of poverty and misery. As a constitution must reflect

F. T. R. G. Júnior (✉)
University Center Christus (Unichristus), Fortaleza, Brazil
e-mail: tarcisio.rocha@unichristus.edu.br; franciscojunior@prp.uespi.br

T. Bustamante et al. (eds.), *Law, Morality and Judicial Reasoning*, Law and Philosophy Library 147, https://doi.org/10.1007/978-3-031-61879-6_16

the social reality of where it is enacted, Latin American constitutionalism represents the desire for social transformation and the recognition of the rights of excluded people.

Recognizing the importance of a theory of legal adjudication for the implementation of constitutional concerns, this chapter raises a discussion about the possibility of using Wil Waluchow's theory of legal adjudication to understand the Latin American constitutional experience. First, I provide a description of the main characteristics and problems of Latin American constitutionalism, followed by a description of the theory of legal adjudication provided by Waluchow. Throughout, questions will be raised regarding what an adequate promotion of the constitutional aspirations of the region might be.

2 A Brief Introduction to Latin American Constitutionalism

Despite its long tradition, there are not many academic texts dedicated to the systematization and critique of constitutionalism in Latin America. Even with different ways of carrying out constitutional projects due to the specificities of each country, there are common characteristics of constitutionalism based on social and political similarities. Debates around different ways of understanding traditional elements, such as the separation of powers and the protection of rights, have followed major political movements since the nineteenth century (Gargarella 2013, p. vii).

One might call Latin America a laboratory for constitutional experimentation. Issues such as colonization, decolonization, the ethnic plurality of the people, the recognition of social and multicultural rights, the importation of external legal concepts, and the typical relationship with authoritarianism and hyper-presidentialism are some of its differentials (Mendes et al. 2022, p. xvi). In this context, it is possible to say that Latin American constitutionalism is a unique constitutional experience whose problems and perspectives deserve to be studied (Gomes Júnior 2022b, p. 160).

2.1 Characteristics and Issues of Latin American Constitutionalism

The phenomenon of constitutionalism began with the promulgation of the US Constitution in 1787. This constitution is a compact written document in which the functions of the three branches are established and certain important individual rights are guaranteed. In addition to constitutionalism, federalism and presidentialism are forms of government that developed during that period. The practice of judicial review, another North American institutional creation, only appeared in 1803 in *Marbury vs. Madison*,[1] which assigned to the Supreme Court the role of guardian of the US constitution (Bickel 1982, p. 1; Gargarella 2013, pp. 1–2).

In the nineteenth century, this complex institutional framework gained a reputation of modernity and was perceived to be a sound alternative to European monarchical absolutism. Thus, virtually all Latin American countries that became independent in that century adopted the American constitutional model.

This first generation of Latin American constitutions differed little from the North American model. A presidential system, federalism, and judicial review were their main features. Over time, it became clear that this model was incapable of solving the social and political conflicts in the region. The established postcolonial model came into crisis at the beginning of twentieth century, and a new institutional framework was needed.

The region's social vulnerability, political conflicts, and difficulty establishing stable governments made the current institutional system insufficient. In response to this need, the 1917 constitution of Mexico was promulgated. This constitution was the result of a revolution and an armed conflict, and it was seen as a moderate model for dealing with the different problems of that period. The main feature of the 1917 Mexican constitution was the constitutionalization of the so-called social question. In this model, the state was recognized as a guarantor of social rights. The American model of a concise constitution was replaced by a new constitutional system that emerged as one of the most innovative constitutional experiments of the twentieth century (Gargarella 2013, p. 106).

This model was replicated by other Latin American countries. They established a new system of individual and social rights but retained a restrictive model of political organization. Among the new rights recognized by this model were the rights to housing, education, health, and, above all, work and social security. A few years later, the German Weimar Constitution, promulgated in 1919, would make this model known worldwide.

Nonetheless, Roberto Gargarella points out three problems in the constitutional theory that emerged from the constitutionalization of social rights. The first problem is the internal structure of the constitution. The recognition of new rights combined with a conservative division of powers resulted in more power for the judiciary and a discredit of the legislature. The second is that of the incorporation new rights into a traditional and institutionally compact constitutional system. Finally, the third is the problem of dormant clauses.[2] As a reflection of the first two problems, several constitutional provisions are understood as merely programmatic and propositional (i.e., as not immediately applicable or as promises for the future). In other words,

[1] *Marbury v. Madison*, Supreme Court of United States, February 24, 1803 (USA).

[2] Gargarella uses the term "dormant" here to mean that these clauses do not have the legal and political capacity to be binding.

there is an implied loss of normativity of the constitutional provisions aimed at achieving social transformation (Gargarella 2013, p. 134).

It could be argued that dormant clauses and the discredit of the legislature are the main difficulties of the Latin American constitutional tradition. The Latin American model can be described as a constitutional framework that relies on a system of individual rights protection to guarantee a complex set of social and economic rights. This creates a high institutional cost, for it puts the sole responsibility for implementing programmatic and social transformation clauses on the judiciary.

In Brazil, the constitutionalization of "social questions" within a democratic regime became more important in the 1988 constitution. After more than 30 years since its promulgation, the Brazilian doctrine is rich in debates regarding dormant clauses and the programmatic constitution. Conservatives criticize this system, saying that these clauses are a form of social demobilization and that they result from a belief that all social problems can be solved by constitutionalization (Díaz 2010, p. 74).

Gilberto Bercovici maintains that an adequate interpretation of the constitution is enough to answer these criticisms but not to carry out the constitutional project. He argues that this belief stems from a theory of the constitution that lacks both a theory of the state and a theory of politics. Only with a committed state and open political debate will the core constitutional commitments be fulfilled (Bercovici 2014, p. 13). To consider constitutional reasoning as something to be undertaken only by judges is to impoverish the problem and its importance. Thus, Bercovici emphasizes that the constitution must be seen as a national project of social development and transformation. This explains the current Brazilian constitutional crisis as a crisis that strips from the constitution its capacity to build a nation of free and equal citizens (Bercovici 2014, p. 15; Bonavides 2011, p. 388).

Another relevant phenomenon in Latin America is the recognition of Indigenous rights within constitutionalism. The constitutions of Ecuador in 2008 and Bolivia in 2009 are examples of this process. They each founded multinational states, recognizing the origin of different Indigenous nations in the country and defining the model of *buen vivir* as a moral principle (Zaffaroni 2010, p. 121). According to Roberto Gargarella, the importance of constitutionalizing the "indigenous question" is offset by the constant problem of the concentration of powers in executive branches. In addition to translating Indigenous rights into a conservative liberal language, the constitutional framework and the concentration of powers make it difficult to realize these rights, leaving citizens out of the constitution's engine room, which concerns the division of powers (Gargarella 2013, p. 186).

Regarding the most recent constitutional events, it is possible to organize the latest constitutions as cycles of pluralist constitutionalism (Fajardo 2016, p. 176). The first is the so-called cycle of multiculturalist constitutionalism, which took place between 1982 and 1988. It has this name because it recognizes multiculturalism and the newly acknowledged demands of Indigenous people. Relevant concepts include cultural diversity, the cultural identities of Indigenous people, and more specific Indigenous rights. The constitutions of Canada (1982) and Brazil (1988) belong to this cycle.

The second is the cycle of pluricultural constitutionalism, which took place between 1989 and 2005. In this cycle, concepts such as the multiethnic nation, the pluricultural state, bilingual intercultural education, consultation with Indigenous peoples, and other guidelines of ILO Convention No. 169 are included in the constitutions. The constitutions of Colombia (1991), Mexico (1992), and Peru (1993) belong to this cycle.

Finally, there is the cycle of plurinational constitutionalism, which took place between 2006 and 2009. Taking place in the context of the 2007 United Nations Declaration on the Rights of Indigenous Peoples, the constitutions of this cycle are characterized by the refounding of the state and the millennial roots of Indigenous peoples who were not recognized in previous republic periods. Some characteristics of this cycle are the recognition of Indigenous peoples as original nations with the right to self-determination, the recognition of the state as being plurinational, the adoption in the constitution of the Indigenous cosmovision of good living (*buen vivir* or *sumak kawsay*), and the rights of Mother Earth. The constitutions of Bolivia (2009) and Ecuador (2008) are the primary examples of this movement (Moraes 2018, p. 44).

This initial information helps to understand the contemporary context of Latin American constitutionalism. This topic aims to briefly develop the context in which these advances are embedded and prepare for an analysis of how constitutional courts can help strengthen democratic culture in the region. Thus, this analysis is both descriptive and normative, given that it advocates a specific role for the region's constitutional courts.

2.2 The Role of Courts in Latin American Constitutionalism

As stated earlier, Latin American constitutionalism is innovative and radical in the recognition of rights, as exemplified by the constitutionalization of the "social question" and the "indigenous question" (Pastor and Dalmau 2011, p. 8). Nevertheless, it remains conservative in the division of powers, making it difficult to implement these rights. The result of this constitutional format is the neglect of legislative power and the increase of demands in judiciary. We can characterize this problem of excluding the population from the political decision-making process as a form of legal alienation (Gargarella 2016, p. 138). This is the starting point for a critical understanding the problems of the Latin American political system.

These failures of institutional design demonstrate that the main problem of Latin American constitutionalism lies not only in how courts deal with their demands, but in the way the state is organized. Likewise, in resolving these political and social problems, one should both consider the role of the courts and develop a model of popular participation. In this context of realizing the democratic role of the judiciary, Roberto Gargarella proposes to understand it according to the model of deliberative democracy. This model rejects judicial activism and the supremacy of the judiciary while attributing to the courts the role of receiving complaints from vulnerable groups and demanding that government officials better justify their actions. Thus, judges would be seen as engineers of public debate (Gargarella 2006, p. 28).

Naturally, the perspective of deliberative democracy does not exclude the possibility of abuse and errors, but it helps to understand the role of the judiciary in relevant social issues, without forgetting that the main focus should be on popular participation and the strengthening of democratic institutions (Gargarella 2006, p. 29). Literature on the role of courts in the model of deliberative democracy is still relatively scarce. The main proposals defend courts playing an important role but place them among several other institutions that also take part in public debate. For this reason, scholars should consider the role of courts but should extend that analysis further (Mendes 2013, p. 84).

There are three ways to characterize the courts in a deliberative democracy. The first is as defenders of an open, public process of deliberation in other arenas. In this characterization, there is no direct participation of the courts in public debate, since the judicial role is limited to protecting the quality of public discourse. The second is to assign the courts more active participation in the determination of the content of controversial rights. Here the court not only engages in deliberate processes as an active participant, but also removes from ordinary politics the prerogative to decide certain issues related to citizens' rights.

The last approach views the court as a relevant deliberative institution, having to comply with guidelines for dialogue internally and externally with society and other institutions. This perspective has not been extensively debated in view of the misconception that court debates, for conceptual reasons, are of higher quality than the deliberations that take place in other institutional realms (Mendes 2013, p. 91).

From the perspective of courts as defenders of the public debate in Latin American democracies, Santiago Nino has important contributions to make. He proposes a conception of rights and a criterion for the participation of courts in the political process. These two proposals are key to understanding and specifying the role of courts in Latin American political systems. Nino's goal is to develop a conception of rights that relates well to the defense of individual rights as the proper distribution of social goods by the state in a democratic regime. In this proposal, the participation of politics and morality are inevitable due to the normative nature of that theory (Nino 1996, p. 46). Highlighting the idea of human dignity, Nino admits that individual acts in deliberative decisions can be sufficiently apt to establish obligations, the loss of rights and the loss of responsibilities. This can happen as long as these acts are performed in favor of other individuals in situations of greater vulnerability (Nino 1996, p. 52).

Another interesting proposal is the conception of equality as non-exploitation, in which human beings cannot be treated as instruments. Denying the need for social leveling, which would be an exaggeration, Nino proposes that people cannot be exploited by others, which does not mean that they are on the same social level. Rather, people must be able to carry out their life projects (Nino 1996, p. 62). The ultimate goal of Nino's construction of a conception of rights is to demonstrate that social rights are not antagonistic to individual rights. In fact, they are extensions of classic individual rights. There is a complementarity, to the extent that one cannot be achieved without the other (Nino 1996, p. 62). We can say the same about multicultural rights.

Regarding the public debate, Nino argues that the majority of the decision-making process on moral and political issues is more efficient in achieving the best possible results. Likewise, he claims that it would be a form of epistemic elitism to put rights-related issues outside of the ordinary political debate. Considering a strong version of the conception of rights, which includes positive and negative actions by the state, almost all major political issues are related to these rights. Thus, removing issues related to rights from the public debate would be to vacate the democratic process. Therefore, while it is not appropriate to defend courts as the only defenders of individual and social rights of citizens, this does not mean that they do not have any role.

The role of courts is to defend the epistemic value of public debate—that is, the quality of the democratic process. To develop an adequate constitutional system, it is necessary to guarantee certain rights a priori (i.e., as preconditions of the democratic process). It is the role of courts to enforce these preconditions. These rights include equal participation in public debate, respect for marginalized groups, and the existence of emotional skills for dialogue (Nino 1996, p. 138). To understand the proper function of courts, examining some points of Nino's proposal helps to demonstrate that understanding the form of rights and the performance of the judiciary differs from what happens in the traditional perspective. It also helps to realize and define the problem related to this institution in the theory of legal adjudication.

During the pandemic, the role of courts has also been relevant (Bustamante and Meyer 2022, pp. 235–236). It became evident that they must collaborate to avoid the abuse of power in the necessary exceptional measures and for the deliberative process to be maintained even at a time of social and health crisis. Together with the other powers, the defense of the democratic process must be a priority in a region with a recent history of military dictatorships (Gargarella and Rao 2020, p. 3).

Within the context of an institutional temptation to concentrate even greater powers in the executive, it is necessary to increase social deliberation so that exceptional measures are not taken due to haste and despair. Organization, dialogue, and social collaboration are crucial for the proper protection of public health, including through prior planning of vaccine distribution. In this context, the protection of freedom of expression and data privacy are essential in view of the proliferation of fake news and the possibility of people being manipulated (Gargarella and Roa 2020, p. 8).

2.3 *The Need for a Theory of Adjudication*

Through this simple explanation of the characteristics and problems of Latin American constitutionalism, some brief conclusions can be reached. The first is that it has an innovative nature in the recognition of social and Indigenous rights, which is extremely relevant for the most vulnerable populations in the region. On the other hand, this innovative language finds opposition in a conservative system of power distribution, which results in some dysfunctionality, such as little popular participation in public decisions, excessive demands on courts, and the discredit of the legislative branch compared to the other powers. All of this results in a lack of efficiency in social projects of inclusion and equality proposed by constitutions (Pastor 2007, p. 2).

Within this institutional and political framework, the role of courts is to serve as a measure of protection and promotion of public debate regarding individual, social, and Indigenous rights, but without becoming a protagonist in their implementation. It is a secondary function but is still relevant within an innovative deliberative system such as the Latin American one. In any case, the courts do participate in the inclusion and protection of vulnerable and marginalized groups. When this is related to deep social issues, the problem tends to expand. As the performance of courts is related to its decisions, these new issues further raise the importance of a theory of legal adjudication (Gloppen 2006, p. 36).

That importance stands out in the traditional function of a theory of legal adjudication, which is to assist judges in their jurisdictional function and to assist lawyers in the evaluation of these decisions (Dworkin 1986, p. 225). In the Latin American context, this is a key role in the recognition of new rights and the democratic role of the jurisdiction in protecting and implementing social development projects established by the constitution. At a time of a global pandemic, enforcement of courts increases, given that, traditionally, constitutional courts have had significant institutional strength in Latin America. A theory of legal adjudication, within a necessary context of clear and democratic social deliberation, is crucial to the due inspection and deliberation of courts (Roa Roa 2020, p. 3).

More recently, the region has also experienced events that fall under what is conventionally called democratic erosion (Dixon and Landau 2021). Although hyper-presidentialism is a reality in the region, recent authoritarian leaders implement their own strategies, with new and relatively more sophisticated political practices. Respect for constitutional parameters has been an effective parameter for evaluating democracies in the region today (Bustamante and Meyer 2022).

Within this regional context, Waluchow's living constitutionalism emerges as an alternative for structuring constitutional decisions in Latin America. As stated earlier, the current Canadian constitution recognizes the multicultural rights of Indigenous peoples and establishes a constitutional court capable of protecting and promoting these Indigenous rights. As Waluchow's theory proposes a model of constitutional adjudication in which these characteristics are sufficiently recognized, and it seems to be a sound approach under these conditions. Before carrying out a critical analysis of Waluchow's proposal, it is important to understand its basic tenets. Thus, a description of its assumptions will be presented ahead of the subsequent confrontation with the reality of constitutionalism in Latin America.

3 Waluchow's Theory of Legal Adjudication

Wil Waluchow begins his seminal book *The Common Law Theory of Judicial Review* by commenting that, in 1982, the Constitution Act was promulgated and declared to be Canada's supreme law; any legislation inconsistent with it was therefore repealed. Its most controversial provision was the inclusion of a bill of rights. The central concern was the fear of these rights being guaranteed by judges who are not directly elected, which raised questions about the legitimacy of the system (Waluchow 2007, p. 3).

Waluchow then develops the standard case for defending constitutionalism, in which traditional arguments are used, such as the protection of marginalized people and the guarantee of authentic interests of society against momentary interests. He then states that the main goal of his book is to develop a reasonable defense of judicial review and to face the most relevant criticisms of this practice, which are those produced by Jeremy Waldron (Waluchow 2007, p. 123). These criticisms are called a democratic challenge.

The first criticism raised is related to the loss of the ideal of self-government. A government that leaves major political decisions about rights to judges cannot be said to be democratic. Another criticism is the image of the human being as a predator who aims to pursue only their own interests. If the human being is really so dangerous that their presence in an open public debate puts citizens' rights at risk, there is no way to justify that the debate between human judges is any different.

Criticism is also raised against the metaphor of a drunk man who asks his friends to take his car keys and the famous metaphor "Ulysses and the mermaids." Neither of these metaphors respects the idea of self-government in a modern representative system, given the fact that the society cannot be compared to a drunk person or someone bewitched. Another criticism is about the irrelevance of moral objectivity in public debate. This criticism argues that even if moral truths were accessible in an epistemically reliable way, it would be impossible to convince all citizens of this.

In the same way, the extreme plurality of worldviews within the same political community makes it almost impossible to reach a consensus on the meaning of the constitution. Together, Waldron calls these conditions the "circumstances of politics." Without a consensus or a method of interpreting and applying a bill of rights, the idea of judicial review is very dangerous. (Waluchow 2007, p. 162).

In defense of constitutionalism and judicial review, Waluchow does not resort to the traditional assumptions of the debate. He proposes a new perspective in which the circumstances of politics (which emerge when there is an acknowledgment of the need for common norms but widespread disagreement about the proper content of these norms) are not an obstacle, but an assumption for judicial review. The legitimacy of judicial review can be justified as a way of dealing with the great difficulties caused by the cultural and political conflicts in the circumstances of politics (Waluchow 2007, p. 182).

Waluchow's proposal is inspired by a Canadian case from 1930 in which two major issues were decided: *Edwards v. A.G. Canada.*[3] The first was the recognition of women as human beings for the purpose of nominating them to the Senate. The second was the reception in Canadian constitutional law of the metaphor of the constitution as a living tree, rather than a document with fixed views.

Henceforth, the Canadian constitution was not seen as rigid, but as a living tree whose meaning can expand within its natural limits. This is an important theoretical tool in adapting constitutional meaning to new circumstances and to issues of social justice. With this proposal, Waluchow aims to defend judicial review and respond to the criticisms raised by Waldron (Waluchow 2007, p. 183).

A relevant point of Waluchow's proposal is that charters of rights are a concession to our inability to understand the nature of rights under the circumstances of politics. Thus, the abstract and incomplete language in which rights are established would represent a strategy to avoid absurd or unwanted results that could arise in the future from fixed and predetermined language (Waluchow 1996, p. 404). Abstract language would be an open door to the development of rights through dialogue, in contrast to rigid language that may be defended by authoritarian judges against the popular will (Waluchow 2007, p. 213). In applying this abstract language, the common law method is suggested. This method is open and malleable, which allows for the flexibility and stability of decisions involving the bill of rights. This is crucial to a better understanding of charters of rights in specific situations (Waluchow 2007, p. 204).

In a brief summary, the proposal has the following tenets (Waluchow 2007, p. 220). First, charters of rights are set forth as the rights of political morality established within the "community's constitutional morality" (CCM). This morality is not that of a specific group, but the result of the reflective equilibrium of convictions in a political community. It represents the authentic interests of the community, which are opposed to momentary interests. Second, the proposal enables us to make sense of the idea that political representatives may be mistaken about what society's commitments require in a given situation. Third, it explains how judges can be correct about the authentic intentions of the community, which are those that can be traced to the community's genuine constitutional commitments. Fourth, the second and third points result in the possibility of judges being required by the charter itself to declare a mistaken view of political representatives unconstitutional. Fifth, when judges do this, they are not appealing to their own moral convictions, but rather to the community's vision of the matter. Sixth and finally, it shows that this attitude does not violate, but rather respects, the democratic principle established in the community's constitutional morality. These points thus constitute Waluchow's response to the criticisms within Waldron's democratic challenge.

Waluchow then explains that the participation of the jurisdiction is relevant and helps the community to develop its own constitutional morality (Waluchow 2007,

[3] *Edwards v. Canada (AG)*, Supreme Court of Canada, April 24, 1928 (Canada).

p. 270). In texts beyond *A Common Law Theory of Judicial Review*, Waluchow further develops his theory of legal adjudication. In these discussions, his position on the neutrality of his method is quite interesting. Considering that CCM is a positive community morality, Waluchow points out that, in some cases, it is possible for judges to find themselves building a CCM instead of applying it. In such a case, they would not be applying problem-solving criteria, but developing a new criteria (Waluchow 2013, p. 210).

In cases like this, Waluchow argues that the democratic principle must be respected even in discretionary decisions. The concept of discretion does not mean complete freedom to decide. Therefore, it is theoretically legitimate to seek democratic criteria to guarantee restrictions that constrain a judge in their discretionary decisions. For example, it would be absurd for a judge to decide a case based on their personal taste or horoscope (Waluchow 2013, pp. 212–213).

In search of a criterion that respects the democratic principle, Waluchow recalls that, in democracies with a deep pluralism, citizens recognize the benefits of living in such a society and that, for this community project to continue, it is necessary to accept that its world vision will not always be honored in public decisions. In the same way, citizens must accept that the commitment each social group has with this community project comes from different perspectives and reasons. Rawls refers to this commitment as the duty of civility (Waluchow 2013, pp. 212–213).

In this context, it is suggested that a discretionary decision within a CCM respects public reason when a citizen cannot disagree with their duty of civility. A disappointed citizen could disagree with a discretionary decision in the same way they might disagree with a vote. In both instances, it would be possible to achieve different results, but it would not be possible to question the good faith and legitimacy of the decision-making process (Waluchow 2013, pp. 218–219).

The argument about the discretion of CCM reaches its ultimate level when Waluchow argues that, even after applying the duty of civility, it is still possible that the result is a discretionary decision. In extreme situations like this, he does not agree with total deference to the legislature. Even making his issues with judicial activism clear, Waluchow argues that this decision must be sincere and seen as part of the duty of civility—that is, one must acknowledge the legitimacy of its procedure (Waluchow 2013, pp. 223–224).

Continuing his theory of legal adjudication, Waluchow argues in another text that, when deciding on CCM, judges should use the detached point of view. This type of view is used when an atheist gives advice to a Christian about Christianity itself. The atheist does not commit themselves to Christianity, but uses the detached point of view to make a value judgment from the Christian perspective.

According to Waluchow, judges should reason about public matters in the same way. They should not use their own point of view or the point of view of a specific social group when deciding on issues related to fundamental rights. They must use the view of the community's constitutional morality. Only this point of view is legitimate and can be used in questions about a bill of rights (Waluchow 2013, pp. 223–224).

These arguments demonstrate that Waluchow seeks to defend the legitimacy of judicial review against what he labeled a democratic challenge. His proposal is that a constitution is not a system of fixed meaning to be defended by a constitutional court and forever understood in terms of its rigid original language. Rather, he argues that the constitution is a living tree whose meaning can be adapted within its limits.

In constructing this meaning, Waluchow proposes that charters of rights are a tool in against misunderstanding of the nature of fundamental rights and that the common law method is the best way to guarantee the security and flexibility of a constitution. He also argues that the constitution is constructed through a community's constitutional morality, which is the result of the reflective equilibrium of its citizens' convictions.

Thus, considering that a CCM represents the authentic intentions of a political community, it is possible to understand that judges can invalidate legislation as long as it goes against these authentic intentions. This method, therefore, respects the democratic principle since it does not allow the implementation of occasional inauthentic interests. Therefore, the democratic challenge is defeated.

4 Waluchow's Theory of Decision in Latin American Constitutionalism

Three questions emerge from the argument developed in this chapter. The first deals with the new dimension of the democratic challenge already faced by Waluchow in his work. The second involves the need for a broader and stronger conception of rights, in which positive and negative fundamental rights are recognized. Finally, the main contribution of the proposal is the guarantee and defense of the authentic intentions of a community. Institutions that reasonably protect and guarantee the positive intentions of the constitution are important at a time of constitutional crisis. Interest groups usually benefit from distancing themselves from constitutional provisions. Protecting the constitution is crucial in this context.

4.1 A New Dimension of the Democratic Challenge

As seen above, Latin American constitutional systems have the characteristic of being pioneers in the recognition of rights. This happened both in the case of social rights in the twentieth century and in the case of Indigenous rights in the twenty-first century. Considering the maintenance of a conservative system of separation of powers, this recognition of rights has resulted in increased demands on the judiciary.

This reality makes the democratic challenge faced by a theory of legal adjudication even greater. The cases that are traditionally dealt with in the legal systems of Northern countries refer to individual rights and not to collective rights in those circumstances. Even the social cases faced such countries are decided through abstract social clauses and are not predictable (Shapiro 2011, p. 248).

Latin American constitutions have ambitious social projects to be carried out. This makes it more challenging to resolve issues related to social and Indigenous rights. A theory of legal adjudication should, in these cases, be able to regulate the reasoning on topics that often go beyond the expertise of judges and are more related to broad areas such as health, education, and the regulation of such public policies.

The large number of demands related to broad topics, in which the discretionary power is often much greater, results in a great power for a constitutional court. The possibility of overcoming the decisions of elected representatives ends up being much greater than traditionally considered, which results in a greater democratic challenge (Waldron 2010, p. 28). To quote Waluchow,

> Charters can and should be viewed as representing a *concession* to our *inability* fully to understand both the nature of fundamental rights and how these might be infringed by government action—and this includes, paradigmatically, government actions premised on the relatively blunt instrument of binding general legislation. Once we see Charters in this very different light—once we, in effect, adopt a Copernican revolution in our understanding of Charters and judicial review—we can begin to see a bit more clearly not only why they might well be good things to have, but we can also see our way clear to answering the various arguments offered by Waldron and other Critics against their adoption. Or at least that is what I hope to show. (Waluchow 2007, p. 127)

This argument reinforces an existing argument about rights that opposes Waluchow's theory of legal adjudication. As Tom Campbell states,

> Moreover, Waluchow does not give sufficient weight to counter vailing factors. Courts are, or should be, con strained by the need to articulate issues and arguments in terms of existing legal statutes and precedents; something which does not apply to democratic discourse which is more open to new demands and arguments. Further, courts do not have policy making competence with respect to information, social science expertise and political efficacy. In these respects courts can be no substitute for governments. Again, these are familiar points, but Waluchow passes over them without acknowledging that such advantages as may arise from using common law methodology in ordinary law do not translate neatly into the sphere of constitutional interpretation. Indeed, despite the attractiveness of common law methodology as gradualist and incremental, he ignores the fact that common law decisions are cumulative and can lead to radical, and, in constitutional contexts, in practice often irreversible changes. (Campbell 2009, p. 29)

This means that in an ambitious and analytical constitution, the guarantee of social and multicultural rights and a conservative separation of powers ends up enhancing the power of a constitutional court and increasing the chances of decisions without proper foundation within a democratic regime.[4] It is important to emphasize that this finding does not mean that this point of Waluchow's theory cannot be improved or

[4]The decisions of the Supreme Court of Canada involving important social rights, such as health and education, are not ignored here. Likewise, decisions regarding Indigenous rights are recognized. Indeed, there are social and multicultural rights in the Canadian CCM. The issue here involves the much greater participation of constitutional courts in the protection and promotion of social and multicultural rights in Latin America. This can happen for several reasons that range from the broad guarantee of these rights in constitutions to a greater need for judicial intervention due to the low representation of the political class. Thanks to the reviewer's comment that allowed me to clarify this point.

adjusted, but it raises the question of whether it may be necessary to deepen the proposal with regard to the deliberative control of judicial decision-making in matters that involve deep social demands, as in the case of structural poverty.

4.2 A New Conception of Rights

When the institutional tradition of constitutionalism was developed in the eighteenth and nineteenth centuries, its apparatus for the defense and guarantee of rights was set forth for individual rights. The inclusion of social and Indigenous rights naturally requires an adaptation of the constitutional system given the emergence of hybrid constitutions. The risk of an institutional dysfunctionality is manifested by ineffective mechanisms for guaranteeing new rights (Gargarella 2016, p. 137).

An important element in solving this problem is a new conception of rights. It is important to realize that the emergence of new rights has an impact on the very idea of a constitution and that a conception of rights appropriate to the current stage of social development is crucial to it functioning properly. On this topic, Santiago Nino developed a thesis about rights that proposes social rights as complementary to individual rights and not as antagonistic to those rights. In this sense, the institutional protection mechanism is shaped to reasonably involve all of the possibilities for the implementation of social rights.

Another relevant point on this theme is the necessity to overcome the dichotomy between principles and policies. Here, while policies are seen as an element aimed at the general well-being of a community, principles represent individual rights and are guaranteed by the constitution. Thus, policies represent the administrative discretion of executive and legislative branches, while principles represent justice and are guaranteed by the judiciary (Dworkin 1977, p. 22). This separation seems to be implicit in Waluchow's theory of legal adjudication.

Nino argues that this proposal cannot be supported by those who defend a strong theory of rights that includes social and individual rights, because it would result in the emptying of public debate and the concentration of political decisions in the judiciary. Furthermore, this separation implies that public debate is dangerous to citizens' rights. A language of rights cannot, therefore, achieve these results (Nino 1996, p. 197).

The need for an adequate vocabulary is increased because the constitutions of Latin America include several social objectives related to vulnerable groups. To consider political objectives set out in the constitution to be outside the judgment of the courts is to make them lose much of their political significance. Positive attitudes from the state are crucial to the existence and strengthening of Indigenous communities, for example. The inspection of a state's positive actions within constitutional parameters is an important element of constitutionalism in Latin America, and a theory of decision needs to place this action within democratic parameters. Here, there is not a contradiction within Waluchow's theory, but a gap in this respect.

4.3 The Importance of Maintaining Authentic Intentions

Waluchow's proposal to defend authentic intentions is interesting, because the current political crises in Latin America are seen as the result of forgetting the social and political project established in constitutions. More than simple commandments without jurisdictional guarantees, the project of eliminating poverty and ending inequality is critical to regional development.

As Waluchow clearly explained, this project represents the authentic intentions of Latin American society and must be remembered by both politicians and judges. Using constitutional jurisdiction as a mechanism to guarantee and promote public and institutional debate about authentic intentions and its consequences is an important goal.

One could argue that Waluchow's proposal has much to contribute to constitutionalism in Latin America. The protection of genuine intuitions is essential for the region, which has traditionally suffered from the problem of democratic erosion (Bonavides 2019). In this process, constitutional guidelines for social advances are forgotten, and advances are publicized as being the result of the intervention of an alleged paternal leader. In this context, defending the genuine intentions present in the constitution is a civic duty not only of the courts, but of the entire population.

The defense of the constitution is an essential instrument against democratic erosion. This must happen within a democratic perspective and without usurping the people's role. Waluchow does not advocate judicial activism, but a mechanism for institutional dialogue in which society itself can participate in its own interpretation of these intentions. In cases of constitutional limitations and the need for discretionary judgments, a clear mechanism of self-restraint is necessary through which excesses can be avoided.

Considering the methodological possibility of these authentic intentions being discovered and protected, Waluchow's proposal already justifies some level of activism. In the context where it was proposed, there was an adequate response to the critic's challenges (Waluchow 2009, p.164). The issue at hand is the importance of presenting criteria for the passive virtues of legislation for the adequate participation of courts in public debate (Bickel 1982, p. 113).

5 Final Considerations

Latin American constitutionalism offers genuine contributions to the global constitutionalism through the recognition of social and multicultural rights. This perspective is opposed to a concentration of political power in the executive branch to the discredit of the legislative branch. The constitution's engine room should also be part of the democratization of the constitutional experience. In this way, it has its specific characteristics and problems that must be considered in the analysis of normative theoretical proposals willing to collaborate with democratic experiences in different parts of the world.

Waluchow's theory of decision is one of these proposals. In an innovative and interesting way, Waluchow has proposed a new way of looking at constitutional jurisdiction in a democratic regime. He denies the image of guardians of the constitution and, instead, proposes a constitutional court open to dialogue with society in the application and construction of the meaning of the constitution. Consequently, judicial activism is rejected, and a clear role for constitutional jurisdiction is ensured in harmony with the other powers.

From the point of view of Latin American constitutionalism, this theoretical proposal has much to contribute; however it is still necessary to analyze it more carefully. There are at least three important concerns to raise. The first is a reflection on social and multicultural rights in the legitimacy of a constitutional court. A longer list of rights results in even greater power for the judiciary. The democratic challenge becomes bigger than it was at first.

The second relates to the theory of rights. It is important to make it clear that social and multicultural rights are not opposed to individual rights. The maintenance of a traditional theory ends up reducing the effectiveness of social and multicultural rights in a context in which they are relevant.

Third, the protection of authentic intentions is relevant when there is political will that aims to vacate the constitution and forget about the social commitments established within it. However, this protection cannot be radical; it has to be dialogical, given its importance in a nation-building project. In this way, a theory that develops the passive virtues as suggested by Bickel would help to predict the action of courts in the defense of the authentic intentions of a society.

At the end of this volume, Professor Waluchow kindly comments on the different comments made regarding his theory in an interview. Its complete reading is highly recommended. With regard to the arguments developed in this chapter, it is necessary to make some notes, but let us first summarize. Initially, Waluchow recognizes that his proposal was developed for what he calls healthy constitutional democracies. This refers to democracies whose most important political actors generally respect the rules of the game, in which there is a reasonable representation of different social groups, and in which there are no attempts to usurp political power. Bolsonaro and Trump are cited as examples of actors who do not respect these premises.

Within these premises, Waluchow continues, judges are reliable actors, and it is reasonable to expect them to make important decisions regarding the rights of vulnerable groups. This would happen because judges do not need to submit to social pressures or run for reelection. Waluchow admits that this perspective influenced him because, with few exceptions such as the treatment Indigenous peoples, Canada closely resembles a healthy democracy.

If that basic institutional trust does not exist, the theory does not work very well, but that is not his final argument. Waluchow says that, at least, his theory may produce a theoretical proposal that serves as a measure of a healthy constitutional system to be built. In this way, this could perhaps serve as a parameter for a theoretically attractive answer. Attempting to go further would reach beyond his theory's limits.

Waluchow's response is provocative and may result in new studies (Gomes Júnior 2022a). In fact, it allows us to analyze a potential path to be taken and answers to be suggested. A representative system that facilitates access for vulnerable groups such as racial minorities and Indigenous peoples may allow more efficient public policies to emerge without the need for pressure from the courts. Another interesting idea would be to insert instruments of social participation, such as public hearings, in structural decisions. On these occasions, social movements and marginalized groups could participate directly in debates about public policies of their legitimate interest. These and other alternatives can be discussed from the point of view of Wil Waluchow's living constitutionalism in future studies.

References

Bercovici, Gilberto. 2014. Revolution through constitution: The Brazilian's directive constitution debate. *Revista de Investigações Constitucionais* 1 (1): 7–18. https://doi.org/10.5380/rinc.v1i1.40249.

Bickel, Alexander M. 1982. *The least dangerous branch: The supreme court at the bar of politics*. New Haven: Yale University Press.

Bonavides, Paulo. 2011. *Curso de Direito Constitucional*. São Paulo: Malheiros.

———. 2019. A América Latina e os 30 anos da constituição. *Revista Acadêmica: Escola Superior do Ministério Público do Ceará* 11 (1): 11–20.

Bustamante, Thomas, and Emílio Peluso Neder Meyer. 2022. Brazil: COVID-19, illiberal politics and the rule of law. In *Routledge handbook of law and the COVID-19 pandemic*, ed. Joelle Grogan and Alice Donald, 225–236. New York: Routledge.

Campbell, Tom. 2009. Slaying the hydra: Living tree constitutionalism and the case for judicial review of legislation. *Problema: Anuario de Filosofia y Teoria del Derecho* 3: 17–36. https://doi.org/10.22201/iij.24487937e.2009.3.8070.

Díaz, Carlos Gaviria. 2010. Los derechos econômicos y sociales em el nuevo constitucionalismo latino americano. In *El nuevo constitucionalismo en America Latina*, 67–80. Quito: Corte Constitucional del Ecuador.

Dixon, Rosalind, and David Landau. 2021. *Abusive constitutional borrowing: Legal globalization and the subversion of liberal democracy*. Oxford: Oxford University Press.

Dworkin, Ronald. 1977. *Taking rights seriously*. Harvard: Harvard University Press.

———. 1986. *Law's empire*. Harvard: Harvard University Press.

Edwards v Canada (AG), Supreme Court of Canada, 24 April 1928 (Canada).

Fajardo, Raquel Z. Yrigoyen. 2016. In *In El estado de derecho hoy en América Latina: Libro en homenaje a Horst Schönbohm*, ed. Helen Ahrens, 171–193. UNAM, Instituto de Investigaciones Jurídicas.

Gargarella, Roberto. 2006. Theories of democracy, the judiciary and social rights. In *Courts and social transformation in new democracies: An institutional voice for the poor?* ed. Roberto Gargarella, Domingo Pilar, and Theunis Roux, 13–34. Hampshire: Ashgate Publishing Company.

———. 2013. *Latin American constitutionalism, 1810–2010: The engine room of the constitution*. New York: Oxford University Press.

———. 2016. Scope and limits of dialogic constitutionalism. In *Democratizing constitutional law: Perspectives on legal theory and the legitimacy of constitutionalism*, ed. Thomas Bustamante and Bernardo Gonçalves Cavalcante, 119–146. Cham: Springer.

Gargarella, Roberto, and Jorge Ernesto Roa Roa. 2020. Diálogo democrático y emergência em América Latina. *MPIL research papers series* 2020–21: 1–30. https://doi.org/10.2139/ssrn.3623812

Gloppen, S.L. 2006. Courts and Social Transformation: An Analytical Framework, *in Roberto Gargarella, Pilar Domingo and Theunis Roux, editors: Courts and Social Transformation in New Democracies. An Institutional Voice for the Poor?. Aldershot/Burlington: Ashgate pp. 35–59*, https://www.cmi.no/publications/2394-courts-and-social-transformation.

Gomes Júnior, Francisco Tarcísio Rocha. 2022a. Poderia o constitucionalismo ser decolonial? In *Decolonização de conceitos sociojurídicos*, ed. Raquel Coelho Freitas, 153–179. Fortaleza: Editora Mucuripe.

———. 2022b. O constitucionalismo como árvore viva de Wil Waluchow: Entre emergência e autoritarismo. Thesis, UFC.

Mendes, Conrado Hübner. 2013. *Constitutional courts and deliberative democracy*. Oxford: Oxford University Press.

Mendes, Conrado Hübner, Roberto Gargarella, and Sebastián Guidi. 2022. *The Oxford handbook of constitutional law in Latin America*. Oxford: Oxford University Press.

Moraes, Germana de Oliveira. 2018. *Harmonia com a natureza e direitos de Pachamama*. Fortaleza: Edições UFC.

Nino, Carlos Santiago. 1996. *The constitution of deliberative democracy*. New Haven: Yale University Press.

Pastor, Roberto Alfonso Viciano. 2007. Algunas consideraciones críticas sobre los procesos constituyentes en Ecuador y Venezuela. *Revista Direito e Liberdade* 6: 375–386.

Pastor, Roberto Alfonso Viciano, and Rubén Martínez Dalmau. 2011. El nuevo constitucionalismo latinoamericano: Fundamentos para una construcción doctrinal. *Revista General de Derecho Público Comparado* 9: 1–24.

Roa Roa, Jorge Ernesto. 2020. El rol del juez constitucional en el constitucionalismo transformador latinoamericano. *MPIL research papers series* 2020–11: 1–16. https://doi.org/10.2139/ssrn.3571507.

Shapiro, Scott J. 2011. *Legality*. Massachusetts: Belknap Press of Harvard University Press.

Waldron, Jeremy. 2010. Socioeconomic rights and theories of justice. *New York University Public Law and Legal Theory Working Papers* 245: 1–30. https://doi.org/10.2139/ssrn.1699898.

Waluchow, W.J. 1996. Indeterminacy. *Canadian Journal of Law and Jurisprudence* IX (2): 397–409. https://doi.org/10.1017/S0841820900003519.

———. 2007. *A common law theory of judicial review: The living tree*. Cambridge: Cambridge University Press.

———. 2009. A living tree constitutionalist replies. *Problema: Anuario de Filosofia y Teoria del Derecho* 3: 147–168. https://doi.org/10.22201/iij.24487937e.2009.3.

———. 2013. On the neutrality of charter reasoning. In *Neutrality and theory of law*, ed. Jordi Ferrer Beltrán, José Juan Moreso, and Diego M. Papayannis, 203–225. London: Springer.

Zaffaroni, Eugenio Raúl. 2010. La natureza como persona: Pachamama y Gaia. In *Bolivia: Nueva constitución política del estado: Conceptos elementares para su desarrollo normativo*, ed. Patricia Montes, 109–132. La Paz: Convergencia Comunicación Global.

Francisco Tarcísio Rocha Gomes Júnior is Professor of Constitutional Theory, Jurisprudence, and Legal Hermeneutics at the University Center Christus (Unichristus), at the State University of Piauí (UESPI), Brazil and holds a Ph.D. at the Federal University of Ceará. He holds a M.A. and was a Teaching Fellow at the Federal University of Ceará, Brazil.

Part IV
Interview

Interview with Professor Wil J. Waluchow

Thomas Bustamante, Saulo de Matos, and André L. S. Coelho

Interviewers: Professor Wil Waluchow, it is a pleasure to have you for this interview and we hope that this book contributes to interpret and disseminate your philosophical thoughts. Let us begin with a short set of biographical questions. What made you become a legal philosopher? Which were the main philosophical debates at your time as student?

W.J. Waluchow: First of all, thank you very much. I'm very grateful to all of you for having the conference, putting this whole thing together, editing the book, and giving me the honor of being able to discuss the work with you here during this interview. I am very pleased and very honored, so thank you both very much. When I first went to university, I intended to study history. That's what I went [there] to do and it was my favorite subject in high school. But when I had to choose courses, some of the courses were new to me, and one of them was philosophy. So I thought "What the heck! This sounds kind of interesting". Really, I had no idea what it was but I thought that I'd try it. The Registrar at the small college that I attended, she had a very forceful personality and she pretty much told me "You are taking philosophy". So I said, "OK, I will". I'm glad she did that because I fell in love with it immediately. I had a wonderful first instructor, Tony Willing, whose method and approach to philosophy I found very conducive and tried to emulate. I was still torn between philosophy and history by the end of the first year, after which you have to declare a Major, and I really didn't know what to do. So, believe it or not, I flipped a

T. Bustamante (✉)
Federal University of Minas Gerais, School of Law, Belo Horizonte, Brazil
e-mail: tbustamante@ufmg.br

S. de Matos
Federal University of Pará, Faculdade de Direito, Campus Universitário, Belém, Brazil
e-mail: saulodematos@ufpa.br

A. L. S. Coelho
Federal University of Rio de Janeiro, Faculdade Nacional de Direito, Rio de Janeiro, Brazil
e-mail: andrecoelho@direito.ufrj.br

T. Bustamante et al. (eds.), *Law, Morality and Judicial Reasoning*, Law and Philosophy Library 147, https://doi.org/10.1007/978-3-031-61879-6_17

coin and it came up philosophy. To be honest, when I think about it, had it come up history I might have said: "The heck with it, I'm going to do philosophy anyway", but it was a conflict because I still really wanted to do history. I also thought at that time that I was ultimately destined to law school, because I found the law fascinating and I thought that it was something I could probably do well. But when I fell in love with philosophy, I thought: "well, maybe I can combine my interest in philosophy with my interest in law." So I took a course or two in legal philosophy and I fell in love with that. I still remember that the very first paper in legal philosophy that I ever read was Dworkin's paper on discretion (laughs) (Dworkin 1963), and I thought: "This is wonderful, I just love this stuff"! And that was it: I was hooked. I still contemplated the possibility of going to law school, but then I soon realized that if I went to law school I'd become a lawyer, you know, dealing with contracts, real estate, and I'd be pining to do philosophy or legal philosophy or legal theory—and realize that only a few who make it to the higher end of appeal courts could actually do that kind of stuff. I realized that in practicing law I'd probably never get there. So, I thought I might as well stick with philosophy and so I became a philosopher who got to study and participate in law instead of a lawyer who wishes he could become a philosopher. That's how I ended up in legal philosophy.

The topics that were hot at the time I was I student, in my undergraduate years, were typical things: the impact of Quine (e.g. 1951)... I remember Kripke's landmark paper on the private language argument, which made a real impact at the time (Kripke 1982). We were doing Gettier (1963) counterexamples until they came out of our ears! That was the big thing in epistemology, and I thoroughly enjoyed it. You know, that kind of analysis has its limitations, but, God, it was fun to do it at the time, and I really enjoyed it! (pause) John Rawls had just come out with *A Theory of Justice* and that kind of swallowed all the energy of everybody in moral and political philosophy. So we spent a lot of time doing that. In fact, my very first reading course in philosophy was on Rawls's *Theory of Justice* (1999). But I have to confess that we only got through about 10% of the book, because it was just so big and there was so much in it that we never finished it. We also did David Lyons' book *The Form and Limits on Utilitarianism* (1965). I'm not sure if you are familiar with that book but I really liked it and I like Lyons' approach. Of course, he is a very accomplished legal philosopher. When it comes to philosophy of law, the hot topic then was, of course, Dworkin's critique of Hart. That's what was occupying all the attention and that's what I did most of my work on. And that's what I eventually ended up doing my doctoral dissertation on.

So I studied legal theory for two reasons. First I find it inherently interesting. Given my prior interest in law, that seemed like a good place to go. The other reason was some advice that I got from that very first philosophy professor that I had, Tony Willing. I remember talking to him and saying "I'd kind of like to do something on the evaluative side, but I'm not sure what". Then he said, "Do legal philosophy. The main reason is because you like it, first of all. But a second reason is you will be more employable". And I think that was sound advice. He said: "If you do legal theory, then you'll be able to do political philosophy and moral philosophy, because legal philosophers are well versed in those areas as well. But it doesn't necessarily work go the other way. You can have a person doing ethics who doesn't know anything about legal philosophy. So if you do legal philosophy, you will have a broader range of specializations and that will make you more employable". I think that this was sound advice and I'm glad he gave it to me.

Interviewers: Well, it was nice to hear that "Discretion", by Ronald Dworkin, was one of the first papers you've ever read on legal philosophy, because that topic will reappear in this interview, and it was there throughout your career.

W.J. Waluchow: Yeah, that paper "Judicial Discretion", that's what got me going.

Interviewers: How would you describe Oxford during your PhD? How was your relationship with Ronald Dworkin and H. L. A. Hart? Could you tell us one or two memoirs about this time as a PhD student in Oxford?

W.J. Waluchow: At the time Oxford was in many ways a very strange place for a DPhil student. That's what we call it: "DPhil," to distinguish it from other degrees (laughs)... Oxford arrogance! But they didn't know what to do with doctoral students. They were kind of an *ad hoc addition.* The university's student life revolved around the undergraduates and their colleges, and so on. I was stuck, well, not stuck, I was in a College, Wolfson College, in which I was the only person who did legal philosophy. And as far as I know there was only one other person in the College who did philosophy. I became a friend of his, another Canadian who ended up teaching in Saskatchewan. But I didn't know one legal philosopher among the graduate students, so it was very strange. It was certainly not what I was accustomed to, and certainly not what you find today in most contemporary universities, the cohort of students who do similar things. So you were always very dependent on your supervisor for any kind of academic, intellectual interchange. When I first went to Oxford I was appointed to R.M. Hare, the famous moral philosopher who unfortunately knew very little about legal theory and really wasn't much interested in what I had to say about it. Had I stayed with him, and given the context that I just described, I probably would never have finished my degree. And I would probably have washed out because I was getting nothing from the experience and I was floundering. But fortunately, toward the end of my second year Hare informed me that he was going off on sabbatical to California for the year. So he said "We are going to have to find you another supervisor". And I thought, "Wow, that's interesting". Luckily, he said: "Do you have anybody you'd like to work with?", and I said "H.L.A. Hart would be nice". I had met him once before and we had a wonderful interaction. Then Hare said, "Well, he's retired, and I don't think he takes on new students, but we can try". So a couple of days later I was sitting in the audience, waiting for the designated speaker to begin, and the guy sitting behind me turned out to be H.L.A. Hart. Hare, who was across the room from us, came up to us and, in front of everybody in the audience, says to Hart: "You know Mr. Waluchow?", and Hart says, "Yes, we met once before and it is nice to see you". And Hare says: "Would you care to be his supervisor next year"? This was in front of the whole crowd! Hart kind of looked a little shocked that he [Hare] asked this question in front of me and in front of all the other people around us. But he said "Yes, of course, if it's OK with Mr. Waluchow"; and I said, "Yes, of course, that would be fine"! So that's how I ended up with Hart. At that point my life, my career, everything changed, because I went from a supervisor with whom I had virtually no meaningful relationship academically to one who became a wonderful mentor from whom I learned an enormous amount and who helped me enormously throughout my studies and afterward as well. Then the absence of people to talk to, fellow students in legal philosophy, ceased to be a problem, because I had H.L.A. Hart to talk to. Hart arranged for me to see Raz a couple of times, and then Dworkin a couple of times. I did meet with both of them. I got to know Joseph very well. Dworkin I only met once or twice. I remember the first time I met with him I sent him a paper to read, and we really didn't end up talking about the paper. Instead, he brought out some wine. He had a wine fridge in his office. So he and I got completely drunk within about 45 min, because he kept pouring glasses. I was, of course, very very nervous, so I kept drinking the wine. By the end of it I was completely blitzed, and he was in his cups as well. We had a wonderful time, and he said a few encouraging words. So these are some of my the experiences from my life in Oxford.

Another feature of Oxford at the doctoral level was that there were no set courses. There was simply a list of lectures and seminars posted at the beginning of every term, and you were free to go to any of them you wanted to attend. You just sat in the audience and either listened to the lecture or to somebody giving a seminar with a couple of other people. So I chose the best I could. I chose a lot of nonlegal philosophy lectures, so that I could get some background in areas other than philosophy of law. And I went to virtually everything that was actually in legal philosophy, including lectures by Dworkin. Everything that Dworkin gave while I was there I went to; Hart had a couple of seminars, I'll come back to that in a minute; John Mackie, I went to every one of his, because he was a wonderful philosopher and I always learned a lot from him; Finnis, and various other people... Derek Parfit! Parfit was running out the ideas that became *Reasons and Persons* (1986), so it was marvelous to be able to go to his seminars every week. There is one seminar in particular that I remember, that ran every year and became known by the label "Star Wars". I don't know if you have ever heard of it, but it was organized, I think, by Dworkin and it always took place at All Souls' Library, which is a beautiful setting. There were always two other people with Dworkin: Mackie, Parfit, Amartya Sen, Charles Taylor, various other people... They would go at it on some topic! It was an incredible experience to watch these giants in the field interacting with each other. The seminar was so popular that you literally had to get there at least 1 h beforehand to even get in the room. And those who weren't there in time would be lining up outside in the quad. I'm not sure if you are familiar with All Souls' College and the Old Library, but there were two staircases going out into the quad, and people would be lined up trying to hear what was going on inside. So I went to those and they were just phenomenal. Another seminar that I went to was also very memorable, given by Hart and Rupert Cross, his famous colleague who wrote the book on the English doctrine of precedent, from which I learned quite a bit (Cross and Harris 1991). I forget the topic they were talking about. I wracked my brain in anticipation of this interview to recall what is was they were talking about, but I can't remember. But I do remember—again, this is one of these coincidences that just stick in your mind—that I was sitting at the table when Hart and Cross walked in. And Hart sits right beside me. This was before I met him, and was the first time I encountered him in person. My first thought was: "This is H.L.A. Hart sitting right beside me!" At one point, during Hart's presentation, they opened things up for questions and so I asked a question. Hart's response always stuck with me. He just stopped, and didn't say anything for 10 s, or something like that, and I thought: "Oh, my God, I really said something horrible". But what he eventually said was: "That's a really good point." And he just kept saying: "Yes, yes". He just smiled at me and kept nodding and saying "Yes, yes". Even after we went on to other things he looked at me occasionally and said "Yes". This is remarkable, you know: this lion of the field who was sitting right beside me, this lowly undergraduate student from the colonies, making me feel like I had something to contribute. That really stuck with me, and, of course, all my other experiences with Hart were similar. He always made me feel like I had something valuable to say, and that he enjoyed talking with me. That's what made the Oxford experience work for me. He really made it work. I can tell you another couple of stories about Hart if you want. Or would you like to move on?

Interviewers: Our more sincere answer would be "both". We want to move on, but we want to hear the stories. I almost regret having to move away from such wonderful remarks about biography and life in Oxford to such a dry subject, that I will ask about now: the methodology of legal philosophy. From the point of view of a non-English speaking country, Brazil, we are used to associating the legal philosophy that is produced in the United States, Canada, and Great Britain to analytical philosophy, or to saying that this tradition holds that legal philosophy is analytical philosophy applied to law. Do you see it that way? Do you think that the methodology is the same, the intellectual devices are the same? Or should we say that legal philosophy takes inspiration from analytical philosophy but is something else, with its own methodology?

W.J. Waluchow: That's a really interesting while very difficult question. I think that there are various methodologies one could pursue and that have been pursued. For example, Brian Leiter's naturalism. That's considered part of the Anglo-American tradition. But I think that for the most part it is analytic philosophy applied to legal problems. And what I mean by analytic philosophy is the kind of conceptual analysis that one finds in authors like Hart and Raz. This is not to say, of course, that value doesn't play a role in analytic philosophy understood in that way, and most, perhaps all, analytic philosophers would agree that value plays a role in the development of theories. And each analyst has complex arguments about that. That whole approach, that is, the thought that value can play a role in the construction and evaluation of analytic legal theory, is developed quite nicely in Julie Dickson's *Evaluation and Legal Theory* (2001), which I think is a wonderful book. I think that her new book that is coming out now (Dickson 2022) will expand on that, to some extent, but her indirectly evaluative approach to philosophical analysis of law is on the right track.

Interpretivism, as Dworkin does it, is something that can of course be done as well. It can provide insights. But I think it is a big step going from saying that values must play a role in the construction and evaluation of theories, to saying that what a legal theorist should do is justify coercion. I think there's a place for an understanding of what law that is different from the justificatory enterprise of justifying some practice and criticizing other practices on moral and political grounds. I continue to think that Hart and Raz and most of my contemporaries are right in thinking that it is possible to try to come to an understanding of a practice like law without necessarily evaluating it in terms of its moral goodness or badness. It might make me a dinosaur to think that way—sometimes I think I am a philosophical dinosaur—but that's the kinds of approach that I've always tried to pursue and that most of my colleagues have pursued. It may well be a matter of preference, but when I read analytic legal philosophers who pursue this kind of project, like Hart, Raz, Coleman, Green, Marmor, Joel Feinberg when it comes to things like the analysis of criminal law, I find that I really get a deeper understanding of law and issues surrounding law, and that that kind of understanding is something that philosophers are good at conveying and trying to develop. It's something that we do well, maybe better than others in other disciplines. The kind of conceptual clarification of the concepts in terms of which we understand and practice law, is extremely useful and it's the kind of thing that we are trained in as legal philosophers. When I read that kind of stuff—again, that might be just a matter of preference, for that's how I was raised philosophically—I find it enlightening, I find it useful, and I find that it is something that philosophers can do reasonably well. Once we start doing other things, and get too involved in social sciences, and so on, then to paraphrase, I think, Richard Feynman, "You just sound as dumb as the next guy." This is because we are not trained in that kind of stuff. I'd like to stick to what I'm trained in, and what I'm trained in is conceptual analysis and the development of arguments of the kind that one finds in Hart, Raz, etc. I hope this answers your question.

*Interviewers: One of the main debates that resulted from the Hart-Dworkin debate (which is taken up in several contributions to this book, e.g., the contributions from Kramer, Ehrenberg, Bix, and Coelho) was between inclusive and exclusive positivists. Exclusive positivists focus on conceptual arguments aimed at proving the impossibility of incorporating moral criteria in view of the incompatibility with some necessary feature of law, such as the claim to authority (*Raz 2009*), the function of conventions (*Marmor 2009*), or the logic of plans (Shapiro* 2011*). Meanwhile, inclusive positivists focus on practical examples of contemporary legal systems at work, particularly the overtly moral language of basic constitutional rights and norms of justice, equity, proportionality, etc. Do you think they are now in a position of stalemate? Or does one of them have now a more powerful argument against the other?*

W.J. Waluchow: Again, that's a very good question. I, in fact, was tempted once to write a paper entitled "Why I am no longer an inclusive positivist". I refrained from doing that, because what I meant was that it has come to the point in this debate between inclusive and exclusive positivism where what we have is a stalemate. The debate has for the most part burned out. There are few fruitful contributions that can still be made to this debate. Now, one of the things that is often said, with regard to this question, is that there might be a confusion between factual questions and conceptual questions, such that inclusive positivists, like me (I'm one of the guilty parties here, if there's a crime being committed), point to certain facts about legal practice supporting ILP. I spent a considerable amount of time, in the early days of my career, pointing to constitutional adjudication on the basis of something like a Charter or a Bill of Rights, as lending some support to the idea that legal validity can depend on moral validity. The accusation can be made: "That's a factual claim, while the exclusive positivists are making conceptual arguments about the nature of law, that is, about necessities, not about contingencies", which is what the inclusive positivist is talking about. I think that [this accusation] mischaracterizes at least what I was up to, and I think there can be a connection between the facts, if you like, that I pointed to and the conceptual claims that are put forward by the opposing parties. Let me give you an example: exclusive positivism says that "necessarily, law can't depend for its validity on moral values or the merits of the law". I come back and ask: What about constitutional adjudication, where it appears as if moral values are playing that role? That's intended to be a kind of counterexample to the necessity claim. If you can point out that in actual fact it is not necessarily the case that "A is B", because "there is an A here and there is no B", then you've got a counterexample. The [exclusive positivist's] response, of course, is that it *looks* like "A and not B", but it's actually "A being B". That's, in fact, what the exclusive positivists did: they developed their "directive powers" account. What do you [an inclusive positivist] do then? Well, the strategy I usually pursued was to point to further facts about legal practice that seem to run afoul of that particular account. So, for example, I asked: "Does it look like judges are changing the law when they strike down legislation?." I then pointed to how legal practice in many jurisdictions seems to assume that the law never did exist at the time before the case was decided and that there is therefore no need to change it. This is revealed by the fact that the court will, for example in a criminal case, treat the so-called offending party as having committed no crime, because the law on which he acted was invalid. If you accept the exclusive, "directive powers" account, then you have to be able to explain that away. So, it's a question of pointing out facts which seem to make the other side feel uncomfortable with its claims. It's not a case of making a knock-down argument, but saying "this looks like data that, so to speak, contradict your necessity claim; this sounds like a counterexample and in fact supports the alternative view, which is, in fact, more consistent with that particular reading of the practice. Hence, when the Canadian Constitution says that a law that is declared invalid is as is of no force and effect, and treats it as if that were the case before the case has been decided, then you've got a recalcitrant fact that has to be accounted for. ILP provides a very nice account of that. You have moral value determining legal validity. That's why nobody can be prosecuted under the law that used to be employed to charge persons, because it never was a law at all. I don't think that this strategy is "mixing up" factual and conceptual claims, or making elementary philosophical mistakes of confusing factual statements with conceptual claims. I think that counterexamples, so to speak, can be a useful way of testing necessity claims. That's how I see a lot of my arguments pertaining to constitutional practice. They were along those lines.

Now, a criticism has been made sometimes—for instance, by Gerald Postema (2011)—that there is no positive argument for inclusive positivism here. What you are doing is just fending off challenges, falsifying the opponent's claims, without providing an argument in support of your own view. Well, I think that objection can be answered as well. In a recent paper that I authored for a Festschrift in honor of Matt Kramer (Waluchow 2022), I tried to develop some positive arguments stemming from things like the conventionality of law, the role that law plays in our practical reasoning, and the possibilities that are open to us in terms of how the law can meddle in our moral and practical reasoning. I develop arguments to show why the law's status as a conventional apparatus that can perform those functions is better understood in the way that ILP describes it, or conceives it, as opposed to ELP. ELP narrows the possibilities too much, whereas ILP opens up more possibilities in terms of how the law can be useful in our practical reasoning. Those are positive arguments, and maybe others could be offered. So even though, as I said, I agree that the debate has probably run its course and people are moving on to other things, I don't think that ILP was guilty of the charge of naïvely or foolishly mixing up empirical or factual claims with conceptual claims.

Interviewers: A controversial point in the debate on inclusive legal positivism, which is discussed, for instance, in Bix's contribution to this book, is whether the rule of recognition can be interpreted as a convention, and what kind of convention it could be. While Marmor (2009) *believes it must be a constitutive convention, other jurisprudence scholars believe it can be a less rigid type of convention (like coordination conventions). Your version of inclusive legal positivism is inconsistent with Marmor's conventionalism, which holds that conventions are the product of arbitrary stipulations and cannot make room for the incorporation of moral principles into the set of recognition criteria. Some think that this brings your view close to Dworkin's philosophy of law. In this sense,* Dworkin (2006, pp. 188-198) *argued that Jules Coleman's interpretation of the rule of recognition dehydrates the notion of convention (making his position indistinguishable from "law as integrity"), whereas natural law authors like Michael* Moore (2000) *think that Dworkin is actually a weak conventionalist. What is your concept of convention? In what sense can one say that your view is different from Dworkin's position about the "paradigms" an interpreter would accept as a general plateau for understanding legal concepts?*

W.J. Waluchow: You are probably going to be disappointed to hear this, but I don't really have any well-developed thoughts on conventions, and on what kind of convention is at the root of the legal system. It is true that I talk about the rule of recognition being a conventional practice. And I agree that ILP is probably inconsistent with constitutive conventions, as Andrei [Marmor] develops them. I've always viewed the conventions at the base of law as pretty much like Hartian social rules, and the analysis that he applies to those is what I mean by the conventionality of law. These fundamental rules of recognition and adjudication—or whatever else that you might wish to put in there—are a matter of social practices which display the internal point of view, patterns of behavior, and so on and so forth, plus the recognition that we are in this together. My adherence to this social rule is at least partly motivated by the fact that other people are practicing it as well, and that's essential to our having been able to sustain that practice. On Hart's account, the practice can be valuable for all kinds of reasons—and Hart was right about that. There are lots of different reasons why people might subscribe to these social rules, or conventional socials rules. I really haven't got much beyond that in terms of articulating a theory of conventions. I certainly don't think that the rule of recognition is purely arbitrary in the sense that it's just an arbitrary choice which rule of recognition we adopt. There are obviously good reasons for having certain features of a rule of recognition rather than others.

Now, whether this collapses into Dworkin, I don't think so. One distinguishing feature is that, under ILP, although there are reasons for the social rules that underlie law, none of them is necessary to law, whereas for Dworkin "law as integrity" purports to describe what is essential to law. The kind of contingency that I found attractive in ILP, and in the choice of the conventions that underlie the law that ILP allows, continues to be attractive to me. So I don't think there's much connection there with Dworkin. Paradigms? I'm not sure if we should call them conventionally agreed; they are fixed points people generally tend to agree with in the practice, and they get us going. They are potentially open to revision and rejection in the practice, and so on. All that stuff is very familiar. But I don't see them as conventional in the sense of a social rule. That's how I distinguish myself from Dworkin. (pause) Or one of the ways in which I do that.

Interviewers: There is a section in your book Inclusive Legal Posivitism especially dedicated to the distinction, introduced by Dworkin in "Law's Empire", between grounds of law and the force of law. This topic reappears in some of the contributions to this volume (viz, chapters from Macedo Junior, Flores, Penna, Bustamante, and perhaps others). Grounds of law are those "circumstances in which particular propositions of law should be taken to be sound or true." But the true propositions of law simply report the law's requirements, which normally should be respected but might justifiably be disobeyed or disregarded in exceptional cases. So, the force of law has to do with whether a legal norm should be obeyed or enforced. This distinction disassociates validity and obligation, or truth and sufficient practical justification. What do you think of this distinction, in light of what you wrote in the book at the time and of what you could add to the reflection since then?

W.J. Waluchow: Yeah, I continue to think it's a valuable distinction. Insofar as the grounds of law are the grounds for establishing what the law is, no positivist is going to deny that picture. As to the force of law, if what is meant by that is the moral force of law, then obviously the positivist is going to keep that separate. So I think it is one thing "what the law is", and that concerns the grounds of law, whereas the question whether it's any good, whether we should obey it, or whether we have an obligation towards it, concerns the force of law. To that extent, I think the distinction is a valuable one. I went back and looked at the discussion in that chapter on *Inclusive Legal Positivism* (1994), and the reason I got into the distinction between the grounds and force of law is because I was responding to a particular claim by Dworkin, that I find puzzling, which is the claim that a legal right is a right to a decision by a court. So, your legal rights are [for Dworkin] those that the court is obliged to give you, so to speak. That struck me as bizarre, because as Dworkin and some others pointed out, you end up, likely, with what he calls the "indexing" of law, which means that your legal rights are different depending on which court you go before. So, if you are in a common law legal system, and you are before one of the lower courts, and there is a binding precedent, then your legal right, on this view, is in part determined by the fact that the court hearing the case can't change the law—can't distinguish the precedent or overrule it. Hence, there you have a legal right to the decision that is established in the precedent. But if you go to higher courts, where the judges have varying powers to overturn or distinguish precedents, suddenly your right to a decision might be different, because if the judge is empowered—or under an obligation, perhaps—to change the law, then you no longer have the right that you might have had at the lower level. Since the court is duty-bound to change the law, you no longer have the right to a decision in your favor. Rather, it's the other guy who has a right to a decision in his favor, because the court is duty-bound to change the law in his favour. So, the result is that there is no longer "the law" governing the issue in Canada, or Ontario, or Brazil, or whatever. There will be a law for this court, a law for the other court, and a law for the third court. That was a result to be avoided, so it took me to the idea that when it comes to the obligations of judges with respect to the law, those obligations vary quite a bit. One way to put this is to say that the institutional force—and by that I meant the force that the law has in relation to an institutional actor at a particular level, say an appeal court versus a court of first hearing—is going to be different. The force that the law exerts over that person's decision—hence the right to a decision on the part of the litigant, if you want to put it that way—is going to vary depending on the level of the court you are at. So the court is subject to different forces that come into play in cases depending upon the court you find yourself in. The law at the lower level has a particular force upon the judge—he can't change it, he's got to apply it—whereas the force is absent or weakened when it comes to an appeal court, where the judge may be able, for various reasons, to get around that, distinguish the case, overrule it, or whatever. So I took that to be an important feature of the law, that perhaps should be taken seriously for legal theories, and should be distinguished clearly from moral force, which has to do with the merits of the law with respect to me, on whether I should be obeying it or not. That's a different question from the responsibilities and the powers of the court, fulfilling an institutional role within a legal hierarchy. That led me to distinguish the grounds of law, the moral force of law, and then the institutional force of law. I still think that that three-part distinction makes some sense, and that it might actually be valuable, but I haven't done much with it since. I hope that answers your question.

Interviewers: Our next question is about moral intuitions and about the role that they play in constitutional interpretation and in the interpretation of a community's constitutional morality. Do they have a role? If they do, do they represent some kind of threat to the objectivity of the interpretation of the community's constitutional morality?

W.J. Waluchow: Right. On the view I defend, as you know, the judge's role is not to draw upon his own moral views or moral intuitions about some matter before the court, the judge's own intuitions concerning what justice demands in a case. For a range of reasons that I articulate in my *Living Tree* book (Waluchow 2007), I don't think that's a good thing. Rather, judges should draw on the community's constitutional morality, or CCM, as I call it. Does intuition play a role there? If intuition plays a role, it is the intuitions of the community, so to speak, that are important here. The judge should not, in attempting to understand, articulate, construct, if you like, the norms of CCM, be invoking or utilizing his or her own moral intuitions. I think judges should try as best as they can to distance themselves from those, because their job, in my view, is to enforce the community's constitutional morality. You can say, if you like, that settled beliefs, as revealed in constitutional practice, and in the precedents and principles that are found there, represent the moral intuitions of the community (again, if you like). It's their beliefs, their true commitments, what they intuitively see as right and wrong. The judge's role is to flesh out these intuitions and then try to establish the relation among them all, try to make them coherent, and purge those that don't meet this test—for instance, beliefs that are the result of hasty judgments, lack of reflection, beliefs that are inconsistent with the well-considered judgments of the community as reflected in other areas of constitutional law. These are all things that the court does, and the intuitions at play here are those of the community, not of the interpreter, the judge who is called on to construct or discover. To the extent that it is possible, it is the norms of CCM that should govern. Now, this is not to say that I'm totally naïve as to think that the judge's moral intuitions won't have an effect on all this. Everybody can agree that we are all hostage to what Rawls calls the "burdens of judgment". We are influenced by our upbringing, by our social situation, by our own innate prejudices, and so on. We are all familiar with how all these things play out, and I don't want to minimize the role that they will play when a judge tries to identify CCM norms and commitments. What I'm suggesting is that judges should try as best they can to keep them in the background and separate them from the convictions and beliefs that should guide their dealings with CCM and the constitutional cases they are asked to decide.

Interviewers: Please allow us to specify this point. One can find in this collection of essays different positions about the role of intuitions in moral and legal reasoning. Although most contributors to the book believe that you are right when you argue that a sound interpretation of the constitution should be based on the "true commitments" undertaken by a community's constitutional morality, rather than the mere "moral opinions" that may be predominant in the community, there is a disagreement about how to determine what these true commitments are. While Bustamante's chapter and Taxi and Matos's chapter advocate a pragmatist interpretive method which holds that these true commitments should be made explicit through a reconstruction of the complex network of inferences among explicit and inferentially-articulated commitments (without resorting to anyone's intuitions or mental states), Sanchez Perez's chapter proposes to turn to a set of "institutionally embodied intuitions" to figure out the intuitions that have a sound interpretive part to play. Do you see an important difference between these two interpretations?

W.J. Waluchow: Let me begin by saying that I find very agreeable the view that you articulate about inferential connections (among commitments). I probably didn't say it as well as I should have, but that's the kind of idea that I had in mind, in employing a reflective equilibrium test upon the norms and beliefs of CCM. That's part of the sanitizing process that one engages in when one is trying to find the true commitments. It's quite conceivable on this view that you end up with one commitment that nobody articulated before. In your construction, you show in fact that given these inferences this is what you are committed to. That is perfectly coincident with the approach that I defend. As for Jorge [Sanchez]'s views, I guess I don't see them as incompatible. I take him to be saying that in the decisions and practices of the various institutions involved you will have certain beliefs and commitments revealed, and these are intuitions that are represented—if I'm right—as the views and the commitments of the community that those institutions serve. So they function as a means through which the community's constitutional morality is articulated and developed to some extent. Again, I think what he was trying to do is to say is that it's not the intuitions of the interpreter that are involved, but rather the intuitions of the community as articulated in its institutional practices and decisions. You can put on top of that the kind of analysis that you offer, Thomas [Bustamante], and you end up with what I think is a very attractive picture. So, I don't have to say which one I think it's better because I don't see any incompatibility! Perhaps they bring out different aspects of the same picture.

Interviewers: Our next question is about the circumstances of institutional design and social conditions on which your approach to constitutional interpretation is dependent.

Some chapters in this collection (viz. the chapters from Sanchez, Guidice and Scott, Gomes Júnior, and Baía Magalhães) claimed that the common law constitutional model provides a plausible theory of interpretation and the nature of charter rights, but that this model must be adjusted to some specific institutional circumstances. Can you enumerate, in an abstract way, some of these circumstances?

W.J. Waluchow: That's a really good question. I have to begin by confessing that, when I wrote the Living Tree book and some of my other early works, I wasn't sufficiently aware of how much I was assuming in terms of the social context—if you like—in which my theory made sense and could be applied. But after having been pushed on this issue a few times, quite often in Brazil and other places, I've come to realize that my view applies only to what I can describe as a healthy constitutional democracy. And what I mean by that is a democracy in which people for the most part play by the rules: there is a reciprocity among the various actors within the political context, there's a willingness to compromise, there's a level of trust among the actors, nobody is trying to undermine the other party, nobody is trying to grasp power at all costs, the views and convictions of the population play a role in government decisions, and there's a commitment (the role of which I came later to more fully appreciate) to the unwritten norms and attitudes that underlie a healthy democracy. Actors like Trump and Bolsonaro are two of the most egregious examples of actors within a constitutional democracy who just ignore these, as if there were no consequences. We can see the result. So these underlying norms have to be respected, and there has to be an element of trust. When I wrote the book I guess I was influenced by the fact that, despite our difficulties—and some of them are rather huge when it comes, for example, to our Indigenous populations—Canada is for the most part a fairly healthy constitutional democracy, in which the parties have this element of trust, the courts are widely respected, both by the population and by other political actors, the members of the legislature, and so on, and vice-versa. There's a kind of willingness to cooperate and cede decision making to another party, in light of the norms that govern the system in which they operate. Those are all things I think are required for the kind of theory that I developed to have purchase. Hence, when I argued that judges are more likely to make the controversial decisions that respect minority rights or the rights of vulnerable individuals, because they are not subject to reelection pressures, and so forth, I was assuming the context that I've just described, where you can actually trust them to do what the theory says they should be doing. Now, if that trust is not there, if it's just a power grab on the part of various parties or antagonists toward each other, and if there's a disconnect between the citizens and the government, then I'm not sure what to say about that. But the approach that I develop certainly will have its serious drawbacks, and probably wouldn't function very well. Now, where does that leave my theory? Well, at least my theory offers, I think, a picture of what it *could* be like if the conditions for healthy constitutional democracies were realized to some extent. But even if you have a society that is not a healthy democracy, then if people can work towards establishing those conditions, then this will be an option that they might find attractive. Now what you would have to do to establish those healthy conditions is something that I don't have a lot to say about. A lot of that has to do with political science, sociology, and not with something that a philosopher can do. I'm just "as dumb as the next guy" when I ask: "How could we possibly get people to cooperate and to trust one another, and so on?" I don't really have a lot to offer there. That's not to say that a lot of other people haven't done that. And I think that they should do it. That really is an incrediblly important project, but it's just one that I'm not equipped to deal with. So I fully appreciate the limitations of my analysis in terms of the conditions that are required for the justificatory moves that I make to make sense and to have purchase.

Interviewers: Some of the authors in the book argued that the model is good, but it doesn't work if two conditions apply. One of these I think you already answered: extreme inequality among people may affect the ethos of compliance (as argued in Gomes Júnior's chapter). But the other point, raised by Baía Magalhães's chapter, is a more procedural comment; it argues that if you have a court with an abstract and concentrated system of judicial review (pronouncing decisions with quasi-legislative character), instead of a diffuse system, then the model would not be applicable. Would you agree with these procedural conditions? Do we need, under the common law approach, an environment that allow judges to dig the concrete aspects of the case in order to gather the commitments implicit in the community's constitutional morality?

W.J. Waluchow: Absolutely. I agree 100%. That's what is required for this to work. It's what I consider to be a highly desirable feature of the approach that I'm developing. Surely, if we simply told judges "Ok, there's a right to equality in the constitution. What do you guys think that is? Go ahead and make grand pronouncements, and then deal with legislation on the basis of those views", I would be the last person in the world to think that's a good idea. Part of my project has always been to show that this is not the only alternative here. But if we do develop this common law, precedent-based, understanding of CCM there's a lot more to be done with CCM than I was able to do in the *Living Tree* book and subsequent writings. I hope that maybe people like you might develop it further. That's absolutely essential. But the point remains: you need that kind of precedent-based practice in order for the benefits of common law constitutionalism to get a grip. It's only in those conditions that the justifications that I offer make sense.

Interviewers: Now we got a question that brings us back to the beginning of the interview, because we go back to discretion. There is a nice opening chapter by Matthew Kramer in this collection, in which he distinguishes between indemonstrability or uncertainty and indeterminacy, when he talks about discretion in law. But we want to ask whether we can say the same about constitutional morality. Is there room for indeterminacy, as opposed to mere indemonstrability, in the community constitutional morality? This connects us to another worry, that has been expressed in another chapter of the book (by Fábio Shecaira, who was one of your students). If we accept indeterminacy in CCM, would this be a source of discretion too? Could that possibility make CCM a less reliable candidate to fill in the gaps that law, strictly conceived, leaves for us?

W.J. Waluchow: Arguments presented by people like Fábio [Shecaira], you, and others—that argued that CCM will not always be determinate, reintroducing the discretionary elements that bring the democratic worries that Waldron expressed—pushed me to try to develop the theory in a way that accommodates some degree of indeterminacy. One of my first moves was to say that if indeterminacy in CCM is encountered, then one approach the judge could make is to appeal to Rawlsian public reason (Rawls 2005, pp. 212–254). That would provide the kind of legitimacy that would be absent if the judge were simply to utilize her own moral views when indeterminacy in CCM is encountered. So, by drawing on public reason, there's a kind of democratic credential that attaches to the reasons cited, even if public reasons fail to precisely determine the right answer to the question before the court. So public reason can add further meat to the bones of CCM by saying that, at this point, we can appeal to a different set of reasons that bring with them a degree of democratic legitimacy that can overcome the democratic worry that motivates this whole thing. I agree that even CCM supplemented by public reasons doesn't always provide full determinacy, at which point the question is once again: "How is the judge to decide?" Now, the first thing to say is: the more constraints on the decision-making process that one can introduce, the less likely it becomes that you end up with indeterminacy in any particular case. So these cases in which indeterminacy is a factor might be fewer the further along you go. In other words, the more meat you put on the bones, the less likely you'll have indeterminacy. But the possibility remains. I was therefore pressed even further on the possibility of indetermincay, and in my latest work, called "The Misconceived Quest for the Right Answer: Dedication to Process, Not Result" (Waluchow 2021), I sketch conditions on judicial reasoning with CCM that apply when we do in fact reach a point of indeterminacy. If these are respected, and even though the decision will in the end be discretionary, in the sense that an underdetermined choice has been made among rival interpretations of CCM norms, that choice can still be justified in terms of the process through which the decision was arrived at. One of the conditions [of this process] is appeal to public reasons, but there are other conditions as well. But the point remains that even though I'm willing to admit that sometimes there will be indeterminacy, it's going to be a lot less than people seem to suggest, particularly those who don't ascribe a role to CCM. If you just say to judges "Tell us what equality means, then decide accordingly", that's nowhere near the kind of decision procedure that I'm advocating. If all the conditions I outline are met, and the arguments are always made from the point of view of CCM, are detached in the way I articulate in other papers, then I think we get a degree of legitimacy that enables us to overcome some of the worries about giving judges discretion in constitutional rights cases, namely the democratic worries. When we add in all the benefits of allowing for constitutional review, conceived and practiced in this way, with judges making very controlled discretionary decisions at the end of the day, I think we can get an overall favorable balance in favor of approaching constitutional rights issues in the way that I sketched. I am assuming, of course, that judges aren't politically motivated, although they quite often may be in some jurisdictions (again, I'm assuming a healthy democracy in which they are not going to be pushing their own political agendas).

Interviewers: This brings us to a related question about procedures in the resolution of interpretive controversies over legal concepts or the norms of a community's constitutional morality. Perhaps this is one of the ideas driving Stevens's suggestion to interpret your model of constitutional interpretation as a rhetorical or argumentative model. Are you comfortable with that characterization? Can a rhetorical model be consistent with your claim to distinguish between true commitments in a community's constitutional morality and mere opinions predominant therein?

W.J. Waluchow: I guess I don't find anything terribly upsetting about Katharina [Stevens]'s take. I think that at least at the end stage that I described, where you've got these procedural conditions upon decision-making, I find what Stevens presents as compatible with my work—it's in the same spirit. So I'm happy to take that onboard, as describing how reasoning takes place in cases of indeterminacy. I don't necessarily have a problem with that. In fact I welcome it.

Interviewers: We are now going to our last question, then we can make some room for another story, if you could tell us one. So here's the last question. For the students interested in philosophy of law, are there five books you could recommend that will take us into your philosophical world?

W.J. Waluchow: I like the way you posed this question [asking Waluchow to explain which books take a student to his philosophical world]. So I'm going to provide five books that I think could give a student a sense of where I'm coming from, the kind of philosophy that I've always found inspirational, valuable and insightful, and so on. Hart's *The Concept of Law* (2012) is obviously at the top of the list. But I'd also put on Dworkin's *Taking Rights Seriously* (1978). That was extremely informative for me. I learned an enormous amount from reading Dworkin's book. In fact, when I was writing my doctoral dissertation, I had *The Concept of Law* on one side of my desk and *Taking Rights Seriously* on the other.

Those were the two books of a Bible, if you will, that I drew on extensively in writing my doctoral dissertation. *Law's Empire* (Dworkin 1986) was another landmark, that really influenced my thinking about a lot of things. Raz's *The Authority of Law* (2009), of all the books that Raz has published in legal theory, that's the one that was most influential in my thinking about the law, and I grappled with it a lot. Many of the chapters in that book are ones Raz was trying out when I went to his seminars in Oxford. Attending those seminars was a very pleasant and rewarding experience too. And the fifth one, well, *The Common Law Theory of Judicial Review*, my own book (2007), if students want to get into my head space, to grasp how I view law. There are elements of what I argue in *Inclusive Legal Positivism* in that book. It serves as a kind of foundation for what is developed there, when I talk about circumstances of rulemaking, and so on. So that would be the fifth one I put on my list. Perhaps a bit of hubris putting that book on the list, but that's what I put on.

Would you still like to hear another story or two? These are stories that I recount, to some extent, in the biography of Hart, by Niki Lacey (2006). I'll tell you one story that really gets to the heart of Hart (laughs), of my relationship with Hart. I think I mentioned earlier that when I went to Oxford the supervisor assigned to me was R.M. Hare. He was a difficult man to deal with. He didn't know much about legal philosophy, and he didn't care about legal philosophy. I was getting no useful supervision from him, at all. And I knew it. I knew that my work was not as good as it should be, but I kept plugging away. Then I had the great fortune of going to a conference in Lancaster, England. One of the attendees was John Mackie, who was a fellow at a University College in Oxford when I was there. We got chatting and he said: "What are you up to?", and I told him about the situation with Hare, and he said "That's terrible". I told him that I wasn't getting much in the way of supervision, that I had these papers, but I didn't think there was much to them, and that I didn't know what to do with them. So he said: "When we get back to Oxford, send me copies of the papers. I'll read them and let you know what I think". So I did that, and after a week or two, Mackie asked me to come by and have a chat. He said: "Yes, I see what you mean. I agree with you. Most of these papers make small points and are not really going anywhere. But there's one paper that I think is really something you can work on". It turned out that that was the paper where I was first dealing with inclusive versus exclusive legal positivism. He said: "You should work on that one". So I did. I produced this mammoth 90-page paper, which turned out to be the skeleton of my doctoral thesis and the book that came out of that many years later. So I was really excited. Mackie thought that was good. I worked on the paper extensively and submitted it to Hare, which was the procedure. [In Oxford], when you are working with a supervisor, you write something up and send it to him. Then you get summoned to his room to discuss it. Much to my good fortune, Hare said at the time: "Maybe we should see what Hart says about this". And I said: "Do you think he will actually be wiling to read it?" He said "We can see". Then he called Hart, who said: "Send the thing to me and I'll have a read through it", which was great. So, anyway, after the requisite couple of weeks I got summoned to Hare's room at Corpus Christi College. The usual procedure was that you waited outside of his office until he summoned you in. You walked in, you sat down in a chair across from another chair in which he sat, and he had your paper and he would ask you questions and make comments. I got to the door, and after I literally moved not more than one foot, he said: "Don't come any further. There's no point in you coming and sitting down". And he handed me my paper, saying: "I haven't read your paper fully. I got to page 2 and frankly I found it all a frightful bore, and I didn't want to go any further". This was the paper that I was really excited about. I had poured my guts into that paper. I was absolutely devastated, thinking my career was over. This was the best work I could produce, and it wasn't just that he disagreed. He didn't think it was worth reading. So I thought: "I'm in the wrong business here". I felt like I had a terminal illness, I mean, the diagnosis of a terminal illness. I felt like my career had been diagnosed as terminal. And so I took the bus back to my college. When I walked in the front door, I checked my mailbox and there was a letter from Hart in the mailbox. Remember that he had been also been sent the paper. The opening line is one I will never forget till the day I die. It said: "My dear Waluchow, I am reading with care and fascination your excellent paper on Dworkin" (laughs). This is the same paper that Hare had said wasn't worth reading. And Hart said he was reading it with care and fascination. I could make that part out, but the rest of the letter I couldn't really figure out what he was saying, because his handwriting was absolutely atrocious. But, fortunately, I had a classicist friend who spent most of his time dealing with ancient Egyptian papyri, trying to discern indecipherable things written on the papyri. He was quite adept at reading unreadable stuff, so I asked him: "What's he saying in the rest of the letter?" (laughs). He said: "He's inviting you over for dinner, to the College, and to give him a ring at this number to set up a time". So I contacted Hart and he invited me to dinner at University College. We were the only two people in the dining hall that evening. And we sat there, it was candle lit, a small dining hall with three waiters with white gloves, chandeliers—the whole thing. And we talked about my paper while we had this wonderful dinner. A short time later, Hare informed me that he would be going on sabbatical, and that's when I hooked up with Hart as my supervisor. When I think back, I realize how fortuitous that was, because I literally went from thinking that my career was over to thinking "I don't care about what this guy is saying – H.L.A Hart thinks this is an excellent paper. I must be able to do the work better than Hare intimated". So he [Hart] was highly instrumental in rescuing me at that point. As he became my supervisor, he was unbelievably helpful. And I just had a wonderful time. That was the highlight of my academic career.

References

Cross, Rupert, and John Harris. 1991. *Precedent in English law*. 4th ed. Oxford: Oxford University Press.

Dickson, Julie. 2001. *Evaluation and legal theory*. Oxford: Hart Publishing.

———. 2022. *Elucidating law*. Oxford: Oxford University Press.

Dworkin, Ronald. 1963. Judicial discretion. *Journal of Philosophy* 60 (21): 624–638.

———. 1978. *Taking rights seriously*. 2nd ed. Cambridge: Harvard University Press.

———. 1986. *Law's empire*. Cambridge: Harvard University Press.
———. 2006. *Justice in robes*. Cambridge: Harvard University Press.
Gettier, Edmund. 1963. Is justified knowledge belief? *Analysis* 23 (6): 121–123.
Hart, H.L.A. 2012. *The concept of law*. 3rd ed. Oxford: Oxford University Press.
Kripke, Saul. 1982. *Wittgenstein on rules and private language*. Oxford: Blackwell.
Lacey, Nicola. 2006. *A life of H. L. a. Hart: The nightmare and the Noble dream*. Oxford: Oxford University Press.
LLyons, David. 1965. *Forms and limits of utilitarianism*. Oxford: Oxford University Press.
Marmor, Andrei. 2009. *Social conventions: From language to law*. Princeton: Princeton University Press.
Moore, Michael. 2000. Metaphysics, epistemology, and legal theory. In *Educating oneself in public*, 247–293. Oxford: Oxford University Press.
Parfit, Derek. 1986. *Reasons and persons*. Oxford: Oxford University Press.
Postema, Gerald J. 2011. *Legal philosophy in the twentieth century: The common law world*. Dordrecht: Springer.
Quine, W.V.O. 1951. Two dogmas of empiricism. *The Philosophical Review* 60 (1): 20–43.
Rawls, John. 1999. *A theory of justice*. 2nd ed. Cambridge: Belknap.
———. 2005. *Political liberalism, Expanded edition*. New York: Columbia University Press.
Raz, Joseph. 2009. *The authority of law*. 2nd ed. Oxford: Oxford University Press.
Shapiro, Scott. 2011. *Legality*. Cambridge: Harvard University Press.
Waluchow, W.J. 1994. *Inclusive legal positivism*. Oxford: Oxford University Press.
———. 2007. *A common law theory of judicial review: The living tree*. Cambridge: Cambridge University Press.
———. 2021. The misconceived quest for the right answer: Dedication to process, not result. In *Constitutionalism: Old dilemmas, new insights*, ed. Alejandro Linares Cantillo et al., 54–70. Oxford: Oxford University Press.
———. 2022. Matthew Kramer and inclusive legal positivism: Dancing on the head of a pin. In *Without trimmings*, ed. M. McBride and V.A.J. Kurki, 125–148. Oxford: Oxford University Press.

Thomas Bustamante is Professor of Legal Theory and Philosophy of Law at the Federal University of Minas Gerais, Brazil, and Senior Research Productivity Fellow of the National Council for Scientific and Technological Development (CNPq), Brazil. He was a Global Research Fellow with a Fulbright Visiting Research Grant at the New York University, from 2020 to 2021, and a Research Fellow at King's College London, from 2022 to 2023, with a grant from CAPES Foundation. He holds a PhD from the Pontifical Catholic University, Rio de Janeiro. Some of his works in English appear in the *Canadian Journal of Law and Jurisprudence, Modern Law Review, Jurisprudence, Australian Journal of Legal Philosophy, American Journal of Compartive Law,* and *German Law Journal.* He has edited the books *New Essays on the Fish-Dworkin Debate* (with Margaret Martin) 2023), *Philosophy of Law as an Integral Part of Philosophy: Essays in the Jurisprudence of Gerald J Postema* (with Thiago L Decat 2020), *Democratizing Constitutional Law: Perspectives on Legal Theory and the Legitimacy of Constitutionalism* (with Bernardo Fernandes, 2016), *Argument Types and Fallacies in Legal Argumentation* (with Christian Dahlman, 2015) and *On the Philosophy of Precedent* (with Carlos Bernal Pulido, 2012).

Saulo de Matos is Professor of Legal Theory and Philosophy of Law at the Federal University of Pará, Brazil, and Vice-director of the Master and PhD Program in Human Rights of the same University. He holds a PhD from University of Gottingen, Germany, and a Master's degree from the University of Heidelberg, Germany. His doctoral dissertation on the legal and political idea of popular sovereignty in modernity ("*Zum normativen Begriff der Volkssouveränität*") was published in Germany by Nomos Verlag in 2015. He was visiting scholar at University of California in Los Angeles (2013) and University of Gottingen (2017).

André L.S. Coelho is Professor of Legal Theory and Philosophy of Law at the Law School of the Federal University of Rio de Janeiro, in Brazil. He holds an M.Phil and a Ph.D in Philosophy from the Federal University of Santa Catarina, Brazil, with a Research Visit at the Goethe Universität of Frankfurt, Germany. He has previously taught at CESUPA and The University of Amazon, both in Brazil.

Printed by Printforce, the Netherlands